Postures of the Mind

The University of Minnesota Press
gratefully acknowledges assistance provided
by the Andrew W. Mellon Foundation
for publication of this book.

Postures
of the Mind
Essays on
Mind and Morals

Annette Baier

University of Minnesota Press *Minneapolis*

Published by the University of Minnesota Press
2037 University Avenue Southeast, Minneapolis, MN 55414
Printed in the United States of America

Library of Congress Cataloging in Publication Data

Baier, Annette.
  Postures of the mind.
  Includes index.
  1. Knowledge, Theory of—Addresses, essays,
lectures. 2. Intellect—Addresses, essays, lectures.
3. Ethics—Addresses, essays, lectures. I. Title.
BD161.B25 1985   121   84-27001
ISBN 0-8166-1326-5
ISBN 0-8166-1327-3 (pbk.)

For my parents

Contents

Preface

I have used Locke's phrase "postures of the mind" to indicate what these essays are about mainly for the anti-atomistic suggestions of the phrase, given its Lockean context. Locke, realizing that at least some words did not name simple or complex ideas which themselves named atomic or molecular things, added a brief chapter on "particles" to Book Three of the *Essay Concerning Human Understanding,* and gave these little non-names such as *but* the job of indicating not ideas but "the actions of the mind relating to those ideas," and "the several postures of the mind in discoursing." He makes no claim to have given a thorough treatment either of particles, or of what they signify, "the several views, postures, stands, turns, limitations and exceptions" our minds are capable of; but by "lightly touching" on this matter, he hopes to inspire others to continue, since "this part of grammar has been perhaps as much neglected as some others overdiligently cultivated." I do little to advance the study of the grammar of particles, and only "Realizing What's What" makes any foray into the philosophy of language. But the following essays in the philosophy of mind and in ethics do try to direct attention away from the overcultivated field of single beliefs, intentions, and intentional actions to the individual abilities, social powers, continuing policies and purposes, virtues and vices they exhibit. A distrust of supposedly discrete events and entities, of Lockean nameables, is one pervasive theme. As Locke wanted us to contemplate not merely ideas precipitated out on some mental microscopic plate, but also ideas "in train," in our discoursing, and to cultivate that *style* in speaking to which, he thought, the right use of particles contributed so much, so I have tried to look at streams of developing and decaying beliefs and intentions, at changes of mind as well as decisions and realizations, and at assessment not just of single actions but of lives and of character, at moral style of life. Locke's trains, of course, are prerailway trains, and lack that railway-track imposed implication of separate but flexibly connected carriages or trucks, all drawn along by some front engine. Although Locke *does* seem to suppose that particles join separate ideas to one another in serial order, as they would if they were like couplings in a railway train, this supposition was and is no necessary implication of the idea that thought forms a train. (Samuel Johnson's *Dictionary* gives, as examples of eighteenth-century trains, bird's tails and the lower back part of bridal gowns, as well as retinues of attendants, and gives *process* as one sense of *train,* and there is no reason to think that seventeenth-century trains were any less capable of continuity than eighteenth-century trains.)

Besides a distrust of mental and moral atoms, these essays also show a distrust of the laws that supposedly govern the behavior of such atoms. Whereas the anti-atomism is a reaction against elements in the British empiricist tradition, the distrust of claims about laws is a reaction against the Kantian component in my philosophical upbringing. Being by nature somewhat contrary (to rhyme with "Mary") was probably what got me into philosophy in the first place—my inclination to challenge whatever anyone else said could there be regarded as a virtue, not a vice. The following essays were written over ten years during which I was still liberating myself from the prejudices acquired during my philosophical upbringing, one which, since it emphasized the virtue of challenging presuppositions, contained the means of its own overthrow. These prejudices were a mixture of Kantian ones and textbook British empiricist ones. They include the following:

(a) Intellect or reason, rather than any other human capacity, is what has intrinsic authority, and its authority extends over all human feelings, and all human customs, traditions, and habits.
(b) The main operation of this authoritative voice is to formulate completely universal laws or rules, which can be nonproblematically applied to give predictions, practical guidance, and practical criticism, in particular cases.
(c) Mental states have a representational function.
(d) All phenomena, psychological and physical, can be analyzed into basic constituents combined according to various rules or principles of synthesis or constitution.

Together these assumptions gave one a nice philosophical agenda—one took, say, a human action and analyzed it into *basic* action, then saw that as carrying various attributes contributed by its relation to its future consequences, to its causes in the motives and beliefs of the agent, its relation to the moral *rules* by which this agent was or should have been guided, and so on. One could do ethics, looking for the best, most reason-supported version of "the moral law," one could do action theory, building up the complex properties of actions from their relation to moral rules, causal laws, psychological origins. One could do epistemology, looking into various representations and how one could analyze them into their atomic parts and basic structures, at what enables them to represent, and enables us ever to know that they did.

The philosophical program looked good, and the fact that one saw all past philosophers to have been busy working at it over all those centuries reassured one, about as much as the divergence of their conclusions worried one. Could they all have been articulating the univocal voice of reason? Whose Logische Aufbau der Welt was the correct version? One put aside these questions with some patter about the eternal questions and the unending dialectic of attempts to answer them, and felt pleased and proud to be in the intellectual company of such great, if disagreeing, thinkers as Aquinas, Bentham, and Kant, between whose versions of the moral law one now gave one's judgment, and such thinkers as Plato, Descartes, Locke, Leibniz, Kant, Carnap, whose deconstructions and re-constructions of the physical world one compared and ranked. One happi-ly picked and chose between Berkeley, Kant, Schopenhauer, and the early Wittgenstein on representation, or between Hume and J. L. Austin on how a promise came to be binding. For even in this last choice one still operates with rules and with the analyzable performances they constituted or ruled on, even if the authority underwriting such rules was beginning to look less like universal reason and more like local tradition.

By the end of my time as a student in Oxford, some of these articles of faith were weakened by the influence of J. L. Austin and his relentless questioning of all easy generalities, his fidelity to complex facts. Then, in 1953, I read Wittgenstein's *Philosophical Investigations.* I cannot say that, even with G. E. M. Anscombe's assistance, the scales fell from my eyes. But I was bewildered, even to some degree paralyzed. If there were no natural kinds to be discerned, nor any inner mental episodes on which to rely as the termini of analysis in philosophy of mind, nor any ultimate self-applying rules, then how could I practice philosophical analysis, and, if I couldn't, how could I earn my living as a philosopher? Paralyzed enough not to write, but still hoping to sort things out in my classes, I began teaching philosophy. A discussion group in legal reasoning at the University of Auckland further shook my faith in the possibility of clear rules whose applicability to future cases was fixed in advance. What Witt-genstein said about rule following seemed borne out by lawyers' practices. Bewilderment continued. Then, a decade later, I decided to include *The Blue and Brown Books* in an introductory course at Carnegie Mellon

University. The students read Descartes, Hume, Kant, James, and the late Wittgenstein. They were very puzzled by Wittgenstein, but I succeeded at least in teaching myself. Then the scales *did* fall, and everything looked different.

Even better, I had a new agenda, at first a somewhat negative one. In a series of articles I attacked the received concept of a basic action and other reductionist moves in the philosophy of action, and tried to make central a more Wittgensteinian concept of culture-dependent competence. Two of these essays, "Mixing Memory and Desire" and "Intention, Practical Knowledge, and Representation," are included here. My work on intention made me want to get its relation to other mental postures clear, and so I was led on to think about remembering, realizing, caring, emotional responses, all in the attempt to get a satisfactory version of the human mind, and one that did justice to its social context and its capacities for feeling as well as its intellectual activities. The first part of this book contains these essays.

My faith in rule-recognizing, atom-finding reason having been shaken, I had returned to another early hero, Hume, for antirationalist aid and inspiration. The various essays on ethics in the second part of this book are guided by my attempts to understand Hume's version of a morality that gave authority to feeling, custom, and tradition. They are also attempts to work out a Wittgensteinian approach in ethics, one less anchored in religion than was Wittgenstein's own approach. I wanted a secular Wittgensteinian ethic, and Hume seemed to be a pretty good guide for getting that. The essays on moral philosophy included here are at first largely attacks on Kantian positions ("Knowing Our Place in the Animal World," "Theory and Reflective Practices"), and later are a little more positive ("Doing Without Moral Theory," "Poisoning the Wells"). Hume is the hero of most of these essays, although none of them deal only with his views. "Secular Faith" is a return to the abandoned tradition of Hobbes and Kant, to retrieve some important truths from them, lest I merely exchange Kantian for anti-Kantian prejudice.

The collection is unified, to the extent that it is, by the groping search for a way to think reflectively about human lives without relying on faith in any sovereign reason, neither Kant's nor the economists', and without oversimplifying the history-bound complexities of human life. That search has not yet been very successful. More progress has been made in ruling *out* methods than in discovering better ones. It is ironic and suitable that the full working out of my "contrariness" should lead me to challenge not only the need for basic atoms and for fundamental laws, both descriptive and moral, but also the value of contrariness itself. In several of my essays on ethics I challenge the assumption that encouraging our students to challenge and seek justification for moral beliefs is helping them to become wiser. So these essays can be read as the record of what seems to be a typically philosophical movement of thought, namely a kind of inverse of a transcendental argument, whereby what is shown is not "how possible," but "how impossible." As Hume pointed out, some sorts of philosophical reflection show us, ultimately, that we cannot establish those philosophically reflective habits as rules. For Hume this coming full skeptical circle was merely the prelude to more constructive philosophy. If any constructive thinking follows deconstructive thinking, in my own case, little of it will be found in these essays. A few tentative constructive moves are made, but the main morals drawn within the essays themselves are negative ones, and the main moral to be drawn from their assembly "in train," may be equally negative. The final posture is less consistently combative than what went before, but also less confident. Construction, although not necessarily harder than destruction, as far as mental and psychic wear and tear goes, demands different and difficult-to-learn postures and actions of the mind.

This overly autobiographical preface has already made clear how much I owe to all those against whose views I reacted, as well as to those who helped me see, however dimly, some alternatives. To all of those authors, teachers, colleagues, students, and especially to Kurt Baier and John Cooper, I express my appreciation. To Collie Henderson, who typed and retyped with skill, patience, and good humor, my gratitude is wholehearted.

University of Pittsburgh

Part I

Varieties of Mental Postures

Kant says that "Das Begehrungsvermögen ist das Vermögen desselben, durch seine Vorstellungen Ursache von der Wirklichkeit der Gegenstände dieser Vorstellungen zu sein." ["The faculty of desire is the faculty of such a (living) being to make its representations the cause of the reality of the objects they represent." Footnote 7 to the Preface to the *Kritik der Praktischen Vernuft*.] This is a perennially tempting view. If one sees the quintessentially mental act to be representation, then, armed with the relation between a representation and what it represents, and the causal relation, one can see mind as playing a causal role in the world both by virtue of the representations the world causes in minds, and by virtue of the effects of mental representations of the desired future state of the world on that world. All my essays here oppose such a Kantian cum Schopenhauerian version of mind as a magic mirror that both reflects the way the world around it is (with some possible "distortion" provided by its own intrinsic features), and also causes an occasional fire or two in the world by its own presence there, its own efficacious representations.

What is wrong with this view of a representable world and a representing mind, in mutual interaction? One thing which is wrong is that the social and cultural dimension of mind seems to be shortchanged by it. All the interactions between minds, and all the influence of custom, convention, and tradition is left out. Nor can we get it in just by adding an extra causal relation between minds. The cultural influence is found, as Heidegger has emphasized, as much in our tools as in what others literally say to us, and in the sort of food we eat, the work we do, the cities we live in, even in the state of our soil, forests, and water. It is not easy in the world around us to sort "nature" out from the contribution of generations of human minds, hands, hearts, and guts. Several of the following essays— "Intention, Practical Knowledge, and Representation," "Realizing What's What," "Cartesian Persons," and "Mind and Change of Mind"—emphasize this interpersonal dimension of mind.

Another thing that I find wrong with the view of mind as representer both of the world and of the way its representations will cause the world to be is the reduction of all relations to logical relations, representation, and causation. (My fascination with Hume's philosophy is due in large part to his attempt at a similar or more radical reductionism of relations, while at the same time saying all the "right" things about the social dimension of mind, and some very suggestive things about representation.) Both in "Intention, Practical Knowledge, and Representation," where I examine Arthur Danto's views, and in "Actions, Passions, and Reasons," where I examine Donald Davidson's developing views about reasons as causes, I try to work out my rejection of such reductionism. I had earlier worked out its implications for action theory in a group of papers not included here (partly to avoid a fat book, partly because I have grown further away from the one who wrote those papers than from the one who wrote these more recent papers, away not from their conclusions but from the manner in which they were drawn). It may help the reader understand the general philosophy of mind that the essays in this book express if I say something about the content of their predecessor essays concerning intentional action.

Several of them[1] investigated the concept of a basic action, as it is to be found in the writings of Arthur Danto, Roderick Chisholm, and Alvin Goldman. Having rejected a reliance on the causal relation to locate what is basic, and the view that bodily movements are basic actions, I went on to try to develop the view, found here in "Mixing Memory and Desire," that any intentional action must be the exercise of some recognizable ability or competence, any intention to act backed up by an action plan connecting the time of the intention formation to the time of the intended action, and consisting of intended exercises of the intender's competences, on foreseen opportunities for their exercise. Such competent doings, rather than bodily movements as such, were found basic, but basic in a culture-relative and agent-relative sense. I appealed to this concept of what is basic to distinguish intentions from mere wishes, or from predictions about one's future, and so to map the relationships among the more or less active mental postures we recognize as our own.

The motive for introducing the concept of a basic or primitive action has, among many philosophers of action, been not so much to distinguish intending from wishing or predicting that one will do some particular thing, as to "reduce" a human action to an event that can take its place in the sequence of causally connected events a scientific observer would record. Whereas my concept of basic action cashes out an action into the currency of recognized human abilities or competences, others, such as Davidson, want to cash it out into the currency of physical events, as seen by what we could call the event-watcher. Since bodily movements or neuron firings do not need redescription to count as data for the event-watcher, if one of them is there at the core of every intentional action, then we have a point of contact between motions in the world of the scientific event-watcher and moves made by agents. I tried[2] to relate these two worlds without treating the event-watcher's version of what an agent does as having any specal basicness or primitivity for our understanding of action. Once we see that event-watching is one of our intentional activities, we see that there is no more reason to single out as basic actions the moves we make which are described in the event-watchers' terminology, than to make the reverse move, and single out as basic or primitive *events* those events that we can intentionally stage, not merely observe, events that do not have to be redescribed, nor dressed up or down, to count as doings as well as events. Bodily movements of selected sorts have a better claim to be "basic events" than they have to be basic actions, but it would be even better to label them in a way that clearly indicates the respect in which they may be special—namely as things we both *can do* and *can see as events* not too unlike nonhumanly staged events. *Robot-actions,* or *humanoid-events,* would be possible labels for them, or some coinage such as *actvents.* Davidson's claim that "we never do more than move our bodies, the rest is up to nature,"[3] expresses nicely the view I tried to replace with the view that we never do less than we can be recognized to have intentionally done, and that is due to the culture as well as the nature of which we are a part. Since I wrote those essays on action, action theory has moved on, both to new versions of basic actions[4] and to helpful new treatments of the intentionality of action.[5]

Another respect in which the philosophical scene has changed for the better is in the treatment by logicians and philosophers of language of the verbal representations of states of mind. That all mental attitudes are attitudes *to propositions* was for a long time an article of faith that was rarely challenged. I challenge it in several of these early essays, and in "Mixing Memory and Desire." I think that the recent work of Barwise and Perry[6] promises a welcome new and better way of regimenting the objects of mental attitudes, transforming them from propositional attitudes to something more flexible, more adequate for capturing the variety of mental contents while also revealing something of the form that guides our inferential and other orderly moves from one attitude or attribution of attitude to other related ones.

My attack on proposition fetishism, representation fetishism, event fetishism, and causation fetishism continues in the essays here. These essays present minds as formed by culture as well as by nature; our mental repertoire made possible by both of these; our beliefs, feelings, intentions, and actions showing that inheritance, as well as contributing to its continuation and to its development. The inheritance includes "reason," a product of animal intelligence plus culture-facilitated self-consciousness, and it includes other such joint mental products of equal importance. I see this view as Wittgensteinian, but it may be safer simply to say that reading Wittgenstein was, as far as I am aware, the main cultural influence leading me to accept such a view. It is less easy to put in a neat formula than the Kantian view it replaced. Instead of causally induced representations of existent facts and causally efficacious representations of future facts, I see mental states as the states of one who learns from others as well as from nature, who trains, criticizes, approves, works with, and receives criticism from others, and occasionally does need a representation of what is not present. Mental states become the states of criticism-sensitive intelligent sensitive beings, characterized in terms that bring out the role such states play in the ongoing activity, receptivity, and responsiveness that displays us not just as intelligent animals, able to anticipate events well enough to survive, but as society-dependent yet often antisocial animals, with inherited standards of correctness that we often try to disown, and with other fairly standard ways of displaying both our self-consciousness and the limits of it. Given these limits, our success in understanding our own states is bound to be partial, even when the attempt at understanding is made within a general framework that acknowledges the difficulty of self-understanding.

Since the view of mind endorsed in these essays is one that sees the crucial mental capacity as a capacity for response to what is itself mind-displaying, it is appropriate that almost all of these essays should be responses on my part to the views of others. "Realizing What's What" responds to Zeno Vendler and Nuel Belnap; "Intention, Practical Knowledge, and Representation" responds to Arthur Danto; "Mind and Change of Mind" discusses several views, including those of René Descartes; "Cartesian Persons" responds to Descartes and to P. F. Strawson; "Caring about Caring" is a response to Harry Frankfurt's views about caring; and "Actions, Passions and Reasons" is a response to Donald Davidson's essays. All these discussed views are widely known, so my partial restatements of them in these essays should suffice to enable the reader to understand my responses and to understand them as responses. Should these essays send the reader back to the authors who drew these responses from me, or on to responses of their own, then they will have succeeded in nurturing the kind of mind they try to display and to analyze.

NOTES

1. "Act and Intent," *Journal of Philosophy* 67, no. 9 (1970): 648–58, discusses Chisholm's view. "The Search for Basic Actions," *American Philosophical Quarterly* 8 (1971): 161–70, discusses A. Danto's, R. Taylor's, and R. Chisholm's views. "Ways and Means," *Canadian Journal of Philosophy* 1 (1972): 275–93, discusses A. Goldman's views.

2. This attempt is found both in "Ways and Means," where I invoke Herbert Simon's distinction between the "state space" and the "action space," and also in "The Intentionality of Intentions," *Review of Metaphysics* 30, no. 3 (1977): 389–414, where I invoke Berkeley's help to relate the worlds of the agent and of the event-watcher. There I also argue for the irreducibility of intending to desiring and believing.

3. Donald Davidson, "Agency," in *Actions and Events* (Oxford: Clarendon Press, 1982), p. 59. Davidson's views on action were not among those I discussed in my papers on basic action. He warns us, in a footnote, that this sentence I have quoted may mislead the reader, if taken out of context, but those who do not wish to be so quoted would be advised not to write such temptingly quotable sentences! In any case my disagreement is with what the sentence says in its context.

4. For example, in Jennifer Hornsby, *Actions* (London: Routledge Kegan Paul, 1980); in Davidson, *Actions and Events*; and in John Searle, *Intentionality: An Essay in the Philosophy of Mind* (Cambridge, Eng.: Cambridge University Press, 1983).

5. For example, in George Wilson, *Intentionality of Human Action, Acta Philosophica Fennica* (Amsterdam: North Holland, 1980).

6. See Jon Barwise and John Perry, *Situations and Attitudes* (Cambridge, Mass.: M.I.T. Press, 1983), and "Scenes and Other Situations," *Journal of Philosophy* 78, no. 7 (1981): 369–97.

1

Mixing Memory and Desire

From Locke to Bernard Williams[1] and Derek Parfit,[2] both memory and desire, or strictly speaking, memory and *intention,* have figured prominently in attempted analyses of personal identity. I shall in this paper offer no analysis of personal identity, nor even attempt to show how memory and intention come together in a person's present awareness of him-or-herself. What I shall do is try to show three features common to the objects of both remembering and intending which mark them off from other intentional objects, yet it is because I believe these features relevant to the more ambitious project of explicating personal identity that I find the parallels worth pointing out. Out of the large range of mental acts, attitudes, and postures, these two, intending and remembering, have a central role to play in any adequate philosophy of mind. I may change my beliefs, expectations, opinions, convictions, but I cannot change my memories. My goals, desires, hopes, regrets, and fears may alter from year to year, or from day to day, but my intentions change only if I change my mind. These surface indicators are not, I think, misleading. Both intentions and memories are, in a special way, personal, and each presents a particularly difficult challenge to the would-be artificial simulator of mental states, or to the materialist who would identify a mental state with a brain state.

I shall first state, briefly and dogmatically, the three features I find in intention and memory. I shall then turn to intending in the attempt to make my claims plausible for it. I shall claim that the three features are integral to intention and, taken together, distinguish it from its close relatives such as expectations and wants. Lastly and more briefly I shall turn to remembering, trace the parallel, and comment on the significance of the parallel itself and of the limitations within which it holds.

From *American Philosophical Quarterly* 13, no. 3 (1976): 213–20.

The three features I find distinctive of remembering and intending are these:

I. What I shall call the *narcissism* of intentions and memories. Where intentions and memories are directed upon objects other than the intender or rememberer, these imply intentions and memories not thus other-directed. (If I intend *you* to go, I must intend to get you to go.) Memories and intentions are narcissistic in a way in which beliefs and expectations are not. My beliefs of course are mine (even if taken from others, on authority), but they need not be of my own forming, and they need not be about me. My intentions must not only be "made" by me, when I make up my mind, they must be directed upon, they must concern, my own future actions.

I take a grammatical indicator of this first feature of intending to be the use of a verb derivative *without any explicit subject governing that verb* in normal expressions of what is intended or remembered.

I intend being there (not "my being there").
I remember being there (not "my being there").

This grammatical feature, which Vendler[3] calls *noun-sharing,* I shall, perhaps perversely, refer to as *self-omission.* So I shall say that self-omission at the surface grammatical level indicates narcissism below the surface, in the mental depths.

II. The second feature is a complement, or compensation, for the first. It is the dependence of individual private intentions on shared common ones, of private memory on group memory or history. For this feature I find no clear grammatical indicator, although the use of the infinitive construction, neutral with respect to persons, could perhaps be the linguistic counterpart of the impersonality or communal character of the essential support of intention, namely recognition of ability. My second substantive thesis, which will need a lot of explaining, is then that first-person singular intentions and memories depend upon first person *plural* ones, and so are *public-dependents.*

III. The third feature I find present in both memory and intention is a certain hard-to-specify connectedness, which is perhaps more immediately evident in memory than in intention. David Kaplan, in explaining the element of vividness in his concept of "representation" (in "Quantifying In"[4]), speaks of the interior story which is formed by a man's beliefs. I do not think the collection of a man's beliefs need form any story, but his version of his own life will. As Leibniz says (*Monadology* § 26), "Memory furnishes a sort of consecutiveness which imitates reason,"[5] where reason, for Leibniz, is grounded in design or intention. Not only does the actual world display sufficient reason, but "Each possible world depends upon certain decrees of God proper to it."[6]

This third feature will need as much clarification as the second feature. For the moment I offer only another gnomic Leibnizian contribution to the topic, if not to its clarification: "*Time* is the order of possibilities which are inconsistent but nevertheless have a connection with one another . . . possibilities which are inconsistent but which we nevertheless conceive of as all existing."[7] I shall eventually try to show how and in what sense temporal continuity is a distinctive feature of the objects of both intention and memory, how all moments of the remembered and intended sequence are held together, conceived of as all existing. The grammatical indicator I tentatively suggest for this continuity is the use of the gerund or participial construction "I intend going," "I remember being there." One cannot make too strong a claim here, since many other verbs, such as *like, dislike, fear, enjoy,* take this construction, and if there is a connection between the different things I enjoy it is not a temporal connection. It seems true that the intentional objects picked out by the gerund construction are always time determinations, ways in which time might be passed, so there will be temporal connectedness within any one intentional object to which the gerund refers. If I enjoy skiing, what I enjoy is a certain way of spending my time; but the different things I enjoy, unlike the different things I remember, and remember having enjoyed, do not exhibit temporal order, let alone the temporal continuity of the intended and the remembered. The many things I enjoy or fear, may, taken together, yield a diagnosis of my hangups, but do not, like my memories or my projected future, yield a story.

So much for the dogmatic statement of my three theses. They can be summed up in the claim that the objects of memory and intention are alike and distinctive in that they are narcissistic, public dependents, and connected. I shall now turn to intending, contrasting it with other forward-looking mental postures and showing how these three features help us to isolate it from other closely related mental states.

How do my intentions differ from my hopes, wants, expectations? It has often been remarked how promiscuous, ontologically and epistemologically, are expectations and wants compared with the selectivity of intentions. Expected and wanted states of affairs differ from intended states of affairs in that they are not necessarily linked to states of *my* affairs. I can want and expect the human race to survive another hundred years without thereby wanting or expecting anything for myself. But my intentions must concern my own future. I can, of course, intend him to revisit Isfahan, but, if I do, this must be backed by my intention to get him to revisit it—to pay him to go, persuade him to go, or lure him there. By contrast, I can expect him to revisit it, even want him to revisit it, without expecting or wanting anything for myself, not even the knowledge that he went there. I need to play no role whatever in his getting there, not even a cognitive role, when fulfillment comes to my want or expectation that he go there. Intentions, however, have their objects ultimately in the intender's own future. This is the first feature I am emphasizing, what I have called the narcissism of intentions.

Since the that-construction after "intend" cannot omit the subject of its verb, cannot exhibit self-omission or noun or pronoun sharing, but only noun repetition as in "I intend that I go," and since even this is nonidiomatic, I shall take the that-construction after "intend" to be dependent on other constructions, and used to express intentions dependent on narcissistic ones, which are not themselves expressed by a that-clause. If I intend that he arrive on time, I intend to drive quickly so that he arrives on time. Philosophers have shown a great partiality for that-clauses, and are disposed to assimilate other constructions to them. Dennett,[8] for example, is so set on getting a unified account of intentionality, and so attracted by the tests already formulated (by Chisholm and others) for that-constructions (referential opacity and nontruth functionality), that he proposes paraphrasing all other constructions following psychological verbs to reduce or expand them into that-constructions. He is willing to accept what he calls the "Runyonesque" sentence "I want that I go," and is worried only by the difficulties of getting "I dislike spinach," "I fear dogs" into that-constructions, but even here his worry does not shake his faith in his program. "Want," "like," "hate" and "admire" reject that-constructions even more flatly than does "intend," and one implication of the analysis I am proposing for "intend" is that tests for intentionality will have to be formulated so that they apply to the constructions which are the primary vehicles for expressing what is intended, namely the gerund and the infinite. Perhaps, once we had such tests, we could turn the tables and try reducing that-constructions to these. This attempt at least could not be *less* successful than the more familiar reverse reductive attempt. My opinion is that what Herbst[9] calls *Q-intentionality* is the fundamental form. Already in Leibniz and Spinoza there is a recognition of the importance of *quatenus* and *quatalis* modifiers, and in Leibniz we even find an attempt to map the details of their logic. Unfortunately for the philosophy of mind, later logicians have not carried on this enterprise Leibniz began. But to say more on this topic would take us too far afield for the purposes of this paper.

One interesting qualification is needed for my first thesis, that intentions for others imply intentions for oneself, and that is for the intentions I have, not as a private individual, but as a member of a group. If *we* intend him to revisit Isfahan, and I, as a consenting and loyal member of the group, also then intend it, it does not then follow that I must intend myself to do anything, other than refrain from sabotaging our attempt, to get him there. If *we* intend him to revisit, then *we* must do something to get him there, but we may have given the task of luring him there to one of us, but not to me. So my intending him to revisit, if I intend it as one of us, is not narcissistic in the way it is in private intentions—or rather the narcissism shifts, in shared intentions, from *me* to *us*. The first feature of intention, then, which marks it off from expectations, hopes, and fears, is that it concerns the intender's own future, whether the intender be an individual or a group. This needs qualification only when the intender is a private individual *as* a member of a group, that is, when a private intention is directly derivative of a group intention.

This qualification provides an opportunity to introduce the second feature distinctive of intentions, and that is their indirect reliance on the existence of group intentions. All intentions, of individuals and of groups, are intentions to do what the intender *can* do, and the concept of competence or ability requires the existence of group intentions (and intentional activities), namely those involved in the policy and practice of training, criticism, and evaluation of the performance of individuals and groups in all the skills and competences which are exercised in the execution of one's plans, the realization of one's intentions. Even if we narrow the range of intentional objects (of expectations, wants, hopes, and intentions) to those in the person's own future, we have not yet distinguished the objects of intentions from those of other mental states, since we have not distinguished them from self-centered expectations or self-centered wants. Yet intentions are surely not identical with self-centered wants and/or expectations. I can want, hope, and expect to undergo as well as to act, to enjoy and to suffer as well as to take initiatives. But if I *intend* to enjoy the evening, I must intend to do something in order that I enjoy it—take a drug, or a drink, or do my mental relaxation exercises before setting out. Intentions to *act* are basic, intentions to undergo must be supported by them. Just as intentions for others must be supported by intentions for self, so intentions for my *non*actions must be supported by intentions to act. A parallel claim would be false for wants and expectations. I may, and frequently do, want to receive without wanting to do what may be needed to produce or to deserve the goods received, and my expectations of my own eventual death need not be accompanied by any expectations concerning actions of mine relating to my death.

Intentions are intentions to *act*. But what is it for me to act? Suppose I want a certain activity to occur, expect it to require movements of my body, expect my body to make those movements, do I thereby intend them? I want my body temperature to be maintained within a certain range, I expect my body to shiver, sweat, etc. so that that end is achieved, but I do not (although members of yoga groups may) intend to shiver or sweat. Why not? Because these are not activities which I have been trained to perform, criticized for performing badly, or praised for performing well. The doctor, observing that the patient's fever is reduced, that the body's mechanisms have begun working after failure, may say "He is sweating nicely now," but such a remark would not attribute to the patient the exercise of any competence, it would merely record the healthy functioning of the patient's body, and might imply an element of self-praise for his, the physician's, part in restoring this functioning. Avowals of intention, as distinct from expression of ambitions, aims, or formulation of resolutions, must be intentions to do such things as others can recognize as exercises of competence on the intender's part, be those competences as simple and basic as walking, as "easy" as consulting an expert or delegating a task. I can intend only what I reasonably believe I can do, and be known to have done.

To recognize an occurrence as the exercise of a competence, one must be able to recognize more than the fact that a certain result has been somehow obtained. If I want and need to find water, announce the intention to find it by divining, and do indeed find it, then for this to count as successful intentional action I must be able to show that not merely did I find water, have success in my search, but that I successfully *divined* water. For this claim to be true there must either be a community of water diviners who could attest to my performance, authenticate my credentials, or else, if I am the first to divine water, it must be possible for me to pass on my skills, to be the founder of the guild of water diviners. Without community intentions expressed and executed in practices of training and criticism, there could be no distinction between what I do and what lucky results I am vouchsafed, nor therefore between what I intend to do and what I expect and want to happen, miraculously and opportunely. Since intentions are different from confident expectation of miracle, the concept of intention involves that of ability, and so of such group intentions and practices as those involved in the creation, recognition, and encouragement of agents' skills and competences (I assume that it could be shown that group competences in criticism, training, etc., do not involve other group intentions in any question begging or viciously circular way, so the general thesis that the concept of intention depends on that of ability does significantly distinguish individual from group intentions, and make the latter the more fundamental. I assume also, what may be more controversial, that there could not be a private practice of self-criticism which was not parasitic on a public one. In assuming this, I do not wish to deny the vital role of individual criticism in the total practice of group self-criticism, nor to espouse any view of the group mind as possessing any wisdom other than the sum of what its members contribute. I assume merely that cooperation between individuals produces distinctive new phenomena, among them those of recognized competences, and intentions, group and individual). Only if the guild of water diviners would back up my claim that *I did it,* can my claim to have intentionally found water by divining stand up. Such assessment by fellow practitioners involves the acceptance of norms and standards of competence, the existence of not just policies but actual practices of criticism, certification and usually of training. Cognition (including knowing how) requires recognition. In some cases, like intending to insult, conventions make the intended action possible for anyone, since they determine simultaneously the point of insulting and what counts as success at it. With water divining, the point is not convention dependent but what is so dependent is the assessment of successful intentional action, as distinguishable from having one's wishes granted.

Intentions are dependent on common intentions in a way not paralleled in expectations, wants, motives, and goals. These latter, if they are to be spoken of, require common linguistic intentions, but do not, for their very existence, require common expectations, wants, motives, and goals as support for their private counterparts. We do, I think, recognize only such motives as we to some extent share, but we share them by all severally, each individually, being moved by them, not by possessing them in common. We need not be co-possessors of group motives. As an aside, and as a reminder that our interest in intentions is partly with their link with memories, I note here that animals are said to have expectations, hopes, fears, goals, and motivation but not, or not without dispute, intentions, nor, I think, memories. There is a difference between attributing memory and attributing *memories,* somewhat like the difference between attributing purpose and attributing intentions. The individuation of memories and intentions is what seems impossible in the case of animals. However purposive the cat's movements, we cannot split up the cat's behavior into a sequence of intended *moves,* since we are not members of a community of practitioners of the cat's skills, so cannot individuate them. (If a lion could speak we would not understand it.) Why we cannot attribute memories to the cat is more problematic. We can of course speak of the cat's remembering how to do things, of its remembering and so recognizing its former owner, but we cannot separate its memory of him from its recognition of him, and we would not happily speak of it having vivid or dim memories. Perhaps the individuation of memories is somehow dependent on the individuation of intentions, and a study of the link between them might throw light on the individuation of memories, and on the absence of animal memories.

Before turning full attention to remembering, I have still to discuss the third claim for intention, the claim that the objects of intending have a special kind of continuity or connectedness. Let us suppose that what I say I intend doing is something you know I am competent to do, could we then perhaps say that an intention is my *expectation* of an exercise of a competence by me, one whose results I welcome or at least accept? Or perhaps that an intention is the desire for an expected exercise of one of the intender's competences? To these questions, I answer "no." We surely need to distinguish intended exercises of a competence from expected ones, however welcome, and from wanted ones, however confidently expected. I may expect to contradict at least ten statements tomorrow (on the basis of my past performance). I may enjoy a good dispute so find this prospect not unwelcome, yet I need not therefore have formed the intention to contradict anyone. It is at this point that we need to bring in the connectedness of the objects of intention. In several recent articles[10] Castaneda has discussed the case of a person whose present intentions presuppose his future predicted but not currently intended actions. I shall consider a variant of his example, the case of Corlissa who on Friday orders flowers to be delivered on Sunday to the friend whom she predicts she will insult on Saturday evening, when both will be at one of those parties where Corlissa predictably drinks too much and insults her friend. Her expectation of the insult is the ground of her present intention to apologize, and of the steps taken to set that apology in motion. But she does not, on Friday, intend to insult her friend on Saturday. She will, no doubt, bear full responsibility for the insult which she has not taken measures to prevent, and she will undoubtedly insult intentionally when she insults, but she does not, on Friday, intend to insult, she merely assumes that she will. What feature of intention is lacking? I suggest that what is lacking is precisely what is present in Corlissa's Friday intention to apologize, namely an implementation plan, a *timetable* linking the present with the intended future. Corlissa sees her way clear to the apology, but the path from the present to the insult need not be clear to her. The inductive evidence, on which her prediction that she will insult is based, need give her no grounds to predict anything that will lead up to the insult. If Corlissa had intended the result, she would have been able to answer the question "how are you going to insult her?" as she can answer the question "how will you apologize?"

What exactly is the force of this question "how?" which the intender must be able to answer? It clearly does not demand a *specification of all events* causally involved in the production, out of the current state of things, of the intended thing. What it does ask for, I believe, is a temporally continuous story consisting of intended exercises of competence, punctuated by expected states of affairs in which they will terminate, states of affairs which provide the opportunity for the next step in the action plan linking the intender to her intended action. This action plan must be specific with respect to competences to be exercised, although it allows for disjunctive sets of such competence-exercises, for contingency plans. The intender must give us her version of her active future, leading up to the intended action. This account must not have gaps, or if it does, to that extent the intention will be faulty, and once such gaps are pointed out the intender must admit that there was something she had overlooked, and either look to it or withdraw her intention-claim. By contrast, Corlissa's *prediction* of her future action is not at all challenged if she can give no predictions concerning events in the intervening time. Her reason for expecting the insult may be simple self-observation, giving her selective, gappy, predictive power. Her intention, however, must be backed by a plan of action, even if it takes a form as noncommittal as "I shall wait for a suitable moment, and then I shall say either A, B, C, or D, each of them suitable as insults." No such linking of the present to the future is needed for my predicted contradictions tomorrow. My predicted acts of contradicting are not necessarily predicted acts of contradicting specified persons, but if I *intend* to contradict, I must intend to contradict either Tom or Dick or Harry, or the next person I meet. Having in advance predicted but not intended them, I do not, meanwhile, watch for a suitable moment to contradict—such moments will present themselves. To spell out, in detail, what counts as an action in the sense needed for the components of an action plan, just how inactive it may be, why watching can count as an action, is a task which needs to be done.[11] In brief, what is essential is that something count as the wrong way to arrive at the state implied in the action verb. Not all ways of coming to be looking are cases of watching, although to watch is to be looking. Not all ways of passing from an earlier to a later time are cases of waiting, and Corlissa's action plan for her apology involved waiting for the flowers to be delivered.

Intentions differ from adopted policies in that their objects are particular, not general, although future particulars have peculiarities. Corlissa intends not a class of actions which would be cases of apologizing, nor even any one of that class, but the particular one which is the outcome of her implementation plan. It is, unlike present and past events, indeterminate in some respects, those irrelevant to its point, or desirability characteristics, and those undetermined by the implementation plan adopted. Corlissa's plan will not determine the number of leaves included in the flowers which will be delivered, nor the precise time of their delivery, so the particular future action which is her intended apology is lacking in the irrelevant details it will possess when it becomes present. But it is not simply any apology made with flowers to this friend on Sunday, it is *the* one she has set in motion. This particularity of the objects of intending demands of the class of all the things I now have made up my mind to do a special sort of coherence not required of all my likes, fears, wishes, hopes, or even of everything I want or everything I believe. My beliefs should not contradict one another, but they can achieve consistency without singling out one temporal sequence which makes those beliefs true. Beliefs can be general, but as Spinoza remarked in *de Intellectus Emendatione,* memory is of particulars, and we remember unique things best. My memories are of one unique narrative. All my intentions, taken together, may not select one unique narrative for my future, since many of my action plans may have disjunctive components. But this disjunctive character of my intended future does not make my intentions general, any more than my general cosmological beliefs determine a disjunctive set of particular histories of this planet. My intentions must be such that they all fit into one future, and that future must be more than possible, must be made continuous with the present by an action plan. The coherence my intentions must have is the coherence of a schema of the actual future. The continuity within any action plan, or internally related set of intentions, must be the continuity of a schema for that determinate time which flows from this present time and from the opportunities it offers. Acting on those opportunities will lead on to further anticipated opportunities which, when acted on, will lead to that for the sake of which the action plan was adopted.

I have tried, albeit sketchily, to indicate the sense in which intended actions involve continuity, involve an action plan bridging the time between avowal and execution of intention. Such an action plan for the future parallels the personal story of one's past which one's memories constitute. And just as the action plans backing one's intentions may be faulty, so memory may fail, and in a similar way. It is time to turn to memory, and see how the three features found in intention are found there. What I have claimed is that the objects of intending are narcissistic, that private intentions depend upon public ones, because of their involvement with the concept of ability, and thirdly that the objects of intention must show the continuity of an action plan. I have not said much about the verbal indicators of these features. I took noun-sharing or self-omission to be an indicator of narcissism, and I tentatively suggested that the infinitive construction links intention with ability and so with common intentions. I suggested also that the gerund construction, "I intend going," indicates the connectedness or continuity, and so I put a little weight on the fact that when we turn from intending to remembering, we find the gerund as a natural vehicle for the remembered—"I remember going."

"Believe" and "know" do not take the gerund construction. What I believe and what I know have the coherence of a set of logically consistent statements, not the continuity of a narrative.

We remember many things, that something happened, how, when and where and why it happened, how to do various things, and we remember to do what we intended to do. We remember the multiplication tables, the kings of England, and surely in these last cases the narcissism thesis fails. I need not remember learning, coming to know, these things, in order to remember them. We remember passions as well as actions, so the link with ability also fails. All this variety in the objects of remembering contrasts with the narrow range of intended objects. Nevertheless I think that, if we take from the wide range of remembered things only what we would include within our memories, the parallel holds. We need and have a distinction between the sort of human memory which is just information storage, just a capacity to regurgitate input, and personal autobiographical memory, one's retention of one's own past. The latter but not the former demands serial ordering, even if it is faulty. In machines which simulate the human mind and its powers, there is a distinction between the "memory bank" which all computers must possess, and the serially ordered record of the machine's operations, its use of that memory bank, which only some computers possess. Only to these latter machines could we at all plausibly attribute memories (and I am not sure how plausibly we could) or speak of the machines remembering having solved a problem rather than its having in fact solved it and recorded that fact.

Even when we narrow our focus to personal memories, does the narcissism thesis hold? Could I not remember, have among my memories, the time when he solved the problem, or when he suffered defeat, without remembering how I came to know of these facts, or remembering any role I played on those occasions? Obviously yes, just as obviously my memory of my own past is gappy. What then comes of the claimed common elements in the objects of intending and remembering, of their narcissism, connectedness, and dependency on their group analogue? To show that the parallel holds, I have to make an important qualification, namely, that it is of remembering-or-having-forgotten that the narcissism and continuity theses hold. The gaps in my memory are not like the gaps in my knowledge of things I am and was ignorant of. The gaps constitute *lapses* of memory, whereas the gaps in my knowledge and the incoherence of my beliefs can be, or be due to, mere absence of conviction, not to lapse or loss. *Pace* Plato, knowledge is not recollection and lack of knowledge is not loss of memory.

It is memory with its distinctive failings, loss, and lapse, which shows the continuity and narcissism which parallels, in the past, that of the intended future. And after all, we have seen that intention itself is subject to the same sort of fault as is memory. The analogue to forgetting is oversight. As forgetting implies having at some time remembered (however briefly), so overlooking a link in an action plan backing an intention requires that one *will* look to that matter once the oversight is pointed out, if the intention is to survive as such. The forgetting and the oversight are separated from the forgotten and the intended action by a remembering of it and a looking to it, respectively. Anything forgotten must have been remembered. Any overlooked part of the action plan of an intended action must be looked to. Given the forward-looking character of intention and the backward-looking character of remembering, the typical faults of each and the compatibility of such faults with continued claims to intend or remember are exactly what one would expect, if looking for a parallel. Once this qualification is made, it becomes more plausible to claim a parallel in memory to both the narcissism and the continuity of the objects of intention. My memory may *now* be gappy, but between the gaps lie once remembered, now perhaps imaginatively reconstructed, stretches of time which fill out a continuous story, and one in which I am the protagonist. However self-effacing my memory is now—if I recall his triumphs but not my reactions to them, I once recalled those reactions and any account of my memories which mentions his triumphs will imply that I did somehow come to know of those triumphs at that time, that I did have some reaction to them. By contrast, in a novel they may be simply not there. The answer to the question "what were her reactions?" may be "none are recorded in the novel so there were none." But if the record is in the form of memoirs the answer will be "none are recorded so we don't know. Perhaps she has forgotten them, or thinks them not noteworthy." The continuity and narcissism theses for memory seem almost trivial. Of course memory is of what happened and so ideally is as continuous as the rememberer's presence in the past which is remembered. Yet it is not an unimportant conceptual truth that memory is of times, while knowledge is of facts, and that times cannot be discontinuous, as known facts can be disjoint. Disjointed memories are necessarily seen as shards of continuous pre-lapse memory. Disjointed facts are not fragments, but building blocks for a system which tries to unify them. *Pace* Leibniz, it is reason which imitates memory, not vice versa.

There remains one feature to examine in the case of memory, the claimed dependence of the private on the public or common. The claim made for intentions depended on their link with ability. Since we remember not only our exercises of competences, or failures to exercise them, but also our sufferings and what happened to us, it will not be via the concept of ability that personal memory will depend on shared memory. Yet, as we needed to bring in the concept of ability to get *verified* claims about intentions, it is in the verification of memory claims that we need to fall back on the concept of *history,* of what according to public record happened. However connected and first personal a man's story may be, unless it is borne out by, or at least not contradicted by, the group's version of historical fact, it will not be an account of his memories. Here we get a parallel with the need to consult the outcome of group activities of testing competence to back up a man's claim that he not merely *aims* at a certain good, but *intends* to reach it. The dependence of private memory on group memory similarly drives us from his or my memories to our historical past. This feature does not distinguish memory from knowledge, but it does distinguish it from belief and expectation. Personal knowledge needs support from common knowledge, but personal belief, hope, expectation, fear, and opinion may go their own idiosyncratic ways. When we combine this feature of memory with the other two features, we can see how it differs also from knowledge, indeed, if I am right, from all other mental states except intention.

Having pointed out the parallels between intending and remembering, I would like to be able to explain them, and to find some present-directed mental state which would serve as the link between narcissistic, connected, public-dependent memories and narcissistic, connected, public-dependent intentions. How and through what mediator does one's past story affect one's intentions for the future? Through what present filter do intended acts, and their failures, become fate? I have no answer to give to these questions. I have spoken of our gaze into the intended future, and into the remembered past, of its continuity, personal character, and public base. But of the present, of the eye which gazes, its identity and continuity, I have said little. My hope is that the parallels to which I have drawn attention may be suggestive for that more ambitious project.[12]

NOTES

    1. Bernard Williams, *Problems of the Self* (Cambridge, Eng.: Cambridge University Press, 1973), first and fourth papers.
    2. Derek Parfit, "Personal Identity," *The Philosophical Review,* 80 (1971): 3–27.
    3. Zeno Vendler, *Res Cogitans* (Ithaca: Cornell University Press, 1972), p. 19ff.
    4. David Kaplan, "Quantifying In," in *Reference and Modality,* ed. Leonard Linsky (Oxford: Clarendon Press, 1971).
    5. G. W. Leibniz, *Philosophical Papers and Letters,* ed. L. E. Loemker (Chicago: University of Chicago Press, 1956), 2: 1048.
    6. Ibid., 1: 511.
    7. Ibid., 2: 949.
    8. Daniel C. Dennett, *Content and Consciousness* (New York: Humanities Press, 1969), pp. 27–28.

9. Peter Herbst, "Fact, Form and Intentionality," in *Contemporary Philosophy in Australia,* ed. C. D. Rollins and Robert Brown (London: Humanities Press, 1969).

10. Hector-Neri Castaneda, "Intentions and the Structure of Intending," *The Journal of Philosophy* 68 (1971): 453–66, and "Intentions and Intending," *American Philosophical Quarterly* 9 (1972): 139–49.

11. I have sketched its outline in "Ways and Means," *Canadian Journal of Philosophy* 1 (1972): 275–94.

12. I have been helped by comments and criticisms by my colleagues John Cooper and John Haugeland, and by numerous others at readings of earlier versions of this paper.

2

Realizing What's What

Vendler, in *Res Cogitans,*[1] contrasts what we believe with what we know, and concludes that it is not possible for what is believed to be known, nor what is known to be believed. Part of his argument depends upon a contrast between the indefinite relative *what,* replaceable by *that which,* and the *wh*-nominalization *what*:

(1) She believes what he believes.
(2) She wonders what he believes.
(3) She knows what he believes.

In (1) the *what* is an indefinite relative pronoun; in (2) and (3) it is a *wh*-nominalization. Vendler's reading of (3) is one which rejects, as a reading of it:

(3a) She *knows* what he merely believes.

In (3a) the *what* is an indefinite relative. If Vendler accepted (3a) as something which can indeed be said, and not said only by linguistically corrupt epistemologists to prove a point, then his main thesis would be exploded. I shall not defend (3a), in itself or as a reading for (3), but shall instead investigate the *what* in (3), on Vendler's reading of it, and compare it with the *what* of (2) and of

(4) She realizes what he believes.

Vendler lists *realize* as an "apprehensive," that is, as a mental act verb, like *find out, notice,* and *discover,* although he notes that it shows some "leakage" towards the state time-scheme. We can ask both "When did you realize that *p*?" and "How long have you realized that *p*?" This use of

From *Philosophical Quarterly* 26, no. 105 (1976): 328–37. Acknowledgment is given to the Editors of the *Philosophical Quarterly.*

realize is the third listed in the *O.E.D.,* "to conceive, or think of as real, to apprehend with the clearness or detail of reality, to understand or grasp clearly." It is given as a mainly American use (although, of course, this is no longer so), and it is the only use of *realize* which takes a subordinate clause as object. Abigail Adams is cited as asking "Can they realize what we suffer?" The "strict" English *realize* takes a noun or noun phrase as object, cited in Johnson's "An act of imagination which realizes the event however fictitious." Vendler's use of *realize* is clearly the "American" use. When he writes "we will be able to achieve a sympathetic understanding of his [Descartes'] views, sharing his momentous insights but also realizing his own biases and prejudices" (op. cit., p. 4), he is not announcing his intention to make Descartes' prejudices real and convincing to us, but rather to convince us that they were prejudices and biases.

Vendler does not explicitly classify realizing as either "objective," like *know,* or "subjective," like *believe,* but in his discussion of knowing he lists it along with *know, tell,* and *learn* as a verb which, unlike *wonder,* takes a *what*-clause which has lost its interrogative flavor (op. cit. p. 95).

What is this interrogative flavor? Vendler distinguishes indirect questions, given in the *what*-clauses following verbs like *ask, wonder, inquire,* from indirect claims made in the *what*-clauses following *know* and *realize.* The difference, he says, is shown in the different *namely*-clauses which might be attached:

(5) She wonders what he believes, namely whether it is *p,* or *q,* or *r.* . . .

(6) She knows what he believes, namely that it is *p.*

Vendler's[2] own examples of the difference are

(7) I wonder what he lost, namely (I wonder whether he lost) a watch, or a ring or. . . .

(8) I know what he lost, namely (I know he lost) a watch.

I shall try to show that the interrogative flavor of the *what* following *wonder* is not always correctly given by the above *namely-whether* strings, and that *know,* far from having lost an interrogative flavor analyzed in this way, is interestingly different from both *wonder* and *realize* in that its *what* always admits of a *namely-whether* expansion. I shall show how *wonder* sometimes rejects such expansion, and how *realize* rejects it altogether. Instead of Vendler's classification of *know* and *realize* as both lacking in interrogative flavor, while *wonder* retains it, my classification will be between two sorts of interrogative flavor, exemplified by *wonder* and *know,* and the lack of an interrogative flavor, found in *realize.* It is realization, not knowledge, which is the state in which the facts one has absorbed have lost their tie to the doubts and questions to which they provided, or might have provided, the answers, and have been assimilated into a background body of information, presupposed in the questions *and* answers one is now concerned with, taken for granted, acted on, in one's cognitive and practical moves.

To make this plausible I must first distinguish two sorts of questions, which I shall call Belnap[3] questions and bewildered questions. Belnap questions are disjunctions, of possibly indefinite length (one proposition and its negation being a limit case, yielding questions with *yes-no* answers), accompanied by a request for a selection of a correct alternative, all the correct alternatives, or a "complete list" in which all given alternatives are explicitly accepted or rejected. Belnap questions are multiple choice tasks. However little the one who asks himself such a question knows, he knows that the answer lies on the list before him, unless the question is a trick question, a disjunction which is false. Contrast the state of mind of the person who asks, in real bewilderment,

(9) Whatever can have possessed him to do that?

This question isn't yet in a position to be given the Belnap analysis, since no suggestions are provided as to how to generate the disjunction of possible answers. The *what* in this question cannot be expanded into a *namely whether*, followed by alternative answers. Bewildered questions are typically asked by a special form of *wh*-interrogatives, *whatever, whoever, wherever, whyever*, or *what the hell, what on earth*, etc. When a person asks

(10) What shall I do?

this might be taken as:

(10a) What shall I do, namely shall I take on task *a*, task *b*, task c . . . ? (select one).

It might however be a bewildered question:

(10b) Whatever shall I do—please suggest *anything*, help me get a list of alternatives started!

Question (10a) is asked by someone who has some properly structured list of alternatives, or some principle for constructing such a list. But the question in (10b) is precisely one of how any such list can be begun. Answering a Belnap question is selecting an (or several) alternative(s); answering a bewildered question is providing a suggestion, something to treat as a member of the set of alternative answers which would transform a bewildered question into a Belnap question. Bell[4] calls questions imprecise when they resist analysis into the disjunction of their possible answers, but there need be nothing imprecise about the bewildered questioner's grasp of his predicament. He may know his problem, even know a procedure for testing candidate solutions, yet not know how to generate a list of such candidates.[5]

Vendler's treatment of wondering, in (7), turns wondering into asking oneself a Belnap question. He supposes that the wonderer has narrowed down the alternative lost items to personal pieces of material property, that he already knows that it is not his faith, his innocence, his confidence in the government, his wife, or his appetite that was lost. Suppose I overhear a reference to what he lost, and wonder what it was:

> (7a) I wonder what he lost, whether it was his nerve or his watch, his faith or his ring, his innocence or his wallet, his taste in wines or his nasty rash, his job, his girlfriend, or his appetite, or all of these, or none of these.

The wondering which is going on in (7a) is very different from that in (7). There is a list, of sorts, of alternatives from which to select a true one. Or is such a list tantamount to no list? Whether we construe (7a) as involving a rather ill-formed Belnap question, or a genuinely bewildered question like that in

> (7b) I wonder whatever it was he lost—I have no idea what it could be,

it is clear, I think, that Vendler's treatment of wondering makes its interrogative flavor too definitely Belnap rather than bewildered. The man who wonders desperately what to do to save his sanity or his marriage or his career may have no list of alternatives, and no way to draw one up.

Where the asking or the wondering is a wondering *who, when,* or *where,* the interrogatives themselves provide a method for generating the list of alternatives, namely lists of all persons, all times, all places. Yet it would be a very poor joke to assist the person who wonders where on earth his key is by transforming his bewildered *wondering wherever* into the more structured Belnap *wondering where,* by supplying the suggestion that the key is either at p_1 or p_2 or p_3 and so on for all places. Certainly with *hows* and *whys* and *whats* and *wherefores,* if not with *whos* and *whens* and *wheres,* what is in question may be the procedure for generating the appropriate list of alternatives needed for a Belnap interrogative, to get from a *wondering whatever* to a *wondering what* with a *namely-whether* follow-up.

So much for wondering and its interrogative flavor. I now turn to Vendler's treatment of *knowing what,* in particular to his claim that the *what* there has lost its interrogative flavor, that it presents an indirect claim, not an indirect question. I shall argue that, on the contrary, *knowing what* is the perfect case for that Belnap interrogative flavor to which Vendler limited wondering and asking. Vendler notes (op. cit., p. 96) that the treatment he gives to *knowing what,* in (8), cannot be given to *not knowing what,* which instead gives us:

(11) I do not know what he ate, whether it was fish or fowl or . . .

Vendler takes this to show "that negation precedes nominalization in the generative process" (op. cit., p. 97). Why not instead conclude that the treatment given to (8) was premature? By removing the *not* from (11) we get the perfectly acceptable sentence:

(12) I know what he ate, whether it was fish, or fowl or . . .

Admittedly (12) would be more natural if one made it

(12a) *I* know, but *you* don't (and I won't tell you), whether he ate fish or fowl or . . .

If we switch from Vendler's preferred first person cases—a preference in keeping with his avowedly Cartesian approach—then we need not supply such indicators of the will to tantalize or to withhold information:

(13) She knows what he ate, whether it was fish or fowl or . . . so we must find out from her if we are to trace the source of his food poisoning.

There is nothing at all deviant about a *knowing what* taken as a *knowing whether,* nor is there any requirement that a given *know whether* claim must be a preamble to a *know that* claim. Where the sentence is a first person one, then we must indeed suppose that the speaker, who is also the claimed knower, does *know that* . . . , whether or not he chooses to share that knowledge with his audience. That he knows that something or other is the condition of the truth of the *know whether* and *know what* claims. But this does nothing whatever to show that *knowing what* is not always *knowing whether.*

I suggest that to attribute knowledge to someone is to claim that they have the answer to some Belnap question. Whenever we can say

(14) She knows that what he lost was the key

we can also say

(14a) She knows whether he lost the key or the watch or . . . (for some well-formed list)

and also

(14b) She knows what he lost.

The full form of the *know* claim, of which (14) is an abridgement, would be

(14c) She knows what he lost, whether it was key or watch or . . . , namely that it was the key.

The *know that* claim climaxes the series, but this does not mean that every *know whether* is the redundant preamble to a *know that*. Every knower must be able to give a *know that* claim, if his *know whether* claim is true, but he need not exercise this ability, and the speaker who is not the knower spoken of need have no such ability to give a *know that* claim to back up his second or third person *know whether* claim. The presupposition of any use of *know*, first, second, or third person, is that the speaker believes it true that the spoken-of knower has the correct answer to some question, but in second and third person *know what* and *know whether* claims the speaker need not know what that answer is. In all first person singular *know* sentences, and in all *know that* sentences, the speaker must be presumed himself to have what he takes to be the correct answer to the question, not merely to take it that the person spoken of has the correct answer. It is perhaps worth noting that, in first person plural *know* claims, a *know that* climax to a *know what* and a *know whether* need not be one the speaker knows enough to give.

(15) We, that is to say our team, know what the enemy's code is, whether it was of type *a* or type *b* . . . , but I myself don't know since I was in on the early, not the final, stages of the code-breaking.

In first person plural cases, as in all second and third person cases, a *know that* climax to a *know* claim cannot be assumed to be in the speaker's power to give.

That *know* claims are always *know whethers* but need not be *know thats* is important for the comparison I shall now make between *know* and *realize*. *Realize* has several interesting peculiarities. Vendler puts it with *know* and *tell*, "objective" verbs, whose *what* clause presents an indirect claim. Kiparsky and Kiparsky[6] treat it as a "factive," along with *know, regret, ignore, resent, mind,* while Karttunen[7] classifies it as a semi-factive. One of the Kiparskys' syntactic indicators of nonfactiveness is the accusative and infinitive construction after the nonfactive verb. By this test *realize* is clearly factive, but many semantically factive verbs, *admit, acknowledge, understand,* and, worst of all, *know,* pass this test of nonfactiveness. It is unclear why the Kiparskys thought that this *was* a criterion of nonfactiveness, since several semantically nonfactive verbs, *conjecture, assent, allege,* do not take the accusative and infinitive construction. Whatever this construction indicates, it is not nonfactiveness, and it *is* something which distinguishes *know* from *realize.*

Although *realize,* unlike *know,* requires a *that* clause rather than an accusative and infinitive construction, it is not restricted to *that* clauses, but can take *who, what, when, where* clauses. The significant thing here is that it cannot take *whether.* While knowing is, as I have argued, always knowing *whether,* whatever else it is, realizing is never realizing *whether.*

(16) When she heard him phoning the locksmith, she realized what he had lost, namely his key.

There is no room in (16) for a *whether* string, as there was in (14). *Know* sentences, because they have a place for a *whether* string, always have a place for one more preamble to their final *namely* phrase than have the corresponding *realize* sentences.

This suggests that *realize* is not tied, as *know* is, to Belnap questions. To know what's what is to have made the correct selection from a set of alternatives, but to realize what's what is to be in the possession of a truth not or no longer seen as the answer to a Belnap question. What is known is no longer in question, but what is realized need not be seen as having been in question, or at least not as having been in the context of any particular Belnap question. If this suggestion is correct, we might have the beginnings of an explanation of the first difference noted between *know* and *realize,* that *realize* does not take an accusative and infinitive construction. That construction is well suited to listing direct answers to Belnap questions, where there will be no need or room for the qualifications introduced by conditional clauses, by distinctions of mood and tense, which an infinitive construction restricts. The accusative and infinitive construction provides room for whatever we need in an answer to a Belnap question, but if the realized differs from the known in *not* being tied to the form of such a question and its answers, then what is realized may be too complex to fit into the form provided by the accusative and infinitive construction, or the form provided by a Belnap question and its answers. Knowledge accumulates in a way which admits of encyclopaedic summation, as well-formed questions get answers, but realization dawns and grows in a different way, and the result is less susceptible to analytic summation.

What is realized, then, is not seen as the answer to a Belnap question, although of course, as in (16), it can provide such an answer, and many things we say we realize are things for which we easily could provide appropriate Belnap questions. It is the fact that *realize* does not admit of *whether* complements which led to this interpretation of realization, but that fact would not rule out a tie between the realized and questions as such, since we have yet to consider whether what is realized could be the answer to a bewildered question:

(17) He wondered what on earth to do, then realized that suicide was the only solution.

(18) She wondered where on earth her pen had got to, then realized that she had given it to Jim.

In such cases realization does look backward to a question, but not a Belnap question. *Realize,* rather than *know,* is the word we should use, I think, when what is solved is the problem of generating any solution or answer, rather than the problem of selecting a solution or answer.

(19) I was really puzzled about how to go about getting a list of candidates; then I realized that the way to do it was . . .

Realization can be more constructive than knowledge, and when what we realize is an answer to a bewildered question, or a way of transforming that question into a Belnap question, then it may well require a form of expression much more complex and qualified than that needed to answer a Belnap question.

So far I have looked at two ways in which *realize* differs syntactically from *know:* at two constructions, the accusative and infinitive, and the *whether* complement, which *know* but not *realize* can take. I have suggested that, if we see *know* but not *realize* as having the background of a Belnap question, these facts fall into place. I now want to look at two related semantic and pragmatic differences between *know* and *realize,* which I believe will confirm the main thesis, and add a new twist to it.

The first new point of difference is that while we can claim ignorance, we cannot claim contemporary nonrealization:

(20) I do not know where it is.

*(21) I do not realize where it is.

The only use for (21) would be as an explicit contradiction of:

(22) You realize where it is.

But (20) can be used not merely to rebut imputed knowledge, but to proclaim ignorance. This difference can easily be seen to be a consequence of the fact that *realize* does not take a *whether* complement. We can expand (20) into

(20a) I do not know where it is, whether it is here, there or . . .

But the only variant of *(21) would be the equally deviant

*(23) I do not realize that it is here.

A similar variant of (20) is

(24) I do not know that it is here.

(23), like (21), can only be treated as a rejection of a "you realize ..."
sentence, but (24) can be either that, or, if the *know* is emphasized, a
partial rejection of a "you know" sentence:

(24a) I do not *know,* but I strongly suspect, that it is here.

*(23a) I do not *realize,* but I am coming to believe, that it is here.

It seems then that while one can spontaneously disclaim knowledge, one
cannot thus disclaim realization. The detective and the eager learner can
list the things they don't yet know, but not the things they don't yet realize.
Since there is no use for "I do not realize that *p*," there is no use either
for "If I later realize, what I do not now realize, that *p* . . . ," nor for the
first person future tense "I shall realize that *p*, though I now do not."

This difference in first person cases is linked to a more general difference
which shows in second and third person cases. The detective cannot list
the things he doesn't realize, but *I* can list the things he doesn't realize,
as well as the things he doesn't know. The difference between my two lists
will be that on my list of what he doesn't realize will occur only things I
myself realize, whereas on my list of what he doesn't know, I may include
both items such as "that the criminal wore sneakers," which I know, and
also items such as "why the criminal wore sneakers," which I may not
know. The pragmatic differences between *know* and *realize* are easily
obscured by concentrating on first person cases, as Vendler's Cartesian
intentions encourage him to do. Both *know* and *realize,* in whatever
person, commit the speaker to the truth of what is said to be known or
realized, but only *realize* commits the speaker to the claim that he is in
possession of that truth.

*(25) She knows where the pen is, but she's wrong.

*(26) She realizes where the pen is, but she's wrong.

The impossibility of each of these shows that the speaker must take the
knower or the realizer to be in possession of a truth, but the difference is
that to use *realize,* in first, second or third person, is also to claim to share
that truth.

(27) She knows where the pen is, but I don't.

*(28) She realizes where the pen is, but I don't.

I can only speak of others realizing what I myself claim to realize. The use of *realize,* in any person, declares the speaker's own realization. Where speaker and realizer, or speaker and knower, are the same, that is in first person cases, this difference is not so easily evident, but the difference in the negative first person claims points us in the right direction. The restrictions on *realize* are stronger than those on *know,* even than those on *know that,* because the pragmatic implications are stronger. These strong pragmatic implications can be linked with the absence of any *whether* complement for *realize,* since the role of such a complement is to present the speaker's question, not his answer. Yet if he admits, by the use of *realize,* that the truth is in his grasp, he has no need for question-raising on that point, except to test or tantalize his audience.

(29) She knows where it is, whether it is here or not, but neither she nor I are telling you, she because she won't, I because I can't.

(30) She realizes where it is, but neither she nor I are telling you, she because she won't, I because I won't either.

A reasonable assumption about normal discourse, outside examination rooms and spy stories, is that what the speaker indicates he knows-or-realizes, that he is also willing to divulge. To use *realize,* in first, second or third person, is to cut oneself off from retreat into a noncommittal *whether,* is to commit oneself either to revealing what is realized, or to admitting to the will to tantalize, as in (30). I take it that the expectations in discourse are that participants should not conceal relevant information they possess, or, if they do, that they should also conceal their concealment.

I have drawn attention to four surface features of *realize* in which it differs from *know*:

(i) Its rejection of a *whether* complement,
(ii) Its rejection of an accusative and infinitive construction,
(iii) The lack, or limitation, of a use for "I do not realize. . . ."
(iv) The deviance of "You, but not I, realize what's what."

The first two features I linked to the weakness of any tie between what is realized and a pre-formulated Belnap question. Whereas to know is always to know the answer to a Belnap question, to realize something may be to grasp a truth without seeing it as an answer to any already formulated question. If it does answer a question, that question may be a bewildered, not a Belnap question, perhaps the question of how to construct some Belnap question, to generate a list of possible answers. To know is to have solved the answer selection problem, but to realize may be to have performed the more constructive task of *creating* an answer, or of generating possible answers.

The third and fourth surface features point us in a different, but perhaps not unrelated direction. They suggest that realization, unlike knowledge, cannot be recognized without being shared. I can envy others the knowledge they possess and keep from me, but I can recognize what they realize only if I also realize it. Realization, if professed, is essentially shared. One can of course have realized something which one keeps secret, just as one can have secret knowledge, but whereas I can be aware that others have secrets from which I am excluded, I cannot express this exclusion from a truth-possessing community by referring to those things they realize but I do not. *Realize* is used when I speak as a member, not as an outsider. If co-operation and truth sharing are essential to the constructive creative advance in which, as indicated by the first two surface features, realization lies, more essential to it than to more analytical advance, then we would have a link between the two "deep" conclusions I have drawn from the two pairs of surface features. To establish that link would be another task.

I have drawn attention to the peculiarities of *realize* in order to try to combat two prejudices in epistemology. The first is the assumption that the cognitive task is to select from among alternatives, to pick out the few truths from among the many falsehoods, to narrow down on the actual, from among the hordes of possibles,[8] to the neglect of the equally important task of envisaging or constructing the possibles. The second is the Cartesian, individualist first person singular bias, which leads Vendler into his sharp distinction between first person singular "subjective" belief and first person singular achievement of "objective" knowledge. *Realize* is in some ways, such as in its rejection of *whether,* as much like *believe* as it is like *know,* and might have provided Vendler with a bridge across his gap from the "subjective" to the "objective." I have suggested that there is a connection between these two prejudices—that while to know what's what it may be possible to go it alone, to select from among the alternatives somehow there before one, without asking how they were provided, to realize what's what we may have to generate alternatives, and that may indeed require that cooperation, that sharing of what is realized, which I have claimed is of its essence.[9]

NOTES

1. Zeno Vendler, *Res Cogitans* (Ithaca: Cornell University Press, 1972), ch. 5, "On What One Knows."
    2. Ibid., p. 95.
    3. N. D. Belnap, Jr., *An Analysis of Questions* (Santa Monica: Systems Development Corporation, 1963). I have profited from discussion with Belnap on this topic.
    4. M. Bell, "Questioning," *The Philosophical Quarterly* 25 (1975): 193–212. See n. 1, p. 204.

5. Herbert A. Simon, in "Discussion—Bradie on Polanyi on the *Meno* Paradox," *Philosophy of Science* 13 (1976): 147–50, points out that to know what one is looking for is to have a procedure for testing what one "finds," to determine if that is what is wanted, but to have any candidates to test one needs a procedure for generating candidates.

6. Paul Kiparsky and Carol Kiparsky, "Fact," in *Semantics,* ed. D. D. Steinberg and Jakobovits (Cambridge: 1971).

7. Lauri Kartunnen, "Some Observations on Factivity," *Papers in Linguistics* 4, no. 1 (1971): 55–69. Kartunnen classifies as semi-factives those propositional verbs which presuppose the truth of their complements, except in the antecedents of conditionals. It is claimed that *realize,* like *discover* and unlike *regret,* can occur in the antecedent of a conditional in a nonfactive way, for example: "If later I discover I am wrong, I shall admit it." I think Kartunnen has an important distinction between *discover* and *regret,* but I do not agree that *realize* is to be classed with *discover,* since, for reasons to be given below, I think "If I realize later . . ." has no acceptable use, and so escapes this Kartunnen test, while "if she realizes later . . ." is factive.

8. Robert Stalnaker, in an unpublished paper on "Assertion," takes the point of the speech act of asserting to be the ruling out of some of the possible worlds in the set of such possible worlds which constituted the initial presuppositions or "context set" of the conversation. But some assertions may be assertions about new possibilities which should be included, some contributions to a piece of discourse widen rather than narrow the possibility-horizons.

9. I have had helpful cooperation from Kurt Baier, Nuel Belnap, Michael Bennett, Steven Davis, and Richmond Thomason while working on this paper.

3

Intention, Practical Knowledge, and Representation

Danto says "that we can change the world to fit our representations, as in action, or change our representations to fit the world, as in knowledge, are marvelous powers, but they require reference to representation." I shall make some fairly obvious points about representation, some more controversial claims about intentional action, taking my cue in both cases from things Descartes says on these topics. Since Descartes is said to have given us the problem of how a movement in the material world can be mind-imbued or mind-informed enough to count as an intentional act, it seems only proper to see what hints he gives of a solution. It is noteworthy that this problem is not a perennial one, it did have to be invented. Earlier philosophers, even those who believed the soul could be separated from the body, found nothing paradoxical in our intentional physical action. It is a special sort of achievement to become puzzled about the most familiar of things, and intentional action surely should be the most familiar of realities, even to a philosopher. Can it really be that the soul spends so much of its time in error, the discrepancy between intention and act so frequent in our "community of spiritual animals" that we can, without special philosophical conditioning, find it problematic that act and intent should ever coincide, that we should find it puzzling when Anscombe says "I do what happens" (*Intention*, p. 52) and "the failure to execute intentions is necessarily the rare exception" (ibid., p. 86)? If our puzzlement is really due to our Cartesian upbringing, then possibly our cure will lie in a fuller realization of what that involved. The way into the flybottle is the way out.

From Action Theory, ed. M. Brand and D. Walton. (Dordrecht: D. Reidel, 1976), pp. 27–43. Copyright © 1976 by D. Reidel Publishing Company, Dordrecht, Holland. Read at Winnipeg Conference on Action Theory, May 1975.

Descartes' own philosophy of action is to be found in three places, first in a few references to the active life of the human person, secondly in his account of divine action, and thirdly in what he says about the actions and passions of the soul. If we want to find Descartes' views about intention and about representation, we must look in all these places.

On the active life of the human person he has a sensible and pragmatic philosophy to offer, one which involves a complete reversal of his official epistemology and metaphysics. When the goal is not truth but the well-being of the whole person, the rule of withholding assent until rational certainty is obtained gives place to this: "we must take sides, and embrace, as regards ordinary affairs, the opinions that seem probable in order never to be irresolute when it is a matter of action. For it is our irresolution which causes us sorrow and remorse." (Letter no. 403, to Princess Elizabeth, trans. by E. Anscombe and P. T. Geach, p. 285.) Whereas in the *Fourth Meditation* sin lay in allowing the will to get ahead of the intellect, here the diagnosis is reversed. Rogues are turned honest, cognitive vices become practical virtues. Whereas for the purposes of the search for truth the ideas of sensation are confused and in need of replacement or regimentation by innate ideas, for practical purposes of harm-avoidance they are clear and in "their own way more distinct than any I myself deliberately produced in my meditations" (*Sixth Meditation*). The reversal is complete in ontology as well as epistemology. That intellectually incomprehensible intimacy between substances with distinct essences, the union of mind and body, is said to be "understood very clearly by means of the senses" (Letter to Princess Elizabeth) and even the dualism gives way to a considering of the person as *one* thing. What is *its* essence? We are not told, but the rules for finding essences seem to be altered, since we are told to feel free "to ascribe matter and extension to the soul" (op. cit.) when our concerns are practical not theoretical. The turn from theoretical to practical reason brings with it a total reversal in ontology, epistemology, methodology. Yet Descartes himself did not in the end see the search for truth as so sharply separable from pursuit of the good. Kenny ends his book on Descartes with a quotation from a letter to Chanut, in which the philosopher complains that his medical studies are less successful than his ethical ones, and says "instead of finding the means to preserve my life I have found another way, far easier and far safer, which is not to be afraid of death" (quoted, Kenny, *Descartes,* p. 226).

What I find instructive in Descartes' few scattered remarks about human action is his clear recognition that his dualistic metaphysics could not there be taken seriously. "The human mind is incapable of distinctly conceiving both the distinction between body and soul, and their union," (Letter to Princess Elizabeth) and, when our concern is action, it is their union not their distinctness which is important. His attempt to save his official dualistic metaphysics by a supporting dualism of theoretical and practical reason presents an interesting foreshadowing of Kant's dualism, but its unsatisfactoriness is obvious and his acceptance of it uneasy and halfhearted.

The other place in Descartes' thought where he gives any attention to action by an agent with a foot in both worlds, thought and extension, is in his claims about what God does. Here Descartes should perhaps be more embarrassed than he is, since his God escapes that intellectually incomprehensible combination of thought with extension which haunts the human person only by a trick, the trick of his "eminent" possession of the attribute of extension. The Cartesian God, an infinite thinking thing, can be the cause and creator of an extended world although formally himself unextended. It is not very surprising that the materialists should turn the tables on Descartes and ask why the extended world should not, in the same mysterious way, contain the power to produce thinking things. For considering God as agent, however, it does not matter much just how he (or she) contains the attributes of thought and extension. What is interesting for our purposes is the fact that all the divine actions are intentional, and there are no failures of performance. To find out what a philosopher thinks successful intentional action consists in, look to his account of divine action.

The Cartesian God stipulates mathematical truths. It creates finite minds to which it gives the power to know and use those mathematical truths, and to share, innately, the divine self-knowledge, both in the finite mind's knowledge of itself, and in its knowledge of God. It creates a divisible and divided extended substance, sets it in motion, intimately conjoins body-sized and body-structured bits of it with finite minds, one per suitable body. All its knowledge is knowledge of what it has done, what it has made. Intention and knowledge go together, but intention or will calls the tune. This means that those disputed concepts, practical knowledge and knowledge without observation, apply to the Cartesian God, and indeed are the only sorts of knowledge that do apply. To act is to know what one is doing, to know what one has done. God needs no representation before his mind to have knowledge, since what he knows is his own work, itself present, needing no representative. Representation comes into the divine psychology not as the way God thinks but as the objective of action. Among the divine products are deliberate copies of other things. Man himself is made in the creator's image, and in him, as in the creator, intention or will dominates intellect. The universe in its variety, including in it man with his imperfections, is said in the *Fourth Meditation* to have a greatness suitable to that of its creator. Descartes, while claiming that it would be rash of him to investigate the aims of God, nevertheless portrays a God who is constantly expressing himself in his work.

Deliberate duplication or re-presentation is found also in man's innate ideas which copy their divine archetypes. But although Descartes' innate idea of tringularity is true because it represents the divine idea, the truth of God's idea of a triangle involves no correspondence between a representation and what is represented. God's idea of the triangle does not represent anything, it makes triangles what they are. God's thinking is constitutive. The divine archetypal triangle is not a blueprint for triangular shaped bits of matter to be cut out from the material world. "When I imagine a triangle," Descartes says in the *Fifth Meditation* "it may be that no such figure exists anywhere outside my consciousness or ever has existed, but there certainly exists its determinate nature which is unchangeable and external." Its nature has been determined. Triangles are no figment of Descartes' mind because they are authoritative "figments" of the divine mind. To the extent that Descartes gives us a correspondence theory of truth, of truth as adequate representation in an idea of the formal reality that idea is of, this theory is supplemented by, and depends upon, a quite different theory of truth at the divine level. Even at the human level, Cartesian ideas "represent" a very mixed ontological array. Geometrical ideas represent divine archetypes, clear and distinct ideas of material substance represent that substance, confused ideas of sense represent it badly but indicate clearly and well the features of it important for action; ideas of self and of thinking are reflexive or self-representational. (Does self-representation differ from self-presentation?) Ideas of God represent, distinctly but inadequately, the divine mind, none of whose ideas represent anything, since their role is to provide originals.

What I take from Descartes' off-guard philosophy of action, that is from his theology, are several truths about human action. The first is that action by the appropriate authority can create, by stipulation, universal rules within the constraints of which other agents will subsequently plan, think, and act. Such institution-creating action has not been much considered by analytical philosophers of action, but has been left to the Hegelians and the Marxists. Secondly there is the Anscombe thesis that skilled successful intentional action carries with it knowledge without observation of what one is doing. If one has the know-how, one knows one has it and so knows that, in normal conditions, one's act succeeds. Practical knowledge is the human approximation of divine knowledge. Thirdly and negatively, I take the thesis that while representation may be the objective of some intentional action, it cannot be the very essence of intending.

This last thesis emerges more obviously from a consideration of Descartes' most direct treatment of action, namely his account of the actions and passions of the soul, or finite thinking thing. Here we do find unsuccessful attempts at action, happenings which are unintended, the full range of deviations from the norm of successful intentional action. One case to which Descartes devotes some attention is that of the failed attempt to imagine a geometrical figure. The mind can, with a special effort, call up the image of a pentagon, but it may fail to get an image of a ten-sided figure whose ten sides it can count, and it will not even attempt to imagine a chiliagon, since it knows its limitations. Descartes provides an explanation of the special effort needed to call up images, and of the limits of the mind's ability to construct images. The mind, he says, needs the cooperation of the body to call up an image. Whereas for pure thought it needs and has the cooperation of the divine mind which supplies those guiding constraints, innate ideas, for image construction it needs a finite cooperator as well. In the *Passions of the Soul* Descartes gives an elaborate account of the reciprocal actions and passions of mind and brain involved in the transaction. Mind is said to "apply itself" to imagine something, say an enchanted palace. This "applying" of itself is an action of the soul which has an effect in the body, namely a movement in the pineal gland which sends the animal spirits scurrying "towards the pores of the brain by the opening of which pores this particular thing can be represented" (Article XLII). This representation is relayed back to the mind, which then passively receives it and has an image to contemplate for as long as the gland sustains the brain motion needed to supply the image.

What is noteworthy about this account is that the calling up of an image is treated as an intentional activity. Not that having images is always intentional—in dreams images come to the mind unbidden, and these are passions of the soul precisely because the soul's desires are not what activates the image-construction activity. The intention to represent is what distinguishes the active from the passive imaginings. The soul's primary activity is willing. Representing, imagining, thinking about, withholding assent, are the things it can will to do. When what it intends to do is imagine, the soul must know, before it receives back the wanted image, what image it applied itself to get, and recognize what arrives as the correct one, or perhaps one too indistinct to be of any use. The representation is acceptable or not, depending on the intentions of the soul.

Could we treat the soul's willings or desirings as themselves representations, as Danto's account would seem to require? For the soul to want or will an image of an enchanted palace would then be for it to have a representation of an image of an enchanted palace, causally efficacious in bringing that image into being. But there would then seem little need for the intention to be causally efficacious, since the intention itself will contain its own fulfillment. By wanting to represent a palace, one will have represented one. And where intentions *are* representations, chiliagons can figure in representations, anything goes. Intentions become magical self-fulfillers, and intending *followed* or *accompanied* by success becomes a pointless repetition or doubling of representations, as Danto himself half-realizes, in his discussion of imagining. (*Analytical Philosophy of Action,* pp. 142–43).

At this point we need to recall Wittgenstein's simple mental exercise, "Consider the order 'Imagine a red patch.' You are not tempted to think that you must imagine a red patch to serve you as the pattern for the red patch you were ordered to imagine." (*Blue Book,* Harper, p. 3) The moral here extends beyond images to anything which is given the role of a self-applying pattern. But, whatever the method of projection, a pattern is inert. A representation requires a representer whose intentions give it its status as representation.

The representations Danto speaks of are presumably not meant to be images, but they play a role suspiciously like that of Wittgenstein's mental samples. The mind Danto describes seems no more than a sequence of pictures or duplicates of states of affairs in the world. Causal relations to that world distinguish representations which are beliefs, caused by the world they picture, from representations which are intentions, exerting a causal force, self-realizing blueprints for future states of the world. But mental states, even mental representations, do not come to us with their causal history or causal future stamped upon them, so it is unclear how I tell which of my representations are my intentions. Must my intentions, like my motives, declare themselves only retrospectively, when their causal role becomes clear? Must I wait to assess that causal role before recognizing my intentions? But who, in any case, am I, and what sort of thing is recognizing? If recognizing is itself representing the recognized, does the recognized occur twice before the mind on the occasion of recognition? Can it be its double occurrence which makes either representation of the twin-pair a case of something recognized? The busy purposeful life of the mind which Descartes described begins to degenerate into a series of self-repeating representations, a perpetual stuttering of images. Every effort to interpret a representation collapses into a duplication of the thing to be interpreted. With the meagre analytical tools of causal relation and correspondence or "fit," the prospects are bleak for an account of the rich variety of the postures of the mind, for expectations, presentiments, forebodings, fears, admiration, hopes, wishes, aims, resolves, imitatings, envy, resentment, pride, shame, regret, remorse, wondering, revising, correcting, rejecting, ignoring, welcoming, repenting, forgiving, redeeming. With intentionality lost, absorbed into representation, the Cartesian active mind hollows out into Hume's empty theater of the mind, devoid of actors, action, and of critical or appreciative audience.

I do not think it unreasonable to test a philosophy of action by applying its analysis to mental acts. There are intentional mental acts which must be accounted for, and whose relation to other intentional acts must be explained. Recent philosophy of action has been polarized into work, such as Geach's *Mental Acts,* which tackles mental activity, and work, such as that of Danto and Goldman, which analyzes physical action. The work of those who have recognized that physical action, in particular speech, is also mental, that is, the work of Austin, Ryle, Sellars, Searle, Vendler, has not been of great influence on the treatment given to nonverbal physical action, nor to that accorded to mental acts. The exception is Vendler's interesting attempt, in *Res Cogitans,* to map the parallels between speech acts and thought acts. But, there too, we are given a parellel rather than a unified theory, and even the parallel does not extend from acts of mind through speech acts to other socially recognized and world-altering action. In Danto's book, *Analytical Philosophy of Action,* the special class of "gestures" are recognized and thereafter ignored. They are even denied the label *mediated actions,* so little parallel does Danto find between gestures and other extensions of the power to act. For Danto, it is not enabling rules and habits of social recognition which mediate between the active subject and his substantial world, the mediators are intractable causal laws. Danto's agents' abilities to act are "gifts," fixed by fate. Had more attention been given to those powers of action we possess in virtue of our necessarily shared ability to exchange and interpret "gestures," to teach, correct and extend our gesture-repertoire and with it our power to cooperatively understand and reshape our world and ourselves, a less blackly Schopenhauerian estimate of the prospects and freedom of the human agent might have emerged.

Danto does not discuss acts of mind as such, although he clearly wants to allow for such things, and instances imagining as an action. Unlike Descartes, Danto treats it as basic, indeed, not surprisingly he calls it the paradigmatic mental event (*Analytical Philosophy of Action,* p. 142). He suggests that imagining or mental picturing, like arm-raising, is to be treated as one among the normal person's repertoire of "gifts," and even suggests that fate has denied this gift to Ryle (op. cit., p. 131). He does not tell us if there are any mind-mediated mental acts, or any mental gestures. His discussion of feelings and forbearances concentrates on our power to inhibit expression of feeling, a power which is developed by socialization. No consideration is given to the possibility that socialization might not merely encourage our nonbasic acts of inhibition, but might enlarge our repertoire of acts, responses, feelings, and recognitions, including those acts and responses which are central to our cognitive life, subject to rational criticism and logical scrutiny. Our ability to think, the conclusions and beliefs which result, are treated as instances of grace or damnation, of that "fatality of gifts" (op. cit., p. 133) which Danto thinks runs deep, deep into mental as well as bodily potencies and impotencies.

The importance of socialized or convention-generated action is more fully recognized by Goldman, who, in his *Theory of Human Action,* has basic actions raised to higher levels by conventional as well as causal generation. But the level-generation apparatus is not applied to mental acts, which, like Danto's "gestures," are mentioned only to be put aside. Goldman treats cases where some overt action, like hiding or fishing, is given its distinctive feature by the wish, belief, or aim of the agent, as cases of "simple" generation, and he emphasizes that wanting and believing are not mental acts. Cases where two basic actions are co-temporal and together generate a higher-level compound act are cases of "augmentation" generation, and this, like simple generation, is mysterious and anything but simple. The cases of compound augmentation-generation which Goldman discusses are ones where two co-temporal bodily movements are equally basic to one higher-level act, such as jumpshooting in basketball. What are we to say of cases where not just a mental state but a mental act gives a distinctive property to an overt action? Suppose I carry a precariously laden tray upstairs, thinking what I am doing and choosing each move carefully. Is my mental attention to my bodily movements basic to them, co-temporal with them, or generated by them? None of these answers seem satisfactory. There are not two independent co-temporal acts. I could not attend to my movements were I not moving, nor could I move with self-conscious care unless the requisite mental actions took place, the acts, that is, of intentionally thinking about the movements one is making. This may be a rare sort of thought, and most bodily movement, however intelligent or careful, need not be accompanied by such mental occurrences, but there surely are cases not just of careful but of self-conscious movement, where bodily action and mental acts cannot be kept segregated from one another. I do not know how a theory of basic actions could cope with such cases, nor give us a unified theory of basicness and of level generation which would cover mental acts and all the varieties of mind-imbued action. Analytical philosophy of action has neglected both the group action or co-operative action which is the prerequisite for "gestures," and has neglected individual mental acts. If one concentrates exclusively on those middle-range actions which exercise neither the individual nor the collective mind, it will not be surprising if one ends wondering how mind can inform action.

I have argued that attention to intentional mental acts shows us that intention cannot be construed as representation of the intended. Whatever intentions are, they are not inner representations. I now want to look at the concept of representation itself, and at Danto's use of that concept. What is it that makes a mental state a representation of a state of the world, rather than the world-state a representation of a state of mind, especially when the mental state temporally precedes and causally affects the state of the world? How can the mind re-present what is not yet present? Representation is a nonsymmetric relation but it is hard to see, on Danto's account, what determines which is representation, which the represented. Temporal or causal asymmetry cannot be what determines it, and the truth relation, seen as correspondence or "fit," will not do the job since fitting too is a symmetrical relation. We need a way of determining what Austin called the onus of fit, but nothing about a state of affairs calls out for a belief to fit it, any more than a nightmare vision calls out for a fact to describe. Danto rightly says that beliefs are not merely inert furnishings of the soul, isolated introspectable interior decorations. "Beliefs spontaneously refer their holder beyond themselves to what makes them true" (op. cit., p. 148). Beliefs may do this, although I would prefer to say that the believer does it, but the content of the belief, the "representation," does not. We need an intender to determine onus of fit, to treat things, mental and physical, as representations, and to decide on the use of those representations. Without intention, without the will to represent, and without recognition of standards of correctness in representations, the world may be cluttered with matching states of affairs but not representations, with endlessly recurring events but, without a recognizing mind, no eternal return.

John Searle has recently[1] argued that within every speech act there is a representation. Completing every utterance which begins "I warn you that," "I assert that," "I promise that" is a clause which represents some possible state of affairs in the world. The illocutionary force operator operates on representations. Searle also suggested that pictures, or even the represented thing itself, might stand in for the verbal representation. Instead of saying "I warn you that the crankshaft is broken," I might, in a foreign country where my vocabulary did not extend to terms for crankshaft or other car parts, but included a few illocutionary expressions, say "Achtung!" then indicate the crankshaft or draw a diagram of it in its broken state. The thesis that every illocutionary act has a representation as its content seems to me to run into trouble when we consider greetings, congratulations, christenings, where the only states of affairs referred to in the speech act seem to be those brought into being by the act itself. If I greet you, you are greeted, and the world changes to that extent. I represent nothing. I need not be glad to see you, nor do I purport to be so, when I acknowledge your arrival with a formal greeting. To construe a farewell as an utterance which really amounts to "I wish that you fare well" is to force the facts to fit the theory, and to turn the distinctive speech act of farewelling into an instance of a different act, wishing. There are many wishes we can make, at the wishing well, or when we get the wishbone, but to wish that someone fares well is different from farewelling them, to wish that they end in hell is different from cursing them, to wish that they will enjoy one's company is different from welcoming them.

If, however, we grant that many illocutionary acts imbed representations of states of affairs independent of the illocutionary act itself, we could use this fact to get a way of distinguishing representations from what they represent. Where we have two matching or isomorphic states of affairs, one will represent the other only if it is imbedded within an illocutionary act. Vendler, in *Res Cogitans,* speak of the modes of thought, in the Cartesian sense, as *frames* for thought. The referents of verbs such as *doubt, intend, conclude, wonder,* will be thought frames. Adopting and adapting Vendler's felicitous term, we could say that a representation is what is inside a frame. The essence of a picture is to be framed.

If we take this line, then it will be true that most if not all thinking involves representing, but representing will now be dependent on framing, that is on the illocutionary acts which provide the frames, and so convert mere symmetric correspondence into asymmetric representation. This will drive us back to the mental and verbal actions and passions, and our account of representation will wait on our analysis of acts and their intentionality. The representations will be what follow the "I think."

The asymmetry of representing is not the only problem Danto's account appears to face. There is also the problem of reference. Wittgenstein asked, "What makes my image of him an image of *him*?" and gave us the beginnings of an answer, "not its looking like him." (*Philosophical Investigations,* II, iii.) What makes one of Danto's representations one of the future rather than of the past? Suppose I think about a painting I have seen and would like to see again. What makes my thought into a memory, or into an intention? A causal link with the past will be there whichever it is. Could one representation serve both as memory and as intention? Memory, as Hobbes said, supposeth the time past. Does the representation incorporate the *suppositio*? Are Danto's representations tensed, and have they mood as well as tense? Aquinas (*Summa Theologica,* § 78, Article 4) discussed the view of Avicenna that the powers of the souls of men and animals include not merely Aristotle's common sense and imagination, to recognize, retain, and revive past perceptions, but phantasy to recombine them, and an estimative and memorative power to use and interpret them once revived, to assign them to the past or project them into the future as goals for action. Danto's representations will get that status only to a soul with estimative and memorative powers. As previously noted, Danto's differentiation of intentions from beliefs by their different causal relation to the world will not help explain how the believer or the intender knows that and what he believes or intends. Danto rejects Anscombe's knowledge without observation of what one is doing, but surely he would want to allow knowledge without observation of one's intentions. But if all our acts are inscrutable to us, our intentions will become equally alien.

Descartes attributes to the soul an immediate perception or knowledge of what it wills. "It is certain that we cannot desire anything without perceiving by the same means that we desire it; and although in regard to our soul it is an action to desire something, we may say that it is one of its passions to perceive that it desires. Yet, because this perception and this will are really one and the same thing, the more noble always supplies the denomination and thus we are not in the habit of calling it a passion, but only an action" (*Passions of the Soul,* Article XIX). Here we have, in its finite Cartesian version, knowledge without observation. This explains how the very concepts Danto criticizes and rejects can come from a translator of Descartes, Anscombe, and from Merleau-Ponty and Sartre, philosophers in the Cartesian tradition. Their Cartesian tradition, however, included its Hegelian development, which analytical philosophers of action have ignored to their loss. In Hegel's writings we find the most sustained pre-twentieth century explorations of intentional action, the varieties of conventional and institutional action, speech acts such as flattery, buying, and selling. Had our attempt to discover what is basic to action taken its starting point in attention to actions of this sort, instead of remaining paralyzed in the hospital room where the amputee tries in vain to move his missing limb, we might by now have analyses of action of more use to the moral and political philosopher. We might have had a conference on transaction, interaction, cooperative action, instead of a retrospective conference on solitary action. Where the Hegelians demythologized Descartes' doctrine of the need for divine cooperation in human action, we imitated the surface individualism of his unhappy consciousness.

I want to conclude by a brief consideration of an action where recognizable intention in acting, practical knowledge, or knowing what one is doing, and knowledge without observation of what one has done, are clearly dependent on shared forms of activity, yet where the achievement is an individual one, no mere ritual act. It is the case of mimicking, an action which also exemplifies that derivative yet peculiarly fascinating family of intentional activities, re-presenting, and shows the difficulty, limits, and demands on cooperation such actions involves.

Suppose that someone entertains us by mimicking Kissinger. This action resists analysis into a basic action root from which sprout causal or conventional consequences. By doing what does the mimic mimic Kissinger? He speaks English with a German accent. Is his speaking basic, or does he do that by moving his mouth and larynx? This case is interesting precisely because the skilled mimic, unlike the normal skilled speaker, may need to make phonetic moves, not to speak English, but to speak like Kissinger. Descartes has interesting things to say about the skilled speaker's bypassing of the "basic act," of his direct access to the language-mediated act: "When, in speaking, we think only of the sense of what we desire to say, that causes us to move the tongue and lips much more quickly and better than if we thought of moving them in all the ways requisite to utter the same words, in as much as the custom which we acquired in learning to speak caused us to join the action of the soul with the significance of the words which follow these movements, rather than with the movements themselves." (*Passions of the Soul,* Article XIV.) The normal speaker will make the movements themselves by speaking English, as well as speaking English by making those movements, if, that is, he has any powers of phonetic analysis he can call on when needed. The mimic probably will attend to some aspects of his phonetic act, not to speak English, but to get the right accent. Is speaking with a German accent simply or augmentatively generated by speaking? If it is either of these, then that speaking cannot have phonetic moves as basic to it, since the phonetic act is involved in the transformation of a case of speaking into one of speaking with an accent. Difficulties multiply when we try to move up the action tree, and ask what sort of level generation gets us from speaking with a German accent to speaking like Kissinger, and from that to mimicking him. A certain effect must be obtained, elicited from the audience, but it is a convention presupposing special effect. The audience must recognize that the mimic is not Kissinger, that he is not impersonating him or piously imitating him, but mimicking him. The prerequisites for the success of this act are a shared language, a shared knowledge that there are other languages, recognition of the distinctive phonemes of one of them, the German language, a shared knowledge of a particular individual and his speech habits, common knowledge of his public role, shared participation in or recognition of related forms of life such as pretending, quoting, playacting. The mimic's act is what Ryle calls a "higher order" act (*Concept of Mind,* p. 193) which depends for its point and recognition on the recognition of a simpler act to which it makes reference. Its generation is complex, not simple. The audience must not only take it as some such higher order act, they must take it as one whose purpose is entertainment, realize that it is not a serious higher order act like legal representation, deputizing, forgery, fraud, or false pretenses. The act of mimicking is one which can be performed and recognized in a community which has a large enough family of higher order relatives of mimicking, including such things as joking, commenting, alluding, practicing, doodling, aping, clowning, re-enacting, trans-substantiating, performing masses both white and black, parading, advertising, self-advertising, confessing, lying, imposture, scandal-mongering, libel, biography, autobiography, parody, metaphor, sarcasm, irony, satire, coverup and exposure, scrawling graffiti, commemorating in plaques and monuments and statues, portraiture, forgery and defacing, making and faking graven images, and desecrating these images.

Mimicking is not gesturing, since no rule of interpretation licenses its description as mimicking, but, like rule-constituted conventional actions, it is necessarily intentional. One might unconsciously or unknowingly *imitate* someone's mannerisms, but one can no more *mimic* unintentionally than one can unintentionally bless, curse, greet, conceal, signal, telephone, pay, sell, buy, hire, dismiss, marry, or contract. (The list is Anscombe's.) There is of course room for failure, for mistakes and misfires. We may telephone or marry the wrong person. We may attempt to mimic Kissinger but succeed only in mimicking anyone with a German accent. Our conventions and shared forms of life make possible not only routine automatically successful intentional acts, acts where the agent must know what he is doing and that he is doing it, but they also give scope and opportunity for special individual talent, for innovative action, for new forms of social comment, new levels of self-reference and irony. The mimic's talents may be rare and distinctive, but he needs our cooperation to succeed in his act, and our cooperation is mediated by our common cognitions and recognitions.

There are, of course, many ways in which persons cooperate or do things together, and many ways in which individual actions and opportunities for action depend on cooperative or collective action. There are the cases which seem to involve the sharing and possibly the dividing and specializing of such action as might have been done singlehanded. If I am cleaning up the garden and you come and help, then I may do all the raking of leaves while you do all the carrying to the compost heap. This division of pre-existent labor, this joining of forces, will give scope for new forms of action and make room for coordinators, conductors, cheerleaders, coaches, coxswains, timestudy experts. When we have new games, religions, cults, we will introduce new forms of action in a different way, not ancillary to the division and specialization of old singlehanded acts. In such cases, doing things together will not be helping one another do more efficiently what some were already doing, but it will introduce genuinely new things to do. Such innovations, new forms of life, will usually involve a plurality of complementary roles, but these will multiply action possibilities without dividing what was already going on. For such roles, teaching and training will be not merely helpful but essential, since what we must learn is *what* we are doing, not just how to do it. The difference between learning how to walk and learning how to pray is that for the former we may use help, but for the latter we need initiation.

Once there are these roles into which new role players must be initiated, they will affect the roles resulting from division of labor. Once we have the roles of priest and penitent there will be room in armies for chaplains as well as for artillerymen, commanders, commissariat, and ship's captains will conduct prayers as well as chart the ship's course. The roles we find in any society will include all degrees of mixing of the natural and the conventional, the solitary and the social, the unavoidable and the arbitrary, of necessarily and of contingently shared actions, of divided tasks and multiplied action possibilities.

Pioneering work in exploring the complex web which results has been done by D. Shwayder in *The Stratification of Behavior,* and D. Lewis has analyzed in detail one form of self-consciously coordinated action in *Convention.* More recent work has been done by R. X. Ware, on "The Mental Life of Groups"[2] and Gerald Massey has explored the logical behavior of sentences with conjunctive subjects.[3] Massey concentrates on sentences such as "Tom, Dick and Harry are shipmates" and "Tom, Dick and Harry moved the piano," which he thinks predicate logic ill-equipped to handle. Adapting the formal tools of Leonard and Goodman, he treats these conjunctive subjects as *sum individuals* and calls predicates *multigrade* at an argument place which admits of terms denoting sum individuals. A predicate such as "presented the calculus of individuals" will be multigrade since it may be true of the sum individual Leonard and Goodman, but not of either singly. Massey suggests that most if not all predicates of natural languages are multigrade, and he notes the "unigrade bias" of much analytical philosophy, including action theory. Now that the methodological individualists no longer have a monopoly of the formal tools, we can hope that this bias will be righted.

Are action predicates multigrade? The only plausible candidates for unigrade status are those mostly unmentionable actions, degenerate cases in that our control over them is limited and partial. Normal bodily functions may be unigrade but, following an operation, Jones' urinating may not be done singlehanded. Apart from such bodily quasi-actions, the other candidates for unigrade status are the controlled bodily movements which have been deemed basic actions. These, in a different way, suffer from unmentionability, since we have no criteria of individuation for hand movements, and a very poor vocabulary for specifying their variety.[4] I think that the search for basic actions has been to some extent motivated by the wish to find something which is unequivocally the doing of an atomic individual, all his own, some act of which he can say "I may depend on the world, and on my fellows, for what comes of this basic act, for the generation of my nonbasic actions, but my basic act is all my own, it is described by a predicate which is unigrade." Since no procedure separates agent from basic act, there is no room for helpers, no labor to divide, no room for shared responsibility or shared glory. The ironic thing is that to bodily movements as such no glory or responsibility attaches. It is for striking the right note, not for vibrating her vocal chords, that we give the soloist credit.

Most of the things we do singlehanded are done, at other times, multihanded, and some of the things we do together, like attending colloquia, are essentially multihanded. Yet others, such as electing a chairman, cannot be done even by sum individuals unless they have some accepted procedure for coordinated action. Whereas I can be said to attend a colloquium, provided others do as well, *I* do not elect a chairman even when I am a member of a committee which elects a chairman. The sum individual, Mary, Jane, and Sally, elect a chairman if they act as members of a committee, but the atomic individual Mary, even as a member of the committee, does not do so. Actions such as electing are more than multihanded since they require, not merely coordination between the hands, but coordinating procedures. They could be called collective actions. The acceptance of the procedures which transforms multihanded action into collective action seems to be essentially multihanded. I cannot, by myself, accept majority rule, and even if I can, by myself, impose one-woman rule, only *we* can accept and legitimate it.

What makes some actions essentially multihanded?[5] I can't move the piano alone, but if I were stronger, I might. I can't play piano music for four hands alone, but if, like Siva, I had many arms, I might. To converse alone or to elect a leader alone, however, I would have to become several persons in one. (Descartes' claim to converse with himself alone is, significantly, preceded by his admission of confusion between his own existence and that of the triune deity.) Do all essentially multihanded actions involve conventions, or is it for collective action that convention is required? The difficulty of answering this question stems in part from that of sharply dividing the essence from the accidents of the human agent. Is it essentially or accidentally the case that human agents reproduce sexually? Were the actions taken in response to the command "Go forth and multiply" essentially multihanded, was the successful action collective? Perhaps, to analyze what is basic to cooperative action, we will be driven back to bodily movements after all, perhaps we will find in the biological realm the basis not merely for solitary but for combined action. It would be pleasing if sex turned out to be the ur-convention.

Whatever we conclude are the proper answers to these questions, I am convinced that if we want to look for something basic to that action which reveals mind making a difference in the world, the direction to look is not towards some elusive basic action core, but towards all the complex interconnections of common knowledge, convention, and recognition of individual originality and achievement which mediate between the individual agent and the world in which he acts. Danto began his presentation with a quotation from Aristotle, and I shall end by re-invoking him, with another passage from *De Anima*. Danto has described for us a mind which, in its representations, becomes all things, reduplicates them in a shadow world, and sometimes botches things, blots its copybook. I have tried to defend the thesis that its power to engage in this highly idiosyncratic act of re-presenting, and its recognitions of its success and failures in the great variety of its reflective activities, depends upon its cooperative, creative, constituting, or presenting power, on that "other mind which is what it is in virtue of making all things." (*De Anima*, 430a, 14–16.)

NOTES

1. In a paper read at the meeting of the Western Division of the American Philosophical Association at Chicago in April 1975.

Since writing the above I have been able to see Searle's paper, whose theses I have somewhat oversimplified. Searle allows that a speech act like resigning brings about the state of affairs it represents, and he has states of affairs *expressed* rather than represented in acts like thanking. But for all speech acts, the form is $F(p)$, and different speech acts are regarded as different modes of representing or expressing reality. For Searle's fully developed view see John Searle, *Intentionality* (Cambridge, Eng.: Cambridge University Press, 1983).

2. Unpublished.

3. "Tom, Dick and Harry and All the Kings Men," *American Philosophical Quarterly* 13, (1976):89–107.

4. I discuss this in "Ways and Means," *Canadian Journal of Philosophy* 1 (1971):275–94.

5. In "Mixing Memory and Desire," I argue that intending, like remembering, is dependent, for its first person singular instances, on its first person plural occurrences, so is essentially multihanded.

BIBLIOGRAPHY

Anscombe, Elizabeth. *Intention*. Oxford: Blackwell, 1957.
Aquinas, St. Thomas. *Basic Writings*. Edited by Anton G. Pegis. New York: Random House, 1945.

Aristotle. *Basic Works.* Edited by Richard McKeon. New York: Random House, 1941.

Danto, Arthur. *Analytical Philosophy of Action.* Cambridge, Eng.: Cambridge University Press, 1973.

Descartes, René. *The Philosophical Works.* Translated by Elizabeth S. Haldane and G. R. T. Ross. Cambridge, Eng.: Cambridge University Press, 1911.

Descartes, René. *Philosophical Writings.* Translated by Elizabeth Anscombe and Peter Thomas Geach. London: Thomas Nelson and Sons, 1970.

Geach, Peter Thomas. *Mental Acts.* New York: Humanities Press, 1957.

Goldman, Alvin I. *A Theory of Human Action.* Englewood Cliffs, N.J.: Prentice-Hall, 1970.

Kenny, Anthony. *Descartes: A Study of His Philosophy.* New York: Random House, 1968.

Lewis, David. *Convention.* Cambridge, Mass.: Harvard University Press, 1969.

Ryle, Gilbert. *Concept of Mind.* London: Hutchinson House, 1949.

Shwayder, David. *The Stratification of Behavior.* New York: Humanities Press, 1965.

Vendler, Zeno. *Res Cogitans.* Ithaca: Cornell University Press, 1972.

Wittgenstein, Ludwig. *The Blue and Brown Books.* Oxford: Blackwell, 1958; New York: Harper, 1965.

4

Mind and Change of Mind

> To possess the right to stand security for oneself ... the right to affirm oneself, this ... is a ripe fruit but also a late fruit: how long must this fruit have hung on the tree unripe and sour! And for how much longer a time nothing whatever was to be seen of any such fruit. (Nietzsche, *Genealogy of Morals*)

I shall take up Nietzsche's investigation into the many things presupposed in the existence of a person with the right to make a promise. He emphasized the selective memory that must be "burned in," the selective ignoring, the regulation, foresight, premeditation that must precede the right to ordain the future in a promise. A promise is not merely a fixing of the future—any intention is that—it is a renunciation of the liberty to change one's mind, to revise that fixing. Where Nietzsche saw the "real problem regarding man" as the emergence of an animal with the right to make a promise, I want to shift the problem back and consider what sort of thing a person must be, what capacities and training one must have, to possess the liberty voluntarily restricted in a promise. It is the "short willed unreliable creatures," who are the forerunners of Nietzsche's sovereign free men of their word, whom I shall take as my problem. I shall investigate the abilities that even Nietzsche's proud paragons must possess before they can selectively inhibit them in their rare reluctant promises.

My concern with change of mind is a concern with *mind* more than with morals or supra-morals, with the capacity rather than the liberty to change one's mind. At a certain point in exploring that capacity, however,

From *Midwest Studies in Philosophy*, Metaphysics vol. 4 (1979): 157–76. This was originally given at the Chapel Hill Philosophy Colloquium, October 16, 1977, where Daniel Dennett replied. His reply, "How to Change Your Mind," is to be found in his book *Brainstorms* (Cambridge, Mass.: M.I.T. Press/Bradford Books, 1978).

the line between abilities and acknowledged liberties will become blurred. Change of mind is a topic worth exploring at this point in the debate in philosophy of mind for a variety of reasons. Some of these reasons will emerge at the end of this paper, after the investigation itself, but one can be mentioned at the start.

One general reason for attention to this phenomenon is methodological. Change of mind occupies an intermediate status, among mental phenomena as we know them, and this very intermediate status promises insight into the *continuity* of human thinking with its animal origins. Change of mind displays less advanced capacities than promising, or scientific theorizing, or examining one's conscience; but it involves a step beyond the purposive monotony of animal intelligence and the seemingly random veering of, say, birds to flight. It is intermediate between intelligent animal goal pursuit and the highest human or "angelic" (and "demonic") understanding, so holds out promise of displaying intelligibly the transitions from one to the other. Its suitability for this continuity-preserving role is increased by its being intermediate along another dimension also, the cognitive-practical one. Change of mind is a change in neither of the philosophers' two favorite states: belief and desire. Like intention, it straddles theoretical and practical reason, and also like it, is concerned neither with the true, *simpliciter,* nor with the good, *simpliciter,* but with a fusion of the two, or perhaps with something more primitive and more fundamental than either, out of which both those two sacred idols of our philosophical tribe are self-conscious and intellectualized abstractions or distillates. To return to Nietzsche's metaphor, they are "*late* fruits," and the flower from which they grow lacks the differentiation to be found in the variety of its final fruits. Or so I shall eventually argue. For the moment I wish merely to recommend the investigation of change of mind because we do not need to speak of either the true or the good in analyzing it. If to believe is to believe true, then by focusing on belief as the paradigmatic mental state we will likely end, like Davidson, concluding that without the concept of truth there can be no believing, so only interpreters of language can be believers. To choose belief as the central mental state is to start on a road that soon forks into the Davidsonian route, of restricting mental states to language users, and the Dennett-[1] de Sousa route, which splits belief into two problematically related sorts— belief in *truths,* or human belief, where degree of belief is inadmissible, and reliance on facts or high probabilities, where there can be degrees, and which can be attributed wherever such attribution helps in the prediction of an "intentional system's" behavior. Unlike Dennett and like Davidson, I prefer to keep the term "belief" for what can be self-consciously assented to and professed by language users; but in what follows I shall be making room for its more primitive ancestors and explaining how their logic can be so different from the logic of belief in truth.

The methodological advantage of attention to intention and to change of mind, rather than to belief, is that, because we can delay the discussion of *truth*-seeking, we can avoid both of these paths which threaten to cut off our mental capacities from anything from which they conceivably might have developed. If one takes the Davidsonian path, then the emergence of a thinking species becomes a real mystery, so different is it from any other species. Those who take the other path, the bifurcation of belief path, need not deny continuity between Bayesian animal belief and Fregean human assent to truth, but making that continuity plain becomes unnecessarily difficult. Since, like Descartes in the *First* and *Third Meditations,* I believe we cannot rest content with any version of *res cogitans* which does not hold out hope that the answer we give to the question "What is it?" can be made to fit with the answer given to "How, and from what, did it come to be?" I prefer to work first on the mental states that seem, while interestingly mental, to be close enough to their plausibly postulated animal antecedents to promise the required harmony between the accepted analysis, or systematic account, of mind, and its eventual phylogenetic explanation. In the end, of course, the story would have to be continued to show how, out of a hunter and food gatherer, there developed not merely a creature capable of intention and of change of mind, but also a promiser and a truth collector. Hume noted, "There cannot be two passions more nearly resembling each other than those of hunting and philosophy." (*Treatise,* 451) The love of truth which he likens to hunting is not that pragmatic belief formation he had described in Book One, but the "love of knowledge which displays itself in the sciences," and in philosophy, that is with self-conscious truth-collecting, a human habit he treats as on a par with hunting plover, or trout fishing, where the catch is the better the bigger it is and where there is an odd need in the huntsman to pretend that the catch is *useful,* intended for someone's consumption.[2] My concern will be not with truth collecting or with the animal beliefs underlying other hunts, but with what mediates between them, with appropriate action and warranted assertion rather than with either purposive action and its implicit belief, or with self-conscious pursuit of the good and the true. It will help my exposition of that often neglected intermediate area to invent a species who develop just that far and do not go on to become truth-seekers. We could call these mythical creatures, who have eaten the fruit of the tree of the appropriate and the inappropriate, the correct and the incorrect, but not yet the fruit of the tree of knowledge, and of good or evil, the "half-innocent," or, following Frankfurt,[3] the "half-wanton." Once they and their changes of mind have been described, we can go on to complicate the story by seeing what happens to them and their changes of mind when the promising and the truth-collecting mania get a hold, when their innocence is fully lost.

One recent attempt to reconstruct our path out of the garden of animal innocence is that provided by Jonathan Bennett, in *Linguistic Behaviour.*[4] Bennett defends a concept of animal belief and develops from that an account of how such belief might come to be expressed and communicated, first by iconic signs, later by noniconic language. His half-wantons indulge in iconic meanings, make snake signs to one another, and so are set on a slippery, sloping path of tempting communication-opportunities which lands them eventually in a speech community. I shall be offering a different account of the half-wanton stage, but in presenting my half-wantons as animals with the ability, not to make icons, but to change their minds, I shall be developing and narrowing a useful concept Bennett provides, that of a "revised registration." If Bennett is right, the capacity for *revision* of a cognitive state, or "registration," is essential to a believer. To have belief states is also to have changes in such states. I think that Bennett is onto something of great importance here, that we can see what a mental state is by attending to its mode of changing. I shall, in what follows, be using the strategy his account suggests, trying to understand mind by understanding alterations in a mind, and in particular those alterations we dignify with the label "changes of mind." My half-wantons are to have the capacity for such changes, and what I shall be investigating is just how much, and how little, that capacity involves. We can, I hope, see more clearly what does and does not count as a mind by seeing what does and does not count as a change of mind. We can understand thought by understanding second thoughts.

I shall at times be using as data our ordinary linguistic usage, but I shall be assembling that because it points us toward a concept of mind that is suggestive and illuminating in its own right, independent of its support from ordinary usage. I shall not be assuming that the only changes in what is really mind are those changes we call changes of mind. Rather, I proceed in the hope that by looking at that narrow class we can get ourselves properly centered, so that we can the better find our way about in the larger field of human mental events and discern true relationships there.

Not every alteration of "cognitive state" or "registration," or "Bayesian belief" is a change of mind. Acquiring new information which pushes back the frontiers of one's ignorance is not, for us or for our half-wanton ancestors, a change of mind, nor is the mere updating of old information, letting one's mind reflect the changes in the observed world around one. A change of mind *is* a correction, but not all cases of mistake-correction, and no cases or ignorance-remedying, count as such changes. If the mistake is corrected by the bitter experience of acting on the mistaken belief, and acting unsuccessfully, then there will probably be what, to use Bennett's language, is a revision of a "registration," but not a change of mind. If I thought the ice was strong enough to support me, skate on it, and sink, I end up knowing better but not having changed my mind. Learning from sweet and bitter experience is what, within limits, all intelligent animals do, but the prerogative of change of mind rests on a different sort of learning. Bitter though it always is to be found to be in the wrong, the bitterness of being corrected *before* one puts a belief to the test of experience, being corrected by *someone* rather than by "experience," is like the bitterness of pills we cultivate a taste for, because of what they save us from, and also because of the sweets such "lessons" make available to us, including that sweet which Hume called "the pleasure of the game alone." (*Treatise,* 452)

But not every case of correcting a belief *before* bitter experience counts as a change of mind. Simply accepting a correction from a teacher or authority is not changing one's mind. If I have misread an atlas, and have a mistaken belief about the distance between two cities, which you correct for me, I do not change my mind about the distance. Why? Is it because of the passive role I played in both the revision and the original belief acquisition? Is it that I never "had a mind" on the matter, if all I did was consult an atlas? If I had estimated the distance, say from the time taken to fly or drive between them, then revised that estimate after considering the fact that the plane's flight was not as the crow flies, that would be a change of mind. What are the relevant differences? Is estimation of distance a *mental* activity while consulting an atlas is not? Or is atlas-consulting an activity beyond the capacity of a half-wanton, excluded because it is too sophisticated rather than insufficiently mental? If the half-wantons are to be given all and only those capacities needed for change of mind, then at this point I must simply set aside, as a problem to be addressed later, the question of whether acceptance of a corrected atlas-reading displays less or more than what is needed for change of mind. For the moment I shall simply point out that although estimation of distance is uncontroversially an activity we share with half-wantons and with other animals, it is not so evident that revision of such estimates can be attributed to mere animals and it is the revisions that are our focus of attention. We want to know which revisions are changes of mind. What, then, is special about such changes, and about the way we form those beliefs, the correction of which counts as change of mind?

One clue here is that we do not need to *make up our mind* what the atlas says, indeed only in exceptional cases would anything count as making up one's mind on this matter. I am not saying that change of mind can occur only after decisions, after datable happenings called "making up one's mind," but I do think that where the latter notion gets no grip at all, then changes of mind are also excluded. We can speak of making up one's mind in judgment of distance, in evaluation of evidence, and in all nonalgorithmic cognitive tasks, including, perhaps, the *making* of maps and atlases, and in some cases, reading them; but the primary cases of this phenomenon are practical ones, where we make up our mind what to *do* rather than what to say or what to think; so it may be best, at this point, to look at cases of change of mind on practical matters, cases of changing intentions.

The clearest cases of change of mind, as of making up one's mind, are practical. One changes one's mind when one changes one's plans. But, as there were cases of belief-alteration that were not changes of mind, so there are cases of change in one's intentions that are excluded, and the exclusions highlight what remains. Two extremes seem to be not changes of mind. On the one hand, variations in how one implements one's intentions—switching a heavy bag one is carrying from the left to the right hand, when the left arm tires, is not a change of mind, even if the switch makes a significant difference, for the agent, to the outcome of the intentional activity—say if it permanently injures an already weak right elbow. Such alterations in what one is doing, substitutions of one bit of one's "work force" for another, are normal semi-automatic happenings in any intentional activity. They indicate no change of mind or plan, if whatever "plan" there was was not specific about such details. What one intended was to carry the bag, with either arm, with whatever switches one felt like at the time, and that was what was done, without any change of mind. A change of mind that is a change of intention is the replacement of one action plan by another. Where there was no action plan, or where it was non-specific on details, no change of mind can occur. I do not change my mind when, walking along a path, I move aside, off the path, to get out of the way of an oncoming cyclist. Most intentions include, implicitly or explicitly, contingency plans for a range of possible circumstances. Varying one's intentional activity to fit varying circumstances, like updating one's version of current circumstances, requires no change of mind.

At the other extreme from such changes in the disjunctively planned or unplanned if sometimes important details of plan execution are some big changes in one's whole goal structure, which are also not what we mean by changes of mind. A radical conversion is different, and not merely in degree, from a change of mind. It would be an insult to the person who renounces his worldly position and turns to a life of poverty and religious devotion to say that he had undergone a change of mind. To call Saul's conversion on the Damascus road a change of mind suggests ulterior motives—it suggests that he made the change for the sake of

power, or for publicity, or for money, or even for treasures in heaven—
that the conversion was phoney. Paul did change his mind when, for
example, after a dream he went to Macedonia, instead of staying in Troas,
as originally planned. A change of mind is a change in one's goals short
or long term, not in that for the sake of which those goals were adopted.

Such radical changes in ultimate values are not helpfully seen merely
as changes in long-range rather than short-range goals. It is not that changes
of mind occur only when there are changes in short-range objectives,
within a stable context of long-term ones. Changes of mind may concern
my longest-term goals and are still distinguishable from radical alteration
in values. If, in my twenties, I buy a piece of land intended as the site for
a retirement home (or, if you insist on longest range, as a burial plot) then
later sell it and buy land, for the same purpose, in another country, then
I have changed my mind about where I wish to live the end of my life.
It would invite confusion to insist that, since my concern to live agreeably
in retirement remains unaltered, the change of mind concerned less than
ultimate goals. Comfortable old age is no farther away from the young
investor than living in the selected retirement home. If we say that the
young person saved in order to invest in order to buy a retirement home,
in order to live in it in old age, in order to have an agreeable old age, the
last member of this ordered series gives, not a further goal, but rather the
reason why the last-mentioned goal, living in the retirement home, is
adopted. Living there is not a means to a good old age, it is a component
of that. That is the good for the sake of which the goals were adopted.[5]

This contrast between change of goals and change in that for the sake
of which the goals are adopted is important for distinguishing us from
half-wantons. We *are* capable of conversion, and even of rational conversion, and this possibility reverberates, as it were, throughout our lower-
level decisions. We can call everything in question. The specter of ultimate doubt haunts our, but not the half-wantons', lives. We need not rule
out the possibility that they too might undergo changes in ultimate values,
perhaps even to know that they do, and wait for the next "switch of sakes."
But if they do undergo such changes, they, unlike us, will be really passive
in relation to such changes, will be slaves of their values if not of their
passions. In even our own case we typically see such radical changes as
forced upon us. Something *happened* to Saul on the Damascus road. But
we take and impute responsibility for such conversions, and it is important that they can be reason-governed. The possibility of such ultimate
change being "our own" is what Sartre, and Charles Taylor,[6] call freedom.
Such higher reflection on that for the sake of which goals are adopted can
lead to risky "bets on the good," acts of commitment, which are beyond
the capacity of the half-wantons. When such bets seem safe or irresistible

bets, we speak, as Descartes did, of a compulsion that is the highest freedom. Religious converts speak this language:

Take me to you, imprison me, for I
Except you enthrall me, never shall be free,
Nor ever chaste, except you ravish me.

(John Donne, Holy Sonnet,XIV)

The half-wantons will have the thralldom without the freedom.

When a radical change, free or unfree, brings in its train more humdrum changes, will the latter count as changes of mind? Can a change of mind be dictated from "above," as it were? I think this depends on whether the higher change is one we feel *we* brought about, one for which we accept responsibility, or whether we feel we had no choice. Since the half-wantons never have such choices, none of their changes of mind will be dictated from above, nor will ours insofar as we exercise only the capacities we share with them. If I cancel my concert subscription because I am retiring to a convent, after a Saul-like irresistible conversion to a life of contemplation, it would be misleading to say I had changed my mind about the concert series. That occurs when I cancel it, say, so that I can be more flexible about *when* I listen to music, or because I find I enjoy recorded music as much as live music, or even because I wish to devote all my evenings to philosophy. Of course, it is conceivable that all along I had planned to switch at this point in life from occasional concert-going to monomanic philosophic endeavors, so the change in life-style would not then indicate any conversion or change of mind. A change of mind must be distinguished from a change of activity that is not counter to previous plan, and also from changes of activity in that for the sake of which we plan whatever we do plan, do what we do. The passively undergone radical change is like a change in the situation. The world of the convert is a different world from that of the sinner. No situation transformations, internal or external, are grounds for change of mind. If, on my way to the bank to deposit some cash I am robbed of it, my not proceeding on to the bank signifies no change of mind. Changes of mind come about after a review, or refocusing, on features in the old, unchanged situation and its options. Saul on the Damascus road was, as it were, robbed of the ability to go on persecuting the Christians. The blinding light and reproachful voice were, like the robber on the way to the bank, not merely unforeseen, they restructured the situation so totally that the agent found himself in a whole new arena.

The border between new light on an old situation and a new situation is no clear border*line*. Suppose I had decided to take a cab to work rather than the bus, but outside my house, before finding a cab, am offered a lift by a neighbor. Do I, in accepting that lift, change my mind about the cab? An unforeseen option is provided, which decides me. It is not clear whether this is a change of mind, whether the neighbor's offer changes my mind for me. I am inclined to say that the appearance of new attractive options, added to the old ones, is a reason for a change of mind, but the elimination of old favored options takes matters out of one's hands, so presents one with a new matter to have a mind on, not reason to change one's mind. What are clearly ruled out as changes of mind, whatever we say on these more difficult cases, are both those alterations of intentional activity made necessary by circumstance, and such alterations as follow, not from the mere addition of a new attractive option, but from some blinding light (but *not* the "natural light" of reason), which transfigures and restructures all the options. Exactly what an option is, and how we divide up the future action-manifold into distinguishable options, is not easy to say. Here I am relying on an unanalyzed concept of an action plan, and its alternatives, which, to be precise, would need to be spelled out as a connected sequence of exercises of distinguishable competences, on occasions specified as opportunities for such exercises.[7]

So far I have claimed that changes of mind, in the practical area, are not changes necessitated by circumstance, nor are they changes in, or normally subsequent upon, changes in fundamental values. It is now time to look and see what does make us, and the half-wantons, change our minds. What does change one's mind? Such things as previously unnoticed relationships, causal and noncausal, ill-appreciated sequences and consequences, overlooked or unrealized meanings, known but forgotten facts. If someone gets me to change my mind, it will be more a case of "You are right. I was forgetting that (or I overlooked that, or I hadn't seen it that way)—you've changed my mind for me," than of "That's news to me—and it changes my mind." If the news is of a new attractive option, or if it is news that makes the existing options look different in order of attractiveness, then it could be the ground for change of mind. But news that merely selects between contingency plans within an option will do just that, not precipitate a change of mind. Suppose a president has decided on a makework program of a certain definite scope to cope with unemployment. News that the unemployment level has dropped may lead to change of mind concerning the scope of the program, or, if the drop is dramatic, to the scrapping of the program. But normally the adopted plan will have been flexible, embedding many contingency plans for changing levels of unemployment, so that news about the current level, as long as it is a change within the range for which the program was designed, will merely select among according-to-plan subplans, not bring about a change of mind. A change of mind is based upon a reviewing of the options facing one, possibly in the light of updated information, including information about new options, but not in the light of news that destroys the originally chosen option, or that totally transforms the situation, so that a new problem faces one. The new light on the old problem can come from new information, but also from remembering previously forgotten relevant facts, or from coming to realize how a rule applies, or from seeing the irrelevance or lesser relevance of what one had previously given weight to. One's previous stupidity need not have lain in ignorance or mistake, but in forgetfulness, a squinting soul, or blindness to what was there to see, or obsession with one thing there to see, in failure to ignore what should be ignored, and to notice what is there within one's cognitive reach, to put it together, realize[8] what it means, to consider it properly. Consider—the original sense is astrological. Change of mind comes after reconsidering, restudying the stars, the entrails, the "costs and benefits" or other auguries. But a radical shift in the method of considering—switching from astrology to rational decision theory—is, like radical change in values, more than a change of mind, transforming as it would the very activity of considering and, with it, what counts as things to consider. Change of mind occurs against a stable background of procedures and in the calm between revolutionary transvaluations of values.

An important member of the list of things that can be grounds for change of mind is a realization that some rule applies, or of the inapplicability of a rule one had tried to bring to bear on the matter. The half-wantons, must, like us, be capable of rule observation. They, unlike animals, have conventions, and these generate reasons for change of mind, as well as providing, when their application is unclear, matters on which to make up and change one's mind. The guest who goes toward his host with hand outstretched ready for a handshake may change his mind when, from his host's stance, he realizes that protocol demands a bow, or a formal kiss. The half-wanton mind that is changed in a change of mind is equipped not merely with purposes and unquestioned ultimate values but with customs and conventions whose bearing on the current situation may leave room for difference of opinion, and for change of mind. Recognition of when and how a law or convention applies exercises one's mind, but need exercise neither reasoning power nor purposive intelligence. The believer, or even exbeliever, who takes off his hat, perhaps also crosses himself, on entering a church, exhibits neither animal cunning nor critical reason, merely a sense of occasion, but, if his companion fails to observe the convention, may appropriately admonish him, *"Think where you are!"* Thinking shows itself and reveals qualities of mind, as much in recognition of occasion as in working out means to ends, or proofs of theorems, as much in observance as in observation. The customs in which we were trained provide us with reasons that complicate, enrich, sometimes override, those which animal purpose provides, and they prepare the way for those *self*-critical conventions, appeal to which we call reason. The half-wantons have customs, but not the custom of custom-criticism. They are pious dogmatists with respect to both conventions and values.

What exactly have we bestowed on the half-wantons in giving them rules and conventions? We have given them an order in their behavior which mere goal-pursuit would not provide. We have given them the capacity for game-playing, and for transferring to their serious life, out of games, some of the structure that obtains in the game. The new order is deontological rather than teleological. Not all play imitates serious pursuit of goals, and it would confuse matters to construe game-playing as teleological, as like an animal's search for food. (Perhaps the term "goal-directed" should be left for activity in those highly structured and usually competitive games where there *are* goals, and where there is winning and losing.) Some play mimics the teleological order of serious animal life, but all play mimics, or exemplifies, the difference convention makes to human life, the constraints and opportunities it provides. Take a simple skipping game, in which a piece of rope is used to provide both the means and the obstacle to success at that game. If a player, frustrated at his companion's greater skills at skipping, uses the rope to beat them or tie them up, he has displayed that versatile instrumental reason Descartes spoke of, but such purposive action puts him out of skipping bounds. Within the bounds, the conventions, of the skipping game, the rope is only for skipping with, just as within the nongame of normal speech, the sounds made are for communication, not for noise or music. Conventions in and out of games provide reasons for conformity to them and a change of mind may often concern, or be due to, a realization of what such conformity demands.

It seems reasonable to suppose that this recognition of the rope's restricted role, in the game, and of the significance of the hat-removal in a religious context, could come about only in a community that trains its members. Our half-wantons, then, are social animals, and their ability to conform to mutual expectations goes along with their ability to train and be trained, to allow "the actions of each of us to have a reference to those of the other, and to be performed upon the supposition that something is to be performed on the other part." (Hume, *Treatise,* 490) Must we give them language? It seems artificial to deny them it, since language-learning is so clear and important an example of initiation into conventions, as Hume noted in the passage cited. Unlikely though it is that the half-wantons will fail to add language-invention to their other inventions and conventions, what seems strictly necessary for their capacity to change their minds on the sort of grounds discussed is not language itself, but any of its cousin conventions. Let us suppose, then, that the half-wantons have conventions but not yet linguistic conventions. They train their initiates in their procedures and can indicate approval and disapproval, encouragement and discouragement. One ground for change of mind will be one's peers' disapproval of actions one is preparing to undertake. The half-wantons care about conformity and attempt to do the accepted thing, to reach approved goals in approved ways. The expression of approval and disapproval, assent and dissent, must, for the half-wantons, take a nonverbal form—head movements, laughter, frowns, raised eyebrows, encouraging smiles. But since even for us language users, the training in our own language must at least begin this way, there is no particular problem in supposing that the half-wantons can train one another without a language to help them do so. And as, in language learning, the pupil learns from the linguistic response as well as from the nonlinguistic response of the trainer, so in any convention-governed activity, the learner will advance by being included in the activity, by being treated as if he understands before he fully understands.

The denial of language to the half-wantons will limit their ability to represent their conclusions concerning matters of fact. They may have maps, like ours a mixture of the iconic and the conventional, astronomical charts, and perhaps pictures of hunted animals. A change of mind about geographical or astronomical fact will show in an alteration of their maps. A corrected map reading, by contrast, will be a correction in the map-guided intentional activity, and it will be difficult to separate out the map-based belief from the intention relying on it. Where the only things read are maps and charts, misreadings will not be easily distinguishable from other sorts of mis-moves in the map-guided activity. But as long as the half-wantons can, not merely communicate their agreement and disagreement with one another's moves, but indicate a variety of grounds for such responses—pointing, say, to the map, not the storm clouds, when trying to dissuade a fellow from proceeding on the longer path to the destination, we can allow them some discrimination of the fact-reliance component in their intentions, and of the fact-representing role of their maps.

We have, then, a community of half-wantons who, while incapable of conversion, of discerning the possible error of their ways, are capable not merely of animal learning from experience, of trial and error, but of discerning and correcting that error which consists in straying from the way laid down by rules and conventions. They can discern the incorrect as well as the unsuccessful. Is it this, the presence of convention, which makes the differene between having and not having the capacity for change of mind? The thesis I want to defend is that change of mind involves but is not the same as revision of rule application. Only because the half-wantons are rule-observers, mutual regulators, have they the liberty of change of mind. But this change is a revision of a decision more involved than simple rule application. It includes deciding whether the rules apply at all, how to combine correctness with success, how to blend one's second nature, as a trained rule-respecter, with one's original nature as an intelligent animal. Because the half-wantons have both intelligence and a sense of what is required, what is proper, but have no inflexible instinct to tell them when the deontological should prevail, and when the teleological, they must somehow make up their own minds about this.[9] They must exercise *judgment*. What is revised in a change of mind is neither simply a means-end calculation, nor simply the application of a rule to a case, but a judgment that such calculation is appropriate, that the rule is applicable, that it should or should not impose constraints on the means-end calculation. Change of mind is revision of judgment, following on a reviewing of the considerations. Considering, forming an opinion, and judging are the thinkings whose rethinking is change of mind. Neither the adoption of necessary means to one's ends nor the observance of categorical imperatives (of morals or manners or mathematics) gives one's mind any room to operate. Where matters are cut and dried, where there is no choice of what to do, we can "use our brains," exhibit intelligence, even conscientiousness, but not wisdom or even prudence. These show only in matters where there is room for difference of opinion, where no problem-solver gives *the* correct answer, where thoughts tend to be followed by second thoughts.

In the special human case where what is judged is a person's status in the eyes of the law, the specialization of function typical of a legal system makes the task of judging the business of an expert, the judge, but the general features of judgment still obtain. The judge is an expert on the law, but the law does not make his decisions for him. A judge, making up his mind on a case, has, to guide him, a stable background of valid statute, accepted precedent, agreement about the spirit as well as the letter of the law; but these give him room for judgment. A judge in a court of appeal may reverse that original decision, change the Law's mind on a case, but not by rejecting that background.

Both in the law and in ordinary life, judgment, like virtue, is not itself taught, but it is intimately connected with what must be taught, if it determines the way in which what we have been taught gets combined with what we knew or learned without teaching. Only if we have acquired a second nature do we have the job of combining that with our first nature (turning eating into dining, and all the other transformations Gass[10] has so brilliantly analyzed), forming a whole person and shaping a life appropriate to persons with such a nature. We are not, and cannot be, instructed in how to make such judgments well, as we are instructed on how to genuflect and how to count. Perennial attempts are made to reduce such thinking to rule—but it resists the attempt. The higher-order activity of criticizing, rather than that of teaching, is what we depend on for acquiring standards of judgment. It is because others once rethought our thinking, reconsidered what we considered, reviewed what we had in view in making up our minds, that we now can recognize reasons for change of mind. Others seconded, or opposed, our judgment, and so we learned when second thoughts were needed. The critic is different from the detector of mistakes, and different also from the efficiency expert. Criticism may be directed at inefficiency, at sloppy procedure, but it goes beyond that and may challenge ends as well as means, the appropriateness and timeliness of procedures as well as their time-saving success. The hard questions requiring judgment rather than know-how concern the appropriate use of conventions and procedures. Here criticism outruns instruction. We can recognize bad judgment without being able to give a recipe for avoiding it. We all expect more of our pupils than we have imparted by instruction. Example, encouragement, criticism, take over where instruction leaves off. Although not instructed in how to make up one's mind judiciously, we are criticized for doing so injudiciously, and we depend on others for the recognition of good judgment, as well as for one precondition of it, initiation into those conventional procedures for which judgment finds a proper place, as it puts animal purpose in its place. The thoughtless person, the fool, fails not in reasoning nor necessarily in goal pursuit, but in proper judgment, of when to calculate, when not, when to genuflect and when to be still, when to speak and when to keep silent.

A machine that simulated even half-wanton thought would need a similar richness of "inputs" into and constraints upon its "thinking." It would need an analogue to animal appetite, to communicated convention, and to communicated criticism of its actions, its way of spending its time. It would need to know, not merely how to calculate and count, but what to take into account, *what* to count, for how much, and when. For thinking beings, for us and the half-wantons, there is a time for all things under the sun; but no clock, and no clockwork calculation or routine, tells that time.

Change of mind, then, is a matter of having second thoughts which are revised judgments, revised to correct faults of judgment which others helped us learn to discern by their response to our unrevised judgments. We revise judgment to avoid anticipated criticism, expecting the revised judgment to be affirmed by our potential critics. What *we* judge *two* times is sound.

For the half-wantons, now revealed as our real Rylean ancestors,[11] criticism will take the form of withholding reassurance or affirmation, and perhaps of indicating the ground for an alternative judgment. Without language they will not have a way of recognizing the general faults of judgment, and what leads to it, faults which we can recognize, like forgetfulness, thoughtlessness, rashness, lack of a sense of proportion, myopia, obsession with one aspect of a matter, inability to ignore distracting irrelevancies. The half-wantons may be able to discern and correct what are, in fact, specific instances of these, but scarcely to discern them as instances of specific sorts of fault, if they have no language in which to articulate either the grounds of their agreement or disagreement, or their detailed assessment of their fellows' judgments. The point of withholding language from them was to discover just how much they might do without it and where its absence would limit them. Without language they can not merely have other convention-guided activities, but they can make up their minds and change their minds, and help one another do so. They can, without language, represent and indicate some facts relevant to judgment; but the sort of representation that would discriminate the thoughtless person from the forgetful person seems necessarily noniconic, and any conventions used to make such distinctions would *be* linguistic conventions. What language can do, which the resources we have given the half-wantons cannot do, is to discriminate and represent norm-governed activities as such, the moves and the reasons for them, the faults and the virtues of the players. Such ability to represent themselves as thinkers could transform the half-wantons into us, since once their own procedures, including their critical responses to one another's judgments, can be articulated and described, the activity of criticism can be directed upon itself.

There is no automatic transfer of the activity of criticism from its usual target, individual performance, including judgment in making up and changing one's mind, to the practice of criticism itself. The thoughtful person applies critical standards to his judgment, so is prone to second thoughts and changes of mind; but more than thoughtfulness is needed to be critical about the standards of criticism themselves, to be critical through and through. Such meta-criticism, criticism directed at itself, is reason's province. The thoughtful person may examine his life, without having examined his method of examination. It remains an open question whether reason pays, by its own coin or any other, whether a life examined by examined standards is better than a less reflectively examined life, whether we lead a better life than the half-wantons. The half-wantons engage in critical judgment of one anothers' judgment, but criticism of criticism requires a language, a way of representing the critical enterprise and articulating its standards, positioning them for critical survey. What we call *rational* norms are standards of criticism that we take to bear, or to have borne, critical inspection. What we say *three* times is *true*? Once we have rational as well as thinking beings, the balance of nature and convention, nature and second nature, established by less critical thinking, can be upset, and then we are apt to get attempts to deny or banish mere less-than-rational convention, definitions of rationality as mere efficient goal pursuit. (Sometimes what we say the third time is simplistic.)

The liberty to change one's mind, then, rests upon membership in a community where there is mutual recognition, which trains its members in some conventions, but not necessarily linguistic ones, and which has the practice of affirmation, of second-thinking an individual's judgment about how to use the training received. Where there is the possibility of such interpersonal affirmation, such heteropersonal second-thinking, there will soon also be auto-personal second thoughts, attempts to improve one's judgment so that it can be reaffirmed by one's potential critics. Second thoughts follow on interpersonal second-thinking. An individual can change his own mind because others once have tried to change it for him, have responded to his judgments with their assent or dissent. The mental events that are changes of mind reveal the interdependence of thinkers, and the limits of the dependence of thought on language. A half-wanton has enough of a mind to be able to change it. The half-wanton mind, and ours in so far as we are capable of just such second thoughts, is mind as Wittgenstein and Ryle presented it, the precariously maintained possession, of some moderately sociable and moderately intelligent animals, of a capacity for minding how their moves measure up to shared critical, but not necessarily *thoroughly* critical, standards.

The view of mind I have endorsed is, then, different from that widely held view that takes language to be essential to thinking. I have suggested that it is essential for fully reflective thinking, for the search for the final truth and the ultimate good, but not for its more modest basis, the attempt to avoid the incorrect and the inappropriate. I shall conclude by making a schematic comparison of the view I have endorsed with that of Bennett and Davidson, and with that of Dennett, using the Cartesian view as the background for the comparison. One can find in Descartes' writings about finite mind a variety of emphases and claims. These can be labeled and expressed thus:

(a) *Reflexiveness:* A thinker is aware of itself as a thinker.
(b) *Heteronomy:* A thinker is aware of a better thinker, in comparison with which its own thinking may be imperfect, and whose reassurance it needs to combat self-doubt.
(c) *Representation:* A thinking thing has ideas with "objective reality."

(d) *Intellect:* A thinking thing discerns truths, can see clearly and distinctly the relations between its ideas.

(e) *Will:* A thinking thing accepts or rejects truth-candidates, or postpones decision.

(f) *Versatile Expressive Speech:* A thinking thing can express its thoughts in speech.

(g) *Response:* A thinking thing can respond appropriately to what is said to it.

(h) *Convention and Custom:* A thinking thing has learned a language, its ability for (f) depends upon "the customs in which we were trained." (*Passions of the Soul,* Part First, XLIV)

(i) *Versatile Intelligent Problem Solving:* A thinking thing can use its reason in all sorts of situations.

These nine capacities of Cartesian mind are not an unordered list, but they are only partially ordered by Descartes himself. The last four are clearly thought by him to be less basic than the first five; but beyond that little can be said, despite his claim to have isolated the essence of mind. If we take (b) seriously, and consider Descartes' views about the nature of truth for that super-thinker, then we would need to make (c), (d), and (e) dependent on a special case of (h), namely on what God decrees to be truth. Truth is correspondence, success in representation, for Descartes but not for his authoritative thinker. Perhaps the best summary formula to extract from Descartes' account would be this:

"I am a thinker. Anyone whom a thinker repeats or reaffirms, or who can reaffirm what a thinker proposes, is itself a thinker."

This would cover the Divine Thinker, but at the cost of narrowing the test for admitting finite fellow-thinkers from appropriate speech response to appropriate assent. Descartes rightly expresses real doubt about which thinker does the second-thinking. "In some way I have the idea of the infinite earlier than the finite, to wit, the idea of God before that of myself." (*Third Meditation*)

Bennett's emphasis on iconic meaning as intermediary between animal belief and full linguistic meaning gives this ordering of the Cartesian features:[12] (i), with modified (d) and (e), then (c) and (g), then (f), then (h) and perhaps (b). Self-consciousness, (a), enters very early, with (g). The early place given to representation makes his view different from both mine and Dennett's, while my view differs from both Dennett's and Bennett's in its emphasis on (b) and on (h).

A view like Davidson's[13] picks up Descartes' emphasis (f) and (g), and makes thinking essentially a matter of the ability to use and interpret speech. His account gives a crucial role to one custom-dependent custom, that of "interpretation," that is to a version of (g) and of (h). He argues for the primacy, among thoughts, of beliefs, and the dependence of belief on "interpretation." To believe is to believe true, and truth enters the picture when the believer is an interpreter of the beliefs of others, expressed in language. Thus "a creature must be a member of a speech community to have the concept of belief" and to have a belief is to have the contrast between true and false belief, and so to have the *concept* of belief.

I find Davidson's account to exemplify what Ryle called the intellectualist legend, the tendency to "suppose that the primary exercise of minds consists in finding the answers to questions, and that their other occupations are merely applications of considered truths, or even regrettable distractions from their considerations."[14] Davidson, I think, confuses understanding with interpretation and unduly emphasizes understanding language, which is merely *one* convention our thought presupposes, essential though it may be for some thinking.

Davidson's account highlights language, one of the external criteria Descartes gave for detecting the presence of inner thought. Dennett's[15] account, like Bennett's, gives priority to the other external criterion, (i), intelligence in behavior. It is taken as basic because the other features presuppose its presence. On the story Dennett gives, they emerge in the following order: from intelligent pursuit of goals, from the sort of rationality possessed by any "intentional system," anything we have reason to treat as possessing beliefs and desires, we move to the special case of the system that *reciprocates* such treatment—that has beliefs about our beliefs, second-order beliefs. Any creature capable of manipulating our beliefs, would have this reciprocity, a special version of (g), appropriate response to other thinkers. From that Dennett moves to the special case of such reciprocity that is involved in linguistic response, where the intentions are Gricean,[16] that is, are not only higher order, but include a reference back to one's own lower-order intentions. Once we have that, we have the seed from which self-consciousness grows. We have persuasion, mutual persuasion, ascription of responsibility, and the attitudes to others taken in such activities can be turned on oneself. "Acting on a second order desire, doing something to bring it about that one acquires a first order desire, is acting on oneself just as one would act on another person: one schools oneself, one offers persuasions, arguments, threats, bribes, in the hope of inducing oneself to acquire the first order desire."[17] Dennett, then, has a Rylean account of Cartesian self-consciousness, (a) which links it intimately with (g), response to others, and with (f) language.

What is not clear to me is exactly how Dennett sees (c), representation, coming into the picture, nor where he places (h), convention, in the developmental story. For Gricean intentions to have a reasonable chance of success, that is for them to be *intentions* rather than wild hopes, there must already be a public language, a set of accepted speech conventions, some version of (h). We cannot get "the meaning" out of "utterer's meaning," if the utterer must depend on common knowledge of *the* meaning, in his intention to produce a specific uptake in the hearer by the hearer's recognition of his intention to get just that uptake. Gricean intentions depend on conventions and do not generate them. So I think that to get individual linguistic intentions one must have some account of convention, of the shared intentions of the group.[18]

About representation Dennett says "we should be particularly suspicious of the argument I was tempted to use, viz., that *representations* of second order intentions would depend on language. For it is far from clear that all or even any of the beliefs and other intentions of an intentional system need to be *represented* 'within' the system for us to get a purchase on predicting its behavior by ascribing such states to it."[19] He says this when discussing reciprocity. I think he would agree that by the time one has persuasion there must be some representation of belief, and, for unspoken self-persuasion, there must be representation "within the system."

Dennett has given us an illuminating way to order some of the Cartesian mental factors. One begins with intelligent behavior, using a crude version of intellect and will as postulates to explain that. The crucial next step is the presence of reciprocal response, leading to linguistic response, enabling mutual persuasion and so self-consciousness. The story I have told is not very different, but it gives more weight to convention and to nonlinguistic conventions and also to a secular version of Descartes' awareness of a superior more authoritative thinker. These differences between my account and Dennett's make my story more heavily indebted to Ryle than is his, though his is certainly not unRylean, given the central place in it of the concept of a higher-order act. Dennett's preference for propositions, and for treating all mental attitudes as propositional attitudes, gives his account the pervasive intellectualist bias against which Ryle warned us, and which my account was designed to avoid. Perhaps if propositions were treated as no more than the formal objects of acts of proposing, with only such structure as such objects need have, then addiction to propositions would be harmless and we could get progressively richer structures as the act of proposing becomes more sophisticated, when language is present. With these reservations about propositions, and about the adequacy of Gricean intentions to generate any conventional meaning, and with my added emphasis on an initially authoritarian training for the eventual thinkers, so that they are forever haunted or reassured by a superior thinker looking over their shoulder, checking up on or endorsing their thinking, my account of what it is to be a thinker is not so different from Dennett's account of what it is to be almost a person.

I have, by inventing the half-wantons, artificially introduced a fairly sharp break between thinking and fully rational and reflective thinking, claiming that it is not necessary for thought as such, for mind and change of mind, to have full self-consciousness, or representation, or language. The half-wanton thinkers have other-consciousness, the desire to think acceptably, that is they have the capacity for appropriate response to fellow thinkers. They have a nonlinguistic version of (h), convention, and they have the special cases of (g), which are responses to training and to criticism, which therefore involve (b) their acceptance of an authority external to their individual thinking, that is, they are heteronomous. Given these three features in addition to their animal base of purposive intelligence, they are thinkers. When they add language, representation, and full critical self-consciousness, particularly consciousness of their own already existent critical procedures, then they will have stepped into the harsh light of reason and can acquire Descartes' version of intellect and will, become seekers of the truth, lovers of the good, and aspirants to autonomy. But this late fruit, reason, ripens from the green fruit of mutual criticism of judgment, and from the flower of animal intelligence only when that is pollinated with conformity to convention. Realization that the conventions and resulting practices are *ours,* and can be changed, that criticism can be turned on articulated practices as well as individual participants in a practice, is the sometimes indigestible late fruit, sour even when ripe. And if the ripeness of that late fruit lies in full self-consciousness, reflexiveness, as the whole modern philosophical tradition from Descartes through Leibniz, Kant, Hegel, to Nietzsche, affirms and reaffirms, then in part that ripeness will show in recognition of one's origins and one's relatives.

To be a thinker at all is to be responsive to criticism, a participant in a practice of mutual criticism and affirmation. A rational self-conscious thinker will turn a critical eye on purported armchair reconstructions of one's ancestry, one's own revisions of them included. Once one has eaten the sour apple of reason, even change of mind becomes reflexive, directed on its own analysis.[20]

NOTES

1. Dennett, in his reply ("How to Change Your Mind," in his book *Brainstorms* [Cambridge, Mass.: M.I.T. Press/Bradford Books, 1978]) to the original version of this paper (given at the Chapel Hill Philosophy Colloquium, October 16, 1977), endorsed a distinction introduced by Ronald de Sousa, in "How to Give a Piece of Your Mind; or, a Logic of Belief and Assent," *Review of Metaphysics* 25 (1971):52–79. The distinction is between Bayesian

animal belief and human assent to linguistically formulated truth-candidates, which must be either assented to or rejected—a version of the Cartesian will that affirms or denies the ideas which the intellect has already scrutinized. Such assent is seen to involve an act of commitment, a bet on truth. Some such bets are uninteresting because sure bets. (Again, compare Descartes in the *Fourth Meditation:* "If I always understood clearly what is true and what is good I would never need to deliberate about what choice and judgment I ought to make, and so I would be entirely free without ever being indifferent." Descartes was no gambler and insisted that any bet on truth be a sure bet, but he did separate out the act of assent of the will from the prior understanding which made it a *safe* bet.) The bets that are risky are the ones we are likely to revoke in a change of mind, according to Dennett. As will become clear, my account of change of mind makes it a second bet, not on truth but on appropriateness; that is to say, I want to delineate a level intermediate between animal Bayesian belief and language-requiring assent to truths.

2. Dennett, following de Sousa, suggests that the distinction between animal belief and linguistically articulate assent gives us the right basis for an account of both self-deception and *akrasia.* The former, presumably, will be the sin of assenting to what one does not believe, the latter the sin of believing and acting on what one would not assent to. Hume clearly thinks the need to try to *connect* intellectual truth-seeking (assent) to pragmatic belief and action is merely itself a bit of self-deception, and that the higher wisdom would lie in recognizing it as no more than a pleasurable game that need connect with the beliefs we rely on no more closely than does backgammon. If we insist on putting something we value at risk in our gaming or our intellectual assent, that is merely to make the game exciting. "Human life is so tiresome a scene, and men generally are of such indolent dispositions, that whatever amuses them, tho' by a passion mixed with pain, does in the main give them a sensible pleasure." (*Treatise,* 452) I have discussed Hume's account of the relation of intellect to passion and action in "Helping Hume to Compleat the Union," *Philosophy and Phenomenological Research,* 41 (1980):167–86.

3. Harry Frankfurt, "Freedom of the Will and the Concept of a Person," *Journal of Philosophy* 68 (1971):5–20. Frankfurt's "wantons" are distinguished by their absence of higher-order mental attitudes of a specific sort, namely desires to desire, higher-order "volitions." My half-wantons have higher-order attitudes, since they want others to echo their own attitudes. Among higher-order attitudes we need to distinguish not merely relative height (second, third, fourth level), but also homogeneous from heterogeneous attitudes, and also self-confined from other-involving higher-order attitudes. Frankfurt is interested in a particular self-confined homogeneous case, the desire to desire. My half-wantons have other-involving homogeneous and heterogeneous higher-order desires, and some of these are indirectly reflexive or self-directed. The hope that others will affirm one's judgment, will judge as one judged, is self-directed without being self-confined.

4. Jonathan Bennett, *Linguistic Behaviour* (Cambridge, Eng.: Cambridge University Press, 1976).

5. The difference between doing something *as a means to* attaining something else, and doing it *for the sake of* some good it contains, recognizes, or celebrates, has been explored and developed, in a perhaps controversial way, by Heidegger, and by Hannah Arendt in *The Human Condition.* She restricts the proper applicability of "for the sake of" to actions in the public arena, in what she calls the space between persons, who have a common conception of a good life. Means-end reasoning, by contrast, is available to the perhaps solitary *homo faber,* whose "work" is goal-directed, guided by the conception of what it is he is making, rather than, like public "action," done for some goodness' sake. More recently, Alan Donagan has spoken up for the irreducibility of sakes, in a section of his *The Theory of Morality* (Chicago: University of Chicago Press, 1977) entitled "The Limits of Purpose." He

distinguishes what he calls purposive teleology from the teleology of ultimate and "non-producible" ends.

6. "Responsibility for Self," in *The Identities of Persons,* ed. Amelie Rorty (Berkeley and Los Angeles: University of California Press, 1976).

7. I have tried to say something about this in "Intentionality of Intentions," *Review of Metaphysics* 30 (1977):389–414; and in "Ways and Means," *Canadian Journal of Philosophy,* 1 (1972):275–92. Harman's account of intention formation, in "Practical Reasoning," *Review of Metaphysics* 29 (1976):431–63, is helpful here.

8. In "Realizing What's What," I have tried to say how realizing is related to knowing.

9. A fascinating alternative account of how our ancestors coped with such situations is to be found in Julian Jaynes, *The Origin of Consciousness in the Breakdown of Bicameral Mind* (Boston: Houghton Mifflin, 1976). Unfortunately, I did not discover Jaynes's book until after this paper was completed. Jaynes's hypothesis is that before the development of conscious independent judgment (in my sense) humans heard voices or saw visions instructing them what to do. These were objectifications of the products of their own brain's right hemisphere, not yet in full communication with the left problem-solving hemisphere. Jaynes's account takes for granted that persons, or proto-persons, with bicameral minds had language, so that, like Saul, they heard *voices* instructing them what to do. My half-wantons are more advanced than Jaynes's bicameral men in that half-wantons can judge for themselves (in a qualified sense) in novel or difficult situations; but they are less advanced in having been, for my special purposes, artificially denied language. But I am in agreement with Jaynes that language is a precondition of full self-consciousness, or what I later call reflexiveness, and I certainly agree that any of our *actual* ancestors who were capable of judgment and revised judgment probably *did* have language.

10. William Gass, "The Stylization of Desire," in *Fiction and the Fitures of Life* (New York: Godine, 1979).

11. I refer here to Wilfrid Sellars's influential paper "Empiricism and the Philosophy of Mind," in *Science, Perception and Reality* (New York: Humanities Press, 1963). Sellars takes the Ryleans to have language but no recognition of unspoken thoughts, nor privileged access to them. My Ryleans depend less on language, more on other conventions and the mutual recognitions they involve. I call the half-wantons our "ancestors," but they might also be taken to be ourselves as children, on the verge of language acquisition. I present them as our forebears rather than as ourselves when children, since children are members of a community containing rational adults, who educate them; so a child's half-wanton mind is, right from the start, affected by the pressure to become a truth-speaking rational adult.

12. Jonathan Bennett, *Linguistic Behaviour,* p. 112.

13. "Thought and Talk," in *Mind and Language,* ed. Samuel Guttenplan (Oxford: Clarendon Press, 1975).

14. Gilbert Ryle, *Concepts of Mind* (London: Hutchison, 1949), p. 26.

15. Dennett, "Conditions of Personhood," in Rorty, *Identities of Persons.*

16. H. P. Grice, "Utterers' Meaning and Intention," *Philosophical Review* 78 (1969):147–77.

17. Dennett, "Conditions of Personhood," p. 193.

18. I do not think David Lewis, in *Convention* (Cambridge, Mass.: Harvard University Press, 1969), gives us what we need, but David Shwayder provides a richer concept, in *The Stratification of Behavior* (New York: Humanities Press, 1965), p. 303. I have begun to discuss shared intentions in "Mixing Memory and Desire," and in "Intention, Practical Knowledge, and Representation."

19. "Conditions of Personhood," p. 185. Dennett refers here to his earlier paper, "Brain Writing and Mind Reading," in *Language, Mind and Knowledge* (Minneapolis: University

of Minnesota Press, 1975). Dennett's quoted recognition that inner representation is not of the essence of intentions, including Gricean intentions, does not itself settle the question of whether he sees language as primarily a means of outer representation. I interpret his account to be giving language a "manipulative" role before it is used for representation, and on that interpretation his position is significantly different from Bennett's.

20. The revisions this reconstruction has undergone owe much to many constructive critics looking over my shoulder—to Daniel Dennett, John Haugeland, John Cooper, Kurt Baier. Obvious, I hope, will have been the influence on this essay in sociometaphysics of the writings of Ryle, Sellars, Davidson, Dennett, Bennett, and also Norman Malcolm's presidential address, "Thoughtless Brutes."

5

Cartesian Persons

Strawson's account of persons, in *Individuals,* highlights the fact that persons have both physical and psychological predicates, and also the fact that psychological predicates have the same sense in their first and third person uses. "It is essential to the character of these predicates that they have both first and third person ascriptive uses, that they are both self-ascribable otherwise than on a basis of observation of the behaviour of the subject of them, and other-ascribable on the basis of behavioural criteria."[1] Strawson contrasts his view with that of Descartes, whom he takes to give priority to self-ascriptive uses and to separate the true subject of the (psychological) P-predicates from that of the (corporeal or material) M-predicates. In a footnote[2] he qualifies this contrast between his own and the Cartesian view, by adding that this reading of Descartes is at least widely enough accepted to justify calling such a view Cartesian. My aim in this paper is to elaborate the suggestion implicit in this footnote, that the real Cartesian view is more complicated and more interesting. Indeed I believe that the Cartesian view, when more fully elaborated, is quite close to Strawson's own view, and also that, when helped along a little, it points us towards some facts about persons which can serve as a basis for supplementing and correcting Strawson's view.

   The popular version of Descartes (dare I call it the straw-Descartes?) holds four questionable theses about mental states—that they are states of something which has no corporeal character, that they are essentially private or first personal, that they are experienced, that they are events or clockable episodes. Strawson is concerned to reject at least the first three straw-Cartesian theses. For present purposes the fact two are the most important. As Strawson notes,[3] Descartes in fact is adamant, even in the

---

From *Philosophia* (volume honoring P. F. Strawson) 10, nos. 3–4 (1981): 169–188.

Meditations whose advertised achievement was to have established the distinction of soul from body, that "I am most tightly bound to it (my body) and as it were mixed up with it, so that I and it form one unit" (117; VII, 81).[4] He can have it both ways, maintain both the real distinction and the "substantial union" (to Regius, Jan. 1642; III, 493) of mind and body, not merely because of his belief that mind and body are in a unique sort of causal and phenomenological[5] relation, but because of the methodological dualism which underlies his metaphysical dualism. Descartes has a distinction which foreshadows and inverts Kant's distinction between practical and theoretical reason, the requirements of action and those of theory. Where Kant saw practical reason as putting us in touch with a world of pure noumena, while theoretical reason explored the order in empirical phenomena, Descartes gives the empirical phenomena the role of guiding our action, while theoretical reason discovers both the pure essences and the things themselves whose essences they are. Descartes believed that it is from the standpoint of practical agents that we know ourselves to be *in* the world, to be so blended with a body that it becomes proper to "ascribe matter and extension to the soul" (281; III, 694). Descartes has two methodological principles, one for theory and its contrary for action, and he has, correspondingly, two opposed standards of clarity and distinctness. In his correspondence with the Princess Elisabeth he advocates not that caution which intellect imposes on the will, but decisiveness in action, since "it is just our irresolution which causes us sorrow and remorse," (285; IV, 295) and in the First *Meditation* he noted that his method of doubt was a justifiable procedure since "I am now engaged not in action but only in thought" (65; VII, 22). This decisiveness in action is to be displayed even when the ideas on which we act are, by the standards of intellect, maximally confused, since, for action, such confusion is transformed into distinctness. The data of the senses, including color, warmth, and all the properties which resist mathematical analysis and so resist intellectual clarification, are indispensable guides to action, and "to this extent (*eatenus*) they are clear and distinct enough" (119; VII, 83). This claim of Descartes *might* be read to mean simply that, by the same standards of distinctness which intellect observes, colors and sounds are not *so* confused to be useless for practical purposes. Sometimes indeed Descartes does want to claim for sensory data a minimal but sufficient intellectual distinctness since such data play a vital role in establishing the existence of physical things, and confirming physical theory. This minimal intellectual distinctness, however, is confined to the sensory presentations of *mathematical* qualities. Descartes does not reveal to us the principle whereby pure intellectual ideas become "schematized" and recognizable to imagination, how extension for intellect relates to extension for the senses, but such translation from nonimagistic thought into phenomena is presupposed in his reinstatement of the senses as aids to intellect, in detecting the real presence of extended things. The main task of the senses, however, is to detect the presence of what is harmful or beneficial to the embodied person, and for that task even sensed secondary qualities, maximally confused-for-intellect, are said to be "more vivid and prominent and in their own way more distinct" (112; VII, 75) than other ideas. I think therefore that Descartes does have, not merely a double standard of intellectual distinctness, but also a standard of distinctness for action which selects, as maximally distinct, the very ideas which are for intellect maximally confused. What is distinct for action is indistinct for theory, and what is distinct for intellect, the real distinction of mind and body, is confused and paralyzing for action. "The human mind is incapable of distinctly perceiving both the distinction between body and soul and their union, at one and the same time" (281; III, 693) and for action it is their union which matters. Indeed Descartes advocates that only a few hours a year be spent contemplating the real distinctness of mind and body and the metaphysical principles on which that depends—and that for the purposes of assuring oneself that the soul's satisfactions are of more worth than worldly pleasures. Descartes' readers may have mistaken a devotional exercise for an all-purpose truth, disregarding Descartes' warning to the Princess Elisabeth that it is very harmful to occupy one's intellect often with contemplating the principles which enable one to discern the real distinctness of soul from body. Of course it is possible that Descartes' advice is intended only for *female* minds, but it is still in order for me to elaborate the concept of the person which Descartes believes should supplement the metaphysical concept of a mental substance. Metaphysical meditation may be needed, occasionally, to combat the fear of death, and to establish the proper subject matter of physical science, but for understanding persons other more mundane modes of thought are available.

Descartes then has a concept of an embodied person, a union of mind and body, which for the purposes of action should supersede the concept of a thinking substance. Strawson gives a special centrality, among the P-predicates, to those which refer to intentional action, and in this sphere he and Descartes are in agreement. The one who acts, who seeks the good and avoids harm, is a union of mind and body, one to whom both physical and mental predicates apply, one whose "whole mind seems to be united with the whole body" (121; VII, 86). The concept of a person to which action predicates are central is a concept which includes mental and physical predicates, for both Strawson and Descartes. For Strawson it is of related importance that the psychological predicates be ascribed univocally in both the first and the third person. I turn now to Descartes' treatment of this issue.

That Descartes neglects third person psychological claims is part of the popular myth—the ghost in the machine is a narcissist if not a solipsist. Strawson, by speaking of "Cartesian egos"[6] implicitly endorses this part of the myth, and links his opposition to over preoccupation with first person ascriptions to his rejection of Cartesian dualism. Is Descartes in fact guilty on this score? He gives surprisingly little attention to the relation of his own status as a thinker, and his awareness of it, to his awareness of other finite thinkers, but he does give a central place to one special case of third person mental attributions, namely those applying to a perfect thinker. "In a way my primary concept is of the infinite rather than the finite, of God rather than myself" (85;VII, 45). Descartes uses the third person when speaking of the divine mind, but, like all present persons, an ever present deity can by referred to in either the second or the third person, depending on whether or not one is speaking *to,* not merely about, the person who is present. I shall eventually suggest that any true account of persons must do justice not merely to the interdependency of first and third persons, but also to the mediating role of second person attributions. I shall argue that persons essentially are second persons, in a sense which will not be made clear until after I have explored some aspects of Descartes' treatment of persons which go beyond his treatment of thinking things.

The first point to be noted is that Descartes acknowledges both the fact that persons speak (41; VI, 56–57) and also that they speak in a customary language, which they had to learn from others (Article XLIV of First Part of *Passions of the Soul*; XI, 362). He sees the role of speech to be the expression and communication of thoughts to other finite thinkers, but he does not see thought itself to be intrinsically expressible or linguistic. It is intrinsically representative, but the representation may be purely private and unexpressed, and need not be in any language. He grants but deplores the fact that "most men's thought are concerned with words rather than realities" (198; VII, 37), seeing this as contamination, a case of that confusion of intellect by imagination which he believes is a source of much error. The ability to learn and use a language exercises imagination and memory, not pure intellect, which can represent realities without imagistic or linguistic means. We need language, on Descartes' account, only to detect other finite thinkers, or satisfy other thinkers that *we* are thinkers, and that is a practical not a theoretical need. Our genuine theoretical need for a standard of excellence, or correctness, in thought, is met, on Descartes' account, not by fellow finite thinkers, but by that divine mind to which we have direct innate nonmediated access.

I find it significant that, while Descartes down plays the place of language in the life of a thinker, he does not minimize the importance for thought of that *correctability by another*[7] which we post-Wittgensteinians find so essential to both speech and thought—the reason, indeed, for their interdependence. Cartesian thinking is intrinsically subject to correction and improvement, but for this purpose the only communication Descartes finds necessary is communication between a thinker and a perfect thinker, and communication between one time and another within the history of one finite imperfect thinker's progress of thought. Strawson's thesis that "one can ascribe states of consciousness to oneself only if one can ascribe them to others"[8] is, therefore, not an anti-Cartesian thesis but a Cartesian thesis brought down to earth. But just because Descartes' third person, or other mind, *is* the divine mind, he has trouble with the thesis with which Strawson links this one, the thesis that intentional *bodily* action, including, although Strawson does not stress it, meaningful speech, is attributed to other finite persons in the same sense in which it is self-attributed.

Strawson makes the predicates attributing meaningful action to a person central because "such predicates have the interesting characteristic of many P-predicates, that one does not, in general, ascribe them to oneself on the strength of observation, whereas one does ascribe them to others on the strength of observation. But, in the case of these predicates, one feels a minimal reluctance to concede that what is ascribed in these two different ways is the same. This is because of the marked dominance of a fairly definite pattern of movement in what they ascribe, and the marked absence of any distinctive experience."[9] Descartes relies on such publicly recognizable patterns of perceptible physical change, namely speech, to get different finite thinkers in touch with one another, but for the communication essential to a thinker there is no such physical intermediary. Strawson, however, emphasizes the importance of intentional action *not* because its recognition involves acceptance of public standards of correctness, but because predicates ascribing it "release us from the idea that the only thing we can know about without observation or inference, or both, are private experiences."[10] Such predicates take us both beyond the essentially private, and beyond "experiences." I have already pointed out how Descartes has his own way of acknowledging the essential nonprivacy of standards applicable to thought, and now I want to suggest that it is a mistake to saddle him with a reduction of thought to a sequence of experiences. His distinction between the active and the passive modes of consciousness just is the distinction between what we mean and what we undergo. Both are modes of consciousness, in that we are necessarily aware of them when they occur, but Descartes emphasizes their difference as well as their common essence. The very intrinsic confusion of the passive modes of sense perception and imagination is due to the fact that they *are* distinctive experiences which, unlike innate ideas of intellect, must be experienced to become familiar. The distinct intellectual ideas we have of mathematical and theological properties are, Descartes says, native to us, so that "my first discovery of them appears not as the learning of something new" (101; VII, 63–34). Redness and pain, however, must be experienced to become familiar. Whereas "discovery" of intellectual essences is discovery of the contents of the treasure-house of one's own mind, phenomenological exploration of the sensory world takes one into new outside territory, the source of genuine experiences. Descartes, then, can agree with Strawson that the intention behind any piece of intentional action, say a stretch of speaking, is not a series of private distinctive experiences. And I presume that Strawson agrees with Descartes' claim that, when such speech occurs, the speaker is conscious of the thought expressed.

Descartes does see particular mental acts and phenomenological experiences as modes which diversify an enduring thinking thing, but there is no reason to treat his "modes" as time slices or time chunks of the history of a thinker, any more than there is reason to treat all modes of thought as distinctive experiences. Descartes is committed to the fairly uncontroversial view that a thinking thing endures through time, and has a variety of active and passive states, some of which succeed others. I began by describing a Cartesian strawman, who held four questionable theses— that thoughts are not states of a body, that they are private or first personal, that they are experiences, and that they are clockable events. I have now distinguished Descartes from this strawman. His recognition of the embodiment of agents qualifies his acceptance of the first thesis, his recognition of the normative heteronomous character of thought protects him from the second error, his distinction of active from passive modes from the third, and only an overly narrow construal of modal diversity as temporal diversity would commit him to the fourth erroneous thesis.

These aspects of Descartes' account of thinking needed emphasis to show how, while he does not see speech as essential to thought, he does see some essential features of speech to be central features of thought. Dependency on another for standards of correctness, and the capacity for meaningful acts as distinct from passive undergoings, are essential to Cartesian thinkers whether or not they are embodied and thinking *persons.* It is not clear whether Cartesian finite thinking things could recognize one another's thought if they were not embodied, whether, that is, any test of appropriate response could then apply. However, there is no doubt that the Cartesian *person,* the one who acts and seeks its good in this world, does speak and engage in other activities whose norms, like those of speech, derive from a human community, not merely from a single creature's intimacy and with its divine creator.

That Cartesian persons and embodied Cartesian thinkers *speak* is the first important positive fact I take from Descartes to supplement Strawson's account of persons. There are some further facts about persons which Descartes recognizes, and which I wish to stress, which concern norm-related variations in consciousness. The difference between being sane and insane, between being awake and being asleep, and being adult and being a child, are not differences reducible to the variety of modes of thought which Descartes recognizes. All the modes of thought—doubting, understanding, assenting, denying, being willing or unwilling, sensing, imagining, occur in childhood, apparently occur in dreams, and occur in some form in insanity. Childhood is not the time when there is a preponderance of doubt, or of certainty, nor can we characterize dreams or insanity by the particular prevalence or absence of some modes of thought, as Descartes characterizes such modes. The fact that persons sleep, that they develop from childhood to adulthood, that they can suffer from bouts of mental illness—all these are facts about persons, and the thought of persons, which Descartes notes, but whose full significance he fails to recognize. These predicates of persons are Strawsonian P-predicates, since they concern variation in type or level of consciousness, but they are also predicates attention to which can call in doubt the very dualism of P-predicates and M-predicates, of psyche and matter. Attention to them is attention to the border between the Aristotelian animal and rational soul, and, as Descartes was fully aware, Aristotle's philosophy of mind is the enemy of Cartesian dualism. It is therefore understandable that the facts which support the Aristotelian view, while not ignored by Descartes, are recognized by him only obliquely and somewhat perversely.

The fact that persons sleep and dream provides the frame, and dictates the form, of Descartes' *Meditations*. They divide into six light-filled, day-long, sleep-interrupted chains of thought. The possibility that he may be dreaming is introduced early in the *First Meditation* and not removed until the last paragraph of the *Sixth Meditation*. It provides Descartes with a ground for doubting his beliefs about the details of the physical world, but one fact he does not explicitly doubt is that there is an alternation of sleeping and waking, that conscious beings *do* sleep and dream. This fact should have given Descartes more pause than it did, for nothing in what he takes to be the essence of a thinking substance explains this rhythm of consciousness, this periodic tiring and lapse into an inferior level of consciousness. Descartes moves very quickly from the possibility that he might be mad to the possibility that he is dreaming, and he thereby fails to do justice both to madness and to dreams. To be mad is to be faulty by interpersonal standards of mental performance, but to be asleep, and to dream, is to sink into a state which is *not* temporary madness, since no interpersonal testing can go on then, but which is, for the dreamer himself, once he wakes, recognized as an inferior sort of consciousness. A solitary person could recognize the fact that he slept periodically much more readily than he could know whether or not he had, in solitude, suffered from temporary bouts of insanity. Descartes calls upon a supermind to validate his reason, to declare him sane, but he needs no direct divine guarantee of his own wakefulness—that he establishes eventually for himself by trusting "Nature's" sense-transmitted lessons, as well as that "Natural light" which has a stronger divine guarantee. The supermind with which he contrasts his own fallible mind is not only the standard of sanity, but also, traditionally, one who slumbers not, nor sleeps. Descartes does not advert to *this* difference between the divine mind and his own, and indeed there was no reason for him to think that if his mind were separated from the body it *would* tire, sleep, or dream. Only its union with a body provides any sort of explanation for the peculiar fact that finite minds take regular recreation, as it were, time off from their regular serious activities of truth seeking. (Angels do not sleep) In the *Passions of the Soul* Descartes explains dream images as due to the body's influence on the mind, but he does not grant that, very early in the *Meditations,* the very fact that sleep occurs could have provided him with evidence that any thinking thing which sleeps *is* an embodied thing.

"Is sleeping," "is dreaming," "is awake," are P-predicates, in that they imply of any subject of which they are predicated, that it is a thing which has conscious states, but they are not predicates which apply only to persons. Animals sleep, dream, wake. If we want a predicate in this group which seems true only of persons then we must turn either to ones like "suffers from insomnia," or to ones like "on waking writes down his dreams, for later analysis by his psychiatrist." The ability to recount one's dreams is one which implies the possession not only of language, but also of a certain sort of memory, namely recollection. Cartesian thinking things have this ability, and, like the ability to sleep, it is *not* one which is really explained by Descartes' account of the essence of a thinking thing. That essence does include the capacity for intellectual advance, for retaining and supplementing rather than losing and regaining the truths previously acquired. But well-trained animals have *that* sort of memory, and so do computers. The only temporal distinctions it requires are between what is past, already done, present, being done, and future, to be done. The ability to give a historical account of one's past, to recall *when* one learned something, whether it was before or after some other past event, is a different ability from that mere availability in the present of a truth one is certain one learned at some unspecified time in the past. Descartes believes that God's veracity guarantees that, if he believes he has already proved, it matters not when, a difficult theorem, then he will not err if he takes its truth as established and moves on to new theorems. He need not keep *repeating* the proofs he has already on some previous "day" seen to be sound. But memory as recollection precisely *is* the repeating and ordering of old things. The intellectual memory Descartes wants validated is not repetition or recollection, but that retention which obviates the need for repeat performances. Human thinking things, however, have both sorts of memory, and the whole of Descartes' "analytic" style of philosophizing exercises the ability to provide a narrative account which recounts, in order, what has already been. That human persons sleep, and that they recall their dreams (or anything else), should, then, for Descartes have been facts about conscious beings as supect as the fact that they sensed and imagined. Like sensing and imagining, sleeping and recollecting are not essential operations of a pure Cartesian intellect. Only a seeker of *historical* truth would need recollection and narrative ability, and only one who tired and was capable of relaxation would be a sleeper, one for whom the question "Awake or asleep?" makes any sense at all.

One crucial achievement of the waking person, for Descartes, is to keep track of where particular physical things come from and go to, and this is both of intellectual and of practical importance. Yet the very concept of a thing's presence or absence is threatened if the intellect is abstracted from the whole person. It is not merely that disembodied intellects could not themselves long be individuated or kept track of, it is that their attention to the physical universe would be transformed so that the distinction between what was present and what was absent would lose grip. Without the limitations of sensation and voluntary movement to localize them, they would be everywhere or nowhere, and, without spatial position they would stand in problematic temporal relations to physical events. Only the sustaining acts of God could link a moment in mental time with one in physical time, if finite minds had no power to act in the world. But there is no need for me to repeat these Kantian and Strawsonian criticisms of the Cartesian position.

The fact that we regularly sleep, that our life divides into nights and days, gives us both that interruption of thought which presents the need for reliance on the sort of memory for which Descartes sought a divine guarantee, and also a division of time whose very monotony helps us with that before-after sequential ordering *within* the past which historical and narrative thinking requires. Planning for action requires the same ordering within the envisaged future. We divide both our past and our future into a succession of days and nights. I now turn to look at a different sort of nonmodal variety within a Cartesian person's passage through time, the (within one life) nonmonotonous unrepeated *stages* through which a person progresses. It cannot be said that Descartes gave this development the emphasis I wish to place on it, but a surprising amount can be gleaned from his writings concerning the typical stages of a thinker's history.

Many times Descartes appeals to the fact that in our early years our mind is "immersed" in the body, and he uses this fact to explain the confusion of ideas which may persist into adult life, so that "there are even a number of people who throughout their lives perceive nothing so correctly as to be capable of judging it properly" (XLV of First Part *Principles*; VIII, 21). Descartes sees infancy and childhood as a time when confusion and prejudice get a hold, a time which sets up the obstacles whose overcoming constitutes intellectual progress. "We were all children before we were men; we must have been governed a long time by our own appetites on the one hand, and our preceptors on the other." (16; VI, 13). Both the child's preoccupation with bodily appetites and the child's docility, acceptance of authority, and impressionability, are seen by Descartes as causes of intellectual error and confusion of mind. From the standpoint of practice they are not so pernicious, since he believed that even in adulthood a person should "obey the laws and customs of my country, faithfully keeping to the religion which by God's favor I was brought up from childhood" (24; VI, 22–3). Neither respect for authority nor preoccupation with one's bodily well-being, and so with sensations which concern that, are harmful to that union of mind and body which is the Cartesian finite agent. From the point of view of intellect, however, childhood seems a disaster from which one may never recover. The enlightened intellect is suspicious both of authority and of the senses, yet has grown up trusting both. Descartes sees intellectual advance to be a matter of liberation from prejudice and from the contamination of intellect by sensation and imagination, a progress from original obscurity and confusion to clarity and distinctness, to intellectual redemption by the natural light.

Now this fact, that we all are children before we are adult, and that certain transformations are possible in the course of the transition, means that not only are descriptive predicates like "young" and "old" applicable, but also normative ones: "has an old head on young shoulders," "infantile," "childish." We have certain expectations about the development which is normal for persons, and these expectations are different from those we have for nonpersons. Any living thing, vegetable or animal, becomes older, changes from being young to becoming old. Inanimate things, if they are artifacts, change from being *new* to being old, and although natural inanimate objects can be geologically young their youth is always qualified. (It is perhaps significant that we use "old" much more freely than we do "young," that we are more discriminating concerning the sort of beginning things have than we are concerning final phases.) When certain transformations normal for a thing of a given type do not occur we may refer to plants and animals as "stunted," but only persons may be retarded or precocious, educable or ineducable, as distinct from trainable or untrainable.

Descartes informed Arnauld that he had deliberately withheld from the readers of the (French) *Discourse on Method* his most extreme metaphysical doubt concerning the origin of his cognitive powers, which was reserved for the "intellectual and educated," (*Reply to Fourth Objections*; VII, 247) to whom the (Latin) *Meditations* were accessible. Since Descartes believed that language learning exercised the imagination and memory rather than the pure intellect, he no doubt took the ability to read Latin as only an accidental indicator of the sort of education which was a prerequisite for understanding his philosophy. But it is worth noting that he does attribute to education some positive contribution to intellect, not merely the implantation of prejudice. Childhood and youth are a time when the mind is first enslaved by the senses and by authoritarian teachings, then may begin to develop some freedom from these false masters, to try out its own powers, move from heteronomy to attempted autonomy. In the *Meditations* Descartes tells us that he waited, before writing them, until "I should reach such a mature age that no increased aptitude for learning anything was likely to follow" (61; VII, 17).

It is today part of commonly received wisdom that distinctive human phenomena, including language and other cultural activities, as well as mathematics and science, depend upon the relatively long period of human maturation, and it is perhaps an ironic fact that the little gland *conarium,* which Descartes took to be the seat of the soul, controls that process, ensuring that maturation be duly delayed. The time for the stocking of the mind with confused ideas and prejudices is measured by the gland which Descartes believed to be organ of consciousness. It may indeed be seen to be the organ of consciousness in a sense Descartes did not envisage, if, as Davidson, Dennett, and others[11] suggest, self-consciousness depends upon exercise of the cultural skills, in particular linguistic ones, acquired during our drawn-out dependency on other persons. A person, perhaps, is best seen as one who was long enough dependent upon other persons to acquire the essential arts of personhood. Persons essentially are *second* persons, who grow up with other persons.

This way of looking at persons makes it essential to them that they have successive periods of infancy, childhood, and youth, during which they develop as persons. We cannot call "young" and "old" P-predicates since they range much too widely; but among the things which can be said to be young only humans (and human persons are the only persons we yet know) can be said to be *in their youth,* or to misspend it, or to come of age, or to have the best years of their life behind them. Persons make calendars, write day by day meditations, celebrate anniversaries, recognize each other's transitions from one stage of life to another, conduct funerals. These typical activities of persons involve recognition of the normal development of a life, as well as of the distinctive way in which a given individual has passed through its stages. The fact that a person has a life *history,* and that a people collectively have a history, depends upon the humbler fact that each person has a childhood in which a cultural heritage is transmitted, ready for adolescent rejection and adult discriminating selection and contribution. Persons come after and before other persons.

Childhood is the period in which are acquired not only those skills essential for persons, but also the experience which generates those ambitions and goals typical of persons. Responses to dependency, and to changing degrees of it, to change of person on whom to depend, define our emotional life, form and display personality. Persons are beings who have some sort of personality, and although one may think of a personality in abstraction from its formation, even suppose it to be eternal, or to have come into being fully formed, like Athena's, all our *understanding* of personality relates it to its genesis, and, for us, that is in the conditions of biological life, in which one generation nurtures its successor generation, preparing it to take its place. Persons are essentially successors, heirs to other persons who formed and cared for them, and their personality is revealed both in their relations to others and in their response to their own recognized genesis. Not only does each earlier phase causally influence each later phase, as in all enduring things, not only is there growth, maturation, and aging, as in all living things, but in persons each later phase is a *response* to earlier phases, caused not only by them but by some sort of partial representation of them and their historical and causal relationships. Leibniz saw this reflective ability as a finite version of divine self-reflection, but if, as I have maintained, it is essential to persons to have had a personal history, then divine reflection cannot be fully personal self-preoccupation. Gods, if denied childhood, cannot be persons. Stories of the Greek gods retain the generational conflicts which form human personality, so that their gods do have personality. In Christian theology the link between personhood and generation is implicitly acknowledged both in the doctrine of the incarnation and in the doctrine of the trinity. To get personhood into an eternal unchanging being a separation has to be effected between the father and the son. (I must confess that my demythologization does not extend to the third person.) The paradigm persons are natural persons, animals whose long and helpless infancy enables them to become educated and cultured and speaking animals. Because they have the time for play, culture, convention, and artifice, they can not only form new natural persons, but invent gods and create artificial persons, corporations, and states. Persons are the creation of persons.

I have emphasized these developmental facts about persons, and it cannot be said that the emphasis is Cartesian. Descartes does, however, show some obscure consciousness of this aspect of persons not only in his picture of the life of intellect as progressive liberation from inherited confusion, but also in his philosophical style in the *Meditations.* It is an essentially narrative and dramatic work, and is divided into six memory-linked acts. It recreates the soul's progress from confusion and dependency on others through rebellion to limited autonomy and clear acceptance of beneficial dependency. What is more the development is not linear growth, even after the *First Meditation,* but a series of reinterpretations each of which amplifies a previous truth, and introduces new distinctions. Descartes keeps recapitulating, in each *Meditation,* what had been thought on previous days, and the recapitulations are also transformations. The *Meditations* rely not only on that intellectual memory which God guarantees, but on the memory of an embodied mind, (which Descartes believed was stored in brain traces or creases) a memory which recorded the *history* of a mind, not merely the theorems it had proved. After the adolescent rebellion of the *First Meditation,* Descartes settles into typically mature development, where successive stages incorporate reflections on previous stages, as well as bringing new developments. I cannot here document and defend this reading of the *Meditations,* but merely draw attention both to the fact that its style was deliberate, self-conscious, and vigorously defended by Descartes, and also to the fact that by Descartes' own definition (190; VII, 23) of that distinctness of ideas which was the goal of intellect, distinctness must increase as ramifications multiply. Although Descartes claims to have a distinct idea of himself in the *Second Meditation,* he proceeds to make it progressively more distinct in each subsequent *Meditation,* as it becomes both more articulated and more clearly related to other things. Without earlier confusion to reflect on, a Cartesian intellect would have no purpose. Its ends, like ours, are set by its beginnings.

I have drawn attention to several features of Descartes' philosophy of the person, to his explicit recognition of the fact that persons act and speak, that they tire and sleep, that between birth and death they grow up from childhood to adulthood. I think all these facts are relevant to that great puzzle, consciousness, which both Strawson and Descartes fail to resolve into anything which explains it.[12] How do these facts about persons help one understand consciousness? The difficulty of that concept stems in part from an endemic confusion between consciousness and self-consciousness, or rather between the simple consciousness which does not require self-consciousness and that Cartesian consciousness which is everywhere infected with it, between the capacity for perception and the capacity for apperception. Since we who seek to understand consciousness are thereby conscious of consciousness, what we find in ourselves is Cartesian consciousness, not simple consciousness. When we seek consciousness of the world we find, in our path, consciousness of ourselves: "No considerations can help towards my perception of the wax or any other body without at the same time going towards establishing the nature of my mind" (74; VII, 33). If we are to see past reflective consciousness, back to its base in simple consciuosness, we must remind ourselves of simple facts such as the fact that we, like other animals, sleep, that we may faint, lose and regain consciousness. What we, and animals, lose when anesthetized, and to some extent lose in sleep, is the ability to respond appropriately to those changes in our environment which are detectable, when we are awake, by our sense organs, or to initiate changes in that environment in response to our own felt needs and wants. The test for consciousness is not appropriate verbal response to a verbal stimulus, but appropriate action and reaction, response to perceptible changes and felt wants. For our sense organs to detect relevant changes, and for the body to act appropriately, not only must the sense organs be unimpaired and the body unparalyzed, but the animal whose organs and body they are must be awake. Anyone who can be known to sleep and wake is not only embodied, but is one who senses and acts. Strawson's emphasis on intentional action is the correct emphasis, if what P-predicates imply is simple consciousness rather than Cartesian consciousness.

Since consciousness is displayed by the ability to form and execute intentions appropriate to one's perceived situation, it involves not only sensitivity to stimuli but also intention formation. In us this may go on autonomously, in the absence of stimuli from the environment, and so we believe consciousness of a sort to be present in the person so abstracted by deliberation or reverie that appropriate response to the immediate environment may not occur. In sleep too, dreams are evidence of the persistence of the conative and affective side of our consciousness in the absence both of input from the current environment and of the ability to carry out any intentions which are formed. In dreams fake input and fake output imbed real wishes and wants, which thereby get expression without satisfaction. A derivative consciousness can continue, then, when full consciousness is lost, and there is no reason to suppose that what holds for us and our dreams does not hold also for dogs and their dreams. The wants which persist in sleep will be different—Fido will not dream of writing the *Meditations* or of proving theorems, but that is because Fido has simple consciousness, untransformed by language, reflection, and self-consciousness.

Being conscious is not enough to make one a person. For that we need Cartesian consciousness, consciousness of ourselves and our place in the world, not merely consciousness of the stimuli relevant to what in fact is self-maintenance in that world. Descartes' test, appropriate verbal response, is the correct test not for simple consciousness but for reflective consciousness. When that is superimposed upon simple consciousness, as it is in us, the manifestation of full simple consciousness, of being awake and alert, will take a self-conscious form, and even our dreams will take a form which reflects the fact that, from being conscious infants, we have become self-conscious adults. Not only do we, like other animals, respond to the things around us and the persons who are present, but we know that we are awake, and what we are doing, and the goods we strive to attain or keep by our actions and reactions are acknowledged, and transformed, by our slow acquisition of self-consciousness. Both our goals and our beliefs, even those which concern satisfaction of our animal needs, take a form which animal intentional states could not take. Unlike animals we have the concepts of self and others, of presence and absence; we can interpret stimuli as the return of identifiable things of concern to us. As Descartes said, we keep track of where things come from and go to, we relate their absence to their presence, see them as the same things in different times and places, continuously existent in determinate places when they are absent from us. A cat can discriminate a dead from a living animal, and a sleeping one from an alert one. It can perhaps be said, therefore, to have a "clear" concept of sleep and of death. But if to have a "distinct" concept of sleep is to know that it is the state when one fails to respond to what is present, when an interruption occurs in the activity of keeping track of things, of relating their presence to their absence, then animals cannot have a distinct concept of sleep. Discrimination of the sleeping from the waking can be performed among the animals present to one, but to discriminate the present from the absent one needs a way of recognizing the absent. Language enables us to do that, and so do certain ceremonies. Without language or some other convention-guided behavior no animal could satisfy us that what it was doing was not merely searching for something not in fact there, but missing what it took to be absent, let alone grieving for the long dead.

Reference to what is absent is reference to what has or could have been once present, so it requires an understanding of the past (and future) tenses. The simple consciousness of others' sleep, and the difference between sleep and the waking state, requires acknowledgment neither of the past nor of the absent—no concept at all of what is "present" is needed for it. But to know *oneself* to be a sleeper, one must be able to understand what is meant when one is told "you were sleeping, it was only a dream." Such understanding involves both a grasp of tenses, and of personal pronouns. We depend upon others for awareness of our own sleep, and without a language learned from others such retrospective self-knowledge would be inconceivable. An animal, without self-awareness, knows lots of things about itself—that it is hungry or in danger. It may, in its confident behavior, show knowledge that it, unlike its competitors, who are present, will be fed by some human patron. Such rudimentary awarenss of itself as one among others, as one having or lacking properties they have, is surely the basis for, but much less than, that real self-consciousness exhibited by the child who has mastered the use of "you," "I," "we," "they." The child who can with understanding respond to "you were sleeping," with "was I?" knows that, as it has found others sleeping and unresponsive, so they have found it—that it was in their presence, without noting their presence. It also knows that "you," spoken by others addressing it, refers to itself, yet also to those others when the child addresses them. Through participation in discourse, through being addressed and learning to address, the child moves from consciousness to self-consciousness, and full Cartesian consciousness.

Because the child may have dreamed, and remember the dream, it can contrast the truth about itself—that it was asleep, in the presence of parents, with its own self-certainty in that same stretch of past time, when it had a sort of consciousness of something else. Truth, learned from parents, contrasts with subjective certainty, reality with appearance. The apparent continuity of subjective consciousness throughout waking and sleeping contributes to that concept of objective continuity of existence in determinate public places and times which eventually is attributed to the things which, in waking hours, we keep track of, both in their presence and their absence. As we seem, waking or dreaming, ever present to ourselves, so any continuant, present or absent from determinate observers, has as it were its own presence. Thus self-consciousness infects consciousness of things.

I have emphasized the concepts of presence and absence, and of the past, in my attempt to distinguish self-consciousness from simple consciousness. I have also emphasized the second personal pronoun. Persons are self-conscious, know themselves to be persons among persons. Knowledge of this shows in the grasp of all the pronouns, none of which has sense except in relation to the others, but there are several ways in which the second person is the key person. My first concept of myself is as the referent of "you," spoken by someone whom I will address as "you." If never addressed, if excluded from the circle of speakers, a child becomes autistic, incapable of using any pronouns or indeed any words at all. The second person, the pronoun of mutual address and recognition, introduces us to the first and third, and to that relationship between first person ascriptions and others which Strawson has emphasized. The univocality of P-predicates which he insists on is as much a univocality in first and second person ascriptions as in first and third. To get at the difference between second and third person uses the child must differentiate between persons and nonpersons, present persons and absent persons, participants and nonparticipants. The correct use of the second person pronoun is the test for that grasp of the concept of a person which is essential to persons.

This grasp of the second person pronoun is vital for self-conscious action as well as for self-concious thought. The standards by which our actions are judged are, like the standards by which thought is judged, interpersonal, and learned from others. The capacity for responsible action grows as we learn to receive and give reproaches such as "But you said you would do it!" By being held responsible, we come to take responsibility for our actions.[13] I began this paper by drawing attention to the discrepancy between Descartes' advice to active persons and his rule for truth-seeking, and I believe that an adequate philosophy of persons will connect self-conscious thought with self-conscious agency, will not, like Descartes, divide persons against themselves by pitting the truth-seeker against the seeker of this world's good. In action and thought about action, as much as in other thought, we are second persons before we are first or third persons.

I have linked this emphasis on the second person with the fact that, in learning from other persons, we acquire a sense of our place in a series of persons, to some of whom we have special responsibilities. We acquire a sense of ourselves as occupying a place in an historical and social order of persons, each of whom has a personal history interwoven with the history of a community. I have tried in various ways in this paper to connect that historical narrative consciousness, that sense of the past, with self-consciousness, with personality, and with consciousness of persons. I am acutely aware that my thinking has been a presumptuous and sketchy rethinking, not only of Descartes' thoughts[14] and of Strawson's, but of the thoughts of others who came between them, in particular Kant, whose thought Strawson has helped us to reappropriate. Such brash plundering of the history of philosophy is at least consistent with my thesis that the shape of the past we reflect on helps explain our ability to reflect on it and on our own relation to it.

NOTES

1. P. F. Strawson, *Individuals* (London: Methuen, 1949), p. 108.

2. Ibid., p. 94.

3. Ibid., p. 90.

4. References to Descartes' writings, throughout, are first, where possible, to the translation by Elizabeth Anscombe and Peter Thomas Geach, in *Descartes' Philosophical Writings* (London: Thomas Nelson, 1970), followed by volume and page reference to C. Adam and P. Tannery, eds., *Oevres de Descartes* (Paris, 1896–1913), to the Latin for the *Meditations* and *Principles of Philosophy,* to the French for the *Discourse on Method* and the *Passions of the Soul.* Where the passage cited is not included in the Anscombe and Geach selection, I refer to it by name, or if by a letter, give recipient and date. Thus this first reference (117; VII, 81) refers to Anscombe and Geach, p. 117, Adam and Tannery, volume VII, p. 81.

5. Descartes' account of the sort of mingling there is between the human mind and the human body includes not only a unique causal interaction, but also a phenomenological relation which is not reducible to a causal one. He characterizes his body as that within which he localizes his sensations. The causal chain leading to the unique body-mind link in the little gland *conarium* extends beyond the body, and no special causal features distinguish physical causation inside and outside the body. Descartes notes the contingency of the limits of one's body, *qua locus* of one's sensations. "God might have so made human nature that this very disturbance in the brain was a sign to the mind of something else (than a painful injury in the foot); it might have been a sign of its own occurrence in the brain; or of the disturbance in the foot, or in some intermediate place; or in fact in anything else whatever" (*aliud quidlibet*) (79; VII, 88). This includes the possibility Spinoza saw, that one's body might stretch to include the entire causal chain relevant to one's well-being, that is the entire universe. Descartes believes that it must be best for the conservation of the body that we localize as we do. He does not discuss the contingencies which Strawson examines—that it is one and the same limited body within which I localize my pains, whose limbs I move at will, whose sense organs' state determines what I see. A helpful examination of Descartes' concept of the union of mind and body is found in Janet Broughton and Ruth Mattern, "Reinterpreting Descartes on the Notion of the Union of Mind and Body," *Journal of the History of Philosophy* 16, no. 1 (1978):23–32.

6. Strawson, *Individuals,* p. 100.

7. I have drawn attention to Descartes' recognition of this feature of thought, and in its importance, in "Mind and Change of Mind."

8. Strawson, *Individuals,* p. 100.

9. Ibid.

10. Ibid.

11. Donald Davidson, "Thought and Talk," in *Mind and Language,* ed. Samuel Guttenplan (Oxford: Clarendon Press, 1975), and Daniel C. Dennett, "Conditions of Personhood," in *Identities of Persons,* ed. Amelie Rorty (Berkeley and Los Angeles: University of California Press, 1976); reprinted in Dennett, *Brainstorms* (Cambridge, Mass.: M.I.T. Press/Bradford Books, 1978).

12. Bernard Williams, in "Strawson on Individuals," *Problems of the Self* (Cambridge, Eng.: Cambridge University Press, 1973), draws attention to the Cartesian features of Strawson's position, and to his failure to clarify the concept of "states of consciousness."

13. Dennett, in "Conditions of Personhood," makes the practice of holding persons responsible an important condition of personhood and of self-consciousness.

14. This paper, regrettably, was written before I had the benefit of the recent burst of Descartes commentary, namely, E. M. Curley, *Descartes against the Sceptics* (Cambridge,

Mass.: Harvard University Press, 1978; Bernard Williams, *Descartes: The Project of Pure Enquiry* (Harmondsworth, Eng.: Penquin Books, 1978); Margaret D. Wilson, *Descartes* (London, Henley, Eng.: Routledge, Kegan Paul, 1978), and *Descartes: Critical and Interpretative Essays,* ed. M. Hooker (Baltimore: Johns Hopkins Press. 1978).

I am grateful to my colleague Richard Gale for pointing out obscurities in an earlier version of this paper. I fear that only some darkness has been dispelled in this present version. As Descartes said at the end of the *First Meditation,* sometimes what we wake up to is darkness.

6

Caring about Caring: A Reply to Frankfurt

In his deep (and, I think, deeply Spinozistic) paper Frankfurt offers us a distinction, which I find important, between the things which are important to us, because they affect our lives in ways we find important, and things or persons we care about, where this caring *makes* something important which need not have been so. We invest ourselves in what we care about, make ourselves vulnerable in ways we need not have been to the losses and griefs we will suffer when what we care about is defeated, or tortured, or dead, or permanently absent from our lives. To care is to make something important, above and beyond what must be important to us simply as sentient beings with desires. I think this distinction is important, and I want to push a bit further what Frankfurt says about caring about our carings in the last section of his paper. He says of the one who cares about his caring about a person or cause, that "he therefore guides himself away from being critically affected by anything, in the outside world or within himself, which might divert him or dissuade him ... from caring as much as he does." This sounds to me like the fanatic, the one whose objects of care are so important to him that he will not risk scrutinizing them. But, for Frankfurt, to care about anything, presumably including one's caring, is to take risks of loss and defeat. The one who carefully insulates herself against losing her loves or cared-about causes, then, is precisely the one who is not willing to take the risks caring involves—in this case the risks of finding out that one's objects of care, and so one's actual carings, are not worth one's while.

From *Synthese* 53, no. 2 (1982): 273–90. Copyright © 1982 by D. Reidel Publishing Company, Dordrecht, Holland. *See also* Harry Frankfurt, "The Importance of What We Care About," ibid., pp. 257–72. Both papers were given at a conference, "Matters of the Mind," at the University of Missouri at St. Louis, October 28–30, 1981, organized by Stephanie A. Ross and Paul A. Roth.

Frankfurt later does want an evaluative dimension to enter into caring about caring, but it seems a very cautious sort of higher-order caring, too cautious to qualify as caring by Frankfurt's own account of that risky investment of self in some other person or cause. He says that

> if anything is worth caring about it must be worth caring about what to care about. It could hardly be the case both that there is something so important to a person that it is worthwhile for him to care about it, but that it is not worthwhile for him to care whether or not he cares about that thing.

It is indeed important to have a way of testing whether one does really care about what one claims to care about, of finding out whether or not one cares. Frankfurt does not offer us any such test beyond the conscious addressing of that question. I suggest that a reliable sign of real caring is the intolerance of ignorance about the current state of what we care about. When a person or a cause is important to us, then we will react with distress to bad news about that person or cause, but we might be content to let no news count as good enough news. The one who cares, however, is distressed at mere ignorance—no news is not good enough. So a sign that a person or cause is not merely important to one, but one which one cares about, is the need for constant contact with and news about the welfare of what is cared about. But if we are to care about caring it is not enough simply to satisfy ourselves that we do indeed care. That is not all that caring about caring need be. A more risky and, I think, a more genuine version of caring about caring is not just checking that one does care, or being certain that one is not hypocritical or self-deluded in one's avowal of love or devotion or concern, but asking whether what one cares about should be cared about. This is the really risky step, since its outcome is either an endorsement and confirmation of one's loves and loyalties, or their alteration, devaluation, or even destruction. And with that last would go not only the elimination of the losses and griefs those loves invited, but also the enrichment and joys they brought. The examined loves may prove not worth continuing. To care about what we care about is to make risky investigations not only into the question of whether we really care, but into why and with what "reason" we care about the persons and things we do.

When I say that to care about caring commits one to evaluation of one's loves and loyalties, I do not mean a specifically moral evaluation. I am willing to leave it to others to dispute Frankfurt's claim that morality need not be what matters most to us, even when it matters much to us. I think my Aristotelian and Humean concept of morality is wider than Frankfurt's, so any differences between us here might be merely terminological.

But whether our evaluation of our loves and loyalties is moral or not, we surely can ask questions as "What sort of a person must I be to care this much about my career, or my children, or some friend who clearly doesn't care as much about me?" To ask such questions is risky, and so meets Frankfurt's test for real caring more than does guiding oneself away from anything which might alter or endanger that caring.

Before I look at ways one might hope to get answers to this risky question, let me first make clear that I agree completely with Frankfurt that the point of such reflection need not be to reach a decision on whether or not to go on caring. I agree that we find ourselves subject to volitional necessity, that we display our wills more in what we cannot but do and feel than in what we can directly control, or do "at will" (although I think Frankfurt assumes too readily that what we cannot stop at will we cannot have started at will). It is not just acts of will, but necessities too which can be criticized—and the resultant raised critical consciousness may break the necessity reflected upon, when criticism is accompanied by understanding of why we were thus necessitated. If I come to see my loves as all fetishes, and see what other possible loves they displaced or disguised, then I may thereby destroy or at least transform my old fetishistic loves, now exposed as such. I need not believe caring a matter for decision to see it as a matter in which there may be faults, indeed the worst faults of all. Seeing them *may* not cure them, and having seen them may not even lead us to want them cured. We do naturally protect existent loves against destruction by probing thoughts. "Lord, let me be changed, but not yet," was Augustine's prayer, and we all know what he meant. Sometimes, however, change does follow an exposure of the hollowness of our loves, or of the self-deceit needed to sustain them. Such change, if it occurs, will also be a case of "volitional necessity," not of a decision or a choice in any ordinary sense of choice.[1] But it may still be in one's control, since one can control in ways other than by a series of effective decisions or acts of will.

Frankfurt says that it is not the special business of ethics to be concerned about what we care about, since ethics concerns what we have an obligation to do, whatever we care about. But if we look to past traditions for help in getting even any vocabulary in which to try critically to categorize our loves and loyalties, then it seems that (in addition to turning to psychiatry) it is mainly to religious or quasi-religious ethics, or to revolutionary politics that we must turn. We find attempts to care about caring in Plato's *Symposium,* in Aristotle's discussion of friendship,[2] St. Augustine's *Confessions,* and in Marx's discussions of fetishism, mystification, and false consciousness, as well as in psychiatric concepts such as sublimation, obsession, displacement. We can come to see our loyalties and loves as sick, or infantile, or as self-deceived, or as perverse or unnatural, or as futile postponements of a too demanding love we are fated to end by accepting. Any one of these findings may transform, degrade, or destroy the caring which, in our loyal confidence that it would stand critical scrutiny, we cared enough about to put at risk by such scrutiny.

But what sort of critical scrutiny can we use? What test should we hope our loves can pass? St. Augustine relates how, after the death of his beloved friend, and after experience of grief and loss, and experience also that time cured that grief, that new friends replaced the lost friend, he turned to love of God. "For he alone loses none dear to him to whom all are dear in Him who cannot be lost. And who is this but our God. . . ."[3] Augustine opted against further risk either of loss or of finding the loss bearable. He turned to a love which was 'true' in that is was an investment of self in what, if real, cannot die or be absent from us, so cannot either cause us grief or give us opportunity to betray it by replacing it once it is gone. Plato's *Symposium* also describes and recommends this strategy, of shifting one's caring from what might one day leave one bereft to what is ever present: not this beautiful person but the form of beauty, not this mortal person, or series of mortal persons, but a safe eternal object of love. Augustine says of the eternal consolation of his fragile, lost, betraying and so betrayable mortal loves, that "No man loseth thee but he who forsakes thee."[4] Better, it seems, to forsake than to be forsaken, or rather, more accurately, better to be the *first* to forsake than to forsake the forsaker.

Is this wisdom, or is this a capitulation to a need for a sure thing, a refusal to love, to put oneself at risk? How are we to tell? There seems some truth in the religious condemnation of "the glue of inordinate affection" for objects or persons we are bound to lose or never to win—this is precisely what makes some loves vain loves. But equally, surely, to react by a refusal to take any risk is to refuse to care, rather than care about "higher" things. I suggest that any critical stance towards our carings and towards what we care about must not lose sight of Frankfurt's truth, that to care at all is to risk loss and grief over and above that which is inevitable to us as beings with desires and sentience. So if we are to judge some objects of loyalty or love more worthy than others, it should not be because loving them is risk-free. That may give them importance for us, but it rules out caring about them, in Frankfurt's strong sense.

Frankfurt in the end suggests that all we can do is find what we *can* care about, and usually there will not be enough of such things to present us with incompatible possibilities. But isn't this too easy? Some people can care about their collection of babies' booties or women's gloves, or other such pathetic substitutes. They *can* do this, and such a care may conflict with no other possibility they see. Again, we all know from our memories of adolescence that one can care desperately about persons one scarcely knows, and who do not know one or scarcely know one. Take Hinkley's supposed love for Jody Foster—this is surely a familiar enough case of fascination with another person, total obsession which has no basis whatever in any realistic hope of returned love—indeed may stem from a fear of any reciprocal relationship. All sorts of investment in other persons' lives are possible to us at various points in our lives—we may progress from hero worship to voyeurism or to hopeless romantic passion. The possibilities just are too many. Frankfurt's counsel, to love what one can love, may be all right for us the middle-aged and soured, but it is not very good advice for the young, or at least for the young before and after the "me generation." Nor do we find it any more satisfactory if we turn from persons to care about to causes to care about. We are not content to say to Hitler, to Sadat's assassins, to fanatical Jewish groups, "Care about what you find you can care about." We must, somehow, be more discriminating.

How can we be discriminating without being ourselves fanatics? I think that, for all their limitations, the traditions which have evolved the concepts of the perverse or unnatural love, and of false consciousness, and of displaced and disguised objects of love, are what we must turn to, at least as a place to start. The Aristotelian-Christian concept of the unnatural love, the Hegelian-Marxist concept of the fetishistic loves of those with false consciousness, and the Freudian concept of the unrecognized oedipal fixation, all offer us ways of seeing loves critically, and offer us versions of improved loves which do not take the risk out of loving, and so do not, like the Christian mystic or the stoic ascetic, tell us in effect to switch from loving, with its attendant risks, to a play-safe policy, to opt for safety, to go for what is deemed necessarily important rather than for what is made important by our loving of it.

The Christian conception of the unnatural love is closely tied to that already suspect Augustinian and Pauline doctrine that we must love the creature only as a way of safely loving the Creator. But if we divorce it from that, and ask why homosexual love was frowned upon, and heterosexual love was encouraged and blessed by the church (or by Aristotle) then we get an answer which I think is helpful in seeing how we might think critically but nonfanatically about possible carings. The homosexual love, even when it dares to speak its name, as it could in Aristotle's time and once again can, no thanks to the tradition I am cautiously raiding for useful concepts, cannot see itself as a means of its own continuation beyond one lifetime. Even if the wholehearted Lesbian who adopts a child, or bears a child by artificial insemination, wants that child also to be homosexual, she depends normally on nonhomosexuals for the continuation of the homosexual community. Homosexual love, however imitable and contagious, is not a love which is fertile when it comes to perpetuating itself across generations. Should this matter? Are we not all dependent on the fact of diversity for the preservation and continuation of whatever sort of caring we do value? Do we not all need others not to be like us as well as needing some others to be like-minded? Yes certainly, but a diversity of loyalties and styles of loving may be more problematic than a diversity of tastes in food, or in career preferences. At the level we are now considering, that of caring about our caring, we may all need to be Kantian, to will as legislators for a system of nature, not necessarily because these are moral willings, (or being-willings) but simply because these preferences are our ultimately reflective ones, and so we are choosing the sort of world we want to continue in being. I suspect, however, that at this level the distinction between when we approve from a moral standpoint and what we endorse simply as reflective beings will tend to vanish.

Why, one may ask, should we not will a pluralistic world in which homosexual loves flourish, but are dependent on heterosexual loves in a way the latter need not depend on the homosexual loves? The heterosexual worried about the population explosion may welcome the increasing proportion of homosexuals, since it may help solve that problem, but he doesn't depend on homosexuals for the very possibility of his love, as they depend on heterosexuals for their own being and the continuation of their community. (Of course they need not so depend—if the human community became like a farm in which all reproduction was by artificial insemination, then no one couple's or group's ongoing sexual preferences need depend on others having other different preferences. Why do most of us not will such a version of a technologically feasible ongoing human community? I leave this question unanswered.) If I see my style of loving as a style which depends on others having different styles, which do not similarly depend on mine, I see my sort of loving as vulnerable, as to some degree a passive and willingly powerless love. Well, why not? Would that not make my love incur risk in just the way I have been complaining that reciprocated love of an omnipotent being avoids it, and so fails to be a case of real caring? The homosexual is taking risks, in that he depends on heterosexuals for the future of his sort of love; if not on their tolerance, at least on their willingness to provide a supply of new potential homosexual partners. Should we not applaud this higher-level risk taking?

Hume, speaking of love, says that, compared with pride, it is an enfeebling passion.[5] It leads to generosity to the loved person and so to loss of prideworthy possessions. But, as Nietzsche pointed out, the person with a superabundance need not lose any of his grounds for pride by overflowing generosity to those he loves. Nietzsche says

Ich lehre euch den Freund, in dem die Welt fertig dasteht, eine Schale des Guten—den schaffenden Freund der immer eine fertige Welt zu verschenken hat. Und wie ihm die Welt auseinanderrollte, so rollt sie ihm wieder in Ringen zusammen. . . .[6]

(I teach you the friend in whom the world is completely presented, a bowl of goodness—the creative friend who always has a world ready to give away. And as the world disintegrates from him, so it rolls again together in rings around him.)

Love and pride can be reconciled, indeed must be reconciled if either is to be stable. Nietzsche says that our faith in others betrays the respect in which we would like to have faith in ourselves[7] so that the best friendship is that between those who *do* have such self-respect, who do not look in their friends for the qualities they fail to find in themselves. Hume too, I think, saw *some* loves, namely the creative ones, as nonenfeebling,[8] as like that of the lover who can declare: "The ripened fruit but falls and new ones rise to take its place, and I grow rich in loving."[9] Thus although the person who cares must "invest" himself in what he cares about, it seems a relevant question, if we are reflecting on such caring, whether this investment is fruitful and so is compatible with pride. I tentatively postulate that a love which is thus compatible is better than one that is not. I suggest that Nietzsche is also right in seeing power as the important thing for pride. Pride is in power, the feeling of pride is a feeling of power, and the feeling of love may be a feeling of shared mutually created power. If this is right, then any "selfless" love, acceptance of which increases nonmutual dependence, and so decreases power, is to that extent a love which competes with pride, and an inferior sort of love. We must find a sort of selflessness which is not self-demeaning.

One might put this alternatively by treating pride as a case of caring, caring about one's own power. Then my claim comes to this, that this case of caring is special, and provides a reflective constraint on all other carings, namely that they be consistent with this one. So I amend Frankfurt's dictum about what we must care about if we care about anything to this: "If we reflectively care about anything we must care about ourselves." Could we say "If we are to selflessly invest ourselves in anything, we must selflessly invest ourselves in ourselves"? Only if the investment is only *apparently* selfless, and really is self-increasing, as any good investment should be.

I now want to stand back and consider if this line of thinking, which began from the Christian concept of the difference between a creative "natural" love and a sterile "unnatural" love, really is one we should use to evaluate loves. Frankfurt has spoken about caring in a way which abstracts from the difference between caring about a person and caring about a cause, and although he compared the personal nonuniversalizable character of the (possibly constraining) love of a person with the universal constraints of rationality, he did not say anything about the relation between love of a person and loyal devotion to a cause, be it family tradition, mathematical truth, or connoisseurship in, say, wines, or in Benin bronzes. I too have followed him by talking in one breath, as it were, of devotion both to persons and to causes. But we surely do want to make different normative demands on loyalty to a cause from those we make on love of a person. Even when the causes are not moral causes, the generality of the object of concern makes generalization tests more relevant here than they could possibly be to love of a person. The test I have been implicitly using in the foregoing discussion is not "can I will that others love this person whom I love," but rather "can I will that others, in particular the next generation, love whoever they love in the *mode* of loving with which I love this person?" Even the first test is not quite as absurd as it might seem—it is absurd as a normative demand on personal love, since as Frankfurt and others[10] emphasize, love need not be based on the independent merit of the loved person, but it is a fairly good criterion for genuine love in Frankfurt's sense, namely, a genuine instance of love—typically the lover *does* want others to find the loved one lovable, wants to sing his praises, repeat his name. This desire can and usually does coexist with the desire for some exclusive or near exclusive enjoyment of, or for some sort of fidelity from, the loved person. The second question, the question of the generalizability of the mode or *type* of loving, is one which shifts the question from the often pointless one, "should I love this person?" to "should I love this person in this way?" But I am not at all sure that there is any good reason to apply even this test to our personal loves. When such loves are homosexual in type, it has been hard in recent times to separate the question of the value of a particular love between two particular actual people from the more general question of the value of that *type* of love, since homosexuals have had to fight for a general cause to protect the particular loves which are of that type. It would not, however, be incoherent to say "I am *not* devoted to the general cause of homosexual rights, nor to making the world safe for homosexual love, nor to the continuation of the homosexual community, but my homosexual love for my friend is the most important thing in my life, and I care more for her than for anything or anyone else." Until we have clearer ideas than I at least yet have on how concern for various sorts of *general* causes should connect with concern for single individuals, it is hard to say what, if anything, is really wrong with such a person's attitude. Once the cause of making the social world safe for homosexual love were victorious, then presumably there would be no more wrong with such an attitude than there is with heterosexuals not devoting themselves to the cause of safeguarding heterosexual love. Nor is it the case that the *only* causes we should and reasonably do devote ourselves to are endangered causes. Those who devote themselves to the protection of wilderness areas may see their cause in that light, but those who devote themselves to community projects such as parent-teachers associations, or hospital visiting, or the United Way, do not and should not see their concerns as endangered causes which need to be fought for against powerful enemies. Those who cultivate their connoisseurship of wines or bronzes also see themselves as continuing and advancing a fairly safe concern. One can safeguard that which is safe as well as that which is threatened—indeed my earlier test for the ongoing *viability* of a form of love practically amounted to a demand that we safeguard only the fairly safe, that we *not* devote ourselves to necessarily losing causes. What I am now suggesting is that this test may be more appropriate to general causes than to individual loves.

Nevertheless, there is surely *something* wrong with the closet homosexual who values his own homosexual love or loves more than anything else but refuses any support to the cause of safeguarding such relationships from political or social attack, or with the parent who never attends a parent-teacher meeting. Some sort of fit between our loves and our devotion to general causes which protect such loves seems a reasonable demand to make. So I return to the question of whether reflective persons should be wholly content with a particular love which is of a general sort which does not obtain their loyalty. Of course one should want to safeguard the right of all persons to love and express the love of whomever they find themselves loving, as long as that love does not infringe the rights of third parties, or harm those (namely children) whose interests should be paternalistically guarded. So whatever the prospects of the long-run viability of the homosexual community, the rights and interests of its present members warrant safeguarding. The question I am here concerned with is not that of political or moral rights, but with the sort of evaluation persons can make of the way they exercise their rights; in Frankfurt's words, of what they do with themselves. This evaluation will and should have no coercive consequences whatever, merely the psychological consequences of self-criticism, if one's loves and loyalties fail one's tests, or similar consequences for one's personal attitudes to others, one's reasoned personal preferences for one sort of person rather than another. Whatever we conclude about what persons should do with themselves, in the sense here discussed, that alone will entail nothing whatever about how the state's or the individual's coercive powers should be used.

With these hesitations and qualifications duly entered, then, I resume my tentative exploration of the question of whether a love which is of a type to whose future we cannot reasonably devote ourselves is less worthy than a love of a type whose future seems more asured. Thomas Nagel, in his essay on sexual perversion, says, "The connection between sex and reproduction has no bearing on sexual perversion."[11] He makes the test of nonperversion that of fully embodied interpersonal reciprocity. "Desire has unity and possession as its object: physical possession must eventuate in the creation of the sexual object in the image of one's desire, and not merely in the object's recognition of that desire, or in his or her own private arousal."[12] This test of a nonperverse desire takes desire itself, and its special characteristics, as a way of testing desires. Perhaps we can let caring itself provide a way to test caring, as Frankfurt himself suggests. If we take Frankfurt's version of care as unlike desire in being prospective, or future envisaging, then we can take Nagel's version of nonperverse sexual desire and transform that into caring for a person simply by introducing the will to continuation. Love has continued unity and continued mutual enjoyment, even perhaps glorification, as its telos or objective. But the moment we bring in the concern with continuation, we are on the way to breaking down Nagel's fence between questions of perversion and questions of reproduction. The connection between sex and reproduction may have no bearing on sexual perversion, but the connection between love and the future of that love, and of that sort of love, does seem to have a bearing on the perversion of love. One must in *some* way intend the love to continue, for it to be love at all. Still, as Nagel says, "Bad sex is better than no sex," and we can add that unnatural loves may be better than none, childless loves better than none, and loves doomed to be the last of their kind better than none.

Are loves incompatible with pride better than none? That is a harder question. The homosexual can of course have personal pride, and can have that outflowing generosity of the proud of which Nietzsche spoke. Can she or he have pride in the ongoing homosexual community? That is less clear. To the extent that the sort of love that community fosters is not able to perpetuate itself, is dependent nonreciprocally on bisexuals or nonhomosexuals for its self-perpetuation, homosexual pride is limited in its possibilities, and so homosexual love is love between persons whose pride in their love is also necessarily limited. To get support from a possibly dangerous source, I quote Plato's Socrates in the *Symposium,* reporting what Diotima said to him about love: "Mortal nature always seeks as much as it can to exist forever and achieve immortality. But it can do this only by procreation, its way of leaving behind another young one against old age" (207 D). "It is in this way that everything mortal is preserved, not by its being the same forever, like the divine, but by what is old and withdrawing leaving behind something else, something new, like itself. It is by this method, Socrates, that the mortal partakes of immortality" (208 B).[13] Attempt at propagation of some sort of continuer of the love between two persons seems an earnest of the genuineness of the love, and success in this attempt establishes a ground for that proper pride which is, for reflective persons, a normative constraint on love. Perhaps the best form of love is that found not in couples, homosexual or heterosexual, but in bisexual unordered n-tuples.

I turn next to the possibility that a love, although nonperverse, may be wanting by Freudian standards, since it may be inhibited, may express unresolved psychic conflicts, exhibit repressed needs, and may involve some form of self-deceit. I will of necessity deal briefly with these faults, not merely because of lack of space but because I can claim no expertise in understanding or recognizing them. Then I shall conclude with a look at the possibility that a love which avoids all these weaknesses, as so far catalogued, may nevertheless be a case of false consciousness, perhaps of fetishism in Marx's rather than Freud's sense.

A love which expresses psychic conflicts of the sort Freud made us aware of will typically be one which brings less than full satisfaction to the lover. If in loving another person I am really trying in a futile way to return to or increase the love my mother showed me in my infancy, then the chances are that my chosen substitute stands in not altogether appropriately for the lost object of the infantile desire or need. If I become aware of the relation between my present attachments and my infantile attachments, this may alter my attitudes now, may transform those attachments, may detach me from some loves and free me for others. Presumably the normative criterion we can get from this possibility that knowledge about, or at least beliefs about, the etiology of our caring may alter that caring, simply is that a love is the better to the extent that knowledge of its history and prehistory does not destroy it and, if it transforms it, does so without degrading it. The test is like that of Brandt's "cognitive therapy"[14] — some loves do and some loves do not survive exposure to facts or purported facts about their own origin and development. This seems a fairly uncontroversial normative requirement to make of caring or loving — that it not depend on ignorance of its own nature and history. Nor is this demand a specifically moral demand, but more a demand of that reason which confronts rather than avoids relevant facts. Where Frankfurt made caring necessarily prospective, future envisaging, I am now making reflective caring necessarily a caring which acknowledges it own *past,* one which looks *before* as well as after.

But maybe this test of full exposure to facts is not so straightforward, nor so uncontroversial. It is not straightforward, since only certain facts, those showing the history and character of my evolving attachments, are those to be confronted. If, as Brandt's test would require, we confronted all the facts conceivably relevant to our emotional attitudes, we would have to consider all those other persons we might have loved instead of the ones we do love, all the facts about the possibilities foreclosed by the actual history of our past loves. How many actual carings would survive this sort of total unselective flood of knowledge is unclear. I surmise that if one really were confronted with full knowledge of all the possibilities and the consequences of their realization, one would go mad and be incapable of any sustained attachment. Among the cognitive skills we have evolved in our species' history is the important art of ignoring what it would really be disastrous to contemplate. I have already quoted to criticize Frankfurt's statement that to care about our caring is to guide ourselves away from anything which would threaten to end that caring. I do not think that such protective maneuvers count as caring about caring, but they might be the better part of wisdom nonetheless. Perhaps it is wiser to protect our carings than to care about them. At least there comes a point where it would seem crazy to risk losing the ability to care simply to indulge the will to know. Where the new knowledge has the effect of destroying any carings, rather than altering the object or the style of caring, then cognitive therapy is no therapy, but itself a disease.

So I cautiously propose that a love which cannot survive a confrontation with its own past is an unworthy love. But may the gods protect us from having to know in detail, rather than vaguely acknowledge the existence of, all those paths not taken, or even to know definitely the future of our actual loves. Even my modest test by selected knowledge may be one Frankfurt will find too dangerous, too much in tension with the self-protective tendencies of genuine caring. If genuine caring does and must protect itself against such knowledge of itself, then caring is not compatible with risky caring about caring, compatible only with regarding one's caring as so important that one protects it against any threat, including threatening knowledge.

I turn last to a third demand we might make if we cared about caring, namely that in our caring we not merely be aware of our own history as particular persons capable of caring or fated to care for someone and something, and not merely be able to take pride in our caring, but also be able to see our sort of caring as one which is free from any taint of false consciousness. For even if my love were a fully "natural" heterosexual love, of whose relation to my infantile needs and whose costs in terms of foregone opportunities I am fully aware, it might nevertheless be a love which depends on another sort of unawareness, namely lack of awareness of the social and economic and human conditions of such attachments. If my sort of love is bourgeois, or if devotion to individual persons rather than to classes or species is typical of capitalist society and expressive of an alienated sort of individualism, then my love may be suspect, open to the charge of false consciousness. But what exactly is such a charge? Is it that my style of loving is doomed to extinction, come the classless society? This would make this demand a variant of the first, that we be able to see our kind of loving as one able to continue into the future. One reason for predicting its demise would be the belief that the economic conditions it required for its nurture were temporary and passing ones. Courtly love was a form of love which flourished only in feudal conditions. The sort of romantic love portrayed in *The French Lieutenant's Woman* may be a kind no longer possible, although the cultural memory of it is fresh enough for us, or at least for those of my generation, to be nostalgic for that lost possibility. There may also be forms of friendship which develop only between companions-at-arms, so flourish only in conditions of war, and there may be forms of male bonding which develop only in the locker-rooms of a sexist capitalist society, forms of female bonding which could occur only within privileged, leisured intellectual circles (Virginia Woolf and Vita Sackville-West). A fuller awareness of the sociological and economic background of one's own sort of caring may lead one to see it as unworthy, as parasitic on injustice or on bloodshed or on powerlessness or on exploitation or on domination. But one might believe and welcome the fact that feudalism will soon pass and with it pass all chances for courtly love, yet remain all the more devoted to one's love, and find the loving more not less precious, because it is fragile and its type is doomed to extinction. Why, after all, and despite my earlier claims, should one value only the love with a future? Even if one disapproved of the social system needed for the possibility of such a love, one could still find the love precious. Lovers always have echoed the sentiment that we should gather roses while we may. "At my back I alwais hear Times winged Charriot hurrying near, and yonder all before us lye Desarts of vast Eternity."[15] We can adapt this from particular loves to culture-dependent kinds of love—if a certain kind is doomed to pass, and if the kind of envisaged future strikes one as promising only emotional deserts, one will find one's passé love the more not the less precious.

But the one who does that can not wholeheartedly care for the cause she believes will triumph, or surely she would welcome the new style of loving and not regret the passing of the old? If I come to see attachment for individual persons as a displaced version of a less individualized love of my comrades in the revolutionary struggle, then presumably I will condemn my old personal loves, rather than make the most of them while they can last. We would find out what we most care about if we had to choose between relinquishing a personal love and loyalty to a cause. But if I understand Marx aright, it is as much a test of a cause that it make possible fulfilling human personal relationships between those of equal power and equal interdependency, as it is a test of a personal relationship that it be a kind which does not require unstable and unequal power relationships in society as its foundation. A general cause which is fully adequate as an object of loyalty will not clash with reflectively affirmable individual loves.

These three tests of our loves which I have culled in an ecumenical spirit from diverse traditions, or diverse manifestations of one tradition, would give us a way of putting our carings at risk, of enhancing them if they stand such tests, damaging or losing them if they do not. But I said that this tradition was the place to *start,* and it still remains an open question whether it is sensible to apply these tests, or indeed any others, an open quetion whether we should thus put our loves and loyalties at risk. The three tests I have explored are all of them, I think, versions of a demand for a certain sort of independence or autonomy in our loves and carings—that our loves not be parasitic and so one-sidedly dependent on other sorts of love, that they not depend on cultivated ignorance or blindness to their past, that they be able to see their own type as the type of the better future. But if caring *is,* as Frankfurt says, a selfless investment of oneself in some other person or in some cause, is this not a willing of loss of self rather than self-fulfillment, of dependence rather than independence? I said earlier that we could, adopting Nagel's strategy and Frankfurt's own intent, try to make love itself the test of love, but have we done this if we have tested the will to dependence by the degree to which various sorts of autonomy or independence are achieved? If loving or caring is accepting *mutual* or equal interdependence, then our tests may be suitable, since interdependence may be joint independence. Frankfurt's account of caring did not address the question of whether the "self-investment" of the one who cares is or should be seen as a case of *mutual* and shared self-investment, whether he or she who loves the proper object of love should hope to be loved in return. My suggested ways of turning caring on caring will be appropriate ways only if mutuality is somehow of the essence of loving, shared concern of the essence of caring.

I began by remarking that Frankfurt's paper seemed to me Spinozistic in tone. It is Spinozistic both in what it does say, namely its acceptance of fatalism, and in what it refrains from saying. In saying nothing about the propriety of a demand that caring be reciprocal, Frankfurt might be seen as agreeing with Spinoza that the highest form of love is love of that which we cannot even hope will love us in return. But even for Spinoza there are lesser but worthy loves which do aim at reciprocity. "If we love a thing which is like ourselves we endeavor as much as possible to make it love us in return." And "the greater the emotion with which we imagine that a beloved object is affected toward us, the greater will be our self-exultation."[16] Again "None but those who are free are united by the closest bond of friendship,"[17] and love itself is defined as joy, or awareness of increasing freedom, accompanied by the idea of another as the cause of that increase.[18] So my emphasis on freedom or autonomy in my tests of a reflectively affirmable love, and my connected emphasis on reciprocity of caring, are themselves Spinozistic in inspiration.

Where I have departed both from Spinoza and from Frankfurt is in rejecting the thoroughgoing fatalism which collapses the actual into the necessary, and the normatively demanded into the one thing possible, at all levels of reflectiveness. In proposing tests we can apply to our loves, and tests which they may fail without thereby ceasing to control us, I have assumed that even if we have no other real choice, we have this choice, whether stoically to accept what cannot be changed, without passing judgment on it, or whether to stand in judgment on our volitional necessities, however powerless such judgments may often be to change them. This is a difference between what we could call the unemotional and the emotional fatalist, or even pessimist. The only consequences of insisting on going on criticizing even when criticism cannot change what is criticized are themselves emotional—one will come to hate oneself for one's unworthy but unchangeable loves. This may be futile or masochistic, and even worse, it may make one a worse companion, friend, or lover than the nonjudgmental stoic, but this seems to me the price we must pay, or rather the risk we must run, when we are constrained not only by love and loyalty but also by reason. And there is always the faint chance that our unavoidable loves and loyalties pass the tests reason imposes, that the outcome of choosing not to cut off reflective criticism is not self-condemnation but self-exaltation. We must risk *tristitia* to make any bid for that self-sustaining *gaudium* which is *gloria*.

NOTES

1. I think that Frankfurt treats Sartre's concept of choice as more ordinary than it is, at least in *Being and Nothingness,* where the "original choice" which explains all the more ordinary choices, such as the decision either to stay to look after one's aged parent or to leave to fight against tyranny, is a descendent of Leibniz's God's "choice" of a determinate "individual concept" to be realized in an existent individual, or Kant's noumenal moral agent's free choice of a whole style of life. This sort of "choice" is not a choice made at a determinate time, but rather the character exhibited in all the actions and responses made in the "chosen" lifetime.

2. See John Cooper, "Aristotle on the Forms of Friendship," *Review of Metaphysics* **30** (1977): 619–48; and "Friendship and the Good in Aristotle," *Philosophical Review* **86** (1977): 290–315.

3. St. Augustine, *Confessions,* bk. 4, Pusey translation, Everyman edition (New York: Macmillan, 1961), p. 60.

4. Ibid.

5. *A Treatise of Human Nature,* ed. L. A. Selby-Bigge and P. H. Nidditch (Oxford: Clarendon Press, 1978), 36, p. 391.

6. *Also sprach Zarathustra,* pt. 1, "Von der Nächstenliebe."

7. Ibid., "Von Freunde."

8. See *Treatise,* bk. 2, pt. 2, sec. 4, "Of the Love of Relations." I have explored Hume's moral psychology in "Hume on Resentment," *Hume Studies* **6** (1980): 133–49, and in "Master Passions," in *Explaining Emotion,* ed. Amelie Rorty (Berkeley and Los Angeles: University of California Press, 1980).

9. I have failed to trace this passage.

10. See Gabriele Taylor, "Love," *Proceedings of the Aristotelian Society* (1975–76); reprinted in *Philosophy as It Is,* ed. T. Honderich and M. Burnyeat (New York: Penguin Books, 1979).

11. Thomas Nagel, *Mortal Questions* (Cambridge, Eng.: Cambridge University Press, 1979), ch. 4, p. 39.

12. Ibid., p. 48.

13. Translation by Suzy Q Groden, in the Bretlinger edition (Amherst, Mass.: University of Massachusetts Press, 1970), p. 87.

14. Richard B. Brandt, *A Theory of the Good and the Right* (Oxford: Oxford University Press, 1979), chs. 5 and 6.

15. Andrew Marvell, "To His Coy Mistress."

16. Spinoza, *Ethics,* pt. 3, props. 33 and 34.

17. Spinoza, proof of prop. 71 of pt. 4.

18. Spinoza, definitions 2 and 6 at end of pt. 3.

7

Actions, Passions, and Reasons

> Between the conception
> And the creation
> Between the emotion
> And the response
> Falls the Shadow
> > Life is very long.

> > > T. S. Eliot, "The Hollow Men"

I. Prima Facie Differences between Actions and Passions

Eliot's shadows fall between intention and action, emotion and response. But there is also the earlier shadow that sometimes falls between reasons to intend and intending. Life being very long, there can be time for deliberation before intention-formation, as well as for conception before creation. Is there any similar formative process for feelings, any room for malformation, for a weakness of the heart paralleling weakness of the will? Reasons for feeling, like reasons for believing, tend to act upon us without our having to do anything except become aware of those reasons. Faced with a reason for feeling anger, straightway we irascible ones feel it. (As Hume pointed out,[1] faced with a reason for *ceasing* to feel anger, we may respond less promptly.[2] Some beliefs show a similar inertia, a resistance to timely termination.) Even those who are slow to anger are not slowed by thinking before they feel. When we feel for reasons, there is no room beforehand, as there can be when we act for reasons, for us to weigh reasons pro and con, and, more interestingly, no need to do so, since we can feel anger or pride in any degree, and we can feel both proud and ashamed of one and the same accomplishment—say a sarcastic witticism about a colleague. Unlike assent, which is supposed not to come in degrees, and unlike an action, which is supposed either to be done or not done, feelings can reflect the complexity of the considerations that led to them. There are mixed, ambivalent, and qualified feelings, and lukewarm ones, whereas there are no mixed, ambivalent, qualified, or lukewarm believings, nor mixed, ambivalent, or lukewarm actions. Or are there? I shall consider how actions and passions are affected by the reasons there were for and against them, and whether Davidson's account captures the complex facts of this matter.

I have brought reasons for believing into the picture, because belief, like feeling, is usually something which responds to reasons without any need or room for choice on our part, yet which may be criticized as unreasonable. We are thought to be at fault when our beliefs are not adequately backed by reasons, and may be at fault when our feelings are out of line with the reasons we have for feeling, just as we are usually at fault when our actions lack good enough reasons, even though we don't decide what to believe, nor what to feel, in the way we can decide what to do. The question "Am I at fault?" is not the same as the question "Did I decide wrongly?" and only divines in disguise suppose that discernment of faults and vices is the same as judging who deserves what punishment. We criticize people for their credulity, for their stupidity, for their sentimentality, for their hardness of heart, without any implied suggestion that they could, at will, have avoided those faults. So it is important to see that the spontaneity of feeling no more exempts feelings from criticism as appropriate or inappropriate, reasonable or unreasonable, rational or irrational, than the spontaneity of belief exempts them from such criticism. Having brought belief and its reasons into this discussion, to make that point, I shall now concentrate mainly on reasons for doing and reasons for feeling, bringing in belief now and again only to help us with that comparison. I postpone the task of looking at a fuller variety of reason-affected mental states, and at the ways reasons can relate to what they are reasons for.[3] The questions I have raised concern the way in which reasons for feeling, including conflicting reasons, affect our feelings, and how this compares with the way reasons for doing affect our doings. On the face of it, I have said, there is not merely the difference that feeling, like believing and unlike doing, is not done "at will," but also three other differences: feelings come in degrees, whereas actions either happen or don't; feelings, like beliefs, can be qualified, but actions are "all out"; and opposed feelings can coexist, (or alternate in fairly rapid succession) whereas in action, as in belief, we seem necessarily unable to say "yes *and* no" to some belief or action candidate. But these are only *prima facie* contrasts, and we need to assemble more considerations.

II. Davidson on Reasons for Action and a Digression on the Demands of Reason

Davidson[4] has used the notion of the *prima facie* to clarify what goes on in practical deliberation, and what is special about the action of the weak-willed person, in relation to the reasons for action assembled in the prior deliberation. He has also suggested[5] that this notion of the *prima facie* can help us see the relation of the reasons for feeling to resultant feelings. I shall examine these suggestions, asking whether Davidson manages to capture the likenesses and the differences between actions and passions in relation to their reason-causes. The first thing to note is that Davidson wants *prima facie* (*pf*) to be an operator not on predicates, nor on single sentences, but on pairs of sentences, related as judgment and ground.[6] In practical deliberation even the agent's "best judgment," his all-things-considered judgment, since it is a judgment with its ground presented, for Davidson counts, like those tentative preliminary judgments after which and in whose light it is made, as a conditional judgment, so far "practical only in its subject, not in its issue," since "A judgment that a is better than b, all things considered, is a relational, or *pf* judgment."[7] Once the agent not merely makes this all-things-considered judgment, but *makes up her mind,* forms an intention, then and only then do we have the unconditional, unrelativized, or "all out" judgment. Since this cannot conflict logically with any conditional judgment, all or less than all things considered, there is no problem about how the *akrates* can say "All things considered, it is best that I do a, not b, but I shall do b." She is weak willed in that her intention repeats the content not of her all-things-considered *pf* judgment, but (usually) of one of her less-things-considered *pf* judgments. We cannot criticize her for contradiction, since there cannot be contradiction between "all out" and *pf* judgments. What we do criticize her for is the "weakness" of doing what she has judged it best not to do, all things considered. Davidson, then, can agree with Hume that it is not contrary to that reason with which *logic* is concerned to effectively prefer one's lesser good to one's greater, to judge "I would do better to save myself and the world, at the cost of a scratch to my finger, but I am going to try to save my finger from that scratch (to perish unscratched)." It may be crazy, shortsighted, weak, self-indulgent, or wicked, but illogical it isn't.

Of course once we divorce a decision's grounds from a conclusion's premises as much as this we face the question of why we should think both that reason requires us to accept only what is consistent with the rest of what we accept, and everything we see to be entailed by other things we accept, and also that it is a demand of reason to act in accordance with our best judgment, where the "best" is often not entailed by its grounds.

What unites these two branches of reason? What links logical consistency to the other demands of reason, including that "total evidence" requirement in inductive reasoning whose analogy in practical reason, Davidson thinks,[8] is the demand that we perform the action judged best on the basis of (where this does not mean "entailed by") *all* the available relevant reasons? In Davidson's terminology, this becomes the question of what links inconsistency to irrationality. Is inconsistency a species of irrationality, if, as Davidson seems to be saying, the irrationality of the weak-willed person is no species of inconsistency? Or are both species of some third more fundamental genus of fault that the possession of reason makes possible for us? We cannot expect to be able to answer this big question, of what if anything unifies the various demands of reason, and what the place of logical consistency is among the requirements of reason, until we are clear about the extent of the variety itself. A look at how reasons for feeling relate to reasons for action will be part of that preliminary survey of the ground, and to that I must return. But I cannot forbear remarking how Davidson's work here shows a steady move away from what (ignoring paraconsistent logics) we could call a logic-centered view of the terrain.

He began, in "Actions, Reasons, and Causes," counting as reasons for an action the premises of practical syllogisms whose conclusion recommended that action, as in his first (and as far as I am aware only) look at reasons for feeling, "Hume's Cognitive Theory of Pride," he finds syllogisms grounding all "propositional pride." Here it seems that these count as reasons, as "rationalizing" as well as explaining actions and passions, only because we can present them in relation to what they are grounds for (or, more strictly, to the judgments implicit in the intentional content of what they ground) in the form of a valid argument. But, in "How Is Weakness of the Will Possible?", the realization that the crucial move, the "weighing" of possibly conflicting considerations, often cannot be presented as the application of some accepted general formula, so is not a matter of some supersyllogism adding up the import of the conflicting bits of prior reasoning, leads Davidson to a down-playing of entailment. Reasons no longer are would-be premises for valid inferences. They are demoted to conditions. Even the ones that *could* be expressed as entailing the judgments they support are expressed instead in conditionals. Where once we had, "with a little ingenuity," the syllogism "Pleasant acts are to be done by me. Act a will be pleasanter than act b, so act a rather than act b is to be done by me," now we have "*pf* (a is better than b, a is pleasanter than b and what is pleasanter is better)." Not merely does this weaken the connection between ground and judgment, by making it *prima facie,* it turns entailment into conditionalization. The same logical form is thereby given for the valid syllogism as for that nonsyllogism in which all the relevant considerations are "added up" and a best judgment mysteriously arrived at.

We have, Davidson says, "no clue"[9] about how we get the all-things-considered judgment from the total of what has been considered. It somehow emerges from those various partial considerations. Tentative conditionals perhaps seem the *right* form for dependencies about whose nature or internal structure we have no clue, or no logical clue. Davidson wants a uniform schema for all the *prima facie* concludings, and since the last, the all-things-considered one, is not entailment, he does not allow the earlier ones to be *essentially* entailments either. Whereas in "Actions, Reasons, and Causes" it was their power to entail what they were reasons for that made them reasons, now reasons have that feature, when they do, only accidentally. More than this, by the end of "How Is Weakness of the Will Possible?" he is willing to reserve the status of a reason for the mysterious condition that is not representable as a logical ground. For finally, to the question "What reason does the weak-willed person have for doing a when he believes that it would be better, all things considered, not to do a?" he answers that he has "no reason."[10] Although the weak-willed agent has a practical syllogism to produce, to give the sort of thing Davidson began by treating as the very paradigm of a reason, now this no longer counts as a reason. It does not have that crucial nondeductive relation to the judgment expressed in the rational action that the all-things-considered judgment (and subsequent normally strong-willed "all out" judgment) would have had. Davidson ends this piece saying that the weak-willed person's intentional behavior is "essentially surd."[11] So far have logical ties been demoted that what has a reason or ground which can be presented so that it entails what it is a ground for, has become "surd," while the mysterious nonlogical connection to its ground now is the *sine qua non* of the rational intention. Logical thieves turned honest! Honest scholastic headpieces and logicians[12] turned into Humeans! (Hume, however, *has* clues about how we get beyond logic to reasons that are real, although he cannot let himself call them "reasons.")

I have noted this change in Davidson's account of what a reason essentially is, a change Davidson himself draws attention to in his introduction to *Actions and Events,*[13] not because I deplore it, but, on the contrary, because I see it as progress. Indeed I am tempted to call it progress from rationalizations to reasons. I see it as part of a more general move away from the equation of human reason with any sort of power of *calculating,* a move that we find also in Davidson's successive accounts of how we understand language, in particular metaphor.[14] Davidson's second thoughts, both in philosophy of mind and of language, seem, like Wittgenstein's, to show a liberation from the tyranny of formalism. But of course it is only a negative characterization of a good or adequate reason to say that it does *not* entail the intention it supports. The real work will come when one tries to say what support is, and when nonentailing support is good, when it is less good. For, after all, the fool, the superstitious person, the weak-willed, the self-deceiver, would have no more trouble in producing nonentailing reasons for their actions, than they would in producing entailing reasons. Some "add up" the reasons badly, some add them up twice, with different results, make a considered judgment about which addition is less suspect, (or add them up a third time) then act on the more suspect addition. (Once we have *really* abandoned the reason-as-calculus view, of course, we will have to avoid speaking of "adding up" and perhaps also of "weighing" reasons. "Considering" is a nontainted word,[15] and we could stick to phases like "my considered judgment," at least until we can say why and when literal additions and weighings, and metaphorical entailments, do sometimes count as compelling reasons. We will be free again to speak figuratively of "adding up" considerations once we see the genus of which addition is a species.)

I return, after this digression, to the question of what help Davidson's version of the *prima facie* gives us in understanding what a reason for action is, and what a reason for feeling is. We have seen how his account of reasons for action uses *prima facie,* as a form of conditionalization. In the last analysis, however, the only *prima facie* conditional that Davidson thinks gives a reason for the action done is the one most users of the language would not call *"prima facie"* at all—namely the all-things-considered, or final judgment in deliberation. Only when this is the one which, detached from its condition, becomes the "all out" judgment, or intention with which the person acts, has that person *any* reason for what he does, if that action is described in a way that makes its relations to the preceding deliberation fully explicit. The difference between the better and worse reasons non-weak-willed agents act on, presumably, will lie in what final judgments they make, sometimes with what went into their making, and with what the agent ignored or failed to consider, at other times with faulty moves from the assembled considerations to the all-things-considered, to what we might call the "all considerations *in,*" or best judgment of the agent.

Davidson ends by dropping the "all things considered" locution as a characterization of the judgment the non-weak-willed person is guided by, and switches instead to saying that he acts on what he sees as the *best* reasons. This does avoid the possibly misleading suggestion not merely that everything relevant has indeed been considered, but also of *serial* assembly of considerations, of the most authoritative "final" judgment always coming later than the less authoritative or more tentative ones.

The weak-willed person's thought can take the form "I know I should do b, but wouldn't it be nice to do a," in which the best judgment precedes the tempting one, at least in mental formulation. Except when new information, or new insight, comes to hand *while one is deliberating,* any judgment, however tentative or weakly grounded, is, as Davidson notes,[16] in a sense made in the presence of all the considerations the agent has. They need not enter his mental presence serially, like witnesses in a law court. Since Davidson ends implying that, for actions, the *only* reasons are what are the agent's best reasons, however bad or faulty they may be when evaluated by some critic, it seems that what can conflict cannot, strictly, be reasons, but merely putative reasons, or inputs into best reasons. Let us say that *considerations* can conflict, and that considerations are what provide Davidsonian reasons, by some mysterious combination we will call considering, about whose nature we have, or at least Davidson has, "no clues," or at any rate no algorithms. So considerations are things to consider, to get a considered or best judgment. And some best judgments are better than others, in virtue of being better considered.

Intentional action that carries out what an agent had been intending to do (as not all intentional action need do) reveals the "all out" judgment the agent had reached if he deliberated, and this, if he is not weak willed, is his best judgment, detached from the considerations that provided its grounds. Having an intention, Davidson says, simply is having an "all out" judgment.[17] Presumably it is only if we ask the agent not *what* he is doing or intending, but *why* he is doing it or intending to do it, that the condition need be as it were reattached, now in a "because" clause or in what can be turned into a "because" clause. Davidson seems to be saying that when we have made up our minds how to act, our reasons for the intention become past history, and are not themselves incorporated in the intentional act, in the way the intention itself is. "Knowing the intention with which someone acted does not allow us to reconstruct his actual reasoning."[18] Nor, it seems, need it allow us even to reconstruct the best or "all in" *prima facie* judgment, the one that gives the *reason(s)* why the agent made up his mind in the way he did, since "the judgment which corresponds to, perhaps is identical with, the action cannot be a *prima facie* judgment; it must be an all out or unconditional judgment which, if we were to express it in words, would have a form like 'this action is desirable'."[19] *What* is desirable about it, and what other undesirable aspects it outweighed, are not contained in the intention, whose form is unconditional, and apparently without "because" clauses.

These claims of Davidson's about the "detachment" of an intention from its support are very puzzling to me. He often cites, with apparent agreement, Anscombe's account of intention, and seems to agree with her that the arm moving, the pumping, the supplying, are the same action.[20] The nested series of intentions with which a person acts, which Anscombe makes definitive of intention, recapitulates at least *some* of the reasons the agent had for forming the more deeply imbedded intention. But if, as Davidson insists, the intention is an "all out" judgment stripped of all its reasons, then we cannot keep Anscombe's account. I for one am loath to abandon it, and see no reason, yet, to do so. For a judgment, in Davidson's extended sense of "judgment," can be "all out," in that it somehow decides matters in a way preliminary trial judgments did not, yet still incorporate both conditions and reasons. When I, after deliberation, decide to snub him if he greets me, my intention can be conditional but quite firm. When, carrying out my intention, I look away from him as he addresses me, my intention is to snub him, and it gives my reason for turning. My discernible intention may be not merely to snub, but to punish him by my snubbing. What is "all out," settled and, once I act, there for the interested world to see, is my implicit judgment "It is good for me to turn away, in order to snub him." This "all out" judgment, my intention, incorporates up to a point the reasons I had for the head turning, and so incorporates the content, or part of the content, of what Davidson calls the *prima facie* judgment in which my deliberation ended—my best judgment, what I called the "all in" one. Watching me, you know what I am doing, and *why* I am turning my head away. You may not know why I judge it best to snub him, although the action might reveal that too—if I turn to speak to his rival, whom *he* has just insulted in a public speech, you may know not merely what I am doing, but most of what there is to know about why I am doing it.

III. Feelings and Their Reasons

I have registered a doubt about Davidson's thesis that an intention is an "all out" but not an "all in" judgment, that our intentional actions do not inherit any of the reasons we had for forming those intentions. Before saying more about what I think has gone wrong here, I want now to turn to what Davidson says about reasons for what he calls "propositional" feelings, such as feeling proud that one won the election. Here Davidson emphasizes that the actual feeling (or the pride that need not be literally "felt" as the agreeable glow Hume took it to be) *does* bring its reason with it, when it occurs. It remains relativized to its grounds. Its grounds, according to Davidson, are a general attitude of *prima facie* approbation towards people of a certain sort, say winners, along with a belief that one is oneself of that sort. The notion of *prima facie* used here seems intended to be the same as that in "How Is Weakness of the Will Possible?". It conditionalizes or relativizes a judgment to its grounds. In such cases "My approval is *prima facie* in character and given only relative to its ground."[21] Yet this *prima facie* judgment, unlike that occurring in practical deliberation, which loses its relativization when it issues in intention and action, keeps its relativization when it issues in feeling. There *may* also be feelings that are "all out," Davidson seems to suggest—he contrasts propositional relativized pride with the "generalized pride" of the proud man, and he chides Hume, as others[22] also have done, for his apparent assumption that all pride, and all love, is relativized to reasons for it. (He says "Hume seems to analyze loving for a reason rather than loving.")[23] Is "generalized" pride pride which has *many* particular reasons, or pride which needs none? "Generalized" suggests the former, but the contrast with "relativized" suggests that it is *plain* Aristotelian pride[24], not pride-in-that . . . in the case where much about the person can fill in those dots. To see what we should say here we must look more carefully at the relation of feelings to perceived reasons for them.

Passions are more immediately linked to perceived reasons than are actions. They do not wait on any making up of one's heart as actions can wait on one's making up one's mind. Nor is there anything to feeling for reasons either as intending is to doing for reasons, or as action is to intending for reasons. Weakness of the will may cause one not to form the intention one has best reason to form, and a change of mind may cause one not to do what one had been intending to do, but feelings are not at the mercy of either of these different swerves of the will. We do not deliberate before feeling, nor intend to feel before feeling. But with intentional action, between the idea and the reality may fall the shadow, and between the deliberation and the intention a prior shadow may have fallen. Reasons for action, to be effective, must sustain themselves across both these dark places, that between deliberation and decision, and that between decision and action. Reasons for believing face only the former danger point. *Pace* Pascal, we do not intend to believe any more than we intend to feel. With feeling there is less room than with believing for any shadow to fall between appreciation of reasons and feeling for reasons, and no room at all for second thoughts between the fixing of feeling and its being actually felt. Both these claims need some comment.

A shadow of sorts can fall between the lack of perceived reasons to feel and an irrational or stubborn feeling. Sometimes we feel what we label at the time as irrational fear, or irrationally continued dislike. But if "irrational" implies "inappropriate," we may be mislabeling it. Visceral fear, as Robert Kraut[25] has pointed out, may be, in a wise animal or person, an appropriate response to a situation which does contain danger, but not danger to which one has intellectual access. The *only* indicator of the danger may be the feeling response of duly sensitized animals. So feeling when we cannot see at the time what the reasons are to have that feeling may be not weakness but strength of the heart. The problem is to tell the strength of heart of the wise and well adapted from the irrationality of the fools and ill adapted.

Are there cases where we do see reasons to feel yet fail to feel accordingly as well as cases where we feel something without knowing why? Repression and inhibition may count as such cases, but usually then we repress the recognition of reasons for feeling as much as we repress the feeling. Should we construe a case where someone faces an admittedly dangerous and threatening attacker with calm confidence rather than with fear as a failure to feel what seems appropriate in the circumstances, or as a feeling of what seems inappropriate? If the latter, then the situation is parallel to that of visceral fear. Here we would have visceral confidence and calm rather than visceral fear. In both cases the feeling response is not supported by reasons the responder can cite. The calm person, in defense of her response, might say "We gain nothing by losing our heads," but that is to shift the confidence from the guts to the head, and in any case the frightened person could (later) reply: "Fright speeds the sensible retreat, so we lose nothing by losing our heads." Sometimes apparently irrational confidence pays off, just as visceral fear can be a healthy reaction. There seems no good reason to reserve the status of "reasons of the heart which reason knows not of" only for the violent passions.

Given these complications, does any truth remain in my earlier claims that faced with a reason for feeling, straightway we feel? If we may feel despite not seeing the reasons and not feel despite seeing the reasons, then the feeling's relation to the reasons has become oblique, not direct. But it is not deliberation that mediates between the reasons and the feeling, rather some visceral-cum-cerebral nondiscursive wisdom (or foolishness, depending on how things turn out) so we can keep the claimed contrast between deliberation-mediated fixing of intention and immediate fixing of feeling. In both cases there may be a discrepancy between perceived reasons and response to them, but with intention-formation the perception of good reasons is drawn out in deliberation. Earlier I said that there was no call for an assembly of reasons for and against a feeling, since we can combine opposed feelings, weaken feelings, and qualify them. No perceived reason for feeling need ever be "outweighed," since we can incorporate response to it into what we feel. Does the person who sees the reason for fear yet stays calm respond in any way to the perceived reasons for fear? Presumably the calm of the person facing the armed robber is indeed different from the sort of calm carrying on she would have shown had the figure in the dark alley not turned out to be a robber—her response precisely is *to the danger,* and so to the reasons for fear. She responds to reasons for fear as if they were reasons for confidence-despite-danger, not as if they were reasons for ordinary confidence. Her confidence will be alert, heightened by the danger. Whether that visceral-cerebral reaction is wiser than that of the person who felt visceral fear so did not enter the dark alley is very dubious, but for the one who has entered the alley, it may be too late for fear to be the optimal response. Perhaps the place for visceral fear is on the edge of dangerous situations, the place for calm courage is in the middle of them, and both reactions are appropriate in their proper place. If danger is unavoided, stay calm and face it.

But the relative appropriateness of particular emotional responses is not my topic. My concern was rather with the difference between a feeling's relation to its perceived reasons, and an intention's relation to its supporting reasons. Both can be out of line with perceived reasons, and sometimes that is due to limits in our ability to perceive reasons rather than to limits in our ability to have appropriate feelings or form appropriate intentions. The same can be said for beliefs—they too can be out of line with our known reasons for them, and that shows either that the belief is faulty or that our ability to discern the grounds of a belief is faulty or limited. Not only the heart, but the mind too, may have reasons that reason knows not. Both with believing and with deciding, we think we know how to "weigh" considerations for and against, whereas we make fewer such pretensions with feelings. But our understanding of how reasons should support belief and decision may be overrated.[26] "When we deliberate, the chips are already down,"[27] and our deliberation does not always even reveal how they really lie. With feeling for reasons, the chips at least appear to be as they are, already down, even if there too we may fail at the time to see how they lie.

The first "shadow," then, may fall between perceived reasons for feeling and feeling as much as between perceived reasons for believing and believing, perceived reasons for deciding and decision, and it can be a beneficent shade. It can fall both when there is and when there is not drawn-out consideration of reasons. But the second shadow, that between a formed intention and its carrying out in action, seems to have no analogue in either belief or feeling.

Beliefs we have assented to may fail to be acted on, and feelings may fail to get any expression, but neither of those failures to carry through into normal effects is parallel to the failure to do what one intended to do. Intentions may be aborted either by change of mind, including cold feet at the last minute, or by frustrating circumstances. There are, of course, changes of mind about what to believe as well as about what to do, and there are changes of heart as well as changes of mind. Whereas a change of mind about what to do is not a change in what one is doing, but only in what one is going to do, a change of mind about what to believe is also a change in what *one believes*. Similarly for changes of heart: they effect a change in actual feeling, not merely in future feeling. There just seems to be no room, with belief and feeling, for the second shadow. Nothing is to believing and feeling as intentional action is to intending.

It might be thought that expression is to feeling as doing is to intending. Between the emotion and the response there can fall a shadow, and it may seem like that between intending and doing. Feeling does tend to its own expression, as belief tends to guide action and as intention tends to its own execution. But only in the last is the "tending" an "intending." The whole intentional content of the intention *is* the purposive action that executes it, but the intentional content of the feeling is not its expression any more than the content of a belief is its role in guiding action. There is a one-one relation between a prior intention and the intentional action that executes it (despite the indeterminacy in many respects[28] of the former, and the fuller determinacy of the latter), but one feeling may appropriately issue in any of a whole spectrum of expression, as any one determinate belief may affect action in countless ways. The countless ways in which one may carry out one's intention to sign one's name on the document are a lower order of uncountability than the countless ways in which one's love or one's dislike may get expressed. Expression is, of its very nature, Protean, giving scope for free choice and even for originality, but carrying out one's intentions is sticking to one's own already fixed instructions. An action doesn't *ex*press the intention it executes—it is more a case of transmitted *im*pression. The prior intention is the intentional action, biding its time, and if no change of mind occurs and no unforeseen frustrating factor intervenes, then the very same intention will be "in" the intentional action, giving it its human face. The expressed feeling is also "in" the expression, in the lighting up of the eyes of the lover on the arrival of the beloved, but what has been in the love before that moment is not just the lighting up the eyes biding its time—it is equally the pain of parting biding its time, the need for news of the beloved in his absence biding its time, and so on for all the possible expressions of the love. They are all some-how potential in the feeling, but because of their multiplicity and unfixity, the feeling is not defined by them in the way the prior intention is defined by the action that executes it.

Since perceived reasons for action have this doubly tenuous tie with action—a tie weakened both at the moment of decision, when things may go wrong, and also at the moment of carrying out the original decision, when other things may go wrong—while perceived reasons for feeling are less separated from feeling for reasons, it may seem a good feature of

Davidson's account that the same judgment which gives the ground for a propositional feeling is found by him implicit in the feeling it grounds. Where an action has, implicit in it, an "all out" judgment, cut off from the reasons which supported it, pride has implicit in it the very *prima facie* judgment which provides its support. Since, according to what I have just been arguing, the transition from reasons for feeling to feeling avoids both the weak bridge of decision and the weak bridge of decision implementation, it may seem right to have feeling automatically incorporate its reasons in a way intentional action, just because of those bridges, does not. Feelings for reasons, unlike actions for reasons, are relativized to their reasons, if Davidson is right. Whether stubborn feelings, like dislike or distrust, which can persist once the reasons that once rationalized them are shown to be false, count as "propositional" and as subject to the same analysis as pride, Davidson does not say. Perhaps feelings, or some of them, can begin as propositional feelings for reasons, but then establish themselves, independently of those reasons, or any others consciously accessible to the person whose feelings they are? Just as love, which can begin as "all out," may shift to being love for reasons, other feelings, like dislike, can begin as dislike for reasons, but progress to being plain dislike. It makes perfect sense to say "I did him an injustice when I believed he had deliberately misled me, and that false belief was my reason for my initial dislike of him. Now I retract the charge of deceit, but I still can't stop disliking him." Nor, as I have emphasized, do we always criticize a person for such a discrepancy between feelings and the reasons they can produce for them. "Trust your feelings" can be sensible advice, and "think before you feel" would be bad advice, were it not already pointless. Although dislike can be a "propositional" feeling, a feeling for reasons, and is sometimes qualified dislike, relativized to those reasons, we do not necessarily trust disliking for reasons more than disliking one knows not why. Often undiscovered reasons for such feelings against apparent reason become retrospectively uncovered by us, and so we have some grounds to regard ourselves as well-calibrated emotional registers. "I always disliked him, although I couldn't have told you why. And how right I was to do so. Now we see him in his true colors." If my feelings can be the *right* or appropriate ones when they were not supported by reasons I could cite, although they are the sort of feelings that often can be reason-supported, what it was appropriate to feel cannot be equated with what we had accessible as reasons for feeling. This is true, I think, of a large range of feelings—dislike, trust, hope, fear, but not for pride, nor for admiration, nor for contempt. These require that we have some reasons in hand, and they do not survive the loss of their reasons. Davidson's account may fit only these few feelings, ones immune from inertia, and also ones there is no question of our trusting or not trusting. I may trust my dislike of him, although I cannot give grounds for it, but my contempt for him must not only have grounds, it must have grounds I can give. There is no such thing as trusting one's contempt. Such feelings—pride, contempt, admiration—are ones that call for justification in a way not all feelings do.

IV. Reasons, Justifications, and a Funny Feature of Feelings

Having justification is not the same thing as being reason-supported. Neither for actions, nor for beliefs, nor for feelings, is it always appropriate to want a justification, even when it is appropriate to expect there to be reasons. Philosophers, in ethics and epistemology, seem to be fascinated by justification, and tend to assimilate all contexts to the context where justification is in order. It is in order when something questionable has been done, something which either draws upon the agent the attention of the law or some moral vigilante, or is itself an action, like punishing, which occurs in such a quasi-judicial context. To show an action to be justified it is not enough to show that there were good reasons for it, one must also show that it broke no authoritative rule, or that, if it did, there was nothing better one might have done, nothing, that is, that had better reasons of a morally or legally acceptable kind. This legal or quasi-legal structure of accusation, defense, and judgment does not normally apply to ordinary action for reasons. One *might* do all one's deliberating that way, anticipating some court that makes one answer for all one's actions, but only divines in or out of disguise will encourage us to force all considering of reasons into this adversarial and officious mold. For beliefs the special features of justification, as distinct from support, come into play when the belief in question is, like the illegal or immoral or official action, socially deviant or a response to it. The flat earther must expect to have to justify his beliefs, but we conformist believers can make do with support for ours, except when we force a confrontation. In a society where there is a minimal body of common knowledge, everyone must expect to be called on to justify some of her beliefs to some challenger, and so epistemology flourishes, and the difference between having grounds for one's belief and having justification gets blurred. Grounding gets inflated to uniquely selecting, justifying gets weakened to having *any* defense, whether or not it would counter the prosecution's case. Moral beliefs often have good grounds, but, in part because they were, until recently, rarely challenged, they rarely can be given successful justifications. Wittgenstein's question of why one looks after one's children can be answered, but the chain of reasons is here very short, and amounts to no real defense or justification of the practice in the face of any serious challenge, any Swiftian modest proposals for alternative ways of living.

For beliefs and for actions, I have claimed, only socially nonconformist ones or official responses to them call for justification, and what provides good grounds or good reasons does not necessarily provide a justification (and vice versa). Whereas any belief, or any action, *could,* given the required social context, be called in question, called into court to justify itself, it seems that, with feelings, some are constitutionally exempt from such answerability, while others necessarily have it. Could it be that our feeling-names incorporate social categories and that the feelings which are tied to justifying reasons are all of them socially deviant, or responses to the socially abnormal? Pride does have a history as a Christian vice, and admiration, shame, and contempt are reserved for those who have been judged to *deserve* them. There is some implication, with these feelings, that some judicial process has occurred to pave the way for them. "Judicial" may be too restrictive—it is perhaps just some process determining what is *due,* on grounds of merit, to a person. A person can feel well-deserved pride or shame, can be the object of well-deserved admiration, respect, pity, or contempt, but not of well-deserved liking, love, or lust, nor of well-deserved envy. We might say, to the callous wife, "Your husband *deserves* your love—look how he has put up forgivingly with all the trouble you have given him," but here we usually would accept the substitution of "devotion" for "love." And to say of someone that he deserves to be liked is usually to emphasize the extent of his efforts to please, rather than any reasons for liking him. Our words for feelings, words like *jealousy, respect, envy, pride, love, trust, fear, hope, suspicion, anger, despair,* are, as Aristotle knew, words for the feelings possible to *social* animals, and social categories often enter into their definition.

It is a peculiar but little wondered at fact that we can draw up *lists* of feeling-possibilities (and of possible propositional attitudes), aiming at a completed list, whereas no one would dream of trying to list all the actions, or all the beliefs, that are humanly possible. Aristotle, Descartes, Spinoza, Hume, all gave us lists of human passions, introducing some sort of systematicity into their lists.[29] Whatever we think of those lists, we need to have an explanation of how it is possible to even attempt them, when no such parallel attempt seems thinkable for actions or beliefs. Action-possibilities seem essentially open-ended, and the questions to which our beliefs give answers just as open-ended. Feelings and attitudes, like colors, seem to come in a limited spectrum. We may discriminate more finely, but not discover or invent a wholly new feeling, as it seems we *can* ask new questions and institute new procedures that make new actions possible. That may be a reason to support the old view that we are in bondage to our emotions, a bondage we can escape both in action and in the pursuit of truth. Creativity seems possible in thought and action, and indeed in the expression of feeling, but only delicacy in feeling itself. Whatever we think or do, however exciting the horizons there, and however inventive our expression of our feelings, our feelings themselves remain unoriginal, restricted to the same old familiar round. Is this really so? Are we necessarily restricted in our feelings and attitudes, not just contingently restricted, as we are in, say, our auditory powers, and, if we are, what explains the necessity? Sociobiological constraints? The very idea of a social animal? I leave this as a question.

V. Due Pride, and Its Justifying Reasons

Davidson restricted his account to propositional feelings, of which pride was his example. I have suggested that pride is among those special feelings-for-reasons in which the reasons are expected to *justify* what they are reasons for, and I have put forward a hypothesis about why such feelings are thought to need not merely grounds but justifications. They are feelings proper to certain *social* situations,[30] so their reasons must establish that one is indeed in that social situation, so can feel "due" pride, or deserved shame, or mete out deserved contempt or due admiration. Davidson's propositional feelings, the ones his account is to apply to, are best seen as only what we could call the due feelings, that is, the ones which *can* be due or undue. They do not exhaust the feelings-for-reasons, but seem to be a subgroup of them. Does Davidson's analysis, in terms of *prima facie* conditionalization or relativization, do justice to these justification-demanding feelings, and to the likenesses and differences between their relation to their reasons, and what we find in actions, and in other feelings? These feelings, Davidson says, remain tied to their reasons, and the tie is *prima facie* conditionalization. They never become "all out," as do intentions and possibly some other feelings. I have already noted that Davidson does not make clear whether reasons for such propositional feelings admit of a contrast between all things considered and this thing considered, as did reasons for action. If "this thing" is my fine house, and my pride is relativized to it, then the "generalized" pride of the person whose pride is based on considering *all* the things that are his should still count, for Davidson, as relativized to an all-things-considered judgment, not necessarily yet "all out." But he speaks as if the significant contrast, for pride, is not between a pride relativized to reasons, including best all-inclusive reasons, and "all out" unrelativized pride, but rather between pride in some particular thing, and a pride that he describes both as "generalized" and as not "relativized." It looks as if Davidson's *prima facie,* for reasons for propositional feelings, contrasts with "all things considered," not distinguished from "all out," whereas for reasons for actions the *prima facie* included the "all things considered," and contrasted only with the "all out." It would be better not to use it for feelings as well as actions unless it can keep the same sense, and mark parallel contrasts, in both places. It seems it does not.

It is possible that the better way to use the contrast between "some thing considered" and "all things considered," in the case of pride, would be to take the "things" in question in a more fine-grained way. Some things about my house might support pride in it, while other features of it do not. I *might* judge "all things considered, its a pretty good house," and feel an all-things-considered pride in it, but no "generalized" pride at all, if a generalized pride is pride *in* every possession or attribute of mine you care to name (Hume's vain man). Then we could get two sorts of pride in x corresponding to the difference between some things (about x) considered and all things (about x) considered judgments. I might be proud of my remark in as far as it was witty, but not proud, perhaps even ashamed, in as far as it was malicious. I suppose one could, in such a situation, judge "all things considered it was (or was not) a good remark to make," and feel some overall pride, weakened by the counts against the remark's malice, or overall shame, but not as intense a shame as one would have felt had one made a malicious remark with no redeeming wit; but it will be more normal to feel not weakened pride or shame, but both unweakened pride *and* unweakened shame. Since each is relativized to its own ground, they can coexist "like oil and vinegar," despite the "intimate connection" between what showed the wit and what showed the malice.

It is, I think, this possibility of coexisting and in some sense opposed evaluations that Davidson wanted to allow for in the judgments he calls *prima facie* conditionalized ones. Both opposed reasons-for-action, and opposed feelings-for-reasons, show this toleration for contraries. And since sometimes feelings are themselves among the reasons for actions, it may have seemed proper to give them the same analysis as had been given for such reasons, namely as conditionalized judgments. (Actually the feelings which motivate, which give reasons for action, are more likely to be the ones Davidson has not analyzed than those he has. One is more likely to act out of love or envy or distrust, than out of pride, contempt, or admiration. These may figure in action explanations, but usually only to explain why one wanted what one did—to boast, to avoid her, to win her approval, rather than also to say, as reasons for action do, what it was one wanted.) But the *prima facie* conditional, as Davidson explicated it, not only allowed us to accept without contradiction both the pros and the cons, it also allowed us to add up the pros and cons into another such conditionalized judgment, which could be accepted even when its "consequent," if we may so call it, is rejected. It was the coexistence of an "unconditional" effective judgment with an opposed conditionalized but "best" judgment that characterized Davidsonian weakness of the will. Three sorts of toleration for opposites were needed—toleration for opposed equally partial *prima facie* judgments, toleration of opposition between a less-than-all-things and an all-things-considered *prima facie* judgment, and toleration between a *prima facie* judgment and an opposed all-out one. We have found scope for the former two, that is for opposition among *prima facie* judgments, but not for the latter toleration in "due" feelings like pride in *x*. So Davidson's notion of *"prima facie,"* even if it did justice to reasons for action, and to weakness of the will, distorts the logic of feelings like pride by introducing unnecessary structure, spare wheels that make us expect contrasts where there are none, or expect the wrong kind of contrasts.

Davidson also uses "in that"[31] to express the sort of judgment involved in pride in one's house. This seems to me a much more promising concept than *prima facie* for capturing the "relativization" of due feelings to their grounds. For pride-in-that need not contrast with any plain pride. *Prima facie* is necessarily correlative to some contrasting category, be it that of the "all things considered" or *tout court,* or that of the "all out" or *sans phrase.* But pride-in-that implies no implicit contrast with any *sans phrase* or *tout court* pride, and that is more what we want for such feelings. What will characterize the vain person is that he feel, not pride *sans phrase,* for we have no idea what *feeling* that could be, nor "pride" *tout court* or general confidence, which is a feeling some are familiar with but one distinct from felt pride, but pride in all he has, pride in that *p,* where *p* is almost any fact about him.

VI. Many (Probably Too Many) Things Considered Judgment on Davidsonian *Prima Facie* Judgments

The concept of a *prima facie* judgment employed by Davidson, originally to characterize judgments occurring in practical deliberation, later to characterize also the structure of some feelings, can be seen to involve four separate aspects. First are the two just distinguished—*prima facie* judgments seen as equivalent to *reason-restricted judgments* of the form "in that *p,* then *q,*" where we can without contradiction (but not always without dilemma) add "and in that *r,* then not *q,*" and *prima facie* judgments seen as compatible not just with opposed *prima facie* judgments, all or less than all-things-considered ones, but with opposed more final judgments. In this second guise, they are equivalent to *tentative* reasoned judgments of the form "As far as *p* takes us, it seems that *q,*" to which without contradiction, even when *p* takes us as far as reason can go, we can add "But in the end not *q.*"[32] Thirdly there is the *prima facie* judgment as that which must keep its reasons in its own internal structure, which does not become free of them, as an "all out" judgment does. I call this the *"reason-incorporating"* judgment. Fourthly, I think, Davidson sometimes thinks of the *prima facie* judgment as not merely not final, but in some sense not *real,* not part of the sequence of real events, or causal network. Before showing how these four aspects come apart, both in intentions and their reasons and in feelings for reasons, I need to say a bit about why I impute to Davidson this fourth sense of *prima facie,* as the possible but not yet actual psychologically real happening.

Actions undeniably occur, and equally undeniably seem to have an intentional face, linking them with the agent's beliefs, desires, and possibly feelings, as well as a physical face, as parts of the causal network. Davidson's anomalous monism is explicated primarily for intentional actions. *They,* with their double face, present the anomaly. What of the things we cite to give the agent's reasons, namely beliefs, feelings, and desires? In "Actions, Reasons, and Causes" it seemed that they must also be *real* happenings, since causes are of course real and the thesis was that "primary" reasons *are* causes, under a description that does not point up their place in a law-governed causal network. "How Is Weakness of the Will Possible?" showed that there were reasons, even agent's best reasons, which were not action causes, and *their* ontological status was left uncertain. In "Mental Events," Davidson says "If someone sank the Bismarck, then various mental events such as perceivings, notings, calculations, judgments, decisions, intentional actions, played a causal role in the sinking of the Bismarck."[33] In "Psychology as Philosophy," Davidson still wants to say that "a reason is a rational cause"[34] (although it has ceased to be a rationalist cause), but showing what is rational about it is no longer a matter of isolating its cause and showing that to have a rational as well as a physical face. Rationality has become not merely logic-transcending, but "holistic"; by citing reasons "we can explain behavior without having to know too much about how it was caused."[35] So is a reason still a rational cause, and therefore psychologically real, if we can know the reason for an action without knowing much about its cause? Davidson considers accounts, like F. P. Ramsay's, which treat wants and beliefs as theoretical constructs for explaining intentional action, itself taken as "the best evidence for desires and beliefs." I am unclear where Davidson ends, in this piece, as far as concerns his answer to the question "so *are* reasons causes?" I think he is saying that to describe the whole nest or sequence of nests of reasons which explain a person's successive actions, over a fairly long period, just is to redescribe the set of causes which determined that person's behavior, in a way which makes that behavior look like the behavior of a fellow person, so humanly intelligible to us. But we cannot go from this identity at the holistic level to any more piecemeal identity—we cannot say "*this* reason, which rationalized this action, is *this* cause, which scientifically explains it." And since science is still taken as arbiter of the real, the moral, I think, is that although in some sense all the reasons are included in all the causes, where action over time is concerned, and so are as real as are these causes, we cannot go from "He felt strongly the force of reason *r,* and did what he did because of *r,*" to "There is some cause *c,* identical with *r* or acceptance of *r,* which causally explains his action." So any individual effective reason is left ontologically insecure. In as far as it is part of the whole network it is real, but in so far as we separate it out, who knows? Davidson's anomalous monism has taken the form of an identity theory that is not merely global, but global across time.

So I see, in Davidson's philosophy of mind, a doubt about the ontological status of singled-out beliefs and feelings and wants, of everything which might count as a reason for action, a doubt which is not extended to actions themselves. Actions seem to be where the action is, in Davidson's philosophy of mind. Were the fit between intentional action and physical event to turn out to be as loose as that between the one's reason, and the other's cause, then the anomalous monism might turn into anomalous dualism. Davidson seems not to be as doubtful of the physical event-action fit as of the fit between an action's reasons and that event's cause, so he does not see any threat to his materialist monism. Given this, we can I think say that the only individuated mental states or events that are taken as *certainly* real, as definitely not mere theoretical constructs, are acted-on intentions. They are "all out," there in actions that are also events in the real physical world's history.

Having tried to ground if not justify my attribution to Davidson of a sense of "all out" that makes unrevised, unthwarted intentions "all out" simply because they are expressed in what undeniably really happens, in those places, namely human actions, where our teleological and holistic or "field" account of rational connections and our atomistic law-invoking account of causal connections make contact with one another, I can now return to my suggestion that the contrast with "all out" in this sense is only one of four separable senses the *prima facie* has been given by Davidson, and that these four come apart both in passions and in actions.

Passions are real, with real physical effects, just as actions are. My due pride, for all its restriction by and incorporation of its reasons, may cause my fall. So the first and fourth, and third and fourth senses can come apart. Not only do "I do what happens,"[36] but in exactly the same sense I feel what happens also. We have already seen also how the first and second senses can come apart, in seeing how the *in that* qualifier can be in place where there is no suggestion that these qualified judgments are either conditional, or less than final. The second and third senses come apart in every case where reason incorporation is a final, not a tentative outcome, as well as in any cases where the tentative judgment is not reason-incorporating.[37] I have already argued that all cases of pride in something are reason-incorporating (as well as reason-restricted) and yet nontentative, and I suggested that intention also has this character, that it is not "all out" in the third sense.

More counterexamples[38] to the coincidence of the four senses of the Davidsonian *prima facie* would merely increase the tedium. I hope the point has now been made, that *prima facie* has to become too shifting in sense to introduce the right amount and kind of structure into our analysis of the way our actions and our feelings, or at least the due or answerable feelings, are related to their reasons. Better to use the variety of expressions we have—"in that," "in as far as," "as far as that goes," "other things equal," "up to a point," and the indispensable plain "as" or "*qua*." But my purpose in this paper has not been simply to reject the terminology Davidson offers us. It has also been to query the data which were to be regimented into the *prima facie* not-so-straight jacket.

VII. Actions and Passions, All Things Here Considered

I have claimed that intentions can incorporate their reasons, as much as do the reason-answerable feelings. This does not make them necessarily restricted by their reasons, and it might be thought that there still remains an important difference between the way reasons for pride limit or restrict the pride, and the way an intentional action resists restriction, even if it does, in its further intention, inherit and incorporate at least some of its reasons. The grain of truth, it might seem, in Davidson's account of how reasons for pride relate to reasons for some action, like showing the house I am proud of, is that the pride is restricted by its reasons, but the showing, even though it has its reasons, and incorporates them into its point, is unrestricted by them—actions break the umbilical chord to ancestor reasons, it might seem. It can continue to seem this way if we restrict our attention to those dramatic cases in which some stark *either/or* presents itself, and some decisive step is taken, whereby we do burn our bridges, cut ourselves off from the old allegiances and half-allegiances that made the decision difficult. Now and then, perhaps, there are such clean moves, when, in St. Paul's words, forgetting those things which are behind us, we march straight forward, accepting what we have prevented ourselves from being able to change. But normal action for reasons is messier and more complicated. There can be restricting reasons for action, and restricted actions, as well as restricted passions. When I am proud of my fine house except for the messiness of my study, and wish to have it admired, I may offer it for the Shadyside Homes Tour provided only that the study not be shown. Or I may blow hot and cold—offer it, then withdraw the offer, or bolt the front door when the day of the tour arrives. My reasons can restrict my intentions, as well as my pride, or can make those intentions unstable, accompanied by conflicting intentions. Philosophers of action, in the analytic tradition, have introduced a grossly oversimplifying *either/ or* structure into their account of our intention-formation, by ignoring all the ways we can and do fit our actions to our mixed and conflicting motives and reasons. I may decide, magnanimously, to forgive you, but do so with a fuss that ensures that neither of us will ever forget the wrong. The oversimplification is aided and abetted by the tendency to look only at isolated time slices of intentional activity, ignoring all the complicating prior reservations and postscripts any single atomic "action" typically has. I may consider whether or not to accept the invitation of someone I don't much like, and decide that I should, since I am a visitor in her department. So I accept, then act in a politely insulting way throughout the evening, satisfying my dislike without sacrificing my sense of social duty. We rarely have to leave a felt motive entirely unexpressed when we act, even when it has been "defeated" by better reasons. There can be a lot of life left in defeated motives, and life that shows in our actions as well as in the sufferings our psychiatrists treat. Even Aquinas' man's choice between pleasure-promising fornication and virtuous resistance to temptation will result, for the normal Christian, either in guilty yielding followed by virtuous penitence and penance, or in self-congratulatory refraining accompanied by pleasantly lubricius regrets. We, or those of us who do not suffer from the symptoms of repression, are experts at getting a synthesis from a thesis and its antithesis. We are practiced in ambidextrous action, in compromise, double dealing, taking back with the left hand what the right has given, not letting the left hand know what the right hand does, not just in letting one hand wash the other. Our actions are rarely as "all out," in any of the senses I have separated out, as simple models of action for reasons would make then appear. What the religious call purity of heart is that rare and difficult virtue which enables some people to love a unified good with *all* their heart and to act wholeheartedly in its pursuit. The varieties of the less than wholehearted are many, among actions as well as among feelings. Nor are they to be wholeheartedly deplored.

One reason why it might be thought that intentions block "inconsistent" or conflicting intentions is that there are times when there is no "going back" on what we do, no more room for changes of mind, nor for undoing what we have done. Points of no return do occur, but we should not let ourselves become hypnotized by them in our action theory, nor think that they are the prerogative of action. They can occur also in our emotional life. We can burn our bridges there too. Once intense resentment has been felt for a person and recognized for what it is, the future course of one's feelings for that person may be set, "poisoned," as we say. We are not always free to have it both ways in our feelings any more than in our actions. But sometimes we can and do have it both ways, in our thinking, including thinking before acting, and in our feeling, and in our intentions. It is for such cases that our rich linguistic resources of what Locke called "particles" have developed to express the various "stands, turns, limitations, and exceptions"[39] we are capable of. "*Prima facie*" was only *prima facie* able to do the whole job. We also need "in as far as," "in that," "so far," "as," or "*qua*," and Locke's versatile particle "but." It helps us express not merely the complex considerations going into a making up of one's mind, but also some outcomes—"I'll go, but not hide my dislike," "I'll fornicate, but punish myself afterwards with agonies of guilt," "I'll forgive, but not forget," "I'll offer the house to the tour, but make sure they can't get into the study." Similarly with feelings, one may feel love but not approval, anger but also attraction, anxiety but also hope, pride but no confidence (in one's latest version of a paper) and so on.

One can also feel some pride, but not much. Not all restriction is due to the relevant considerations pointing in opposed directions. When I feel a *little* proud, because my house has some fine features, and lacks any really shameworthy features, my pride is restricted by its reasons' *intrinsic* limits. When I don't really have any reasons *not* to accept the invitation, but no strong ones to accept either, I may end going, but going apathetically. Unlike the case in which I go taking my dislike of my hostess with me, this time I go, expecting the pleasures neither of my likings nor of my dislikings. Actions can be lukewarm, as well as half-hearted. When the reasons that went into the formation of the intention were nonconflicting, but not very strong, I form an unenthusiastic intention, and act accordingly.

Intentions and actions not only incorporate their reasons, but can be restricted by their reasons, both by the limits of their intrinsic strength, so be lukewarm, and by the limits imposed by opposing reasons, so be qualified or ambivalent, just as feelings can. These are the substantive points I have tried to make. I have rejected Davidson's suggestion that *prima facie* will serve to capture both the incorporation of reasons into mental states and the sort of restriction they can bring, and I have mentioned some better alternative for some cases.

Many other questions about reasons for action and for feeling remain unasked as well as unanswered. One of these is the question of just what reasons *are*, whether, as Davidson supposes, for action they are desirability judgments, a psychological or social-psychological reality if a reality at all, or whether they are the *content* of those judgments, the recognized desirability itself, rather than just the imputation of it. Another question,[40] to be left unanswered, is whether reasons can always have reasons, and what different sorts of *chains* of reasons we get. For Davidson feelings can be reasons for actions, and can themselves have reasons. Are the reasons for my jealousy-for-reasons the more ultimate reasons for my jealousy-motivated action, and is the adequacy or goodness of those reasons inherited by the reasons for the action? It would seem, on the face of it, not, since many different actions, some better justified than others, could all have jealousy, for the same reasons, as their reason. But since I have not even begun the real work, of looking at the variety of what makes reasons better or worse reasons, for actions or for passions, my view about the heritability of the goodness or appropriateness of reasons by reasons must at this stage be merely *prima facie*.

NOTES

1. David Hume, *A Treatise of Human Nature,* ed. L. A. Selby-Bigge and P. H. Nidditch (Oxford: Clarendon Press, 1978), pp. 440–43.

2. Amelie Rorty, "Explaining Emotions," in *Explaining Emotions,* ed. Rorty (Berkeley and Los Angeles: University of California Press, 1980), discusses this phenomenon, which she likens to *akrasia.*

3. In "Hume's Analysis of Pride," *Journal of Philosophy* 75 (1978): 27–40, I criticized Davidson's account of Hume's analysis, in his "Hume's Cognitive Theory of Pride," *Journal of Philosophy* 73 (1976): 744–57, and also began to criticize Davidson's own implied view about reasons for propositional feelings. There I said "Reasons for feeling are significantly unlike reasons for acting, and both differ from reasons for believing. I cannot here offer a total theory of reasons . . ." (p. 37). Not only do I fail here to look at all at reasons for wanting, and look only very superficially at reasons for believing, but my look at reasons for feeling and for acting itself seems regress rather than progress, since I now seem to be emphasizing similarities, not differences, so apparently challenging my own previous views, as well as Davidson's. However, I still do think there are significant differences, and that an adequately comprehensive theory of reasons would get them right. I still leave that for another occasion, but I harbor suspicions concerning my repeated postponements. The task may just be too difficult.

4. See Donald Davidson, "How Is Weakness of the Will Possible?" in *Actions and Events* (Oxford, 1980). Originally this appeared in *Moral Concepts,* ed. Feinberg (Oxford, 1970). In what follows I shall cite page references in *Actions and Events* for this and other essays in that volume.

5. See "Hume's Cognitive Theory of Pride," in *Actions and Events,* p. 285.

6. "How Is Weakness of the Will Possible?" p. 38.

7. Ibid., p. 39.

8. Ibid., p. 41.

9. Ibid., p. 39.

10. Ibid., p. 42.

11. Ibid.

12. Hume, *Treatise,* p. 175. Aristotle too saw the limits of our ability to represent our recognition of rational action in practical syllogisms. David Wiggins, in "Deliberation and Practical Wisdom," *Essays on Aristotle's Ethics,* ed. Amelie Rorty (Berkeley and Los Angeles: University of California Press, 1980), has emphasized the limits to our ability to make explicit what it is about a given choice that makes it a wise choice. He finds in Aristotle's concept of "intuitive reason" a recognition of this fact, that practical wisdom outstrips the wise person's ability to analyze his or her reasons. He quotes Aristotle: "Therefore we ought to attend to the undemonstrated sayings and opinions of experienced and older people of practical wisdom not less than to demonstrations; for because experience has given them an eye, they see aright." (*N.E.*1143611ff.)

13. Davidson, *Actions and Events,* p. xiii. Further light is cast on Davidsonian reasons in his "Paradoxes of Irrationality," *Philosophical Essays on Freud,* ed. Richard Wollheim and James Hopkins (Cambridge, Eng., 1982). Unfortunately, this came to my attention after this paper was completed.

14. I am thinking of the striking change from "What Metaphors Mean" (1978) and "Communication and Convention" (1982), both in Donald Davidson, *Inquiries into Truth and Interpretation* (Oxford: Clarendon Press, 1984), to "A Nice Derangement of Epitaphs" (1982, unpublished).

15. Its taint, if that is what it is, is rather in the opposite direction, given its astrological etymology. I comment on this in "Mind and Change of Mind."

16. *Actions and Events,* p. 40.

17. "Intending," in *Actions and Events,* p. 99.

18. Ibid., p. 98.

19. Ibid.

20. See especially "Agency," in *Actions and Events,* where he says (n. 19, p. 59) that he is following G. E. M. Anscombe in the treatment he gives to actions displaying the "accordian effect," as Joel Feinberg called it. Feinberg's discussion is in "Action and Responsibility," *Philosophy in America,* ed. Max Black (Ithaca, 1965), and Anscombe's, in her *Intention* (Oxford, 1957). !N"Hume's Cognitive Theory of Pride," in *Actions and Events,* p. 285.

21. See Gabriele Taylor, "Pride," in Rorty, *Explaining Emotions,* and "Love," *Proceedings of the Aristotelian Society* (1976–76), reprinted in *Philosophy as It Is,* ed. Ted Honderich and Myles Burnyeat (New York: Penquin Books, 1979).

22. Davidson, *Actions and Events,* p. 278.

23. What Aristotle means by *megolopsychia* seems to be self-assurance, a confidence in one's own worth that does not need to be supported by keeping a tally of what things one has to be proud of.

24. Robert Kraut, "Visceral Fear," a talk given at the APA Eastern Division Convention, Boston, December 29, 1983.

25. David Papineau, in a paper entitled "Why Truth?" at the APA Eastern Division Convention, Boston, December 30, 1983, suggested that to understand the success conditions of both belief and desire we need to look at their role in our teleological behavior, and eventually at the natural selection of the various human factors determining that.

26. Jean Paul Sartre, *Being and Nothingness,* trans. Hazel Barnes (New York: Washington Square Press, 1966), p. 581.

27. I discuss the sort of determinacy that must be present in an intention in "Ways and Means," *Canadian Journal of Philosophy* 1 (1972): 275–93, and in "The Intentionality of Intentions," *Review of Metaphysics* 30, no. 3 (1977): 389–414.

28. Amelie Rorty, "Explaining Emotions," p. 104, says, "Emotions do not form a natural class." But they might still form a sort of system.

29. Philippa Foot, in "Approval," *Virtues and Vices,* (Berkeley and Los Angeles: University of California Press, 1978), makes this point for approval and disapproval.

30. Davidson, *Actions and Events,* p. 285.

31. Davidson, in "Intending," *Actions and Events,* uses "in so far as," not "in that," to characterize *prima facie* judgments as they are found in reasons for action. "Let us call judgements that are desirable in so far as they have a certain attribute *prima facie* judgements" (p. 98).

32. Davidson, *Actions and Events,* p. 208.

33. Ibid., p. 233.

34. Ibid.

35. G. E. M. Anscombe, *Intention* (Oxford: Basil Blackwell, 1957), p. 52.

36. I might reason this way: "Somehow I got the idea that one shouldn't consume both cucumber and milk at one meal. Maybe Paracelsus said so, though I've no idea what reasons he would have had for thinking this. Still, in as far as they *are* combined in cream of cucumber soup, maybe it isn't a good idea for my dinner party." Here the in-as-far-as judgment fails to have any reasons to incorporate into itself—it is tentative, and can be formulated as "In as far as I have this idea, of uncertain reliability, I should not serve cream of cucumber soup," but such thinking has scarcely yet got as far as *reasons* for not serving it. Not all thoughts influencing outcomes are reasons.

37. The remaining cases to consider would concern the first and third senses of *prima facie,* and the second and fourth. For any tedium-tolerant readers I offer the following cases. Restricting reasons for action fail to be incorporated when the reasons are outweighed by counter-reasons and when the agent acts only on those weightier counter-reasons. Then reasons would be *prima facie* in the first sense but not the third. This is a rather trivial counterexample. A better case would be when, after considering some conflicting reasons, like the reasons for going to concert A rather than concert B tonight, one in the end despairs of choosing, so stays home. This is doubtless irrational, but would be a case of an intentional action that did not incorporate, in its intention, any of the pros and cons considered in the prior deliberation about whether to go to concert A or concert B. This sort of counterexample is needed, of course, only if it is agreed that rational intentional action *does* incorporate some of its restricting reasons.

In the same case the restricting reasons considered would, in a sense, explain the action done, but not by giving *supporting* reasons for the choice of staying at home. So they do not get derivatively "realized," shown to be real by their rationalizing an action, as do those reasons that explain by "rationalizing." The real cause, even when it involves reasons, is not always a very rational cause. In a parallel way tentative reasons for action may fail to leave their mark on the final real outcome, so the second and fourth senses of *prima facie* can also come apart.

38. John Locke, *Essay Concerning Human Understanding,* bk. 3, ch. 7.

39. A much discussed issue I have not addressed is what *more* there is to feelings than judgments. A parallel question arises for actions, and for beliefs. It seems easily answerered for actions, and seems too rarely asked for beliefs. (Hume of course asked it, and answered it at length but not to his own satisfaction.) Another question I have not raised here is whether one distorts intentions for reasons and feeling for reasons by forcing their intentional content into propositional form, that is, into *that* clauses. I have discussed this in "Mixing Memory and Desire," in "The Intentionality of Intentions," *Review of Metaphysics* 30, no. 3 (1977): 389–414, and in "Hume's Analysis of Pride," *Journal of Philosophy* 75 (1978): 27–40.

Part II

Varieties of Moral Postures

One could make a rough division of moral philosophers between those who feel the need to connect their moral philosophy with their epistemology, and those who feel the need to connect it with their philosophy of mind. If one thinks, like Kant, that we are confronted with something called the moral law, as we are with the starry heavens, then we will need a way to discern it clearly, we will want in both cases to check our cognitive telescopes. The terms *reason, law,* and *episteme* belong together. By contrast, if one's "epistemology" gets submerged in one's study of believing, realizing, ignoring, verifying, testing, correcting, approving, licensing, authorizing, regulating, appealing, resisting, defying, wanting, intending, convening, and agreeing, then one will want one's account of morality to cohere with this larger investigation. One will want to show of all norms, moral ones as much as those of logic, science, or any skill, how they can grow out of the process they govern.

The following essays put up a Humean resistance against a Kantian version of morality that sees moral norms as carrying the authority of some divine reason whose job it is to issue laws which control but do not grow out of natural human sources of motivation. But there is much more in Kant's ethics than just the dualism of rational *Wille* and passionate *Wilkur,* and in both the first of these essays, "Knowing Our Place in the Animal World," and in the last, "Secular Faith," I look to other elements of Kant's ethics for guidance.

"Secular Faith" also accepts more from Hobbes than is usual for me. Hobbes does soundly base his moral philosophy on his account of human nature, but I side with Hume on all points where he disagrees with Hobbes—in his rejection of Hobbist egoism, in his insistence on the possibility of a social order without magistrates, and in his rejection of contractarianism. As "Promises, Promises, Promises" shows, I agree with Hume about the limited and convention-dependent role of contract in generating obligations. Indeed I follow Hume on most of the issues I discuss. One point on which Hobbes and Hume agree is in recognition of the virtue of agreeability, and "Secular Faith," which makes some concessions to the Hobbists and Kantians, can be read as an attempt at obedience to Hobbes' eighth law of nature (neglected by most Hobbists, along with all the others after the first three), that requiring mutual accommodation.

Some of these essays deal with specific moral questions—what our attitudes should be to organized religions, to animals, to promises, to practices increasing the risk to human lives. Several of the essays, in particular "Knowing Our Place in the Animal World" and "Frankena and Hume on Points of View," discuss the scope of moral concern. But in writing about these issues I also raise methodological questions, ones that I face head on in two papers about so-called applied ethics, "Theory and

Reflective practices" and "Doing Without Moral Theory?". These two papers advocate Hume's method with what may be unreasonable and unHumean aggressiveness, also to be found in "Civilizing Practices," where Hume is defended against Alasdair MacIntyre's charges against him. In these essays I question the assumption that moral philosophy should be moral theory. It may in the end be an uninteresting verbal question whether the sort of reflection on morality which I am in favor of does or does not itself count as moral "theory." If one chooses to say that what Aristotle, Hume, Hegel, MacIntyre give us are moral theories, the question I have raised has to be reworded. Should we have nonintellectualist "theories" like theirs, or theories like those of Aquinas, Kant, Hare, Brandt, Rawls, Gauthier, which both exercise and recognize the sovereignty of that reason which the others supplemented or transformed in various ways? In my present accommodating frame of mind I am willing to consider the possibility that I have overdrawn the contrast not merely between theory and nontheory, but also between reason and less intellectualist reflection. But any interest these essays have will lie in their attempt to draw those contrasts. Inconsistently, they argue in support of those moral philosophers who did not rest everything on arguments, who looked to psychology and history to find out what sort of good we have any chances of successfully attaining, creating, preserving, and recognizing as our own.

8

Knowing Our Place in the Animal World

Rawls, in *A Theory of Justice,* says that "a correct account of our relations to animals and to nature would seem to depend upon a theory of the natural order and of our place in it. How far justice as fairness will have to be revised to fit into this larger theory it is impossible to say" (1971, p. 512). Rawls had not felt the need for a theory larger than his Kantian interpretation of fairness when, earlier, he had discussed principles of right for individuals, such as duties not to injure and duties of mutual aid. Such duties, when due to other humans, can be seen as arising from principles that would be chosen in the original position. But since, in that position, the hypothetical choosers are self-interested rational persons, duties to animals, or to anyone or anything not party to the hypothetical agreement, cannot be derived from that starting point. Rawls recognizes this, and recognizes it as a limitation on his theory. He does *not* conclude that since the theory shows nothing wrong, there *is* nothing wrong with testing our drugs at the cost of animal suffering and contrived death, nor with destroying whole species in our determination to convert their bodies into materials that increase our profit, comfort, or pleasure. He acknowledges the need for a larger theory that would accommodate at least some beliefs concerning wrongs to animals.

Rawls' own account of what a moral theory is, and how it is related to the moral beliefs of nontheorizers, allows for the possibility that a good theory may have implications that clash with some moral convictions, both with some convictions the theorists had before working out the theory, and perhaps with some still held after the theory is developed. A

From *Ethics and Animals,* ed. H. B. Miller and W. H. WIlliams (Clifton, N.J.: Humana Press, 1983). Read at Ethics and Animals Conference, Virginia Polytechnic Institute and State University, May 1979.

theory may lead us to revise our earlier judgments, to change some of our convictions. It should be in "reflective equilibrium" with our considered judgments, and part of the consideration and reflection to which those judgments are submitted is provided by the theory itself, and by alternative competing theories. I agree with Rawls that a good moral theory should not merely systematize existing intuitions on particular matters, but deepen moral insight, and even correct moral error. The trouble comes when there is conflict or disagreement in "considered" beliefs. Some people, like Rawls, noting that a given theory cannot account for the belief that some ways of treating animals are wrong, conclude that the theory therefore fails to maintain reflective equilibrium with the full range of one's considered beliefs, and they therefore look for a "larger theory." But others, enamored of their theory, dig their heels in and insist that since the theory shows nothing wrong in exploiting animals for human ends, there *is* nothing wrong in it; thus, they believe that those who disagree, even they themselves some of the time, are sentimental or unrealistic, and that their beliefs are not properly "considered" ones.

Should we, when faced with an array of moral theories *none* of which, as Narveson has argued, provide a theoretical basis for worrying very much about the fate of animals, give up worrying? Or should we declare the theories all inadequate precisely because none of them *do* accommodate the belief that we are not morally free to torture, hunt, and kill animals as we please? If there were unanimity in moral belief—if everyone agreed with Rawls that there are wrongs to animals—then it would be very clear that the theories, not the intuitions, are what need revision. But there is no such agreement. What we need, in this situation, is a reasonable way of deciding whose intuitions to discount, since *no* theory can hope to accommodate the intuitions of both the animal lovers and their enemies. If contemporary scientific experimenters, heirs of those Cartesians who nailed living cats by their paws to a wall, then slit them open to study the circulation of the blood in a living creature, are strongly convinced that the advance of science demands and justifies similar practices, while those who protest are equally strongly convinced that only moral monsters could act this way, then no theory can hope to gain acceptance by both parties, unless the theory also succeeded in converting one of them. But on this issue, as on some other moral issues—for example abortion— feelings run very high, and the chances that any mere theory will convert anyone are negligible. I am not content, like Rawls (1971, p. 50), to retreat to the aim of finding a theory that accommodates all *my* considered judgments, while resigning myself to the likelihood that yours are different and may require a different theory. I see no point at all in having a moral theory unless it can serve to help us live together more successfully and, therefore, unless it *aims* at general acceptance. Private moral theories, like private moralities, are more likely to divide us further than to harmonize our differences. So I see as unavoidable the issue of how we can with good conscience discount the moral convictions of some of our fellows and adopt a theory that has implications they reject. Even if one did adopt Rawls' modest program of squaring a moral theory with one's own ineradicable moral beliefs, one is likely to find oneself ambivalent on some issues, to find that one's own mind reflects the disagreement in the culture that formed one's intuitions. When am I thinking straight and feeling appropriately: At those times when contrived animal suffering for human ends, whether frivolous ones such as the taste for hunting, or more serious ones such as testing medical drugs, seems clearly wrong, seems as firm a moral given as any could be, and seems finally a decisive objection to any moral theory that would allow such practices? Or at those times when the claims of self-conscious human purpose seem to drown out, if not silence, all others, times when a moral theory that bases duties on mutually acceptable ties between persons seems obviously correct? Which side of my ambivalent mind should I suspect of muddle or ulterior motive, and so reform or control? Who, in the community of moral thinkers, should I heed: those who, like Stephen Clark, suggest that no one has "any standing" in discussions about our duty to animals unless they have taken "the simple minimal step of abandoning flesh-foods" (Clark, 1977, p. 183), that "those who still eat flesh when they could do otherwise have no claim to be serious moralists" (ibid.), or those who tell me that I indulge in anthropomorphism and sentimentality when I worry about the fate of animals at human hands, that on "lifeboat earth" serious moral thinking is restricted to the question of how humans can save themselves from self-destruction, that "animals are not self-conscious and are merely means to an end" (Kant), so that it is only right and proper that they serve the ends of rational beings like us, thus becoming our food, our clothing, our playthings, our prey, our experimental subjects, our guinea-pigs, and our sacrificial lambs. Both to cure the instability and incoherence in my own beliefs and to attempt to face up to the real disagreement in the community of moral thinkers, I must raise the issue: When is there good reason to discount moral intuition, however recalcitrant and ineradicable it may be? I shall list some sources of likely prejudice and moral error on *any* issue, and so on this issue, before turning to the question of which moral theory squares best with the intuitions we have least reason to suspect.

One ground for suspicion of apparently sincere moral convictions is their link with some special interest of those who hold them. The questions *cui bono* and *cui malo* are appropriate questions to raise when we are searching for possible contaminants of conscience. Entrenched privilege, and fear of losing it, distorts one's moral sense. Just as, on an issue such as abortion, we should not listen too respectfully to the views of those who derive special profit from the legality or illegality of abortion, so on this issue of human treatment of animals we must be on the watch for special interest. We need to ask who has something special to lose or to gain from any change in our practices. As far as special gain goes, I see no interest group whose views ought to be treated with suspicion. Animals themselves cannot plead their cause, and those who plead it for them have no obvious financial or other selfish interest in the issue, although many may have "vested" their emotions in it. When we turn to special gain from maintaining existing practices, special loss if they were to be changed, we find a large number of groups whose views might be discounted. Butchers, furriers, hunters, cattlemen, chicken farmers, scientific experimenters on animals would, unless compensated, all have to suffer significant personal loss if we were to change our practices. They cannot therefore be expected to see the moral issue without the distortion of special interest. The scientists might claim that in *their* case their own interest coincides with a universal human interest, but I think the butcher and the furrier could make a similar claim—that their private gain from their occupation comes from their success at providing a public benefit—the food the rest of us want to eat, the sort of clothes we wish to wear. Even if some case can be made for giving a special place to the scientific and health professions, for seeing their practitioners as providing what is more obviously a public benefit than butchers and furriers, who simply meet a public demand, and I am not at all sure this case can be so convincingly made, it would not affect the claim I am making, that since private personal gain, and group interest, is also involved, the views of scientists who use animals in research ought to be discounted. The public benefits they supposedly offer can more impartially be weighed by other members of the public, not by those whose individual reputation, privilege, and income are tied to the practices whose morality is in question.

At this point it may be objected that my procedure in eliminating from the serious debate all those who stand to gain or to lose from a change in practices is itself contaminated with prejudice, namely a prejudgment of the relation between morality and interest. To avoid this objection let me emphasize that it is not interest, but *special* interest which I am citing as a disqualification. I am indeed assuming that the point of morality is to harmonize and advance interests and other components of the good of those concerned. But I am also assuming that one is not in the best position to judge overall or long-term interest, nor to appreciate the value of some proposed measure that will harmonize interests, when one is threatened with loss of what one has come to count on and depend on.

It is not *interest* that interferes with moral vision, it is the threat of loss of special privilege, of short-term loss, or the lure of special privilege and of short-term gain. I follow Hume in thinking that the moral point of view is "steady and general" and that such a point of view is one from which I "prefer the greater good whether at that time it will be more contiguous or remote" (T. 536),[1] a view that gives both contiguous and remote goods their due weight. But, as Hume noted, the "violent propension to prefer contiguous to remote" makes it difficult for a person whose near interest is involved to adopt this point of view, to "overlook our own interest in those general judgments, and blame not a man for opposing us in any of our pretensions . . ." (T. 583). A realistic assessment of the difficulty, for any of us, of adopting the moral point of view when our own immediate profit or loss is at issue lies behind commonly accepted rules such as those requiring judges and politicians to disqualify themselves when private and special interest may conflict with the public interest their role requires them to consider.

It still might be objected that this disqualification of all especially interested parties is a hopeless measure when the issue involves a possible clash of "interest" between all humans and their animal victims. Must we disqualify ourselves because our species' advantage is at issue? This would indeed reduce *ad absurdum* my suggested way of discriminating between conflicting intuitions. They cannot *all* be suspect if moral theory must square with some of them. If moral theory is more than a rationalization of superior advantage in a competitive struggle between would-be exploiters of others, then there must be some way, not merely of fairly adjudicating, but of avoiding irreconcilable conflicts of interest. If there is an unavoidable conflict between our human interest and that of other living species, then it is unlikely that, in that battle for survival, we will (of necessity unilaterally) tie our hands with moral bonds. Yet can we really still call a theory a moral theory if it openly avows itself as a self-serving justification of ruthless acquisition and retention of group or species advantage? If morality is to be neither an ineffective guilty gesture in the direction of those who must lose so that we may win, nor a glorification of the advantage of the stronger, there must be some faith in the possibility of a harmonization of interests, in some way of preventing the moral game from being itself a zero-sum one. I find it no more idealistic or utopian to believe that we do not *have* to choose "animal interests or our own interests" than to believe that we do not *have* to choose between the interests of males and of females. The moral enterprise is built on the faith that interests can to some extent be reconciled, that flourishing need not always be at the expense of others. I am supposing that such a faith in a peaceable kingdom is no more utopian when extended beyond the human species than it is within the species of us moralizing animals. The fact that we can theorize, moralize, accuse, and condemn does not itself make our different individual self-perceived interests any easier to harmonize than they would if we did not. Our special human skills give us ways of seeing solutions to the difficult problems of coexistence, but the mere fact that we are talkers, theorizers, and political and religious zealots creates as many conflicts as it solves.

I therefore do not need, absurdly, to conclude that because human interests are involved, humans must disqualify themselves from the moral debate. If the moral discussion aims at a harmony of interests, only those with a vested interest in avoiding harmony, or in what in fact prevents harmony, need to be disqualified. On this issue, as on any other moral issue, we need not listen to the gunrunners.

So far I have suggested only one ground to discount a belief—its contamination by vested special interests. There are, of course, other sources of moral prejudice and error. Besides perceived immediate special interest, there are also tastes and likings that might warp one's moral judgment. One hangs on tenaciously to the pleasant, as well as to the profitable. Those who just *like* eating meat, although they have no special interest in eating it, may disguise from themselves the full costs of catering to their tastes. Should we therefore, as Clark suggests, disqualify all meat-eaters and fur-wearers from the debate on this issue? It seems to me that many of us who eat meat do not even believe our lives would be any worse if we did not. This may make continuing to eat it all the more inexcusable, but at least it will not be our tastes that, by their strength, distort our moral perceptions. (If distortion is there, it will more likely come from guilt, and the defensive mechanisms that burden brings with it.) So I am inclined to think that our present tastes are a much less important source of contamination of conscience than our present vested interests, some of them interests in catering to tastes that could fairly easily be changed.

Another possible source of prejudice is dogmatic attachment to some set of beliefs that one keeps safe from critical examination. If, as I have suggested, our moral intuitions derive from our moral upbringing, then a particularly rigid one may indoctrinate a person so successfully that no serious rethinking is possible. I do not think it is easy to detect such inflexible commitments to *inherited* theory in one's own set of beliefs. If a particular moral intuition survives confrontation with a theory one explicitly considers, that might be only because one's loyalty is already irrevocably enlisted by the theory one's parents held, which one received before critical reflection was a possibility for one, and which therefore became an incorrigible belief. It is theoretically possible that any stubborn moral intuition is of this sort, and not really susceptible at all to "consideration." One may hope and believe that all one's beliefs are sensitive to rational criticism and challenge, but this too seems to me part of the faith on which moral philosophy is built. It is not, therefore, easy to tell the dogmatists from the open-minded, in order to discount the intuitions of the dogmatists. Presumably if there were a religious cult fanatically dedicated to animal sacrifice, their beliefs would be suspect, and so equally would those of fanatic Hindus, hopelessly prejudiced on the other side of the issue. We will suspect and discount those recalcitrant moral intuitions that are clearly tied to dogmatically held theories we do not accept. But one possibility that we must face is that *all* recalcitrant moral intuitions are tied, perhaps not obviously, to some older moral theory, so that all the "data" against which we might test a theory are vestiges of the faith of our fathers. If that were so, then the only external contraint on any moral theory would be that of conservatism. To demand that a moral theory square with incorrigible or invincible moral intuition will then be to demand that it not depart too radically from its predecessor theories.

I have tentatively suggested some reasons we might have for discounting some moral intuitions—the taint of special interest, the less powerful poison of special tastes, the contaminant of obvious and dogmatic prior theoretical commitment. The last may be only an obvious version of an unavoidable component in every moral intuition, but I shall nevertheless treat avowed dogmatism as a reason to discount a moral intuition, while not discounting the intuitions whose dogmatic component is hidden and unavowed. If one is to avoid total moral skepticism one must salvage some intuitions as less suspect than others. "Byasses from prejudice, education, passion, party, etc., hang more on one mind than another" (Hume, E. 107 note.)

Where does all this methodological preliminary leave us with respect to intuitions concerning duties to animals? It seems to me to leave us with most of the intuitions of most of the defenders of the cause of animals free from suspicion, or tainted only with the suspicion of religious or prior theoretical prejudice, while most of the intuitions of their opponents are tainted with special interest, over-attachment to their current tastes, or a combination of these. These may also be a large dose of religious prejudice, in the form of a commitment to the view that humans are the crown of creation, uniquely made in the image of God, behind many of the intuitions of those who would subordinate animals to our subjective ends. So the result of my "method of doubt," applied to moral intuitions, leaves me in agreement with Rawls and others who share his intuitions here, that these intuitions are as *nonsuspect* a foundation for a moral theory as any we are likely to find.

What moral theory has any hope of doing justice to these intuitions?

If Narveson is right, none of the serious contenders among existent moral theories accommodate even a fairly weak set of beliefs about the scope of our duties to animals. Utilitarians may be able to derive a *prima facie* duty to avoid making animals suffer, but it is only *prima facie,* and usually easily balanced by some promised "higher" pleasure for us, the cost of which is animal suffering. Utilitarians can derive none but prudential reasons for not destroying whole species. I suppose the consistent utilitarian would keep in existence such animal species as serve our needs, or as we find cute, and would have no objection at all to the preferably painless destruction of the rest. Contractarians, as Rawls has pointed out, cannot see any duties as owed *to* animals since they are not and cannot be members of a moral community who formally enter in into agreements, actual or hypothetical, with one another. They may be the *beneficiaries* of obligations accepted by members of a moral community, but if the reason for accepting such obligations is the perceived rational self-interest of the contractors, then only enough seals to stock the zoos and nature reserves will be the beneficiaries of our hypothetically contractually based obligations, and the rest will be fair game for the fur trade.

Is there then no moral theory on the horizon that might accommodate the intuitions of those who, like me, believe that it is primarily for the *seal's sake,* not mine or yours, that one should desist from bashing baby seals, however much profit it might bring, for the cat's sake, not mine or yours, that one should not slit it open while keeping it alive and unanesthetized, however much one might learn from the vivisection? I think there is at least one moral theory of respectable lineage and good independent credentials that can accommodate such fairly minimal intuitions about us and animals.

This is the theory Hume offers us. I do *not* consider Hume a forerunner of utilitarianism, and therefore what I shall go on to say in defense of Hume is not intended as a defense of any version of utilitarianism. I see Hume to be much closer to Aristotle than to Mill, to be offering us a theory about human virtues, not a theory about utility maximization and the duties that might involve.

Let me first say something about the basis on which Hume rests his specifically ethical views. Rawls says that any moral theory that generates duties to animals will have to be based on a metaphysical theory of the "natural order and our place in it" (1971, p. 512). Hume cannot be said to give us a metaphysical theory of the natural order, but he does give us a psychological theory, which with a bit of exaggeration can be said to be a theory of the animal order. In his section "Of the Reason of Animals" in Book One of the *Treatise* and in the first *Enquiry,* he relates human cognitive powers to animal intelligence, and in Book Two of the *Treatise,* he applies his account of both pride and love to animals. Indeed one might say of Hume's version of human nature, in all its aspects, that it presents us as not radically different from other animals. Hume emphasizes the continuities, and these continuities go well beyond shared sensitivity to pleasure and pain. Both in our cognitive habits and in our emotional range, human nature as Hume sees it is a special case of animal nature. Not merely the direct passions of desire, contentment, and fear, but the idea-mediated indirect passions of pride and love, and the spread of all these passions to others by sympathy (T. 363) are attributed by Hume to animals. Since the moral sentiment, on Hume's account of it, depends both on the capacity for pride and love,[2] and on the capacity for sympathetic sharing of another's feelings, it is quite significant that Hume attributes to other animals all the basic emotional prerequisites of a moral sense, including some, such as pride, that require a sort of self-consciousness. Hume says that "all the internal principles that are necessary in us to produce either pride or humility are common to all creatures; and since the causes which excite these passions are likewise the same, we may justly conclude that these causes operate after the same manner thro' the whole animal creation" (T. 327–28). He had previously allowed that some causes for human pride cannot be causes for canine pride, that we must make "a just allowance for our superior knowledge and understanding. Thus animals have little or no sense of virtue or vice; they quickly lose sight of the relations of blood, and are incapable of right and property. For which reason the causes of their pride and humility must lie solely in the body, and can never be plac'd either in the mind or external objects . . ." (T. 326). Animals, Hume says, have no sense of property or right, and so there can be no question of any obligations, based on convention or agreement, either on their part or owed to them. Hume would reject any attempt to give sense to the concept of rights of animals, since all rights arise from artifice. But since the artificial virtues are only a small subset of the virtues, the fact that animals have no obligations or rights would not mean that no moral wrongs can be done to them, nor even that they themselves can have no "duties." Hume significantly says not that animals have no sense of virtue or vice, but that they have "little or none." He is, of course, both in these sections in Book Two, and in the earlier section on "Reason of Animals," deliberately debunking the inflated rationalist conception of a mental substance uniquely capable of truth-seeking and a moral life. He demotes human truth-seeking to a version of instinct, and likens the philosopher's love of truth to the passion for hunting (T. 451), the desire to *collect,* and to get prize catches. Similarly he is intent on de-intellectualizing and de-sanctifying the moral endeavor, in presenting it as the human equivalent of various social controls in animal or insect populations. So he may be merely teasing us when he tells us that animals have little or no sense of virtue and vice. But he is in earnest in presenting human capacities, including moral ones, as special cases of animal capacities.

One curious feature of Hume's discussion of the "indirect" passions of pride and love is that he both says that their "object" must be a person like ourselves, with a sense of self (T. 329), and also says that animals feel both pride and love. What is more, in the case of love, it is not only that they, in their fashion, feel, towards something like them—a member of the same species—a version of what we feel towards creatures like us, Hume goes out of his way to say that "love in animals has not for its only object animals of the same species but extends itself farther and comprehends almost every sensible and thinking being. A dog naturally loves a man above" his own species and very commonly meets with a return of affection" (T. 397). Hume might be said to imply, by these claims, that animals *are* persons, but it would be more reasonable to interpret him as pointing to a very strong analogy between human emotions, of the most self-conscious and personal kind, and their animal equivalents.

At this stage of my exposition of the "theory of nature" on which Hume's ethics are founded I need to say something about his treatment of self-consciousness. As is known, if anything too well, Hume in Book One gave a skeptical account of our consciousness of ourselves as enduring persons. But that was an account carefully restricted to intellectual self-consciousness, or "personal identity as it concerns our thought and imagination," as distinct from "our passions or the concern we take in ourselves" (T. 253). When it comes to the latter he shows no skepticism at all—pride involves the occurrence of an "idea or rather impression of ourself" that he says is "constantly present to us." "The immediate object of pride and humility is that identical person of whose thoughts, actions, sensations we are intimately conscious" (T. 329). Because this self-reference is part of a *passion,* not the culmination of a merely intellectual search for self, Hume treats it as escaping the incoherences of attempted intellectual self-survey. Indeed part of his case for claiming that animals can feel pride is that his account of it "supposes so little reflexion and judgment that 'tis applicable to every sensible creature" (T. 328). These words, however, should not be taken to deny what Hume has previously insisted on, that all passions are "reflexive impressions," and that pride in particular involves a special sort of reflexion, namely reinforcement of one's own self-assessment from the respect others pay one. Hume does not believe that pride requires any *intellecual* reflexion, any reflective or thoughtful ideas, but, like all passions, it does involve a reaction, or reflex, to a given pleasure, and for its own prolongation it requires reinforcement from other passionate beings, it calls out to be "seconded by the opinions and sentiments of others" (T. 316). So Hume in fact has quite an intricate account of the varieties or levels both of "reflexion" and of the self-consciousness reflexion may involve.[3] The pride he attributes to animals involves both nonintellectual sorts of reflexion—both the capacity for passion, or reactive sentiment—and also the need for reinforcement from others of the passion of pride, which involves nonintellectual self-consciousness. He has therefore provided us with an account of human and animal psychology that gives us a basis for an ethical theory that can say something much more interesting about our relation to animals that Bentham's simple-minded trichotomy: "The question is not can they *reason*, nor can they *talk*, but can they *suffer?*" It is the range of feeling and suffering, the presence of self-conscious and social feeling, which is important for deciding the moral issues. I believe that Hume gives us a plausible and discriminating account both of what we share and of what we do not share with other animals (and, of course, how much we share will vary from species to species).

To turn at last to the moral issue itself. What sort of account can a Humean moral theory give of the place of animals in a moral order? Hume's version of a moral order is of a community of persons who assess one another's virtue by shared standards. The virtues that are prized include both "natural" ones, which presuppose no convention, and "artificial" ones, which are displayed in respect for conventions. The qualities of persons that count as virtues are those that are agreeable or useful to oneself or to others. Agreeable or useful to which others? To those who recognize the virtues, but they are of necessity persons who can sympathize with a wider circle of others, who can appreciate what is agreeable or disagreeable to others, whether or not those others are approvers and disapprovers. The virtue of kindness, for example, is displayed in one's treatment of children, long before they are themselves aspirants to and judges of virtue. It seems to me a virtue of Hume's account that there is absolutely no need to say that the only reason we should not be cruel to infants is because they are potential full members of a moral community. That fact may point us to some specific harms that we should avoid doing to them—for example exclusion from the circle of those who are mutual approvers and disapprovers—but it is not itself the reason for not harming them. The harm *itself* is the reason for that, and our sense of its disagreeability. So although Hume himself does not address the question of whether vices and virtues are shown in our treatment of animals, it seems quite evident that his answers would be "Of course." The duties of justice will not be owed to them, but all the natural virtues will cover our treatment of animals. Because we can recognize what constitutes harm to them, because they, like us, are potential victims of human vices, we have both sympathetic and self-interested reasons to condemn humanly inflicted harm to them. Hume makes only a half-hearted attempt to separate out the self-interested from the altruistic component in his account of the natural virtues, and I find this a strength not a weakness. Sympathy with others is, for Hume, both altruistic and also an indirect way of getting what one needs oneself, insight into how others react to one's own character, and their approval. Because Hume believes not only that "the minds of men are mirrors to one another," but also that each person needs such a mirror to sustain self-confidence, as well as to make confident cooperation possible, it is impossible to separate the self-concerned from the other-concerned reasons for regarding a particular character trait as a virtue.[4]

Only when we turn to Hume's account of justice, that is to the group of artificial virtues comprised of respect for property, promises, and governmental authority, do we find a rationale that is based only on utility or interest, and even there it takes artifices to *create* this interest that is a share in a public interest. Clearly animals cannot have either the obligations or the rights that the artifices of property, promise, and government give rise to, but when one looks at Hume's general definition of a convention, rather than at the specific conventions he discusses, I think one finds that, in his sense of convention, we could have conventional obligations to animals. A convention involves both a mutually expressed sense of common interest, and mutually referential intentions. "The actions of each of us have a reference to those of the other, and are performed on the supposition that something is to be performed on the other part" (T. 490). A horse and its rider, or a man and his dog, seem as good an example of this as Hume's boatload of rowers. For simple "conventions," involving no symbolic expression such as money or promise, the higher animals seem not disqualified from inclusion in the conventional agreement. As long as the expression of the mutual interest and interdependent intentions can be natural, surely Hume's conditions can be fulfilled, are fulfilled, in every case when humans and animals can be said to cooperate for common advantage. The fact, which even Kant recognized, that a man who can shoot his trustworthy and trusting dog shows a bad character, can be given a quite straightforward interpretation on a Humean theory. It is *not* because such a man might well also shoot a trusty and trusting human companion, it is simply because he betrays the animal's trust, breaks the "agreement" with the animal. I see nothing at all anthropomorphic or in any other way absurd in saying that one may "break faith with" an animal, exploit its trust, disappoint expectations one has encouraged it to have. I see no reason at all to treat such a case as discontinuous with breaking faith with humans. Hume half-recognizes that the virtues of honesty and fidelity and loyalty extend more widely than respect for property, for promises, for governments, since he on one occasion includes fidelity on a list of natural virtues (T. 603). The distinction between artificial and natural virtues may not be as sharp as Hume sometimes makes it appear, especially when one realizes the broad scope of his official definition of a convention. (After all there surely is some link between the agreeable and what has been agreed on.)

I have suggested that all the Humean natural virtues and vices, and a primitive informal precursor to the artificial virtues and vices, are as much displayed in our treatment of animals as in our treatment of fellow humans. Indeed, if we are to believe Hume, some animals may themselves display a rudimentary sense of virtue. It would I think be absurd to suggest either that we morally assess an animal's character, or that we should be sensitive to the "disapproval" of animals. Animals can not disapprove, but they can complain and protest, at least until their vocal chords are cut to spare experimenters their protests. Children too have complaints heeded before they are capable of disapproval.

One question that still remains is why, granting that we *might* treat a virtue's scope as extending to our treatment of animals, we should not narrow it to exclude them, if that appears to be easier or more convenient for us.

To that question I answer: for almost the same reason as we do not exclude future generations of humans from the scope of our moral concern.[5] We gain nothing from considering them, and, if we harden our hearts, we *need* not consider them. Rawls makes his self-interested contractors heads of families, in part to ensure that there will be some self-anchored reason for each hypothetical contractor to care about some of those in the next generation, to let concern spread. To make the contractors heads of families, caring about the members of their families, is to modify the claim that it is *self*-interest, in the right conditions (the veil of ignorance), that generates agreement on moral principles. We could perhaps extend the same tactic and make the hypothetical contractors heads of households that include domestic and other animals tolerated in the household, a group of Noahs each with an ark of humans and animals in his or her care. The principles then agreed on would include ones that would accommodate Rawls' intuitions about duties to animals.

Would anything be gained by approaching the matter this way? Hume, as I have already argued, could have let the agreement-based artificial virtues include more than he did, by a strict application of his weak definition of agreement or convention. Had his parties to the agreement been taken to be, not individuals, but heads of households, or, to get the effects of Rawls's veil of ignorance, spokesmen for "the party of human-kind," all the virtues could in a vacuous sense be seen as artificial virtues, ones founded on agreement. There would still remain the important differences both between nonformal agreements and symbol-involving formal agreements, and the even more important distinction between the cases where the agreement is possible only because of the artifice that agreement creates, and the cases where the parties agree about what was and is agreeable independently of their agreement. Would anything be gained, is anything gained, by forcing all moral demands into the mold of agreement-based demands?

The gain, as Rawls' work shows, is the availability to the moral philosopher of the formal techniques of game theory and the theory of rational choice. One can *calculate* what would be agreed on by one's hypothetical contractors, given their hypothetical preference-based interests. One thereby gets at least the appearance of greater precision in one's moral theory than is present in, say, Hume's theory as it stands. But we should not aim at a greater precision than our subject matter admits of, and I am not at all convinced that the precision gained by any moral calculus, utilitarian or contractarian, is more than a surface one. What is more, it is gained at the cost of what might be seen as a false pretense that moral reasoning is just a special case of individualistic self-interested reasoning,[6] a special case of a competitive game. It may be a hard historical fact that the developed formal techniques in decision theory are those developed to meet the needs of capitalists and heads of armies. But that is no good reason to make ethics the moral equivalent of war, or of business competition. The hard questions about the relation between moral reasoning and the calculations of individual self-seekers are pushed back into the description of the contractors, their primary goods, and the circumstances of the contract. It would seem to me better if they were directly addressed. A moral theory that makes the admittedly fuzzy concepts of virtue and vice the central ones at least openly avows both the imprecision concerning the relation between individual interest and the interest of others that is at the heart of the theory,[7] and also the imprecise guidance the theory yields both concerning the details of moral duties and also concerning the proper limits of state coercion. On the last question, Hume speaks as if magistrates are invented to clarify, formulate, and enforce already existent conventions and the conventions creating government—to prevent theft and fraud and treason. But clearly he expected them not only to do this, as well as to organize cooperative enterprises of "complicated design," to "build bridges, open harbours, raise ramparts, form canals, equip fleets and discipline armies" (T. 539), but also to prevent assault and murder. The "care of the governments" includes care for the persons as well as the property of their subjects, so they must treat some manifestations of some natural vices as criminal, in addition to making the artificial vices punishable by law.

What guidance would a theory of virtues and vices give us in deciding what treatment of animals is wrong, and which wrongs ought to be made into criminal offenses? Hume's list of virtues includes, besides the artificial or convention-dependent virtues, the natural virtues of generosity, humanity, kindness, friendship, good nature, considerateness, prudence, benevolence, good sense, economy, all of which would be involved in appropriate treatment of animals. Lists of virtues and vices in themselves do not also embody decisions on what degree of vice is sufficiently evil to render an action criminal, but we surely could and should forbid the obvious manifestations of extreme cruelty as well as of extreme lack of ecological good sense. And the less formal sanctions of disapproval and withdrawal will be directed at those who display less than criminal degrees of that cold insensibility, and that foolishness, that is involved in treating animals as mere things for our use. Hume describes (E. 235) as a "fancied monster" a man who has "no manner of concern to his fellow-creatures but to regard the happiness and misery of all sensible beings with greater indifference than even two contiguous shades of the same color" (ibid.). To limit one's concern to those sensible beings who are of one's own species is to be part-monster, but such monsters, alas, are not merely fancied ones.

Hume's moral philosophy, then, gives no very precise ruling on wrongs to animals, either to individuals or to legislators. But I think that the serious guidance given by other theories in real life situations is equally vague. So the wish for definite guidance provides no reason to switch from a theory of virtues to a theory of agreement-based obligations. When we are trying to find a theory that holds out some promise of accommodating widely shared nonsuspect moral intuitions about how animals may and may not be treated, a theory such as Hume's seems at least to contain no theoretical obstacles, even if it gives us no very precise guidance. The more difficult question that I have still not answered is whether the theory not merely fails to present obstacles to extending moral concern to animals, but gives us positive reason to do so. Hume's version of human nature is a good basis from which to start, since it encourages us to respect, not to downgrade, the capacities we share with other animals, to recognize that what we respect in fellow humans has its basis in what we share with other animals. When we refrain from hurting an animal, it will not be because by hurting it we would "damage in ourselves that humanity which it is our duty to show towards mankind," (Kant) it will rather be because important elements of the humanity we respect in our fellow humans are also really present in the animal, and so demand respect in their own right. It is also intrinsic to any theory of virtues to include some, such as Aristotle's equity and practical wisdom, that discriminate among the relevant *differences* between cases, and are displayed in good judgment concerning how they should be treated. A theory of virtues must give an important place to such discrimination and judgment, and a Humean theory that extends our moral concern from those humans (future generations, idiots, madmen) who cannot have a return concern for us, to animals who must fail to reciprocate that moral concern, will value as a special virtue that "delicacy" and judgment that is shown by a thoughtful appreciation of the difference between proper treatment of a child, an adult, an idiot, a mad person, an ape, a pet lamb, a spider (and the proper appreciation of the differences between eating human and other flesh).

Does a moral theory that, like Hume's, bases discernment of approved character traits on sentiment build on a nonsuspect foundation? If tastes and perceived interests can poison our moral intuitions with prejudice in our own favor, may not sentiments do the same? Why should human sentiment, even when it is moral sentiment, be a reliable guide to the good of a larger than human community of morality-affected beings? As I have already acknowledged, emotions *can* be invested in a cause, good or bad, and so distort perception of issues. And one sometimes suspects that some of those who plead the cause of animals are as much human haters as they are animal lovers. Sentiment, as much as taste or perceived interest, can contaminate one's conscience. But if Hume is right, certain sentiments have both a built-in potential for enlargement by sympathetic spread, and also a built-in need for reinforcement from others, so that there can be a genuinely moral sentiment that results from the correction and adjustment of more partial sentiments. For this moral sentiment to arise, "much reasoning should precede" to "pave the way" (E. 173). Hume does not believe reason alone can discern what is right, since he sees reason as always serving some sentiment or passion. But no sentiment can count as the moral sentiment unless it is "steady and general," unless it does arise from a reflective reasoned consideration of the good of all concerned, since "I am uneasy to think that I approve of one object, and disapprove of another . . . without knowing upon what principles I proceed" (T. 271). The moral sentiment, to *be* moral, must be one "in which every man, in some degree, concurs" (E. 273). Hume speaks of this shareable sentiment as the sentiment of *humanity,* not of animality, since it is only humans who approve, or are themselves objects of approval. It does take some reconstruction of Hume's theory to ensure that the scope of moral concern extends to animals, but I believe this can be done. As long as we distinguish the community of moral judges and judged, restricted to humans, from the wider community of those with whom some sympathetic concern must be felt in order to do the judging, then we can find in Hume's moral theory at least the basis for an adequate account of proper attitudes to animals.

Nevertheless I want to end by admitting that I do not think that a Humean moral theory can show anything positively incoherent in refusing to consider the fate of animals or animal species,[8] that is, in restricting the scope of a virtue's reach to humans. To get any strong reason why we should extend our concern to animals, I think the best theory is one that is Kantian to this limited extent, that the moral order is seen as continuous with a natural order, that the question to ask is "Can I will this as a law in a system of nature?" The reference to system, the insistence on seeing human good as the good of a being who is part of a wider system that is a system of *nature,* a nature containing a great variety of beings of different kinds, was only one component in Kant's theory, one that owes much to Leibniz and Aquinas. If Rawls looked to that element in Kant's ethics, rather than to Kant's dualistic Cartesian refusal to respect anything we share not with God, but with animals, then the larger theory he needs may be surprisingly close at hand.

NOTES

1. References to Hume's works are to the Selby-Bigge and Niddich editions: *A Treatise of Human Nature* (T) and *Enquiries* (E) (Oxford: Clarendon Press, 1978).

2. I have discussed the relation between Hume's version of the moral sentiment and Humean pride in "Master Passions," *Explaining Emotions,* ed. Amelie Rorty (Berkeley and Los Angeles, 1980), and in "Hume on Resentment," *Hume Studies* 6 (1980): 133–49.

3. I have discussed the intricacies of Humean self-consciousness in "Hume on Heaps and Bundles," *American Philosophical Quarterly* 16, (1979): 285–95.

4. Both in the *Treatise,* and more thoroughly in the *Enquiry Concerning the Principles of Morals,* Hume does attempt to classify virtues by asking whether their beneficial effect falls mainly on the virtue-possessor or on that person's associates. A virtue is a character trait that, by corrected sympathy, we see to give pleasure or to advance the interest of "the person himself whose character is examined; or that of persons who have a connection with him" (T. 591), where the "or" is definitely not exclusive. As Hume says, a virtue may have "complicated sources" (E. 328) so that, although the main reason for approving of persons who are kind and generous is the good they do others, still these virtues are also "sweet, smooth, tender and agreeable" (E. 282) to the kind and generous person, and "keep us in humor with ourselves" (ibid.) as well as others. In the *Enquiry* Hume is at pains both to show that we do not need a self-interested motive to cultivate the virtues, and also to show that we need not lose by cultivating them.

5. I have discussed obligations to future generations in "The Rights of Past and Future Persons," *Responsibilities to Future Generations,* ed. Ernest Partridge (Buffalo: Prometheus Books, 1981). See also "Frankena and Hume on Points of View."

6. As Hume put it, "It is not conceivable how a *real* sentiment or passion can ever arise from a known *imaginary* interest" (E. 217; see also, E. 300).

7. Hume sees a need to distinguish *mine* from *thine* with definiteness only for those scarce alienable goods that are covered by the institution or artifice or property, not for such benefits as accrue from the cultivation of natural virtues. Those who insist on sharply distinguishing benefits to oneself from those to others, and on making narrowly self-interested calculations, may find themselves the "greatest dupes" (E. 283). Because of this view about convergence of interests, Hume can afford to say what he does about motivation to virtuous action: "It seems a happiness in the present theory that it enters not into that vulgar dispute concerning the degrees of benevolence or self-love which prevail in human nature" (E. 270).

8. The fate of the human species may be more bound up than is immediately obvious with that of other species. Although *this* generation would probably live well enough if it exterminates species as it pleased, the long-term effects on the human environment of human policies of "improving" their natural environment have almost all been bad. So if we *are* considering future generations of humans, we might do best for them by not attempting to pit their interests against those of other species. We know too little about our own species' interests to rest our policies on fallible calculations aimed to advance only them. Consideration of other species may be the best policy, whoever and whatever we care about. At least we do not know Hume to be wrong in thinking that those who take a universal moral point of view will not be the greatest dupes.

9

Frankena and Hume on
Points of View

Frankena sees moral point of view theories as steering a middle course between skepticism or relativism in ethics and absolutism or dogmatism.[1] The constraints of a distinctive point of view limit the range of moral judgments, provide some basis to expect agreement between different moral judges, and generate standards if not of moral truth at least of moral acceptability. Since however these constraints arise only from the moral point of view, they are avoidable if the point of view is avoidable, and do not impose absolute inescapable demands on every person. Frankena sees the judgments made from the moral point of view to include categorical ones, but since he does not characterize the point of view itself as either the final court of practical reason or as an inevitable point of view, the categorical judgments made from that point of view are themselves externally conditional on taking that viewpoint. The most that can be said is that when and if one takes that viewpoint, certain demands are inescapable and unconditional. The whole illocutionary act of making the categorical moral judgment is as it were limited by the condition that one's hearers, including oneself as hearer, share the point of view. Made fully explicit, what I am calling the external conditional would take this form: "Provided that one takes the moral point of view, one must acknowledge the unconditional obligation to. . . ." This is quite different from claims like "If one is a parent one has obligations to one's child," which is itself presumably a claim which may have an implicit initial qualifier of the form "From the moral point of view . . ." or "From the legal point of view. . . ." It might of course also be saying "From the point of view of practical rationality as such, a point of view which one cannot refuse to take, and beyond which lies no more comprehensive or corrected point

From *The Monist* 64, no. 3 (July 1981): 342-58.

of view. . . ." Frankena distinguishes this ultimately authoritative practical judgment from a moral judgment, while nevertheless suggesting that practical reason will normally endorse what morality has decreed. It is not, however, part of the very meaning of "moral point of view" that that point be final or inescapable for human persons.

I shall explore Frankena'a version of the claims of morality by comparing his characterization of the point of view of morality with that of David Hume, who has certain claims on that concept, if not on that phrase. Hume speaks of the need for a moral judge to depart from "his peculiar point of view" as a private person, and fix on some "steady and general points of view" (T. 581–82).[2] Again, in the *Enquiry Concerning the Principles of Morals* he speaks of "the point of view of humanity" (E. 272) as that from which the moral sentiment is felt and from which one speaks the moral language, the language of virtues and vices, obligation, desert, and merit. There is no doubt that he distinguishes moral judgments from private interested or partial judgments by the point of view which must be adopted before any sentiment counts as moral, any judgment as a moral one, expressive of moral approbation or disapprobation. Morality is for Hume a matter of sentiment, not reason. "But in order to pave the way for such a sentiment, and give a proper discernment of its object, it is often necessary, we find, that much reasoning should precede, that nice distinctions be drawn, distant comparisons formed, complicated relations examined, and general facts fixed and ascertained." (E. 173) All this reasoning, comparing, distinguishing, discriminating, examining, fixing, and ascertaining, as well as the final feeling of expressing, must be done from the correct point of view and in the correct terms—"When a man denominates another his *enemy,* his *rival,* his *antagonist,* his *adversary,* he is understood to speak the language of self-love, and to express sentiments peculiar to himself and arising out of his particular circumstances and situation. But when he bestows on another the epithets of *vicious* or *odious* or *depraved,* he then speaks another language and expresses sentiments in which he expects all his audience are to concur with him. He must therefore depart from his private and particular situation and choose a point of view common to him with others; he must move some universal principle of the human frame, and touch a string to which all mankind have an accord and symphony." (E. 272)

Even these few quotations from Hume show both that he has what Frankena calls a "point of view theory" about moral judgment, and also that his version of such a theory is different in some ways from Frankena's own. I shall point to some likenesses and differences, in the hope that the comparison will both highlight some of the distinctive characteristics of point of view theories, and also highlight some of the more controversial aspects of Frankena's version of such a theory. I shall first discuss the relation of Frankena's "caring" to Hume's "sympathy," then turn to Frankena's distinction between the moral point of view and the point of view of practical reason, looking at the avoidability or unavoidability of these viewpoints, and relating the discussion to Hume's account of the various "corrections of sentiment" and the nature of practical agreement. Finally I shall discuss just what the "point of view" metaphor does and does not do to help us understand the phenomenon of moral judgment and what it expresses.

I. Caring and Sympathizing

Frankena characterizes taking the moral viewpoint as "caring" about persons and conscious sentient beings, where such caring is "more neutral than benevolence, love or sympathy." It involves an imaginative realization of the lives of persons other than oneself, but in theory might take the form of hate and malevolence. What is ruled out is indifference. One cannot take the moral point of view and not care one way or the other about the quality of the lives of others. Frankena contrasts what he means by "caring" with Humean sympathy, and rightly so, since to feel sympathy in Hume's sense one must feel about another's life in the *same* way they feel. Hume, of course, does not believe that the capacity for sympathy is enough to produce the "moral sentiment" (animals, for instance, often exhibit sympathy but not the moral sentiment). Sympathy must be "corrected," to eliminate a bias towards those close in some sense to one, before it can count as moral feeling, and it is precisely this correction of partial and biased sympathy which Hume thinks the moral or "steady and general" point of view achieves (T. 581). By sympathy one feels pleasure or pain by "contagion" from others, directed at whatever pleases or pains the other, but the moral sentiment can be directed only at motives (T. 477), as displayed in actions, and even sympathy-mediated reaction to motives must itself be corrected for bias before it counts as *moral* sentiment. So Frankena's "caring" is, in one way, no more "neutral" than is Hume's moral sentiment, although it is more neutral than Humean sympathy. Suppose that a Humean considers the ambition of a son-in-law. Sympathy with one's daughter's attitude to this ambition, be it pleasure or distress, may have to be corrected by considering the ambition from a more "general" angle, before it becomes moral feeling. The sympathetically felt fear for the more ruthless ambition of this son-in-law's competitor may also have to be corrected before arriving at a moral judgment of that competitor's character. Considerations of personal interest, Hume says, are to be "overlooked" in moral judgments, (T. 582) and since the negative reactions of daughter and son-in-law with which one naturally sympathizes here *are* interested feelings, one has to correct or at least discount that sympathy. Hume's "moral sentiment" has as tenuous a relation with real occurrent sympathetically communicated feeling, or "fellow feeling," as has Frankena's "caring" with love. What Hume in the *Enquiry* calls the "sentiment of humanity" is just this corrected or due sentiment, whatever sentiment *would* be expressed in a considered moral judgment, and this, I think, is not so different from Frankena's "caring." It is to be felt by the magisterial punisher for the punished, as well as for the victim of the punished offense, felt as much by the judge taking money from a poor man to repay debts owed to the rich as by the generous warmhearted benefactor.

Hume does acknowledge a sort of imaginative realization of the lives of others which is less "vivacious" than sympathy. Before one is moved by sympathetic feeling one first has an *idea* of what the other is experiencing, and sometimes this idea, say of the distress of another, instead of spreading the distress itself to one, rather enhances one's own sense of well-being, by comparison. Hume believes that this "principle of comparison" works against, not for, morality, creating jealousies and conflicts of perceived interest where they need not exist. But in allowing for this effect, he does distinguish the imaginative realization of another's feelings from a sympathetic sharing of those feelings and concerns. Nor is this idea of others' lives as they seem to them a perfectly inert idea, amounting to Frankena's "indifference." Hume speaks of a set of *passions* belonging to the imagination (T. 585, 594–95) so that even when my thought of another's distress does not rise to sympathetic distress, it does occasion what Hume calls "uneasiness." This uneasiness may not control stronger passions such as the will to victory, to subdue the enemy, nor will, say, the punisher's uneasiness at the distress of the punished stop him administering the fair punishment, but it does rule out indifference. What makes the moral point of view possible, for Hume, is the imaginative reconstruction of the passions of others, the uneasinesses and fellow feeling that produces, and the ability to correct bias and "contradiction" in such reactions. Hume agrees with Frankena that the moral point of view cannot be taken by those who are altogether unmoved by the feelings of others, by any "fancied monsters" who "regard the happiness of all sensible beings with greater indifference than even two contiguous shades of the same colour" (E. 235). But the way in which the moral judge is moved must be "calm," "steady," "corrected," and "general." I turn next to look at the relation between Hume's explication of these requirements and Frankena's version of the rationality of the moral point of view.

II. Morality and Reason

Frankena accepts it as a "postulate" that in the final analysis by the final court of practical reason, a person will be found to have done well by adopting a moral action guide, by cultivating concern and care for others. It is not a matter of definition that moral reasons are overriding reasons, more a matter of faith that they converge with the overriding reasons recognized by what David Falk calls "a man in his wisdom." Frankena, like Hume, builds into morality, by definition, a certain range of concerns and considerations—a concern with actions and the springs of action, an evaluation of these by a consideration of the difference they make to the well-being of persons and conscious sentient beings. But Frankena does not wish to make it a matter of definition that morality be egalitarian, nor a matter of definition that its word be the last practical word. Indeed he clearly makes it the penultimate, not the ultimate judgment. The ultimate judgment is that of practical reason as such, considering *everything,* not restricting its concerns and its aims as morality does. The moral point of view is not the most comprehensive point of view, but a selective and discriminating point of view which highlights some considerations and dims others. Frankena says that the idea of morality represents a wager that man and the world are such that the desiderata of social concern and of rationality will be found eventually to coincide. In the nonmystical this-worldly sense which Frankena gives to to this wager (unlike Butler and Kant), he is distinctively Humean. Hume spoke of the sensible knave's choice of a way of life which represents the opposite wager, the wager that judicious dishonesty is the best policy, and agreed with Frankena that we cannot *show* such a person to be wrong. But nor can the sensible knave show that those who opt for morality are wrong, and the way of life they choose does tend, Hume believes, to confirm its followers in their choice, to convince them that the "greatest dupes" (E. 283) are the sensible knaves, the ones most determined not to be society's dupes.

It might seem that Hume cannot be either in agreement or in disagreement with Frankena over the coincidence of the "sentiment of humanity" and ultimate practical rationality, since he has rejected the latter concept. It is true that Hume says that it is not contrary to *reason* to prefer the destruction of the world to the scratching of one's little finger. Reason, for him, can by itself determine no preferences whatever, it can merely select beliefs about matters of fact or relations of ideas. But Hume's anti-rationalist campaign in ethics can now be declared won, so we can relax his terminological tactics, and use "reason" in what he allows is its common and "vulgar" sense, to mean whatever does control our violent passions. The "calm passions" which include what Hume calls the moral sentiment are tantamount to practical reason—they are reflective, they consider remote as well as contiguous concerns, they overcome the "contradictions" which more partial passions generate. To rephrase the question in strict Humean terms we could put it this way—*which* calm passion is the ultimately corrected passion, the one Hume calls the moral sentiment, or the calm self-love of the sensible knave, or some further yet more reflective policy-generating sentiment?

There are several questions to be sorted out here. One, which I shall postpone, is whether whatever is the final and most authoritative sentiment-or-reason is to be characterized as felt or recognized from a point of view, or whether "mere" *points* of view are ultimately transcended. Other questions, which I shall now address, concern the sort of correction which is involved in moving from the self-love or partiality which is not, like the sensible knave's, beyond morality, but rather is *pre*-moral, to the corrected moral sentiment. To consider if anything could correct morality itself, we must first try to be clear what counts for Hume as a *correction* of sentiment.

In Parts II and III of Book III of his *Treatise*, Hume describes the way unreflective spontaneous motives and sympathies get altered by a "reflection" which follows on experience of both the conflicts and "contradictions" which spontaneous passions engender, and also of the benefits of the cooperation made possible by some shaping and smoothing of passions in family training and education. Experience, both of the "rough corners" (T. 486) and of the "smooth" cooperative social sentiments, persuade us of the advantages of giving some passions, in particular avidity, an "oblique" direction, and of cultivating other natural passions of a less "interested" nature, such as parental love, compassion, or pride in virtue. Why, according to Hume, do we transform avidity into justice, and why do we cultivate some forms of natural passions and give them the status of natural virtues? Because, Hume says, of the "contradictions" which occur if we do not, and because "the least reflection" (T. 492) shows us the "infinite advantages" (T. 489, 498) which we gain by the cooperation with others which is made possible by the artifices and the "artificial" virtues. We are *driven* out of pre-moral points of view by their instability and by the promise of a firmer and more sustainable position. Only if morality itself proves unstable, or generates "contradictions," would we have any parallel reason to desert its point of view for any further or different viewpoint. Of course one might not require of a reason for abandoning morality that it be parallel to the reason for first embracing it—one might just get bored with stability and steadiness, nostalgic for conflict and contradiction, so get beyond moral good and evil precisely to avoid the very things for the sake of which one accepted morality. I see no indications in Hume, however, of any such Nietzschean swerves, which in any case would be more upsurges of will than movements of Frankena's practical rationality. Hume rejects the sovereignty of "reason," but he does not reject the ideals of consistency and integrity. In Books One and Two of the *Treatise* he explored the contradictions into which both the "understanding" and the pre-moral human passions lead one, and in Book Three he shows how the moral sentiment can reconcile these contradictory drives in persons. The contradictions play their part, but only to set the stage for morality and for the civilized pleasures it makes possible. The only sort of consideration which could for Hume count in favor of moving away from morality would be a "contradiction" at the heart of morality itself, an internal incoherence or self-destructiveness in the cooperative enterprise as Hume understood it.

Could there be such a contradiction? The contradictions which morality overcomes, on Hume's account, arise both within one person's preferences and also arise between persons, either in outright conflict over scarce goods, or as "contradictions to our sentiments in society and conversation" (T. 583). Part of his characterization of the viewpoint of morality is that it is one from which one expects to agree in judgment with others, as one does in judgments of size and shape (T. 603), despite the various and fluctuating appearances of objects to observers at different positions. The *point* of the moral point of view, for Hume, is agreement and lack of contradiction, both with oneself at a variety of times and with one's fellows on whom one depends. One depends on them for cooperation, for reassurance, for that "seconding' of one's sentiments which even nonmoral human sentiments require for any steadiness or persistence, on Hume's analysis of them. "Let all the powers and elements of nature conspire to serve and obey one man: Let the sun rise and set at his command: the seas and rivers roll as he pleases, and the earth furnish spontaneously whatever may be useful or agreeable to him: He will still be miserable until you give him some one person at least with whom he may share his happiness, and whose esteem and friendship he may enjoy" (T. 363). If the sensible knave is really to be sensible, he must contrive his life so that he gets the friendship and trust of some of his fellows, and avoids the resentment and jealousy which could motivate others to threaten him, and he must contrive things so that he not merely feels proud of his knavery but finds others to echo and sustain that pride. To succeed in this last requirement, he must reveal himself sufficiently to some for them to know his special achievement. "There are few persons, that are so satisfy'd with their own character, or genius, or fortune, who are not desirous of shewing themselves to the world, and of acquiring the love and approbation of mankind" (T. 331–32). The sensible knave must either make a false show to get general approbation, or restrict himself to a few intimates who know his real achievement, namely "to cheat with moderation and secrecy" (E. 283). Hume clearly believes it unlikely, but perhaps not altogether impossible, for a person to succeed in sensible knavery, for such a knave not only to maintain secrecy where necessary, but to find sufficient scope for self-*expression* to others that his sense of self-value can be sustained. Hume speaks of the knave as sacrificing "consciousness of integrity, a satisfactory review of his own conduct," but the knave was supposed to think that he "conducts himself with most wisdom, who observes the general rule and takes advantage of all the exceptions." He may have traded consciousness of integrity for consciousness of successful trickery and superior wisdom. If there is a fatal weakness in his position, it lies in the combination of a need for secrecy and the common human need for self-expression and reassurance. Hume's case for morality, as against the sensible knave's choice, depends more than he acknowledges in the final section of the *Enquiry Concerning the Principles of Morals* (where we are introduced to the sensible knave) on the interdependence of human passions which he had explored in Book Two of the *Treatise.* Could the knave manage successfully to do without reassurance, or to get it only from wholly loyal intimates, then his "heart" would have no reason to rebel against the maxims he adopts.

Similarly, if there is to be a Humean correction of morality, in favor either of sensible knavery or some other position, it will come from some instability which appears when we take into account that really happy times are not merely those when we can believe or feel what we wish, but when we can express what we feel. (See the title page of the *Treatise*'s first two books.) To mold our life policy to our fully informed wishes is not enough—we must be able to express what we are doing, to make it known. The expression of our policy must support not undermine the policy itself. Does Hume's expression of the moral enterprise strengthen that enterprise? If not, then the moral point of view as Hume describes it could be corrected by some more reflective viewpoint which achieved greater reflective and expressive stability.

There is some evidence that Hume later in his life had doubts whether his analysis of morality had furthered the cause of morality itself. Hutcheson had complained that Hume in Book Three of the *Treatise* had lacked warmth in the cause of virtue, but his real worry was not lack of warmth but the openly secular nature of morality as Hume portrayed it. One frequently advanced candidate for a point of view which transcends the moral point of view is the religious viewpoint. If Hume, in divorcing morality from religion, had weakened morality, his own version of secular morality would fail his own test for expressive coherence. If recognizing the *human* origin of moral demands deprives those demands of authority, then Hume's moral point of view is as unstable as any partial point of view. A certain decent "disguise" of the human basis of morality might promote the cause of "humanity" better than full exposure, at least in Hume's own time.

Hume believed that his works on religion had shown how religion engenders conflict and contradiction both between people and within each person. But of course this result is not the *aim* of any religion—like Humean morality, each religion puts forward a banner to unite persons in a true faith. If there are as many contrary versions of the "true" secular morality as there are of the true religion, then for all the *talk* of moral agreement and contradiction avoidance, morality could prove as divisive when secular as it proved when tied to religion. The religious wars to which Hume drew attention have, after all, in our time been to some extent replaced by wars between secular ideologies, between morally self-righteous communist and equally self-righteous capitalist powers. Hume was well aware that to actually reach agreement and overcome contradictions it was not enough simply to announce that aim, but the actual machinery of secular morality which is to do the work of turning disagreeing egoists and fanatics into agreeing cooperators is not described by him in sufficient detail to assure us of its chances of success, nor has the course of history done anything to reassure the pessimist.

To say this is not to downgrade Hume's achievement in attempting to describe social practices, mutually correcting conventions and customs of moral education, which do *something* to minimize some sorts of possible conflict. That those very practices might engender new forms of possible conflict is not so surprising, nor necessarily fatal to a Humean view of morality. As long as each new form of threatened conflict can be matched with a new peace-making convention or a new peaceable virtue, Humean morality could be saved. But if the very exposure of the psychological and social bases of morality worked against its success even at the most basic levels—that is in disciplining unreflective appetite and greed, or if the zeal of secular moralists promotes war, then the whole Humean attempt to correct sentiment by reflections which need no "false glosses of superstition and religion" fails dramatically. What the wise person would *then* do is quite unclear to me—if secular morality is internally incoherent, given the facts about human nature and the limits of its malleability, I suppose we must expect "wise" religious bigots as well as "wise" irreligious knaves and profiteers. But their "wisdom" would *not* lie in their having corrected an incoherence which weakens the secular moral person's position, since their positions are merely repeat versions of the very inadequate positions which drove Humean persons towards a moral point of view in the first place. So perhaps all we can have is a cyclic alternation of inadequate incoherent views, with the only "progress" being an increase in self-consciousness of the process, and in consequent pessimism. What Hume said in his *Natural History of Religion* about religions, namely that fanatic intellectually respectable but morally barbarous monotheism alternated with a tolerant polytheism which was intellectually ridiculous but morally harmless, may also be true about practical points of view—there is a recurrent drive towards monistic "common" moral viewpoints, and an equally recurrent collapse into a variety of religious cults and versions of opportunistic nihilism. The latter "flux and reflux" however, would be humanly harmless in *neither* of its phases, since in both there will be destructive conflict. Going to war because our cause is just kills and maims people and destroys cities just as barbarically as going to war for fun or for profit or with God on our side. Moral zeal and rancor may be as furious and implacable a human passion as that "sacred zeal" which Hume tried to reveal in its true colors. He tried to describe a version of morality which was a "calm" passion, which would keep persons in humor with themselves and with one another, but could he have seen the twentieth century fruits, in colonial Africa or Central and South America, of the capitalist artifices he described so appreciatively, or the communist version of a secular state, he might well have wondered whether his honest anatomy of morality had not indeed made it "something hideous" (T. 621). The cost of not being duped may be very high.

My discussion of where Hume stands on the question of whether any point of view is *more* final than the moral one is therefore inconclusive. There may be no final view at all, nothing which counts as the ultimate correction, as Frankena's "ultimate" rationality, or as Hume's "steady" view. Falk's man in his wisdom may be as flighty and inconstant as the traditional silly woman. Hume may have been wiser than he realized in avoiding talk of practical reason, since nothing may satisfy the requirements of "reason," of absence of contradiction, full generalizability, and full disclosure.

III. A Provisional View of the Point of "Points of View"

What does the visual metaphor of points of view add to the other ways available to us in practical discourse of indicating both the extent to which a recommendation is provisional, the sorts of grounds on which it is made, and the sorts of considerations which might override it? We have "*prima facie,*" and "*ceteris paribus*" to indicate provisionality, "if you want X" and "for the sake of Y" to indicate the sort of grounds for hypothetical and assertoric judgments respectively. What more, or what which is different, does mentioning a particular point of view do?

According to a recent useful article by Robert Brandom,[3] the specification of the point of view determines a range of relevant reasons which would support or defeat the judgment given. It tells us which other "*facies*" need to be added before the *prima facie* judgment becomes a judgment all things considered (from that viewpoint), which other matters might or might not be relevantly equal. Specifying a point of view is specifying both a range of relevant possible truths and how they bear on action. But Brandom's examples suggest that the point of view specification does nothing which could not be done by specifying a goal. He is willing to speak of the point of view of getting to the station on time, and of the advisability of castling early from the point of view of control of the center. Such use of the idiom to limit the immediately relevant considerations and counterconsiderations does nothing which could not be more natually done by a Kantian hypothetical imperative: "If you want to control the center, castle early," nor, when the idiom is used to justify an action already taken, which could not be done by an assertoric judgment: "Since I wanted to control the center . . . ," or a possibly equivalent judgment of the form: "I castled early for the sake of center control."

The sort of things for the *sake* of which we adopt or eliminate goals are typically things we never get so securely that we can say "That's that. Now I can turn to other matters." We do things for the sake of our health, our financial security, our friends' welfare, our reputation, our souls' eventual salvation. Goals, by contrast, can be reached once and for all, and replaced by new ones. Hobbesian persons who pursue power after power never really get once and for all what they pursue, not even in one of the many forms of it which Hobbes catalogs. They may of course get some particular prize they aim at, some honor they covet, the extra supplies they wish to store away. But these are mere goals, which are set for the sake of the good whose insecurity they diminish but never eliminate. That for the sake of which one pursues some goal is of a different type and generality from the goals and subgoals it makes worth pursuing.[4] Do we get a variety of different points of view from the variety of the different goods for the sake of which we bother with pursuing the goals they light up with value? A list of things for the sake of which persons act, plan, adopt and eliminate goals, sacrifice, and die, would give us a list of things of the appropriate generality and elusiveness to distinguish points of view from mere goals. We would have the points of view of health, of wealth, of salvation, of national honor, of family honor, of sheer enjoyment, of longevity, of morality. Does Frankena see points of view as individualized by that for the sake of which one would act from each point of view? This seems too narrow, since from within the moral point of view, as he conceives of it, one might act either for the sake of others' welfare, or for the sake of harming them. It is nonindifference to people, not concern for their *good,* which defines Frankena's moral point of view, although he believes that in fact this "caring" *will* take a benevolent not a malevolent form.

Do sakes individuate points of view for Hume? Since we can speak of acting for the sake of this or that individual, this or that interest group, the plurality of the partial or "peculiar" points of view which Humean morality transcends can be specified by saying that, before morality, each individual or each group acts for its own sake. Among the things for the sake of which we can act are private and group interests. But when we are in what Hume calls the common or steady point of view, is there one interest, or one thing for the sake of which we commend actions? Hume might reply "Yes, humanity," but he equally might reply "No, there are *many* things for the sake of which the moral person acts, for the public interest, for justice, for friendship, for a whole variety of excellences which are useful, for a whole range of agreeable things, like good company, literature, witty conversation." Any and all of these can be that for the sake of which a particular decision is advocated from the moral point of view. Indeed Hume speaks of "steady and general *points* of view." (T. 581–82) as involved in moral judgment, so there may be for him a separate general point of view from which to consider each virtue.

We do not need to talk of moral or of other points of view if we can translate what we are saying into "sake" talk or into hypothetical or assertoric imperatives. If points of view are *merely* points from which we group subgoals under more comprehensive goals, or nest sakes within sakes, then we can simply switch locutions and eliminate the metaphor without any loss. The metaphor suggests a plurality of more or less definite viewing places from which one might view either one thing, say the temple of Ankor Wat, or simply take in "the view," where this changes from point to point, as we get views of different things—as one climbs up a mountain new peaks and ranges come into view, and the valley one began by viewing may be hidden.[5] Those who want to speak of a moral point of view need to make clear whether what is considered from that point is in any sense the same thing as is considered from the points of view with which it is contrasted, or whether each point brings with it not only its own view but its own objects viewed. There is no doubt, I think, that for Hume the things viewed from the moral point or points of view at least *include* things viewed from other nonmoral viewpoints, although the focus may be different. Underlying motives must be viewed, but they can also be viewed from a private angle, as well as lost altogether to view as they would be to views incapable of the sort of postulation of causes Hume thinks involved in the attribution of motives to others (T. 576). Does Frankena think that from the moral viewpoint one sees the same things one sees from at least some other viewpoints? Are the lives of others as experienced by them viewed with indifference from nonmoral viewpoints, or not viewed at all? I am not sure what Frankena's answer is. He certainly seems to think that the final authority of ultimate practical reason is linked to its comprehensive view, as if it sees what is seen from the moral and other viewpoints and more besides. With things in space, a suitably distanced aerial view may allow us to see, say, *all* sides of the Temple of Ankor Wat (in a particular perspective) but not all of its foundations nor the reliefs in its interior corridors (unless recent warfare there has left these open to the sky). Hume, although he speaks of "remote" views as correcting the faults of contiguous views, and although he thinks that a moral view considers *all* not only some of those persons affected, characterizes the moral point of view, which is for him as authoritative as Frankena's ultimate rationality, as much by what that view eclipses as by what it takes in. It considers nothing except the character of persons, and considers them in the light of nothing except their agreeableness and usefulness as fellow-persons, where this is as much a matter of their providing agreeable company as it is of their "useful" accomplishments. Hume's finally authoritative point of view is one which is shareable, which takes in a view of the character of all those who can share it, and from which no contradictory views arise. Achieving this viewpoint is as much a matter of what *not* to attend to as of attending to more. Yet it is not really that in moral judgment and in the moral language one does not recognize self-interest— Hume's artifices regulate self-interest, so must involve seeing people as competitors, adversaries, and sometimes enemies, people needing rules of competition and magistrates to settle disputes. When speaking the moral language as a moral judge I do not see my fellows as my competitors or enemies, but I may see them as one another's competitors or enemies. So what I see somehow includes the way they see each other from nonmoral viewpoints, without my having to take that viewpoint. I do not think that any playing with point of view metaphor quite captures this sort of comprehending. We could try talking of mirror reflections—as when, say, from a favored viewpoint in Switzerland I not only see the Matterhorn in the perfect symmetry of that mountain's northern aspect, but also see its southern aspect reflected on some mirror provided by unusual light and atmospheric conditions. Thus I might both have a direct view of the mountain as the Matterhorn and also a derivative view of it as Monte Cervinio. This contrived extension of the spatial metaphor really does nothing that could not as well be done by talk of remembering or somehow knowing the way a thing looks from other perspectives. One can know one has a point of view only if at least some other points of view are familiar to one. A point from which one cannot conceive of moving is not knowable *as* a point, but is indistinguishable from omnipresence, from a god's eye view. In any case even this contrived way of letting the view from other points enter into the view from one point cannot capture the way that from the Humean moral point of view we not only comprehend the enmity between two competitors, we also take action to change it, to eliminate the destructive potential of the conflict. It is as if, from my Matterhorn view, I not only see the crags of Monte Cervinio but somehow smooth them out. Here the point of view metaphor shows its limits. Only for a Leibnizian, for whom the plurality of spatial points is itself derivative of the plurality of monads, each with its more fundamental than spatial point of view, can viewing from a variety of points be an adequate metaphor for the variety of ways we can organize our thoughts.

For Hume if not for Frankena the moral point of view is not related to that of self-interest or group interest merely as are the northern and southern views of one mountain, even when one of those views yields a more pleasing aspect. Hume does liken the moral point of view to an optimal point for judging the color or beauty of some object (T. 582), where light and distance must be just right, but he also likens moral judgment to judgments about size or shape (T. 603), where in fact no one optimal viewpoint exists. Such judgments depend not on proper viewpoints but on interpretation of the data got from any one viewpoint in the context of what we know could be got from others.

Indeed I think that Hume's talk of different points of view and different languages is best replaced by more Hegelian talk of less and more corrected or developed attitudes, by less and more expressive languages. It is not just that some people, some of the time, prefer agreement and so take a position which makes that possible, while others or the same ones in other moods, opt for conflict, and speak the language of self- or group-interest. If the moral viewpoint is a *correction* of peculiar partial and contradiction-ridden viewpoints, then it is not simply one viewpoint among others, a northern rather than a southern approach to some subject/object. Hume describes a "correction" and a "progress of sentiment," and different so-called points of view are merely way stations on a journey to a destination where the mind can "rest." Hume's use of point of view talk, although it is not, I think, reducible to talk of goals and interests and sakes, is reducible to talk of correction and of dialetical progress, or at least movement. Only if the resting place of morality proved unstable and there were the perpetual seesaw envisaged in the previous section would there be two roughly co-equal different real points of mental view within which arise all the other distinctions of means and end, *prima facie* and *tota facie, ceteris paribus* and *sans phrase,* for the sake of this or of that, in X's or in Y's interest, in so far as this, that, or the other. Hume does not expect this seesaw, and so the moral point of view really is for him a privileged point, an Aristotelian peak or *center* around which other lesser points of view can be ordered.

For Frankena this privilege is not given to morality but to "ultimate rationality." What then are the other points of view which are mere points of view, origins of less than ultimate practical judgments? Frankena does not tell us, and what he does say about the distinctive features of the moral viewpoint allows us to consider a variety of alternatives. One might see morality as one form of control of persons, along with others such as the criminal law, economic institutions, the press and the media, religious institutions, sexual response, all of them concerned with or "caring" some-how about how persons live their lives. We would then get an economic, a legal, a publicity, a religious, a sexual point of view from which roughly the same things, actions and policies, could be evaluated. Are these the fellow points of view to the moral point of view which Frankena envis-ages? Or do we vary not the human control system but the *object* of our care—and so see the point of view from which we care about the impact of our actions on people as one among other points of view, such as that from which we assess action and events for their effect on forests, or on birds, or on dolphins. The "space" in which we find "the point of view of humanity" might contain also the point of view of dolphins, or of whales, or of lichens, or of redwoods. In a book about New Zealand's national parks, I recently read the remarkable claim that the responsibility of the park rangers is to the land itself, and to the forests which cover it—so that even grazing animals or human admirers are possible enemies, not primary objects of the rangers' "care." Frankena characterizes the moral viewpoint by the nonindifference we feel, when there, to the lives and experiences of persons and conscious and sentient things. Possibly the coordinate points of view are to be got by varying this indifference— becoming indifferent to human experience and caring only about dol-phins, or whales, or about the "life" of redwoods and lichens. Or we might become indifferent to all life and "care" only about the preservation of a full variety of minerals and "precious" stones. These imagined view-points, in which human lives cease to be precious to us while other things are made precious, seem unreal and not sustainable. Those park rangers must care, at least derivatively, not merely about the land but about park rangers, not merely about the cared-for but about those who feel and provide the care. To care *only* for things which cannot themselves care seems to reduce "caring" to fetishism. The only plausible variety of points of view we can get by variation of the objects of indifference and nonin-difference is got by varying *what more* we care about than just ourselves. There will then be the point of view of me for me alone, for me and my family, for me and my country, for me and my fellow-persons, for me and my fellow sentient beings, for me and my fellow living things, possibly for me and the world which sustains me and all my fellows. These points of view, which include Frankena's moral point of view, seem more like a progression than a variety of coordinate alternatives in any one of which we can somehow choose to stand. We will *find* ourselves on one or other of them, driven there by the impossibilities of our former temporary resting points. It is not clear to me from Frankena's version of the moral point of view whether it is supposed to be a *correction* of self-interest or a co-equal alternative to it, or an alternative to other equally limited points of view like the legal or the economic views, or to differently limited but implausible views like "humans for humans" versus "humans for redwoods," or "humans for gods or angels," or "humans for unborn foetuses" or "humans for extraterrestrial beings" or the progressively more inclusive concerns just discussed.

If the metaphor of points of view is really to do some work, the plurality of points of view of which the moral point of view is a member should not be either simply the plurality of possible goals, nor the plurality of interrelated sakes or aspects of the human good, nor yet a plurality of stages in a dialectical development. For Hume I think it was this last, and morality was the most advanced stage, a stage where we are both able and motivated to overlook self-interest and to look behind the actions of our fellows to the motives and characters those actions display, the kind of company such persons provide. There sentiment becomes reflexive, is turned on sentiment, and both the durability and the general acceptability of the discerned character traits match the "steadiness" and the universality of the point of view from which they are discerned. Frankena's version of the moral "point of view" makes it sound more a real point of view, one among other alternatives, than is Hume's, but I suspect that, when the relevant alternative points are clarified, we would find that for Frankena too there is a progression. From caring about one's own concerns one comes to care about those who care, whoever they are, and to share their concerns and their care. The concerns may extend to those who cannot or do not care, and even to lichens and to the land, but the primary focus will be on those, the moral agents, capable of caring and secondarily on the moral patients, those capable of that less reflective "caring" which is desire, and the capacity for pleasure and pain. There may be no plurality of real alternative viewpoints, except the twins of moral optimism and pessimism cited in the previous section. Before we get to either of those we have only less or more corrected versions the self-concern we can expect others to tolerate or support, and the range of others with whom we have a common interest or an interrelated fate, so properly include in our care. The range of beings with whom we have what Hume called "an accord or symphony" will indeed affect the stability of the ground morality stands on, whether it is a point which we must periodically abandon in pessimism or a homeground on which we can remain and build. Seeing ourselves as having more than ourselves, "the party of humankind," in our care, may indeed be just that inverse equivalent of religion which is needed if a secular morality is not to degenerate into self-indulgent license or its bleak aftermath. Perhaps when we cease seeing ourselves as sheep with a caring shepherd we need to see ourselves as shepherds with sheep in *our* care. An extension of moral concern could save moral concern itself from the incoherence I found to threaten Hume's version of a secular and undeluded morality. Frankena's inclusion not merely of persons but of "conscious and sentient beings" in the scope of moral care suggests that he too wants an extended version of morality in which there are more who cared about than there are doing the caring. This asymmetry of care, rather than the reciprocity so emphasized in recent moral theory, may be itself a source of strength for a secular morality for beings with our nature and religious ancestry.

NOTES

1. I shall be relying on Frankena's two published articles entitled "The Concept of Morality," and on a paper, "Moral Point of View Theories," given at the Humanities Institute, North Carolina, in fall, 1979.

2. My references to Hume are to pages in *A Treatise of Human Nature* (T) and to *Enquiries* (E), both edited by L. A. Selby-Bigge and P. H. Nidditch.

3. Robert Brandom, "Points of View and Practical Reasoning," *Canadian Journal of Philosophy* 12 (1982): 321–33.

4. I have discussed this difference in "Mind and Change of Mind." I have discussed some of the features of Hume's version of morality, which I am here emphasizing in "Master Passions," in *Explaining Emotions*, ed. Amelie Rorty (Berkeley and Los Angeles: University of California Press; 1980).

5. Alexander Nehamas, in "Immanent and Transcendent Perspectivism in Nietzsche" (read to the North American Nietzsche Society at the APA meeting in Boston, December 1980), in *Nietzsche Studien* (1982); provides an illuminating discussion of Nietzsche's view that "we cannot look around our own corner," that each "perspective" has its own "world," viewed only from that perspective.

10

Promises, Promises, Promises

I. Various Views about Promises

A promise, according to Hume,[1] Austin,[2] Searle,[3] and Anscombe,[4] is a speech act whereby one alters the moral situation. One does not merely represent some possible state of affairs, one brings it about—makes it the case that, from being free in some respect, one is thereafter unfree, until the obligation taken on in the promise is discharged.

This is surely correct, as far as it goes. To give a promise is to alter one's moral position, to take on a new responsibility. But, as Cavell[5] has objected, one does not need anything as elaborate as a special ritual act, with well-defined roles or offices, the "promisor" and "promisee," to do that— we are continually altering our moral situation by what we do, committing ourselves or extricating ourselves from commitments, and it seems absurd to suppose that we need a special "institution" or "convention" to do this. It is the norm in human life that our actions change the moral state of play, as it were. I injure someone, either knowingly or unknowingly, and so owe that person at least an apology and perhaps reparation. I bring a new person into being, intentionally or unintentionally, so incure parental responsibility. I oppose some plan of a colleague, so owe the colleague an explanation of my opposition. I allow someone to come to depend upon me, so owe the one who depends upon me the gentlest of abandonings, if I leave him. Almost everything we do or say alters the moral situation

Versions of this paper were given at the Oberlin Philosophy Colloquium in 1981, where David Falk disagreed constructively with it, and at CUNY Graduate Center in 1981, where several people, in particular Arthur Collins, made helpful comments. I am also indebted to Robert and Carolyn Birmingham for their legal as well as philosophical advice on an earlier attempt to relate Hume's account of promise to what he might have learned while a law student.

between ourselves and some other, so we either distort the nature of moral responsibility if we suppose we need a special form of words to incur it, or we have not yet found what is special about the form of responsibility incurred by saying "I promise."

Cavell tries to show us that promising is not "the golden road to commitment"[6] by drawing attention to all the other roads. A different sort of challenge to the standard philosopher's account of promising as taking on the obligation to do a particular specified thing, has been posed recently by Atiyah,[7] who charges the philosophers with "an apparent or overt belief in the sanctity of promises and contracts which is no longer to be found in the value systems of modern England at least."[8] The charge here is not that promising and contracting do not alter the moral and legal situation, but that they do not make the *sort* of difference the philosophers have claimed. To oversimplify Atiyah's view, what one must do, if one has given a promise, is nothing at all unless one has also received some consideration from the promisee, and, if that condition is satisfied, then one must either do what one promised or pay damages. For Atiyah (and, he claims, the common law) promises are merely fragments of an agreement to an exchange and admission of that agreement. What one is committed to by a promise is the same as one would be committed to without one, namely to do one's part in some reciprocal transaction, to complete some exchange. "The English common law has never treated the mere fact that a promise has been made as even prima facie a sufficient condition for the creation of a legal obligation. . . . To them [the common lawyers], it was of vital consideration to ask *why* a promise had been given. A promise made for a good reason—a good consideration as it came to be said, was prima facie enforceable. Very roughly, it could be said that a promise was only legally actionable if the promise was to do something which the promisor should have done anyway."[9]

Do promises create new obligations? Is there anything special and unique about promising—is it the golden road to anything of special moral interest? Does a promise create an obligation only if there is some intended *exchange,* and is it a matter of moral indifference whether one keeps one's promise or breaks it and pays fair damages? I shall address these questions, and I shall claim that the correct answers to them are to be found most perspicuously not in any of the recent discussions but rather in the account given two and a half centuries ago by David Hume.

Atiyah cites Hume's account as a "utilitarian" one, which sees promising as a useful artifice. I find Hume's account of all the artificial virtues (of which "fidelity to promises" is one) to commit him not to utilitarianism but more to a sort of enlightened egoism,[10] since he requires that for any social convention to give rise to an obligation each person must find himself (or herself?) "a gainer, on ballancing the account" (T. 497). He does also say of promises that they are "an invention for the interest of society" (T. 524), but this general social interest would not give rise to any individual obligation, for Hume, unless "the whole system of actions, concurr'd in by the whole society, is infinitely advantageous to the whole *and every part*" (T. 498, my emphasis). This is a particularly strong egoist constraint on any supposed requirement to promote the interest of society. Hence my defense of Hume's version of what a promise is, what it obligates us to do, and how it does that, is not intended to be a defense of a utilitarian account of promising.

It is, however, an account which, like that of Austin, Searle, Cavell and Atiyah, rejects the natural law account of promissory obligations. In its usual religious version, this view held that all obligations are obligations to obey God's laws, one of which forbids promise-breaking. On such a view, obligations are all of the same sort, dependent on a divine law somehow promulgated through natural human reason. One is obligated to do what God requires of one, and that includes whatever (not otherwise forbidden act) one has promised another that one will do. Anscombe may perhaps have a way of seeing the sort of non-natural "logos"-discerning "reason" she recognizes as the vehicle for a divine law, but she does not see divine law in the way Hume's main opponents in ethics did. When Hume denied that justice or promise-keeping were natural virtues, because their virtue was not "naturally intelligible," and when he nevertheless called the obligations they gave rise to "natural obligations," the human artifices they depend upon "natural artifices," their content the three "laws of nature," he is arguing with and to some extent mocking the natural law tradition in ethics. He is keeping the terminology of this tradition but emptying it both of its theological implications and of its rationalist implications.

Today, in our post-Wittgensteinian philosophical times, both "reason" and "God" can appear in guises Hume would not have recognized. His battles both with old-style rationalists and supernaturalists in ethics seem largely won, and the issues today are ones which arise within an area of agreement that morality is a human cultural phenomenon, that discerning its content is not much like using reason to discern order in nature. The starry heavens above and the moral law within have drifted further apart than they were to Hume's opponents, despite Kant's efforts to bring them together as both recognized by human reason. If they come together today, it is not through Kant's or Aquinas' notion of reason or of law, not because we think that, as the heavens can be charted by law-recognizing reason, so too can morality. It is rather because we see in any law-discovery (or law-following) that norm-recognizing, correction-sensitive participation in a form of life, or practice, which is also needed for morality and its understanding. The fact-establishing, fact-connecting, law-discovering work of science requires and presupposes both rule-following and the more primitive social capacities that involves. When Hume opposed rationalism in ethics, it was reason as nature-representer that he dethroned, in favor of corrected sentiments and reflectively approved customs and conventions. Today's version of reason, whether it be Anscombe's or Cavell's, is not the reason Hume tried to dethrone. It is much more like that capacity to acquire what Hume called "habit," to learn and operate with "customs," "conventions," and social "artifices." This was a capacity Hume usually contrasted with "reason." Custom is the great guide to human life, and has "equal weight and authority" (E. 41) with reason. Among the customs Hume analyzed were those which, unlike the habit of ordinary causal inference, required a certain "agreement" between those following the custom, an agreement "changeable by human laws" (T. 528). One such agreement-based custom, or convention, is that recognizing the special force of the words "I promise."

II. Representation and Commitment

Hume's discussion has been cited by writers like Anscombe as recognizing the important fact that the words "I promise to help you with your harvest" change the moral situation and do not merely represent such a change, or represent the future help that is promised. They create the obligation to help, and represent that obligation. Hume clearly recognizes the situation-altering power of promising, and what is more he also makes clearer than recent accounts just how, in a promise, the act of representing is linked to the act of binding oneself. He shows us what commitment it is to which explicit promises are indeed the golden road.

Promising, like articulating one's intentions, seems both to describe or represent an action, and also to do something to ensure that the described action become actual.[11] It also declares itself, the verbal act, for what it is, and simultaneously makes it that. "I promise" makes it a promise, and in a different way from the way in which "I am speaking" makes that statement a true one. Promising therefore is one of those verbal actions J. L. Austin called performatives, a species of illocutionary act. It is one of the things we can do with words, and it is a particularly interesting case of an illocutionary act. Unlike congratulating or greeting, promising must be promising something, and what is promised must be represented or signified. Hume has an interesting account both of how the signifying in a promise differs from that in an intention-avowal, or even in such "symbolic delivery" as may attend barter and gift, and of what it is that a promise does which gives an important job both to the verbal representation of what is promised, and to the words "I promise." He says: "When a man says he promises any thing he in effect expresses a resolution of performing it; and along with that subjects himself to the penalty of never being trusted again in case of failure. A resolution is a natural act of the mind, which promises express: But were there no more than a resolution in the case, promises would only declare our former motives, and would not create any new motive or obligation. They are the conventions of men, which create a new motive, when experience has taught us, that human affairs would be conducted much more for mutual advantage, were there certain *symbols or signs* instituted, by which we might give each other security of our conduct in any particular incident" (T. 522). The key elements in this Humean account, ones I shall be alluding to in what follows, are the promisor's explicit expression of *what* she resolves and binds herself to do; subjection to the penalty of distrust, should she not perform just that; the "new" self-interested motive to avoid this penalty; the community's conventions recognizing the force of those "symbols or signs," the words "I promise," and so recognizing the promisor's obligation and also empowering the promisee to initiate the withdrawal of trust, should the promise be broken. This account makes both the words "I promise . . . ," and the exact words completing the utterance begun thus, of significant moral importance. Is Hume right about this?

Cavell and Anscombe both say that we do not need to use the form of words Hume attributes such force to, nor to perform any other particular ritual act, to make a promise. Cavell believes that, in any case, a promise, however given, gets its moral force from being a case of "commitment," and commitments require neither ritual acts, nor the sort of explicitness about what one is committed to which promises usually involve, nor any constitutive rules. Promising, he says, is not a social "institution" that defines roles with rights and obligations attached to them. Indeed, he suggests an indicator of a real institutional role involving obligations, namely that one can take an oath of office on assuming it.[12] The implication is that we take no such oath when we become promisors. As Hume noted, "we are not surely bound to keep our word because we have given our word to keep it" (E. 306). For Cavell, to give a promise is to spell out a commitment, but what binds is the commitment. Spelling it out may make it more easily ascertained, later, whether the commitment has been kept or not, but the commitment itself does not depend upon the spelling out nor on any implicit oath. "There is nothing sacred about the act of promising which is not sacred about expressing an intention, or any other way of committing oneself. . . . If it is important to be explicit then you may engage either in the 'rituals' of saying 'I really want to . . . ,' 'I certainly

intend, will try to . . . ,' or the ritual of saying 'I promise.' It is this importance which makes explicit promises important. But to take them more
seriously than that, as the golden path to commitment, is to take our
ordinary nonexplicit commitments too lightly."[13] This makes the crucial
act commitment, and promising becomes just one form of it. Cavell says
"The appeal (to rules) is an attempt to explain why such an action as
promising is *binding* upon us, but if you *need* an explanation for that, if
there is a sense that something more than personal commitment is necessary, then the appeal to rules comes too late. For rules themselves are
binding only subject to our commitment."[14]

Has Cavell a disagreement with Hume? Hume can agree with Cavell
that unless we already understand what it is to be bound (for example, by
one's consent), or to be under obligation (for example, to respect the
property rights of others), the question of how promises can bind can
never be answered, since on Hume's view the force of promises presupposes prior convention-generated obligations, those of property and consent to its transfer. But Cavell's point is *not* that promising is one of a
mutually referential family of conventional acts, all of them rule- or convention-dependent. That is Hume's position. Cavell's point seems rather
to be that we must understand how individual commitment can bind to
be able to understand how any rules or conventions bind, since they bind
only if accepted by individuals, only if individuals *commit themselves* to
those rules. Here too we can find partial agreement between Cavell and
Hume, since Hume of course supposes that the conventions of property,
its transfer by consent, and by promise or contract, must be somehow
accepted before they can generate obligations. Hume calls this acceptance
"agreement," not "commitment," and this may not be merely a terminological difference from Cavell.

The "agreement" on the first rules, namely property rules, Hume says,
is a matter of an expressed sense of common interest and of mutually
referential intentions, but it "arises gradually and acquires force by a slow
progression, and by our repeated experience of the inconveniences of
trespassing it" (T. 490). There is no dateable occurrence when all persons
commit themselves to all the rest, nor any occasion on which each new
member of a society commits her or himself. Agreement and acceptance
can arise gradually, but it is less easy to see how individual commitment
can arise except by some definite acts of the committed person. I can find
myself in "agreement" with my fellows, in Hume's sense, if I find myself
willingly doing something, like rowing, or talking, or using money, which
presupposes "that something is to be perform'd on the other part." It
would take a deliberate act of disengagement to avoid being caught up in
the general cooperative practices of the community into which I am born.

How could I show that I was not in agreement with others in accepting the current language, monetary system, or set of property rules? By a deliberate proclamation, or public act of disrespect? If I take no such measures, then I am presumed to be in agreement, and to have an obligation to respect the currently recognized rights. I am born into obligations. I do not need to take any initiative, nor do anything to *commit myself.* Indeed, if Hume is right, the very possibility of an individual act of commitment, consent, or refusal to consent depends upon general acceptance of some recognized ways of making individual adjustments. Once there *is* the general practice of property recognition, it takes new general practices to enable individuals to make individual adjustments, to relinquish or exchange property. The binding general practice precedes the binding conventional acts by single individuals. Cavell asks how a general rule can bind unless individuals bind themselves to respect it. Hume's (implicit) answer is that individuals can *agree,* and express agreement, by something less individualized, and less definite than is needed for an individual commitment. Hume describes a bootstrap operation whereby from an informal general agreement on a convention that invents rights, namely property rights, his convenors move on to another informal general agreement to recognize the force of a more formal and more individual act, consent to transfer property, and from that to another informal agreement to recognize a more explicit and more formal individual act, namely promise. The issue between Hume and Cavell is not whether rules bind only if accepted, but rather what counts as acceptance; what the relation is between acceptance and commitment; what moral difference is made by different degrees of initiative, formality, and explicitness in acceptance; and what the relation is between acceptance of a general practice and acceptance of a particular understanding with specific persons.

Only if one sees all obligations as incurred by avoidable commitments on the part of the obligated persons would it be necessary to reduce the obligations engendered by generally accepted rules to a series of acts of individual acceptance or commitment by individual persons. Does Cavell believe that about obligations? I do not think so. The existence of an established practice, cooperative scheme, or form of life, establishes a presumption of acceptance by new members of the society. They may do things that rebut this presumption, but there is no need for any oath of allegiance to established customs nor any acts of commitment before persons can acquire the obligations of participants. This is part of Cavell's own point—that obligations are not something one can avoid simply by avoiding certain ritual acts or oaths. They are the normal accompaniments of normal relationships with others, relations that do lead to gradual acceptance of accustomed ways of acting to one another. One can agree with Cavell about this yet still see a place for *special* obligation-assuming acts, and for oaths to solemnize those acts, be they ones of commitment to individual persons or commitments to uphold laws or rules.

Hume sees promise as a special sort of act whereby a new obligation to a specific person or persons is taken on, where this sort of individual act is possible only because people in general recognize the force of such a verbal act. To agree with him one need not claim that all special obligations to particular individuals arise from promises (he believes that subjects have special obligations to sovereigns, with or without an oath of allegiance), nor that without promise there could be no commitment-dependent special obligation to particular people (he believes that parents owe a "fidelity" to one another that is distinct from "fidelity to promises"), nor that obligations arising directly or indirectly from an acceptance of a general convention such as that making promises possible have any greater moral seriousness than a two-person nonpromissory and informal agreement, such as that between friends or lovers whose "intercourse" is "more generous and noble" (T. 521) than that of the parties to a promise. Hume believed that there must have been limited cooperation and trust between persons, in the family, before any conventions could arise (T. 490), and he insisted that promise, a convention-dependent explicit agreement between private individuals, "does not entirely abolish the more generous and noble intercourse of friendship and good offices" (T. 521). There is the natural duty of parents to care for children, of friends to be true friends, and so on, independently of all the artifices. So Hume certainly does not treat promise as the golden road to commitment. But he does treat it as a rule-dependent or convention-dependent road to commitments beyond family and friends to those whom we bear no "real kindness."

III. Symbolical Delivery of the Absent and General

Hume sees promise as an obligation-creating device that is useful between strangers and especially when they wish to transfer either *future* goods or services, or *distant* goods, or a certain definite *measure* of goods. Without promise, with only the artifice of transfer by consent, even when that is embellished by the lawyers' superstition of the symbolical delivery (T. 515) of what is present but too bulky to literally hand over, "one cannot transfer the property of a particular house, twenty leagues distant, because consent cannot be attended by delivery, which is a requisite circumstance. Nor can one transfer the property of ten bushels of corn, or five hogsheads of wine, by the mere expression and consent; because these are only general terms and have no direct relation to any particular heap of corn or bushel of wine" (T. 520). Hume sees a need for promise, with both the penalty it involves and the verbal representation of what is to be transferred that it involves, for transfers, between strangers, of absent (distant or future) goods, and of precise amounts of some general type of goods. This limited rationale does make Humean promises "mere contrivances for the convenience and advantage of society" (T. 525), clarifying as it does both the convenience and the fact that what provides it is described by Hume not, like the artifice of property, as "infinitely advantageous" (T. 498), but as a *mere* contrivance, albeit a useful one for limited purposes. The rationale also explains the special features Hume finds and emphasizes in the artifice of promise, and in particular that of penalty, and of explicit statement of what the promisor must do to avoid that penalty. To see exactly how the explicitness of promises connects with the obligation to perform them, it will be helpful to consider Anscombe's treatment of Hume's account of promising.

Anscombe praises Hume for seeing that there were two problems, "one, what sort of beast a promise is; and the other, concerning how, given that there is such a thing, it can generate an obligation."[15] She goes on: "One may fail to note that there are two problems, because a promise signifies the creation or willing of an obligation. It might be thought that if you could show that there were a sign with that signification, you would be home and dry: the obligation is generated by giving the sign which has that signification! Hume's clarity of mind perceived that this is not so."[16] Anscombe regards Hume's thesis of the "natural unintelligibility" of promissory obligations as a great discovery. She also says that this thesis has wider application than Hume gave it. But he in fact gave the thesis a fairly wide application—to all agreement-based or "convention"-based obligations (including the obligation to keep rowing in stroke). To be not naturally intelligible, in Hume's sense, is to be intelligible only once we understand what a convention or "artifice" is. He discusses a limited number of social artifices—property, its transference by consent, government, some forms of marriage. But he makes it quite clear that he regards money as another case of something not naturally intelligible, and he also regards words as cultural and convention-dependent things, to be understood only by reference to human artifice. "In like manner (i.e., to property conventions) are languages gradually established by human conventions. . . . In like manner do gold and silver become the common measures of exchange" (T. 490). So the application of his thesis of natural unintelligibility is fairly extensive, and Hume is in explicit agreement with Anscombe that "no language is in Hume's sense naturally intelligible."[17]

Anscombe sees what is peculiarly puzzling about promises, among what she calls the naturally unintelligible things, to be the fact that "a promise is essentially a sign, and the necessitation arises from the giving of the sign."[18] Social or "artificial" necessitation can arise, say within a game, without any sign-giving by the party under the necessity or by other parties. In the children's hand-piling game Anscombe discusses, one must lift one's hand from the bottom to the top of the pile when it is on the bottom, and musn't lift it before then. No signs are given by the players, their moves in the game are determined without the need for signs. But in a promise words are used, and used to signify both a future action and the non-natural necessity to perform it. Because the giving of a promise simultaneously creates an obligation, and signifies the precise obligation it creates, it is easy, Anscombe thinks, to suppose oneself home and dry if one can account for the feat of signification, and so miss the deeper problem of the very possibility of what is signified, a non-natural necessity. She credits Hume with seeing the deeper issue.

So, I think, he did. But he addressed this "deep" issue of how it comes about that one must repay a loan, or keep one's promise, why one can't take another's property without their permission, in his general account of "convention," and of the sort of "agreement" involved in that. His thesis of the natural unintelligibility of promises is simply an application, to this case, of his general thesis about all the "laws of nature" and the "natural" obligations they engendered. They are, all of them, intelligible only when we see that conventions or general agreements are involved. Property is unintelligible until its conventional character is acknowledged, consent could not alter rights unless it were recognized to do so, promises could not bind unless a convention enables them to bind. Hume continues to call these convention-dependent obligations "natural" obligations partly because of their link with the "laws of nature," and his usage is ironical. Natural obligations, for him, are precisely the obligations that are natural law-dependent. Since the only natural laws are human customs, they are *not* naturally intelligible, and no rational motive to perform them can exist until there is an agreed custom or convention. When Hume gets to the third artifice he discusses, namely promise, he does make some puzzling departures in his terminology, claiming that because there is no convention-independent motive to keep promises, there is therefore *no* "natural obligation" (T. 525), as if he had forgotten that in his ironical usage (at, for example, T. 498) a natural obligation just *is* a convention-dependent one.[19] This may have misled Anscombe into thinking that, for Hume, promises are more "naturally unintelligible" than is property or consent to its transfer. But Hume in the next section resumes his ironical usage and speaks of the three "laws of nature," or pregovernment sources of obligation, as "that of the stability of possession, its transference by consent, and of the performance of promises" (T. 526). He does admittedly go out of his way to emphasize the "contradictions" in promise, if we try to treat it as a natural phenomenon, and to emphasize its family resemblance to religious practices such as baptism, the mass, and the laying on of hands, which he characterizes as superstitious artifices. He had earlier (T. 515-6) likened symbolic delivery in transfer by consent to religious ceremonies. It may well be that he did wish to make some special point about promises, and all cases of symbolic delivery, over and above his general point that all the "natural obligations" of justice arise from artifices: "Unless we will allow that nature has establish'd a sophistry, and render'd it necessary and universal, we must allow that the sense of justice and injustice is not natural, but arises artificially, tho' necessarily, from education, and human conventions" (T. 483). Hume may be emphasizing the oddities of promise, as an artifice, and its link with the lawyers' superstition of symbolical delivery, in order to combat the tendency to see it as the fundamental source of obligation. A few sections later, in "Of the source of allegiance," he argues against Hobbes, Locke, and all contractarians, that there is no good reason to assimilate other obligations to that of promise.

Because Anscombe sees Hume's achievement as the recognition of the natural unintelligibility of promises, she misses his more detailed thesis about how *this* naturally unintelligible thing differs from its close relative, "mere expression and consent" (T. 520). Both consent and promise[20] are artifices, but to understand what promise adds to consent Hume has to give a fairly detailed account of how representation enters into these two artifices. Both the common elements linking promises to other grounds of non-natural obligation, and those special to it, are fairly clearly laid out by Hume, but we do not see these clearly unless we read his section on promises in its context within his total account of human social conventions and the natural order in which they develop. If one reads only the section on promises, and not the preceding section on transfer by consent, one may not understand the emphasis given by Hume to the role of the verbal signs in promising. If one reads the account in that one section of the unintelligibility of the idea of willing an obligation, without the more general earlier account of the unintelligibility of any obligations of justice, until we invoke the existence of conventions, we may be misled into thinking that promises are more "unnatural," or more naturally unintelligible, than is property, or than is permission to take or borrow. To see what Hume is saying about promissory obligations one must see it in the context of what he is saying about property rights, rights transferred by owner's consent, and about magistrates' rights. None of these are naturally intelligible, all of them depend on general social "agreements" or customs. Some but not all of these, as I shall shortly go on to emphasize, involve provisions for sanctions against those who fail in their obligations. Some but not all of these involve the power of individuals to alter rights and obligations. Some but not all of these, like both consent and promise, involve the giving of signs. Some, like promise and some forms of transfer by consent, involve symbols or representations.

Hume, unlike both Anscombe and Cavell, sees what makes promises puzzling and to some extent suspect as the element of symbolism they involve, and what makes them distinctive and distinctively useful as the element of *verbal* representation or signification they involve. Where contemporary philosophers, accustomed to attending to language and particularly to the representational function of language, had a sense of puzzlement and of "deep" discovery when they saw that a verbal act could create an obligation and not merely represent one, Hume came to the matter the other way around. Having satisfied himself that what he called "conventions" create obligations, he then went on to look at how conventions governing the use of sign and symbols extended the scope of non-natural obligations, and how words came to play a vital role. He began his discussion of promising already clear that there could be what Anscombe calls non-natural necessitation (indeed, in a sense, it is for Hume the only kind of necessitation there is),[21] and that it could come into being by an individual's voluntary act within a context of social customs (as the giver is necessitated, by his act of giving, not to later attack the recipient of the gift to regain what was once his property). The only puzzling issue facing Hume when he came to discuss promising was how its being a ritual *verbal* act made a difference, and what difference it made. Where later philosophers, thinking they understood the phenomenon of language, hit on non-natural necessitation or obligation, and found it a deep, puzzling phenomenon, Hume, having understood artifice-based obligation, then hit on the role of signs and language, and had to account for their special contribution there. It was part of his genius to be puzzled by the role of representation, not to take it for granted. His account of promising, taken with his earlier account of the role of symbols in transfer by consent, gives representation in language a vital role, and shows how there are some things we can do with words only by acts of representation, by using words to represent what is not present. For Hume representation in language was more not less of a mystery than was obligation-creation. That linguistic representation could be given an intelligible role in obligation-creation demystified it, gave it its place among other useful artifices.

Hume begins his discussion of sign-giving in his account of transfer by consent, the artifice that enables persons to acquire wanted property of others with the owner's "consent," often in exchange for something they want. His first artifice was property, whereby possession became stable.

His second artifice is consent to transfer, whereby it becomes less stable again, but is transferred voluntarily and to mutual advantage. Barter, gift, and loan are now possible because the owner can signify consent to transfer of his property. The first complication to arise is what is to happen when you give me, say, gold in exchange for my land or my herd of cattle. I cannot literally hand over my land as you can your gold. What do I do to give you any security? Unless you want to make a gift, you would be a fool to relinquish your gold without getting something more than the hope that I will vacate my land for good, or not reclaim my cattle. Hume says that, once there is the convention of property, we should be able to see that what you get is the *right* to the land or cattle, but since rights are abstract entities we don't easily understand how they are transferred when nothing perceivable is transferred. So we, or the lawyers, invent symbols that can be literally transferred. "Men have invented a symbolical delivery, to satisfy the fancy, where the real one is impracticable" (T. 515). I hand you a lump of soil or stone from my land, and it symbolizes the land itself, the right to which I relinquish by handing over the stone. Or I give you the key of my granary, when the wheat that is in it is too bulky for me to literally hand over to you. Hume describes as "a kind of superstitious practice in civil laws and in the laws of nature, resembling the Roman Catholic superstitions in religion" (T. 515) all these symbolic transfers, these ritual acts with their sometimes elaborate rules. (For land transfers in Scotland, the stone had to be handed over in daylight, on the land to be transferred, in the presence of the workmen who had worked on that land.) All they do is mimic the important thing, the transfer of rights, by a physical delivery of something. The whole act symbolizes the transfer of rights, and the stone symbolizes the transferred property. "The suppos'd resemblance of the actions and the presence of this sensible delivery deceive the mind and make it fancy that it conceives the mysterious transition of the property" (T. 515). This description is of what happens once law and lawyers get into the act, and it is unclear if Hume thinks that there were prelegal precursors of such symbolical delivery not yet amounting to giving a promise.

When Hume turns to promising, he already has an account of how consent creates or transfers rights, and of how a superstitious practice of symbol-giving can accompany the transfer of rights. The first question he raises is whether a mere act of mind, a willing to be bound, could make one bound, and he dismisses this as impossible. What he had called "consent," in the previous section was no mere mental act, but a public, social one—transfer by consent is a new artifice, a second "law of nature." "The translation of property by consent is founded on a law of nature as well as is its stability without such a consent" (T. 514). Consenting is not mere willing. As Hume puts it in a footnote, the individual will would merely return on itself *in infinitum,* would never find its own object, what it willed, in trying to will a right or an obligation. Only within a social practice and by a social act can a new obligation be created. Only then could one effectively will to assume a new obligation. But there is another reason why the individual will cannot produce the obligation of a promise, one that Hume puts in the main text, not merely in a footnote. This is that "a promise always regards some future time and the will has an influence only on present actions" (T. 516). Humean will, like Hobbesian will, is the transition from deliberation to action. I can now will to say "I promise," and do so, but that doesn't explain how promising now makes me bound later, how I get a grip now on a "remote" future time, the time when I must do what I now promise to do.

At this point, I think, someone like Cavell might object and say that our language does refer to future time in many of its uses, and so do we in our commitments, nonverbal and verbal, nonpromissory as well as promissory. A commitment must include some future, however brief, in its scope. Has Hume any problem with deciding to promise that is not also present when we decide to utter a prediction, or a generality, or even when we decide without words to go on a journey and so knowingly prevent ourselves from being here tomorrow? Isn't every willing, for an intelligent creature, a plunge into the future, a ruling out of possibilities for tomorrow? Isn't every use of language a use of a language with future and continuous tenses, so that claims about the future and commitments concerning it are given and implied constantly?

I think we see where promises involve future time in a way other agreements or commitments need not when we remember what, on Hume's view, promising enables a person to do, and look at his implied account of how the community as a whole is involved in making that power possible for individuals. A promise, Hume says, enables a person to transfer not merely particular goods in his possession at the time of transfer, but "absent and general" possessions. Tomorrow's labor, or next year's corn, or the cargo in ships still at sea, can be transferred to someone who accepts one's word when "consent *cannot* be attended with delivery" (T. 520, emphasis added) of those goods. The rights are transferred, but what they are rights to cannot be delivered now if they do not yet exist, or are too far away. A promise is something that must *later* be performed, and then the promissory obligation is discharged. When one makes a gift, or barters something, immediate delivery obviates the need for any later "performance," and such obligations as the giver takes on, in virtue of having made the transfer, are never "discharged," since they stem from the standing obligation to recognize the altered property rights. But a promise provides, as it were, the script for its own future performance, and that performance can fully discharge one's obligation. The future time a promise regards is the time of a performance that terminates the obligation the promise created. A promise creates a limited obligation for a limited time. The obligation ceases to exist once the promise is performed, or once one is released from one's promise by the person to whom it was given.

IV. Threats and Promises

This bond for a limited future, for "*some* future time" (T. 516, my emphasis) contrasts with the obligations created by the general agreement which constitutes the convention of property, or of consent as a way of transferring property, or indeed of the convention which gives the words "I promise" their special force and so enables anyone to make a promise. In all these cases of Humean conventions everyone in a society agrees to recognize certain rights—of ownership, of transfer with owner's consent, to performance of promises. This recognition of rights, in Hume's first two conventions, brought with it only negative correlative standing obligations—the obligation not to steal, nor to interfere with voluntary transfers, nor to reclaim the property one consented to be transferred. But to recognize the rights of someone to whom a promise has been given, noninterference is not enough. The promisor must perform, and everyone else must demand that he does, on pain of "never being trusted again in case of failure" (T. 522). This introduces an element of threat into the basis of an obligation to perform according to one's promise, a threat that the promisee alone could not convincingly make. That I won't trust you again if you break your promise to me is fairly easy for me to ensure, unless you disguise yourself when you return with tempting offers, but is no great threat to you, if you do not need me to trust you again. But if I can have you as it were stigmatized, so that others recognize you as someone not to be trusted, then you have a fairly strong self-interested reason not to break your promise to me. Can I do this? If we are talkers, as we must be to give or receive promises, then I can harm your reputation, I can spread the word that you are not to be trusted.

Without promises, on Hume's account of them, trust would be more restricted—one might trust one's family, friends, or neighbors to do what they know one expects them to do, either from their established habits and customs or from their statements of intention, but one will have no such reason to depend upon some stranger's future action, even if he expresses an intention. He may change his mind, or forget, or have intended to deceive one. But if he promises, gives his word, one has some hold over him. Promises are "the *sanction* of the interested commerce of mankind" (T. 522, my emphasis). What one "holds" in one's power is his reputation as a reliable person of his word. Should he break his promise, his reputation, at least among those one can communicate with, can be ruined. Thereafter others will not accept his promise, and so his dealings with them will be restricted to simultaneous, direct exchange, if indeed they will be willing to have any dealings with him. He will have lost what Nietzsche called the permission to make a promise.[22]

Hume sees promise as an "invention" which comes about after consent and before government, and which by its "sanction" facilitates, in fairly small communities, cooperation between nonintimates. What makes government necessary is the growth of wealth and of community size, which makes it possible both for thieves to escape proprietorial vigilance, and for promise-breakers to move on to new victims, to move away from their bad reputations. Only when magistrates are invented to receive complaints and to keep official track of a person's record can persons in a large society count on a promise-breaker being generally known as such, and/or effectively punished. Hume says that it is "possible for men to maintain a small uncultivated society without government" (T. 541), that is without any official whose job it is to detect, declare, and punish those who break the generally accepted rules. In such an uncultivated society, he says, there will, before government, be justice, "and the observation of those three fundamental laws concerning the stability of possession, its translation by consent, and the performance of promises" (ibid.). What induces people to institute government, to divide off the task of stigmatizing and punishing the untrustworthy, is the increase of successful theft and fraud; and this comes with the change from small to large societies, and with the change to more cultivated societies in which individuals achieve such "encrease of riches and possessions" (ibid.) that their transfers typically are transfers of "absent and general" goods, requiring contract, and where these same absent goods provide both targets for easy theft and opportunities for lying promises. The informal enforcement of promises by withdrawal of community trust from the word of a known promise-breaker works only as long as the community is small enough for word to get around when anyone proves not to be a reliable person, not a "man of his word."

Thus, on the story Hume gives us, threat is an essential element in promise, and it takes community cooperation in the relevant convention or practice to pose that threat of destruction of one's power to ever have one's promises accepted. "They are conventions of men which create a new motive, when . . . certain symbols or signs (were) instituted by which we might give each other security of our conduct in any particular incident. After these signs are instituted, whoever uses them is immediately bound by his interest to execute his engagements and must never expect to be trusted any more if he refuse to perform what he promis'd" (T. 522). Hume here quite clearly refers both to the community interest in giving each other security by "instituting" these signs, with backup penalty of withdrawal of trust from those who take them lightly, and to the individual promisor's interest in performing what he promised, so as to remain in good standing, to keep his reputation as a trustworthy person. The conventions of men give the promisor "a new motive" to perform according to his promise. Hume slightly obfuscates his account of exactly what sanction and what new motive a promise introduces, when in the next paragraph he describes the practice of a promise-recognizing society as based on a obvious interest in the "institution and observance of promises" (ibid.), but then seems to confuse the interest all have in the institution with the interest a given promisor has in observance. "When each individual discovers them [the advantages of the institution and observance of promises] to every mortal, and when each individual perceives the same sense of interest in all his fellows, he immediately performs his part of any contract, as being assur'd that they will not be wanting in their part. All of them, by concert, enter into a scheme of actions for common benefit, and agree to be true to their word, nor is anything requisite to form this concert or convention, but that everyone have a sense of interest in the faithful fulfilling of engagements, and express that sense to other members of society" (ibid.). This seems to say that the interest each person has both in the institution *and in the performance* of promises is simply the common benefit, and that the only threat or worry on the horizon is that others might be "wanting in their part" of any contract or mutual promise. It would have been better if Hume had separated out the motive each has for the institution of the whole scheme of action that sets up promise as "the interested sanction of mankind," and the motive each *then* has for performing anything he may go on to promise, once he uses the instituted practice. The interest in the institution is an interest in the common benefit, and this interest is conditional on general conformity to the rules of the institution. Penalty helps ensure this conformity.

The interested motive to perform one's part in any contract one has made includes a wish to avoid the sanction that has been instituted, but of course it need not be the whole of the motive. As Hume emphasizes, one condition on one's willingness to fulfill engagements is the expectation that others will do likewise, as well as one's belief that the whole scheme of actions is for common benefit. Whether or not one can expect others to conform depends not just on the expected common benefit of "correspondence of good offices" (T. 251), but on the penalty for promise-breaking, and the assurance that it will be levied. So for the expectation that others fulfill their engagements one needs also one's own and their willingness to exact the penalty for nonfulfillment. Once the penalty ceases to be effective, and violations of equity become frequent, then "your example both pushes me forward in this way by imitation, and also affords me a new reason for any breach of equity, by showing me, that I should be the cully of my integrity, if I alone shou'd impose on myself a severe restraint admidst the licentiousness of others" (T. 535). This is Hume's description of what happens when riches and population have increased, and a need for magistrates as official rule-declarers, rule-appliers, and rule-enforcers becomes evident. At the earlier stage, when the artificial custom of promising "arises gradually and acquires force by a slow progression" (T. 490), there is no reason not to expect the informal victim-initiated penalty of withdrawal of trust to be workable and efficacious, so that there can be assurance that others will fulfill their engagements. Their interest in so doing, like one's own, can be threefold, to help keep a useful custom going, not to disappoint the other party, and to avoid the penalty for promise-breaking.

Hume's account of promise-keeping is like Hobbes' account of obedience to any of his "laws of nature"—one needs assurance of others' conformity, for obedience to have point, and one needs not just conditional reciprocity but the institution of a penalty to get that assurance. But unlike Hobbes, Hume saw that promises themselves had to be "invented," along with their penalty, and unlike Hobbes he seems to think that this need for penalty is special to promises. We need to keep the threatened *penalty*, withdrawal of trust from individual promise-breakers, distinct from the equally important foreseeable danger that promise-breaking brings, namely collapse of the climate of trust, as promise-breaking spreads by imitation. The interests everyone has in "the faithful fulfilling of engagement" are interests in three distinguishable connected policies.

(a) In principle willingness to accept the mere word of another, unless that one is known to be a promise-breaker. (Of course whether or not one actually accepts a promise will depend not just on one's confidence in the promisor, but in whether one wants what that one offers.)

(b) Providing an interested motive for all promise-givers to keep their promises, by participating in the practice of making a public record of a person's performances, letting each have a reputation that can be ruined by failure to keep promises.

(c) Being faithful to one's own word, as long as others can be expected to do so, and giving weight to the interest one now has in maintaining one's status as a trustworthy person. (This interest is among those Hume later describes as real but "remote" ones, which in some conditions are outbalanced by the more immediate advantages of "violations of equity"(T. 535).

One might perhaps think that the element of community-levied penalty for disregard of obligations is not a special element in promise but is involved in all convention-based obligations, even if one does not agree with Hobbes in thinking it a necessary backing for every moral requirement. Will we not communicate to our fellows our knowledge that Jones is a thief, as well as that Jones is not a man of his word? Surely we will, and surely the threat of withdrawal of trust provides some motive for refraining from stealing. In Hume's account of acceptance of the convention of property, and of transfer by consent, there is no mention at all of penalty, nor any reliance on the existence of it to motivate the convenors to conform to the convention. Their self-interested reason for conforming is not fear of penalty, but the "infinite advantages" of the whole "system of actions" whereby stability of possessions is achieved. When Hume considers how "a man may impoverish himself by a signal instance of integrity" (T. 497), he does not cite fear of penalty as the self-interested reason why such a one should accept impoverishment—the threat is not of a contrived cost to the individual thief, but merely his share in the loss, or diminishing, of "peace and order," and of the infinite advantages that brings. When this loser by integrity balances his account, fear of reprisals need not go into the balance on the side of conformity.

This may seem just a mistake on Hume's part—why should threat of penalty be needed to motivate promise-keeping, but not needed to motivate honesty? Here we must remember that the question is not whether, in some conditions, the threat of penalty is necessary to motivate honesty—Hume grants that when societies become large, and individual holdings also large, the "artifices of politicians" (T. 523) will be needed to bolster both the motive to be honest and the motive to keep promises. The question is whether Hume is right in thinking that promises require some penalty, in all conditions, before and after magistrates, whereas property does not. Why should one think there is a real difference? Is the difference just an accident of Hume's expository fiction of a step-by-step development from a hypothetical state of nature, or is it one of the truths that fiction is intended to reveal? I think that there is reason in Hume's order of exposition, which places property before promise, and promise before government, and there is also reason in his introduction of penalty only when he gets to promise. This new element of penalty comes in along with two other new elements—the essential reliance on linguistic representation, for incurring the obligation and transferring the right, and the inclusion of particular remote and general goods within the scope of voluntary transfer. I suggest that the full utilization of language, by the promisor and his fellows, makes possible the sort of penalty Hume makes part of the interested obligation to keep a promise, and that the special reference to the future a promise involves makes the threat of that possible penalty necessary to provide self-interested motivation to keep a promise to a stranger (and strangers will be the ones Humeans reserve their promises for).

Do not the trusting always need protection from those who might exploit their trust? Do not property owners, who trust their neighbors not to steal, need protection? Is protection by the contrivance of a penalty not needed wherever persons risk something by trusting others? Hume seems to be saying "no," that protection by penalty is needed when what we trust someone to do is not merely what we trust all our fellows to do, namely to refrain for the indefinite future from stealing, or in other ways violating our property rights, but is some special individual "performance," in "some future" that he and only he owes us. In virtue of his promise, we expect more of him than of others, and we expect a definite "performance," not merely a refraining. We need protection because we are at special definite risk from a special definite person. The existence of the penalty of victim-initiated general withdrawal of trust, made possible by the ancillary linguistic invention of "reputation," gives us this protection.

What would it be to withdraw trust from a person who had proved a thief, as Hume supposes we withdraw trust from the promise-breaker? If someone steals some object while in my home and if I know this, I can try to keep this person out of it in the future, and warn others to do likewise, but I surely cannot, short of banishing or deporting the thief, remove him from all opportunity to steal again. The promise-breaker can be prevented from having a promise accepted again, but no such "suitable" penalty exists for the thief. Promise-breaking presupposes both a prior promise-giving and a prior acceptance of one's promise, but theft has no parallel presupposed prior actions on the thief's or his victim's part. We cannot deprive him of the opportunity for further thieving by the sort of relevantly specific incapacitation we inflict on the promise-breaker when we refuse to accept further promises from him.

V. Acceptance

Accepting and rejecting are actions that are of vital importance to all agreements and all agreed transfers. For Humean conventions there must be general acceptance, and a theoretical option of rejecting disadvantageous or exploitative schemes of action. His second convention, instituting transfer by consent, enabled persons to make gifts, loans, and to engage in barter. The "consent" whose force is thereby recognized is the consent of the one who gives up what was hers, so that the relevant actions seem to be requesting, consenting, and refusing. Must something be offered before anything can be refused? Once we see gift and barter as made possible by this second convention, then we will find offer and acceptance of individual transfers as well as request and consent to transfer as made possible by it. The right of refusal by someone to whom one wants to make a gift, loan, or with whom one hopes to engage in barter could in theory provide a way in which one's fellows could relevantly incapacitate those who had broken the rules of giving, loaning, and bartering, but only the barterer and the recipient of a loan, not the giver or the lender, is likely to have any motive to break these rules. It is much more likely that the costs of bad behavior as a party to gift, loan, and barter will be a drying up of offers to one, than of refusal of the offers one might make. Only with promise does the right to refuse an offer give one any significant power in dealings with one's fellows.

Of course a penalty, even a "fitting" one, can always be *contrived*, if one wants to contrive one. One might cut the hand off the thief, and some communities do just this (but usually only by means of magistrates' powers). Had Hume's initial convention of property included a right of the victims of theft to attempt such retribution as dispossession or maiming, then it is certainly not clear that either private or public interest would be furthered by such an agreement. It simply would not qualify as a scheme that would arouse "a sense of common interest," especially as the levying of the penalty would recreate the very violence and disorder the convention is supposed to end. "To ... allow every man to seize directly what he judges to be fit for him wou'd destroy society" (T. 514). Hume speaks here of acts of redistribution of property, but the claim holds good as much when the reason for my judging it fit that I have your goods or your hand is that I reasonably believe that you took my goods, as when the reason is simply that I would like your possessions. Revenge by victims simply cannot be made a part of an acceptable convention of property. But some form of revenge by victims might be made part of an acceptable convention of barter, or exchange by consent, and must be made a part of any acceptable convention whereby strangers are induced to rely on another individual's performing a specified future act that is not obligatory on other grounds. The cluster of special features Hume associates with promise—namely linguistic representation, acceptance, acknowledged threat of victim-initiated penalty for nonperformance, trust in future or delayed delivery—are an interdependent group of features. Language makes the penalty possible, as well as making possible both that exact (possibly conditional) undertaking a promise typically involves, and the sign that it is solemnly undertaken. The penalty and the solemnity and the precise spelling out of the obligation (which facilitates later determination of whether or not it has been discharged) are needed because someone, the accepter of the promise, is relying on that performance or "delayed delivery," is trusting the promisor, and so needs protection.

There are three features promissory obligations have, which make penalty both something it is safe to allow victims to inflict or initiate, and also something it is advisable to institute. First, there can be no doubt who the promise-breaker is, as there can be doubt who the thief is. With promise-breaking there can be no detection problem. Second, since promises must be accepted before any obligation arises, there can be such a thing as the power to make a promise, and threat of forfeiture of that power. Suitable incapacitation is therefore possible for promise-breakers but not, for example, for thieves. Thirdly, there is the fact that promissory obligations are each of particular content, owed by a particular person to some particular other, and are dischargeable within some limited time. This means that, especially when they are not part of a contract or mutual promise, they put the accepter of a promise in a position where some more security is needed than one needs where one relies on others "doing their part" in some open-ended scheme of reciprocal services. I can expect my neighbor to continue not blocking my driveway if I don't block his because this is a private "scheme of action" we have for an open-ended future, one in which "I foresee that he will return my service in expectation of another of the same kind" (T. 521). It is not an obligation dischargeable once and for all, like that which a promise typically creates. Just because an individual promise need *not* be part of a mutually advantageous reciprocal transfer, and because even when it is part of a mutual promise it is possible for one party, before he does his part, to have already *obtained* all the "goods" that the other is to transfer, that other *needs* the security which penalty provides.

VI. Deposits, Penalties, and Oaths

Hume studied law and practiced commerce before writing the *Treatise*, and his discussion of promise shows both an appreciation of the importance of this device for commerce and trade and also a familiarity with lawyers' inventions, both superstitious and fanciful ones and useful ones. One concept he would have encountered in his law studies was the canon law notion of *interpositio fidei*,[23] the doctrine that a promise is binding because the promisor puts his Christian faith and salvation at risk, since in promising he invites the promisee to call down damnation upon him should he fail to perform his promise. This interposition of a threat of divine punishment, cued by a human accusation, turns promise into a case not only of delayed delivery but also of simultaneous delivery of something, namely the promisor's status as a Christian in good standing, into the power of the other party, the receiver of the promise. This amounts to a pawn or deposit, recovered when the promissory obligation is fulfilled, and the threat of losing one's deposit operates as an interested motive. A penalty for nonperformance is created by this handing over, by the promisor, of his moral status. Hume's version of promise includes a secular version of *interpositio fidei*—the promisor, in promising, "subjects himself to the penalty of never being trusted again in case of failure" (T. 252). It is not merely that the community will thus react to his failure, but that he acknowledges that fact, he "subjects himself" to the penalty as he himself takes on the obligation it enforces. Were there no such penalty, why should anyone accept and rely on any promise?

This subjection to acknowledged conditional penalty, levied by some higher power, is exactly what an oath is. Hobbes says that an oath is "a form of words, added to promise, by which he that promiseth signifieth that unless he perform he renounceth the mercy of his God, or calleth to him for vengeance on himself."[24] Hobbes believes that "oath adds nothing to the obligation," but that may be because "there are no oaths but of God," and Hobbes has the sovereign's sword to make promises more than mere words, so needs no invocations of *divine* punishment. Hume, like the canon lawyers, makes oath (or secular oath-equivalent) a necessary part of promise, not a superadded extra. Of course an oath can be added to solemnize any obligation, and so once there *is* a power of penalty, it can be conditionally invoked to solemnize standing obligations as well as dischargeable ones. If Hume is right, however, it *must* be present in promises. The threat of the penalty of loss of reputation as a reliable promise-keeper, to which the promisor knowingly subjects himself, provides that "new motive" without which promises would not differ from "mere expression and consent." And without the community's practices of promise-receiving only from those not known to be promise-breakers, and of reputation-giving, the threatened penalty would be nonexistent. So Cavell's *reductio* of promising to entering an "office," and so taking an *oath* of office, turns out to be, for Hume, no *reductio* at all. To promise *is* to take an oath of performance. Hume finds a third alternative between the punitive power of God and the punitive power of magistrates—the punitive power of one's fellows, the keepers of one's reputation. The "word" without the sword is enough to bind, when words are available and used not only to undertake and to solemnize undertakings, but to communicate a person's positive or negative record as a "man of his word." Truth or fidelity as the virtue of those who are true to their word needs the assistance of truth-telling about persons, of truth in reputation-giving, and this requires the practice of keeping track of a person's moral performance. Representation in language is not only needed in the very act of promising, to specify a future act that becomes obligatory, but is also necessary to provide the motive for keeping promises. Past performance or nonperformance must be represented and conveyed in reputation for it to be possible for the giving of a solemn representation of a future action to bind a person to perform that action. J. L. Austin, arguing for the binding force of the word "I promise that . . . ," said "Accuracy and morality alike are on the side of the plain saying that *our word is our bond.*" [25] We can now say, not so plainly, that the bond is our word, given the background uses of other words to keep and destroy reputations.

Cavell claims that a promise does not bind one any more than does an expression of one's intentions. We need to see how the representation of a future action, in a Humean promise, binds in the way the representation of a future action, in a statement of intention, does not. In a community where reputation is kept track of, one may get the reputation for fickleness as well as for infidelity, for being a person whose plans and intentions change rapidly and inconsiderately. Cavell is surely correct in saying that one can commit oneself to another by saying "I intend to . . . ." Austin too lists "I intend," with "I promise," among the speech acts he calls "commissives." But the commitment of a serious avowal of intention to another is not that of a promise, as can be seen if we look at what discharges the obligation in the two cases. If having said to you that I intend to attend the meeting and support your proposal, I find it very difficult to do this, I am at moral liberty to change my mind, but I surely should let you know and apologize. Had I promised to attend, letting you know I will not attend and saying "sorry" may be better than breaking my promise without warning, but certainly does not discharge the obligation I took on. A statement of intention made seriously to another *limits* my freedom to change my mind. I need good reason, but not necessarily in the form of another overriding obligation, to change my mind, and I owe it to you to keep you informed, so that your plans, where they depended on mine, can also change. I may even owe you some help in your efforts to make compensatory changes of plan, so that a serious statement of intention attaches *costs* to any subsequent change of mind. But if I *promise* you to attend, I have no freedom to change my mind. A more important moral necessity or a physical necessity may prevent me doing what I fixedly had a mind to do, and so excuse me, or you may release me; but if I simply decide that on second thought I won't go, I must acknowledge that I fail in my obligation, whatever I do to let you know or to help you to find other support for your cause. I have no excuse, and must accept the penalty of being "branded" as unfaithful, of having others in future refuse to accept my promises. I changed my mind after renouncing my liberty to do so, after giving you both the go-ahead to count on me and the connected right to penalize me by withdrawal of trust if I change my mind. In a promise, *what* is promised is what is obligatory. Change of mind is not allowed.[26] In an intention-avowal, what is obligatory is to either fulfill the stated intention or to let the other know of one's change of mind. The obligation is explicit in a promise, not fully explicit in an intention-avowal. Of course in both various possible excuses for nonperformance of one's obligation are tacitly understood—that inability excuses, that some moral emergencies may override the obligation. But these are standard excuses in moral matters, not special to obligations originating in acts of individual commitment, so they can go without saying. Hume points out some invalidating conditions special to verbal obligation-incurring acts like promises— for example, that one did not understand what one was saying; or that the words, although spoken with understanding, were spoken in obvious jest, that is with "contrary signs." The best contrary sign is "That's not a promise." Since promises can be given without saying "I promise," we can cancel the apparent commissive force of a serious "I intend to be there" by adding "but that's not a promise."

Hume is quite clear that the conditions invalidating apparent promises do not include deceit or insincerity, even when they are detected or suspected. "Withdrawing one's intention" while apparently expressing it in words does not invalidate a promise, as long as it is accepted by the other party. One is bound by it whether or not one intended to keep it when giving it. Hume takes this as an indicator of its being contrived for social convenience, unlike those other less useful ceremonial acts like baptism, the mass, or holy orders, where the priest's "withdrawal of intention" destroys the force of the act, takes the magic out of it. The magic of a promise is carefully contrived for the convenience of a trading society, and its purpose explains its intricacies, even what Hume calls "all these contradictions" (T. 523)—that for a valid promise one must understand what one says, but need not mean what one says, that withdrawal of intention by "evident signs," but not secret withdrawal of intention, invalidates the act.

A promise, then, on this slightly reconstructed Humean account, is a convention-dependent, two-party verbal act, in which several things happen at once. The promisor expresses a serious intention to perform a particular future action that the second party wants her to perform. She makes that very action obligatory, one she is no longer free to decide not to perform. She does this by introducing the verbal representation by a special ritual act or "sign," the words "I promise," which get their force from community recognition and enforcement of the obligation thereby created, once the promise is accepted. By this act, or oath equivalent, the promisor acknowledges the other party's right and power to destroy her good standing as a promise-giver, should she fail to perform as promised. She ritually hands over her reputation to the other party, as a pawn or security, to be redeemed by her performance of her promise. There is both representation and what Anscombe calls "the giving of a sign." The latter makes obligatory what the former represents. The non-natural necessitation is done by the giving and receiving of the sign, and what is necessitated is elaborated in the representation. But the sign gets its power to bind from other acts of representation—from the public representation of a person's moral record and character, and from the general agreed intention to receive promises only from those not known to be promise-breakers. These background representations of character and conditional intentions to withdraw trust make it possible for the promisor to *have* a reputation to pawn, and for the promisee to ruin it should the promisor not perform.

The penalty for nonperformance of a promise might therefore be seen as forfeiture of one's deposit, what one gave as security. Once one has not merely the social practice of promising, and of mutual promises, but the legal institution of contract, with magistrates to enforce contract, then a failure to honor one's contractual commitments may be responded to in several ways:

(a) Forfeiture of whatever security one gave,

(b) Enforced performance according to the contract (an edict *ad factum praestandum*),

(c) Payment of damages (reliance or expectation damages),

(d) Penalty (fine, imprisonment, deportation, disablement from future contracting).

The latter three depend upon the victim's initiating some legal action, but (a) is more automatic. In promise, (a) and (d) are fused, since the deposit forfeited is one's good name as a promise-keeper, and one's ability to give promises in future. This disablement is the form penalty takes, before there are magistrates, and in some cases after there are magistrates. Because of the special nature of *what* is "deposited" in a promise, forfeiture of deposit is also social disablement. No prelegal forerunners of enforced performance or of damages are present, unless the promise included a penalty clause that the promisor observes in order to retain reputation, to recover deposit.

VII. Promises and Exchanges

This way of looking at promise as essentially involving not merely the representation and simultaneous creation of an obligation, but also subjecting oneself to a penalty that the victim can initiate, makes the apparent one-way transfer of rights to what is to be delivered later into a case of two-way transfer of something, and of immediate delivery of something, namely power to harm. The promisor delivers her good name into the power of the promisee, the promisee receives it. The promisee puts the success of his future plans into the power of the promisor, he gives her his trust. There is an immediate exchange of powers to harm, but not of the same sort of power to the same sort of harm. The promisor gives her "word," and that word both spells out her obligation and subjects her to a penalty made possible by the power of words the other party has, the power to accuse, to brand, to disable. But all these social powers are dependent on the nonpromissory "agreement," or as Cavell might call it, "commitment," of the community to cooperate in giving persons "repute" and in refusing to accept promises from those with a bad repute in this respect.

Atyiah says[27] that "gratuitous" unilateral promises do not bind at all, especially if not relied on. The two-way voluntary transfer is a natural place to start when thinking about what makes a transaction between persons just, and the simplest case is a simultaneous immediate transfer. There are no outstanding obligations if you and I swap, say, pens, each getting what we want and giving what the other wants. Commitments and obligations arise, or seem to arise, only when there is *delay* in delivery, or when only one party receives something (or one receives more than the other). "Artifices" are needed to make possible transfers *other* than simultaneous immediate two-way transfer, and on Hume's account, which *does* make unilateral promises binding, this is done by inventing a "fiction" of immediate delivery when there is not immediate delivery, a fiction of simultaneous transfer when there is not simultaneous transfer, and a fiction of receiving something when one party does not receive anything, or anything of the same sort. The handshake, the mutual giving and receiving of hands, symbolizes all these fictions. For them to be useful fictions they must be backed by socially conferred powers, and recognized obligations. The obligations "tie," as it were, the fictions to the real thing; they enable cooperative transfers to stretch to include the nonsimultaneous transfers, the delayed delivery, and the one-sided delivery. Hume derides the "lawyer's superstitions" which demand immediate delivery of some physical token, and which insist on some *causa* or "consideration" to make a deal seem to be two-way immediate transfer, but his account of the obligations of promises retains a "spiritualized" version of what the lawyers wanted. "Words" are given to effect immediate delivery, powers are exchanged to make a promise a mutual transfer. But Hume shows how the words "I promise" can do their magic, what makes these exchanged powers real powers.

He locates the convention of promise-receiving within a family of other obligation-generating conventions or agreed forms of life. He distinguishes the cooperation through contrived vulnerability of promisor and promisee from the more generous cooperative practices of friends and loved intimates, who need no conventions to help them become mutually trusting and so mutually vulnerable, who as he says "do services" without "any prospect of advantage," and "make return in the same manner, without any view but that of recompensing past services" (T. 521). The friends' and lovers' reciprocity is not a penalty-backed exchange of definitely specified future-including services, but a natural response to love and kindness. It creates its own vulnerabilities, but Hume neither confuses them with those of the parties to a promise nor does he confuse the latter contrived trust and concomitant vulnerability with other contrived dependencies on others, those produced by the conventions of property, consent, and authority. He showed how, in promise, our word is our bond—how there we use the powers language gives us to represent the future, the general, the conditional, to keep and make known an individual's moral record, to explicitly commit ourselves, subject ourselves, denounce others. This enables him, I think, to account for all the features of promissory obligations, both those shared with other obligations and those peculiar to promises. He can agree with Cavell[28] that we should not construe all ties between persons on the model of promise, let alone on the model of bargain. Some personal ties are natural, and depend upon no general rules nor any contrived penalties. Neither all the natural ties nor all the contrived ones are voluntarily assumed or taken on by those who are tied, and not all the voluntary assumed ones are penalty-backed, nor all the penalty-backed ones contracts or bargains. Hume can agree with Anscombe that the non-natural necessity to keep one's promise is like the non-natural necessity to obey rules, such as property rules or rules of a language, but he can show how in this special case of promise language must *both* do what other rituals might do, change the moral situation, and *also* do what only language can do, represent the precise conditions under which the ritually invoked penalty will be avoided, if promises are to play their special and limited role. Hume shows us what sort of beast promise is by putting it in its natural habitat—trust-requiring cooperation, on a limited matter, within a limited time, between particular strangers, who need no greater cooperation with each other, and need the presence of penalty to make possible even such limited trust.

Such individual binding agreements occur not only when labor is contracted for harvests, before magistrates are invented, but in commerce, after their invention. Hume's year in Bristol must have made clear to him both the extent to which commerce depends upon the convenient contrivance of legal contract, and also how frequent breach of contract is in that sphere, breach which is *not* always followed by exclusion of the contract-breaker from the community of traders. For, as Atiyah has emphasized, as long as one collects enough reliance damages when the other party breaks his contract with one, one may have no occasion to shun further equally profitable deals with that contract-breaker. Does this mean that the preceding account makes no sense of the very commercial activities in which promise and contract are such convenient contrivances that without them the activity would be scarcely possible? Atiyah's charge that philosophers in their treatment of promising have shown more belief in the force of "bare" promises than does English law appears to apply to Hume, as I have understood him. Hume must have become familiar with English law of contract, as it was in the eighteenth century while he was in Bristol, if he had not earlier become familiar with it as a law student in Edinburgh. That he was reacting to the natural law tradition in his account of all the artifices is quite obvious, and I have claimed that he puts to his own secular uses the canon law concept of *interpositio fidei*. But the influence of the English common law must also be presumed present, given Hume's legal studies and apprenticeship in commerce. Atiyah has helpfully traced the changes that the concept of contract underwent and Hume lived during one of the periods of fairly dramatic change. According to Atiyah, before 1600 the common law treated as legally binding only such promises as were given in return for a "consideration," and only such as had in fact been relied upon. But by 1800 "the common lawyers had largely come round to the modern viewpoint that promises *per se* are morally binding." By "modern," Atiyah here seems to mean the "classic," not the contemporary lawyer's view. Atiyah sees the later legal development, in the nineteenth and twentieth century, as a return to the earlier view. Hume lived and wrote after the rise and before the fall of freedom of contract, and so one must expect in his account of promising to find "the modern viewpoint that promises *per se* are morally binding" that concept which, if Atiyah is right, contemporary philosophers but not contemporary lawyers still hold. And, if the preceding interpretation is right, we do indeed find that in Hume. Does this mean that Hume's account cannot explain the fact that sometimes a tradesman accepts a promise that he will happily see not performed, as long as he collects enough in damages? Is he pleased at the "immorality" of the contract-breaker, from which he may reap good profits? There is no need at all for

Hume to have to say this about the sort of commercial exploitation of the device of promise with which it is reasonable to suppose him familiar. The account he gives us in the *Treatise* is not an account of what becomes of promise once there are magistrates, but of what it can be without them. Once the full panoply of the law is there, everything is changed by its presence. Only when there are magistrates can damages be assessed or awarded, so contract-making with an eye to the other party's expected contract-breaking, followed by one's own receipt of reliance damages, is a form of life made possible by Hume's fourth artifice, the invention of magistrates who declare and administer the rules, as much as by his third artifice, promise.

What is good about his account, however, is that it does contain the germs of all these later developments, and of the various possibilities that Atiyah sees realized at different times in the history of the English common law's attitude to promise and contract. A promise is given in return for receipt of something, namely trust, which the promisor is presumed to want, so there is an element of "consideration." The promisor receives this and in return she gives her word, thereby giving the promisee both a right to future goods or services, and putting her reputation in the promisee's safekeeping, giving him power to initiate the penalty of harm to reputation resulting in a general refusal to accept her promises, should the promise not be performed. The promisee relies on the promise being performed, if he really gives his trust. He may, if he is as scheming as some later tradesmen, rely not on the main performance but on the performance of a penalty clause or even on his power to blackball the promisor when she fails to perform. He cannot rely on performance-or-damages, before there are magistrates, but he may rely on performance-or-ruin of the nonperformer's chances of trading again. Since this penalty, of "never being trusted again in case of failure," is a very drastic one, which it may not always suit the interests of the promisee to inflict—he may after all *need* to make deals again with the promise-breaker—it is to be expected that a community of wise Humeans will go on, once they invent magistrates, to include, among their powers, power to substitute a less drastic and more generally beneficial contrived consequence of nonperformance, namely monetary damages. The law of contract, unlike the natural artifice of promise, enables us to cooperate with those who are known to be untrustworthy, known *not* to be "men of their word." Hume's account is of the convention of promise, not of the legal institution of contract, but the account he gives us shows how the latter could develop from the former, as well as making it understandable that promise survives as a convention alongside legal contract. After all, there are spheres of life where we do not want to cooperate with the untrustworthy. Promise helps us cooperate with strangers, on a limited basis, and the penalty it incorporates helps us limit that cooperation to strangers not known to be untrustworthy in the relevant respects.

Like Atiyah's account, Hume's is a historical account of how a certain contrivance comes to be invented and used because of its usefulness. Promise takes varying forms in different societies, and has changed in ours. But I think we nonlawyers and nonbusinesswomen do still, sometimes, give and accept promises that are still recognizably Humean.[29] To be recognizably Humean a promise must not be the golden road to commitment, must not be as basic as contractarians must make it, but must be what we can resort to for some of our dealings with strangers, and it must differ from a serious statement of intention. It need have no more "sanctity," to use Atiyah's phrase, than any other useful artifice. But to see it as the artifice it is we need to see the traces in it of the older sanctity of oath, as well as of the eternal apparent sanctity of mutually profitable exchange. Better, I think, than any more recent account, Hume's helps us put promises in their proper and properly restricted place.

NOTES

1. David Hume, *A Treatise of Human Nature*, (ed. L. A. Selby-Bigge and P. H. Nidditch, (Oxford: Clarendon Press, 1978), bk. 3, pt. 2, secs. 4, 5, and 8. My references to Hume are to pages in *A Treatise of Human Nature* (T) and in *Enquiries* (E), both edited by Selby-Bigge and Nidditch.

2. J. L. Austin, *How to Do Things with Words* (Cambridge, Mass.: Harvard University Press, 1975).

3. J. R. Searle, "How to Derive an 'Ought' from an 'Is'," *Philosophical Review* 73 (1964), and *Speech Acts* (Cambridge, Eng.: Cambridge University 1969), ch. 8.

4. G. E. M. Anscombe, "Rules, Rights and Promises," in *Midwest Studies in Philosophy,* vol. 3, *Studies in Ethical Theory*, (Minneapolis: University of Minnesota Press, 1980).

5. Stanley Cavell, *The Claim of Reason* (Oxford: Clarendon Press, 1979), ch. 9, and also chs. 5 and 11.

6. Ibid., p. 298.

7. P. S. Atiyah, *Promises, Morals and the Law*, (Oxford: Clarendon Press, 1981).

8. Ibid., p. 7.

9. Ibid., p. 3. Atiyah's final account of a promise as admission, a form of consent that there is already an agreement to reciprocal transfer, is given later, in ch. 7.

10. See David Gauthier, "David Hume, Contractarian," *Philosophical Review* 88 (1979): 3–38, for a persuasive account of Hume's nonutilitarianism. (I do not, however, think that Gauthier succeeds in showing that Hume in his account of obligation is a contractarian. Not all enlightened egoists who believe in cooperation are contractarians.)

11. I discuss the way intention-formation does this in "Mixing Memory and Desire," and also in "The Intentionality of Intentions," *Review of Metaphysics* 30, no. 3 (1977): 389–414.

12. Cavell, *Claim of Reason*, p. 297.

13. Ibid., p. 298.

14. Ibid., p. 307.

15. Anscombe, "Rules, Rights and Promises," p. 318.

16. Ibid., p. 319.

17. Anscombe, "Rules, Rights and Promises," p. 318.

18. Ibid., p. 322.p

19. A "natural obligation" at T. 498 is one that is not yet a moral obligation, since not yet approved or disapproved by the moral sentiment. But it *is* one done from a motive that is "not naturally intelligible," since we must refer to an artifice or convention, as well as natural self-interest, to spell out that premoral motive. Hume had warned us, at T. 474–75, that no word is more ambiguous and equivocal than "nature," and his own usage in what follows displays this ambiguity. Although he officially opposed "natural" to "artificial," he also opposes it both to "moral" and to "civil." "Natural motives" and the "naturally intelligible" are what involves no necessary references to any artifice. "Natural obligations" at T. 498 are those which involve no necessary reference to the deliverances of the moral sentiment, but may refer to artifice. "Laws of nature" are rules of pregovernment artifices, contrasting with laws. But Hume seems to speak not merely ambiguously but equivocally when he says "where an action is not requir'd by any natural passion, it cannot be requir'd by any natural obligation" (T. 518, repeated at T. 523). Natural obligations here seem to exclude artifice-dependent ones, whereas at T. 498 they included them. As for the *moral* component in promises, Hume also says some puzzling things. At T. 516 he says "If we thought that promises had no moral obligation we shou'd never feel any obligation to observe them." This seems to contradict both his later spelling out of the "new" motive that subjection to threat of penalty brings, and also his statement at T. 523 that "Afterwards a sentiment of morality concurs with interest, and becomes a new obligation on mankind. This sentiment of morality, in the performance of promises, arises from the same principles as that in the abstinence from the property of others." It is hard to save all these textual phenomena, but I think that the interpretation I am offering involves minimal reconstruction.

20. Like Atiyah (see n. 9) Hume sees consent as more "basic" than promise. Unlike Atiyah, he does not reduce promise to a form of consent. Atiyah sees it as irrevocable consent to the existence of some other obligation owed by the promisor (see Atiyah, *Promises*, p. 184). The explicit promise has merely an evidentiary function—it is an irrevocable and conclusive admission that there is an obligation. "A promise is an admission concerning the existence and extent of other obligations which either pre-exist the making of a promise, or which anyway would arise before, or at the same time as, the promise becomes obligatory" (ibid., p. 193). This view seems to conflate consenting into *assenting* to a *fait accompli*, and Hume's question of what obligation it is to which our will supposedly assents in a promise arises. Atiyah has an answer to that—namely a whole range of obligations arising out of receipt of benefits and a basic moral requirement of reciprocity, but he has to strain hard to find one of these prior obligations in every case of an apparently binding promise; and he has to dismiss some gratuitous unilateral promises as "senseless act(s), not capable in a rational world of creating an obligation at all" (ibid., p. 214). Hume remarked that, on the view he rejects, in which the assent of the will is what binds in a promise, this will "must be express'd by words or signs, in order to impose a tye on any man. The expression being once brought in as subservient to the will, soon becomes the principal part of the promise ... " (T. 523). On Atiyah's view, the subservient *evidentiary* function of the representation of an obligation in a promise becomes the principal part of a promise.

21. I think that Hume's treatment of the "fiction" of causal and of logical necessity (T. 166) in bk. 1 should be linked to his account of the distinctive sort of "inflexibility" (T. 531–33) that the social artifices introduce into morality.

22. Nietzsche discusses promising in the second part of the *Genealogy of Morals*. See the quotation with which I begin in "Mind and Change of Mind."

23. My information about this and other facts about Scottish law comes from James Dalymple, Viscount of Stair, *The Institution of the Laws of Scotland*, ed. David M. Walker (New Haven: Yale University Press, 1981), and from Richard Keith and George Clark, *A Guide to Scots Law* (London: Johnson and Bacon, 1978).

24. Hobbes, *Leviathan*, ch. 14.

25. Austin, *How to Do Things with Words*, p. 10.

26. I discuss change of mind, and treat promise as a renunciation of the right to change one's mind, in "Mind and Change of Mind."

27. See Atiyah, *Promises*, pp. 212ff.

28. Cavell, *Claim of Reason*, p. 299, says that utilitarian accounts of promising (such as that offered by John Rawls in "Two Concepts of Rules," *Philosophical Review* 64, 1955, pp. 3–32) not only make commitments more like explicit promises than they are but make promises more like legal contracts than they are, adding that the central idea underlying the English law of contract is that of a bargain.

29. Charlies Fried, in *Contract as Promise* (Cambridge, Mass.: Harvard University Press, 1981), accepts much of Hume's account of what a promise is, but differs from Hume on why it binds. Fried's account of that appeals to "basic Kantian principles of respect and trust" (p. 17). As his title indicates, Fried holds that the law of contracts is rooted in promise.

11

Theory and Reflective Practices

The usual assumption, when one speaks of "applied ethics," is that there is something called moral theory, and that such a theory can be applied to give guidance in concrete human situations, perhaps with the help of a body of professionals, heirs to the casuists, whose job it is to show how a given moral theory applies to a case. I want to challenge the value of that assumption, and, very sketchily, to suggest an alternative idea of how we can, by taking thought, act more wisely than we might otherwise have done.

The casuists who applied Christian moral teaching to concrete, sometimes to novel, human situations, were a bit like judges who, given an accepted body of statute law and precedents, applied these to the case before them to get a decision on what should be done. What they applied was not a theory but a set of commandments. Philosophers may try to turn such a set of laws into an "ethical theory" by supplying unifying principles or background assumptions, but those who gave the guidance did not see themselves as drawing out practical guidance from a theory.

In any case, whether what the casuists had was a body of law or a moral theory, they had only one such body or theory. The obvious trouble with our contemporary attempts to use moral theory to guide action is the lack of agreement on which theory we are to apply. The standard undergraduate course in, say, medical ethics, or business ethics, acquaints the student with a variety of theories, and shows the difference in the guidance they give. We, in effect, give courses in comparative ethical theory, and like courses in comparative religion, their usual effect in the student is loss of faith in *any* of the alternatives presented. We produce relativists and

Read at Applied Ethics Conference at Rutgers, October 1980, organized by Fadlou Shehadi and David Rosenthal.

moral skeptics, persons who have been convinced by our teaching that whatever they do in some difficult situation, some moral theory will condone it, another will condemn it. The usual, and the sensible, reaction to this confrontation with a variety of conflicting theories, all apparently having some plausibility and respectable credentials, is to turn to a guide that speaks more univocally, to turn from morality to self-interest, or mere convenience. In what conceivable way have we helped, say, hospital administrators make a difficult decision if we have given them, in their course on medical ethics, the awareness that a contractarian would do x, a believer in natural rights would do y, and a utilitarian would do z? What guidance is that?

Most of us do not aim to produce moral skeptics when we teach introductory ethics. But that is what we do, with most of our students, when we teach moral theories and their different applications to cases. What we aim to do is increase reflective awareness of what is at stake in difficult decisions, to produce more thoughtful, better informed, and presumably wiser people. The best reason to believe that there is something amiss with the whole procedure is that it is defeating its own ends. In attempting to increase moral reflectiveness we may be destroying what conscience there once was in those we teach.

Such moral convictions as people have before studying moral philosophy were not acquired by self-conscious acceptance of a theory. Most parents lack the intellectualist's compulsion to transform their moral beliefs into theories. What they pass on to their children may be a few slogans or principles or commandments, but mainly they impart moral constraints by example and by reaction to behavior, not by handing on explicit verbal codes of general rules, let alone moral theories. Now if philosophers choose to see implicit rules wherever there is a tradition and a teachable practice, and implicit systems or theories wherever there are general rules, that is their hang-up (and one that a reading of the *Brown Book* might cure). It is a mere Kantian dogma that behind every moral intuition lies a universal rule, behind every set of rules a single stateable principle or systems of principles.

In a pluralistic society like this one there is no escaping the fact that there are a plurality of moral traditions, that what people learn at their parents' knees varies from one ethnic or religious group to another. This substantive moral disagreement is a fact that no reforms in the teaching of introductory ethics will conjure away. Catholic hospitals will make different decisions from non-Catholic hospitals on many cases, whatever we philosophers do in our classes. What I am deploring is not the variety of moral traditions, and the disagreement that brings when these traditions coexist in one nation. I am deploring the additional and unnecessary

variety and conflict produced by insisting on turning every moral judgment into an instance of a law or principle that has its niche in a moral
theory. The array of moral theories that philosophers have produced does
not match the array of working moral traditions in this society, or in the
world at large. It is not as if a rights theory fits the Catholic tradition, a
contract theory the Protestant, intuitionism the Moslems, utilitarianism
the atheist residue. Cultural historians may discern some genetic linkages
between ethical and metaethical theories and cultural moral forces, but
the moral philosopher who is, say, a contractarian, does not see him or
herself, when putting the theory to a class of students from all sorts of
backgrounds, as either trying to convert some of them from Catholicism,
or as saying "this view will suit those of you who come from a Protestant
background." The result of the teaching of moral theories is that, in
addition to the variety of cultural traditions initially there, we add a
variety of theories. So we might expect to end up with Catholic utilitarians, Catholic contractarians, Catholic intuitionists; Protestant variants of
all of these; atheist variants of all of these. In fact the alternatives tend to
cancel one another out, leaving a moral vacuum.

All intelligent persons—aware that the tradition in which they have
been reared is one of several, that it is the lottery of nature-cum-culture
that has made one Catholic, another Muslin; made one believe that eating
pork is unclean and wrong, the other believe only that eating pork on
Fridays is wrong; one believe that adulterers should be stoned, the other
that adultery is preferable to divorce—must entertain some doubts about
the point and validity of the constraints they have been trained to observe.
They come to us, into our introductory ethics classes, with some questions
in their minds about the rationale for their moral beliefs. We offer them
a variety of rationales, and a correspondent variety of decision procedures, no one of which may justify all their pre-philosophy-course moral
beliefs. By then they are thoroughly confused. To the variety of cultural
traditions we have added, crosscutting that, a variety of "rational" procedures, each backed by a theory. A better recipe for moral cynicism could
scarcely be deliberately devised.

Before suggesting what we might do which would be less counterproductive, I want to raise some questions about the very idea of a moral
theory. Even if we had no problem of choosing between theories, even if
only one were available at a time, or if one were by common consent
superior to its competitors (which is decidedly not the case at present),
there would still be room for questioning the point in having a moral
theory at all. A theory, in its traditional and oldest sense, is an outcome
of contemplation of some world or independently existing reality, a way
of representing what it is, how it works, how its various different parts are

connected, how its different aspects hang together. The paradigm object of contemplation in traditional theory was God, and derivatively the world seen as the creation of God, an expression of the divine nature. In that nature different attributes flowed or emanated from a center, a point of unification. It is quite understandable that the idea of a scientific system, in which different laws hang together in interdependence, with less fundamental laws hierarchically dependent on higher laws, was the natural model for those who contemplated the universe as heirs or successors to those who saw it as the expression of its creator's nature, a world in which there was the maximum of order along with the greatest plenitude or variety of manifestations of that order. This theological paradigm of *theoria* has some plausibility where the task is to understand an already existent reality, a system of nature; to predict its new manifestations; to codify its features in a succinct, coherent way; to concentrate its essence into a basic formula or name, a secular version of Yahweh, that which is what it is. But normative moral "theory" does not describe an existent world, at best it guides the conduct of one species of living things within that world, a species a little prone to hubris and megalomania, to treating their own guidelines as world blueprints, to confusing the attempted articulation of their taboos with the description of a contemplated world.

Some moralists *have* sketched utopias, written as if they have contemplated a ideal society which they then describe for us—its laws, its unifying structure, its unity in variety. But Plato's *Republic*, or More's *Utopia*, or Rawls' well-ordered, just society with full compliance, do not guide us in the actual world. The real moral guidance comes when we are told not how the law of an ideal community would apply to a concrete case in that ideal world, but when we are told that we should therefore do, in this nonideal world. The description or contemplation of an imagined utopia is an escape from, not a solution to, the problems of this world.

Actual moral traditions—the Christian, the Buddhist, or the Bantu ethos—for all their limitations, do address directly the question of what to do now, and do not retreat into accounts of what one should do in hypothetical conditions such as just institutions or full compliance by others to ideal moral constraints. Indeed Christian attempts to describe heaven, a world in which there are only conformist saints, typically yield very thin accounts, and do not get much beyond talk of singing in harmony. Full compliance by one's fellows may transform morality into music, rather than inform us what is basic to morality. Detailed advice for here and now may imply nothing about what a heaven would be like, and descriptions of ideal societies imply nothing about how to act in this society. Even if one derives the vague injunction to act so as to change the actual society in the direction of the ideal one, one is still left with all the hard questions concerning how one is to do it—by revolution, by gradual qualitative improvement, by making things so intolerable that everyone will opt for drastic change? Is one to sacrifice only oneself for one's cause, or drag others with one? Is one to lie, cheat, and kill so that there can be a society without liars, cheats, or killers? Knowing what sort of society a utilitarian or a contractarian would deem satisfactory tells us nothing about our or their duty now, in this society. Richard Brandt takes the brave but implausible Kantian line that "in a situation like the present in which the 'ideal' moral code is not accepted . . . a person is nevertheless morally obligated to do what would be required by the rules of a rationally supported code for his society."[1] But John Rawls, and most others, suppose that there is no simple step from knowing what would be right in some ideal world to knowing what should be done here and now. For Rawls one must know that one's society, although not perfect, is well ordered in its basic institutional structure before his principles of justice can guide behavior within it.[2] But although Rawls believes that this society is thus well ordered, many do not, and I wonder whether the most basic structure of our society, that governing relations between parents and between parents and children can be well ordered by principles of justice, when a theorist like Rawls can so uncritically suppose that a family has a "head" who can articulate its interests.[3] I mention Rawls and Brandt at this point as typical moral theorists, although their approaches are very different, and I find much to admire and accept in Rawls' theory, especially in his account of the sense of justice, and of social union and the unity of good. My criticisms of Rawls concern mainly the first two parts of his *A Theory of Justice*, the codification of the principles of justice by working out the content of a hypothetical agreement between hypothetical beings in unreal circumstances.

My complaints about Brandt's theory are different—he has actual people in real conditions, and has them formulating moral codes that take account of the likelihood of compliance and the cost of having codes at all. Some of the criticisms of the codification business that I shall make do not apply to Brandt, since he keeps his eye on the real world in selecting his code. But the general criticism I am making, that philosophers' codifications of the moral law increase rather than decrease moral disagreement and conflict, does apply to Brandt. Although a moral code has as its supposed *point* the coordination and fair adjustment of different persons' concerns, Brandt advocates that each person form an ideal code for the real conditions and act on that, regardless of the lack of coordination and unpredictability and unreliability which would result. One may know the chosen moral codes of those closest to one, and so allow for their idiosyncrasies in dealings with such persons, but I cannot possibly know where

I am with the mailman, the shopkeeper, the bus driver, or my new employer, if each has her own operative code. To avoid the conflict of a state of nature, moral theorists in effect give us the basis for a recurrence of the war of all against all within society, when each person has her own version of the rules by which the fight is conducted. A battle of rival umpires and adjudicators replaces the Hobbesian state of nature. Even if the battle is now more civilized, because within legal bounds, it is just as futile. With or without hypothetical contracts and imagined full compliance, such ideal codes, if produced by single persons or even single heads of families, will decrease, not increase, coordination between persons. The search for an ideal fair mode of cooperation and coordination, if pursued by independent thinkers, can make cooperation more difficult and unlikely, and can decrease the level of that minimal fairness which consists in having fair warning of what response another will make. Brandt gives as an example of unilateral compliance to an ideal moral code, the keeping of a promise in circumstances of such difficulty that conventional morality would have excused nonobservance.[4] But this is to cheat a bit. Suppose it went the other way, as with a utilitarian it is more likely to—suppose that the ideal code observer feels morally free to break promises in a wider range of circumstances than do I, to whom the promise was made. Must I ask each person to recite his particular moral code before ever relying on him? It would be simpler never to accept a promise or an agreement, but to insist on contract, where the small print and the law of contract ensure *standard* conditions of validity. If everyone has his own moral code for dealings with others, soon no one will have any morality, all will rely entirely upon the criminal law and the law of contract and torts. Private moral codes, like private languages and private legal systems, fail the first principle of practical reason, that she who wills the end should not will the means that destroy that end.

Most moral theorists who outline and defend norms which are valid in conditions of full compliance, which can be willed to be universally followed in some system of moral nature, give some recognition to the need for supplementary accounts of what norms hold good in more realistic conditions, and give some promisory notes about working back from the world they have presented in their theory to the actual world. Maybe such promises can be kept, but only when they have been kept will we know just how much guidance the full-compliance world provided in the journey away from it, back to the actual situation in which we act. Suppose we imagine a simplified ideal world in which there is full compliance to the norm of not inflicting bodily injury on others, and so there is no question of compliance to norms concerning responses to injurers or their victims, since by hypothesis there are none. This world represents (by depicting ideal compliance to) one norm we might think is valid (with qualifications) in this world. But this world cannot *similarly* (that is, by full compliance) represent any norms concerning the punishment of offenders or aid to their victims, or other responses to noncompliance to this one norm. For that we must add additional worlds to the world of the noninjurers—the world of the perfect punishers, the world of the good Samaritans, or the world in which aggression and malice and other drives to injure others are"treated" in some way, in which there are norms for the rehabilitation or reforming of the injurers, or for seeing to it that the next generation has such drives diverted into harmless channels. Are we any closer to this world, or to representing all the injury-related norms valid in it? We have represented no norm telling us how to respond to the presence of bad punishers or bad Samaritans, or unsuccessful reformers of aggression, no norm telling us what to do in situations of imperfect compliance to what we could call the responsive norms. So we can imagine another world in which all the norms so far represented by perfect compliance in one of our earlier worlds are now imperfectly complied with, but this time we represent some norm concerning response to faulty *responsive* action, to the presence of corrupt police, unjust judges, brutal prison officials, bad Samaritans, ineffective psychiatrists, poor parents. This norm might be one demanding a corrective response to these evils, or one permitting conscientious disobedience to all bad authorities, or demanding acceptance and forgiveness. We add the Platonic world of perfect responders to imperfect responders to the worlds we already had. In principle, we could continue indefinitely. But would we by this procedure be representing norms accepted in this world? Do we have a moral norm specifically covering responses, individual or collective, to those who are, say, unforgiving to bad Samaritans? Do we have a moral norm dealing specifically with hypocritical conscientious disobedience? Our hierarchy of possible worlds quite quickly loses contact with the norms it was to represent. It might represent legal norms, which, because of their deliberate formulation and making, are likely to have a structure that "fits" the sort of structure which modal logicians, moral theorizers, and intellectuals generally find graspable and eminently representable. In the case of legal norms (leaving common law aside), representation and promulgation must accompany the demand for conformity, so human tastes in representation do dictate the structure of the law. A significant fact about moral conscience is that its deliverances need not come in verbal form, that it is often a difficult task to articulate what it is we are certain is wrong in an action, let alone what universal rule we think it breaks. In moral philosophy courses we insist that students make their moral intuitions articulate, that they represent them and "defend" them by subsuming them under some universal rule that coheres in some system, and we make them feel that they must have been muddled if their moral intuitions are inarticulate or resist tidy codifications. But it may be we the intellectualizers who are muddled, not those whose consciences we insist on tidying up. It is as if we are claiming that if you can't wear your heart on your sleeve then you haven't really got a heart (or perhaps that *all* you have is a heart, unaccompanied by a mind). In law it makes eminent sense to insist that, unless it is verbally represented and promulgated, it is no law. But it also makes good sense to have courts of equity to deal with grievances that cannot be represented as breaches of law. There is no reason to believe that actual moralities mimic legal systems in the way they control or regulate action, and it is only a dogma that we would improve actual moralities by making them mimic legal systems.

Moral theorizers usually appeal to clear moral intuitions as confirmers of their theory, which is presented as a systematization of and endorsement of such intuitions, and as a way of deciding cases in which no clear intuition was forthcoming, a way of inducing intuitions in a wider range of areas. I do not want to assert dogmatically that this cannot be done, merely to challenge the assumption that it must be possible, and that any person whose moral intuitions are not so systematized, and may not even be coherently statable in the theorist's preferred terminology, has an inferior moral capacity. That theorizers appeal to intuitions at all is a sign that they do recognize some pretheoretical faculty, call it conscience, as a touchstone for their theory, that with which it must maintain "reflective equilibrium," but such a conscience is expected to deliver its judgments in the right form of words, in some ready-made representation. If all moral training took a verbal form (as some, surely, must), it might be reasonable to expect that anyone who finds some action wrong must be able to say "It's a lie," "It's cheating," or "It's stealing," since in learning to avoid such behavior, that person learned to avoid precisely the behavior which would count as "lying," "cheating," "stealing." Some moral training is of this form, but surely some is not. A parent has not failed to give a child some sense of right and wrong simply because neither parent nor child can tell us what rules the child has been taught to obey, nor even which virtues the child has been encouraged to cultivate.

This lengthy insistence of mine on the dogmatic character of the assumption that a genuine morality must be codifiable, and in particular the assumption that it will, like a Kantian world or a legal system, be codifiable in terms of general rules, with hierarchies of the sort we can design and tidily represent, was prompted by my parody version of what happens when we try to represent moral demands by imagining worlds in which there is strict compliance to them. We can get an ordered series of worlds if norms are classifiable into different levels, with the higher levels containing norms for response to noncompliance to lower-level norms. The order we get, however, is not an order of approximation to this world, since here the likelihood of immoral officials seems if anything higher than the likelihood of immoral nonofficials. All these strict-compliance worlds are about equally far from this world, and it is dubious if the norms represented really are our moral norms. I suggested earlier that they might be expected to represent legal norms, but even there one would need to complicate the picture a lot to get the full variety of ways in which one law may be a response to some imperfection in another law's operation. We have laws not only for dealing with noncompliance, but for dealing with uncertainty, conflict, and immorality in laws, regulating our response to needless laws, to the need for some law in a new area, to faulty administrative machinery or procedures, to corrupt officials. In each of these dimensions of imperfection we can in principle go, as before, to higher and higher levels—responses to uncertain laws about the removal of uncertainties and other imperfections, responses to conflict in the laws concerning the settlement of conflict and concerning other imperfections, and so on. Whether we actually need to go to such higher levels to represent our own legal norms is not so clear. We may soon reach a ceiling, a supreme court of ombudsman whose job it is to respond to all imperfections, including imperfect supreme court or complaints about the ombudsman. Actual rules don't exhibit as many levels as logicians' possibilities —because, as Hume said, the normal human mind soon loses track. We need a legal order in which at least some of us can understand our way around.

Do all these dimensions of imperfection diverge from one perfect world, that in which there is full compliance to needed, clear, nonconflicting, perfectly administered, morally acceptable rules, none of which need regulate our response to noncompliance, to uncertainty, to conflict of laws, to imperfect administrative machinery, to immoral or unnecessary laws? To say "yes" is, I believe, to express faith in the unity of justice. If that faith is reasonable, one might get insight into the structure of a legal order by contemplating a possible world, ideal in respect to compliance, definiteness, coherence, etc., and moving out from there in different directions to consider all possible deteriorations from this, in all the listed respects. One might even find a sketch of the actual world among those possibilities, so find a path from it to the "ideal" world. To call that world one with an ideal legal order, however, would be very strange, since it seems to have no legal order at all, if it has and needs no police, no courts, no appeal and adjudication procedures. To *add* idle police, judges, etc., to the perfect world is to destroy its perfection by adding wasteful public expense. If in that world there is no noncompliance, any norms specifying the duties of these needless officials will be unnecessary and so bad norms. The perfect world cannot contain them, any more than a perfect moral code contains rules whose inculcation is an unnecessary cost. Every accepted prohibition has its cost, either in frustration or in guilt, and in their unlovely offspring.

Here it might be objected that imagining full compliance to a contemplated norm is a preliminary test of the *fairness* of that norm, not the final test deciding its adoption. It will not matter, then, that we cannot imagine simultaneously full compliance to two fair norms, one forbidding assault, another specifying proper punishment of assaulters. But to imagine full compliance to any rule we must imagine *some* background conditions, or we have nothing dense enough to count as a world. Kant's test, which is a simultaneous test for fairness and for adoption, is "Can I will this as a universal law in a system of nature?" or "Can I will this as a member of a kingdom of ends?" I must, to use this test, fill in the other laws with which this one coheres, I must imagine a *system* of laws. What can be willed in isolation from the other things that are willed is not yet morally tested, for fairness or for any other virtue.

Whatever we say about imagining "perfect" worlds as a way of clarifying or representing the structure of a legal code, I think that this sort of hierarchy of possible worlds, even a complex hierarchy, cannot be used to represent the content of morality as understood by ordinary people. This is not simply for the reason already given, that in morality, unlike law, the representation of a norm may lag behind the recognition of its force. It is also because of a feature or moral demands once we do get them verbally formulated. This is that, in terms of the above notion of nonresponsive and responsive norms, all moral norms are responsive, yet they can be given no determinate place in a hierarchy of the sort sketched, since they refer back to no zero-level demands. I shall try to explain and substantiate this claim.

We do not in fact endorse a moral demand of the absolute form "Do not injure others," or "Do not kill." We accept killing and injuring of, for example, all animals when and if it suits our purposes, culinary, recreational, commercial, or whatever. So is it "Don't kill or injure other humans"? Not that either, since self-defense, war, judicial punishment, abortion, dumping nuclear wastes, making dangerous cars, allowing too many at too high speeds on the roads, and so on, are all accepted. We may need, as has often been suggested, to revise the formulation of these rules to "Do not kill or injure the innocent." But "innocence" is a norm-referring concept, and it may seem at this point that a norm like this one does indeed resolve itself into "Do not kill, unless *x, y, z*," where *x, y,* and *z* specify various ways in which the one we are licensed to kill has forfeited the right not to be killed—by being himself a killer, by being knowingly engaged in a high-death risk occupation, like war, or driving, or just living in an industrialized nation, or in an overpopulated world. We soon see that, in addition to specifying the forfeiters (not all of whom have broken this rule or any other we can cite), we must add some clause of the vague form "or unless you can't help killing them," where "can't help" never means literally can't help, but "can't help except at unreasonable cost." The "innocent" who are protected by this rule turn out to be a dwindling group, those whom we choose to save, just as "Don't eat people" can be accepted by cannibals, who protest that they eat only their enemies, who are not real people, not *fellow-persons.*

Is every rule about killing or eating of flesh then empty? Certainly the statute forbidding murder is not empty—in the law we make quite precise what the exception clauses are, and give unequivocal licenses to kill to certain classes of people (soldiers, executioners, hunters, sometimes doctors). They are licensed to kill only specific classes of living things, or of human living things. The legal rule against murder is a rule against unauthorized or unlicensed killing, but the constraints on the recognition or issuing of licenses are fairly weak.

When we wish to express moral outrage at the licenses tacitly given to, say, dumpers of poison in places whence it will get into human food, or into the air we breathe, we want to use words like *murder* to describe what the poisoners are doing, knowing quite well that it is not murder in the legal sense, since we know that the poisoners of our wells may have broken no law. We want a new law, revoking their license to kill or cause death. But what was their license? Only a tacit one, that they were merely going about their legitimate business. But now it looks as if all businesses, however predictably death-dealing, are licensed or legitimate unless explicitly forbidden, so we seem to come full legal circle. Can we both have a rule of the form "Don't kill unless authorized to do so" and another rule that says "Everything is authorized unless it is specifically prohibited"? If legal norms have this circular character, this provides further reason for claiming that the parody hierarchy of possible worlds sketched earlier does not represent *their* content any more than it does the content of morality. Neither morality nor the law are properly seen as comprised of straightforward zero-level directives, supplemented by fallback responses to noncompliance to these basic ones.

Whatever the complexity of the legal norm concerning murder, it does rule some action out, and *moral* attitudes to killing can take the form of a demand that more cases get counted as manslaughter or murder. What other form is taken by our moral attitudes to killing—do they take the form of definite prohibitions? When we morally condemn some actions of others as murderous, as showing a disregard for human life or for other animal life, we criticize the way such persons conduct themselves in a situation in which, given the press of human and other animal populations, and the strain on the resources, material and emotional, that living things need, the mere existence of another living thing is a sort of evil for every other—a threat to the size of my share of food, power, prestige, or other goods. Given the sometimes unavoidable competition for scarce resources, any response to another living thing is a response to what is, among its other aspects, a threat in this extended sense to oneself. Morality controls our responses in this situation of vulnerability and danger, staving off the outright barbarity of the unregulated way of all against all. Our moral feelings concerning when we may destroy other living things vary from one moral tradition to another, and are all controls of some sort on our response to the evil of a precarious life in conditions of scarcity.

Those who justify abortion by treating the human fetus as an attacker on the mother's resources, as an enemy within, could perhaps try treating the original offense as the offense of being alive at all. The zero-level rule would be "Don't come into existence," and all other rules could be treated as rules responding to offenders. Maybe the original sin is existence, and all morality is for sinners? This seems to me self-evidently absurd. The fact that overpopulation is a problem, and that even in conditions of underpopulation there may be competition and scarcity, does not make being alive something that is an initial count against one, an offense against others. For to cope with scarcity, vulnerability, and powerlessness, we need the cooperation and help of the very ones who also pose the threat. The good and hopeful aspects of our condition, as much as the evils, stem from the fact of interdependence. Moral feelings control by positively reinforcing our responses to the good of cooperation, trust, mutual aid, friendship, love, as well as regulating responses to the risk of evil.

"'Tis impossible to separate the good from the ill."[5] I think that this is as true of the conditions giving Hume's natural virtues their rationale as it is true of the conditions brought into existence by what he called the "artificial" virtues, namely conformity to the constitutive rules of well-functioning human institutions. A natural virtue like "gentleness" is a controlled response to conditions in which the good of cooperation and trust is inseparable from the evil of vulnerability and competition, since the ones we must work with are the ones who may, sometimes, through no fault of theirs, prove our enemies. We have to love our possible enemies, if we are to love anyone. The gentle person is, as Aristotle's analysis of virtues showed us, between two extremes. He is neither the coldhearted, self-defensive one, nor the willing slave, all loving service to others. Gentleness is a willingness to take a risk of exploitation and betrayal of trust, but not of course when it is more than a risk, but a certainty. It is a standing response to standing conditions of life in which the chance of good cannot be separated from the risk of evil. The gentle person is not gentle only to those known to be also gentle, or known to be trustworthy, but is gentle to all unless known to be violent. Some, such as Christians, may encourage us to behave to a person as if he were cooperating in the attempt to keep violence at bay, even when we are quite certain that he is guilty of, or intent upon, violence towards us, that is, to turn the other cheek and love our *declared* enemies. One question that a study of evolution, anthropology, and history as adjuncts to moral philosophy would force us to consider is that of what happens when a Christian community encounters one with less self-sacrificial norms, of what way of life succeeds in getting passed on to descendents when it competes with a more violent way of life. The study of history might tell us something about the survival value, for a community, of different sorts of norms. It isn't an *a priori* truth, indeed it seems not a truth at all, that the less violent go under, when we look at the moral community rather than at its individual members. Christianity made as great or greater advances when, in its early years, it was the way of life of a persecuted and apparently powerless group than when kings went to war for it, when it absorbed the martial virtues into its list, when it imitated its enemies. It may be, of course, that the way of living which keeps a community going in some conditions will not do so a century later, or that the only way of living which can continue is one we would, from within our own moral tradition, find abhorrent and immoral. But it is an important fact about any moral beliefs which anyone has acquired from parents that they have passed at least a minimal test for viability—they are two generations old. That is more than can be said for many philosopher's moral theories, which are entirely untested as respects their transferability to new members of a community at the age when such learning is still possible, the age of innocence, early childhood. Whatever else an acceptable morality must be, it must be in some sense "teachable" to young children, and understandable by nonintellectuals. Understanding is not the ability to verbalize, let alone to systematize, any more than acceptance of a morality is lip service to its slogans.

A moral virtue like gentleness seems to resist analysis into rules. We might try a rule of the form "Act towards others in a friendly and nonhurtful way, unless they are known offenders against this rule," or, for the Christian rule, "Act towards others in a friendly and nonhurtful way, even if they are known offenders against this rule." But what typifies the gentleperson is that they do not approach another intent first on getting clear whether they are or are not offenders against this or any other rule, insisting on seeing the other's moral credentials, even if willing to give them the benefit of any doubts. To frame a rule which explicitly either excludes or includes offenders seems to contradict the virtue which lies in acceptance of others as fellows, not in passing judgment on them. It is a response to others in conditions of risk, risk that the other may exploit that friendly response, but part of the friendly response is nonsuspiciousness, an avoidance of spelling out the risk, of seeing the other person as one who might return evil for good. The gentleperson acts as if there is no risk of return violence when there is such a risk. But that cannot be quite right either, if gentleness is a virtue, an *appropriate* response to others. Or is it that the appropriate response to those who do pose some risk to us, as everyone does, is to act as if they didn't? Are virtues ways of shutting one's eyes to danger, seeing the good not the bad prospects? Maybe they are. And certainly they seem to involve one another—a gentleperson whose gentleness is a virtue must also be patient and must have some courage and some pride, some sense of herself as a person the other would properly hesitate to insult or exploit.

I insisted earlier that we should not assume that moral norms can be easily represented in the forms of representation that have developed in the making and administering of written law, nor in the scientific description of a world assumed to be orderly and law governed. Norms in the form of virtues may be very difficult to formulate, while being not so difficult to recognize and encourage. It is not part of my purpose here to attempt to formulate the content of any one virtue nor to show the virtues to be a system, on some possibly new paradigm of "system." I want merely to contrast some features we do seem to find with those more easily represented features to which normative theorists seem attracted. Norms in the form of virtues may be essentially imprecise in some crucial ways, may be mutually referential but not hierarchically orderable, may be essentially self-referential. But then again all these categories may be unhelpful ones to apply to such norms. I think we still need to learn how best to reflect on morality.

If we see morality essentially as control of our natural responses to the mixed risk of evil and chance of good inherent in our interdependent situation, we can see moral response, in the form of training, criticism, and so on, as a response to a natural response, and we can see the evils and goods which come from morally disapproved and approved action as themselves the offspring of those evils and goods responses which morality controls. Suppose that what a child naturally fears includes withdrawal of trust and love from a person on whom he depends, for example, from a mother. Trust and love are natural goods, suspicion and hostility natural evils. Once moral training enters the picture, the child may be encouraged to become more confident of parental love in some conditions, more certain of a partial withdrawal of manifestations of love in others. The conditions will be determined by the parents' reactions to *other* fears and hopes the child has—his hope to take what he wants from his brothers, his fear that they will treat him similarly. The child's various natural hopes and fears are played off against one another, so that some become faint hopes, others confident expectations. The goods originally sought were love, food, and playthings. But the reaction to that search makes him also seek and hope for parental approval, and eventually he may have to choose between the approval of parents and the approval of his siblings and peers. Approval is not simply a means to more secure possession of love, food, and playthings, it becomes a good in its own right, and eventually he may be willing to risk his lower-level possessions to get it—he loses parental love and home comforts, for instance, by some daring exploit that gets him the approval of his gang. When any conflict develops within the group he now looks to for recognition, or when he confronts many rival sources of wanted approval, he may come to some choice among them, or possibly to renunciation of all of them, a response to the high risk of offending someone he would like to please, whatever he does. He develops loyalty to a cause, a party, a set of principles, a way of life. At this point he seeks a nonarbitrary way to either select among or reconcile the many possible claims on him, to make his choice seem nonarbitrary, as uniquely "selected" as the parents he initially looked to for love. He now secures one source of approval and if necessary sacrifices the rest—he moves from needing general popularity to needing general respect, just as earlier he moved from needing parental love to needing popularity. Respect too has its potential for conflict and it can be reflected upon, turned on itself to produce some more reflective response to a new risk, but most moral theory seems to have been produced by those at this respect-needing point in their moral development—they have elaborated and defended the cause which they have made their own, without much concern about the process by which that occurred (Rawls is an exception). They have rationalized and intellectualized their response to a common human predicament, that of reconciling, compromising, or selecting among the various conflicting disapprovers who function as forces in our lives. At each stage some possible response from others, be it withdrawal of love, of peer-recognition, or of respect, serves as a threat to train us to behave in certain ways, to cultivate certain virtues, certain habits and attitudes, as the hope of the opposite response, love, acceptance or popularity, respect, encourages those virtues. To the extent that we are loved, accepted, respected, we win some of the sweets of cooperation, and we also risk the evils of abandonment, betrayal, injustice. We begin wanting merely what one could call the first derivatives of the mother's breast—love, food, playthings, but we go on to want approval, justice, respect, and allegiance, all the higher derivatives.

I have sketched an *individual* development that in its own way is as oversimplified, overintellectualized, and hierarchial as the parody systems of norms I sketched earlier, and it owes much to Rawls. Because I looked only at the individual's response, not at the collective response of his family, his gang, his party, or his nation, I have distorted the picture. We would need to supplement the sequence of responses I have just sketched with one that begins from the parent's point of view, not the child's; proceeds to a reflection on parental influence, on school influence, on gang influence, on patriotism, on political parties; and then recall that at each point the two processes intersect. The parent has known what it is to be a child, and the child can, to some extent, see the parents' point of view; moreoever, the child responds not only to parents but also to those forces which come about by reflection on and correction of parental guidance—to welfare officials, to schools, to television, and so on—at each point with a partial ability to see the rationale for whatever pressures are being put upon him. He anticipates his adult role as the adult recalls and still half-understands the child's outlook.

Moral development is at least as complex as psychologists who have studied it have claimed, but no *a priori* hierarchy captures its complexities nor represents all its possibilities. The sketch I have given is intended merely to show how new "moral" goods grow out of natural goods, not to display all possible moral goods nor to show the only possible form of moral growth. What form that takes in an individual person depends in part on the direction social reflective growth has taken, on whether the child grows up in a kibbutz or in a one-family home; in the care of parents, grandparents, or nurses; if in the care of parents on whether one or both are working outside the home, and, if both are working, on what sort of day-care facilities they have available, and so on. The direction taken by the social reflective development, as revealed in the history of childcare, schools, child psychiatry, juvenile courts and crime procedures, political and legal institutions, will in turn depend upon the sorts of persons who are designing and operating these, on whether one's school teacher is, say, a Marxist, or a born-again Christian, or a Kantian respecter of persons.

What I have tried to make persuasive is the suggestion that morality begins in a response to a natural response to a situation in which hope and fear are properly inspired by one and the same situation. Morality is a proliferating succession of responses, individual and collective, to those primitive responses to the risky adventure of interdependence. Morality then becomes a bootstrap operation. It starts from natural responses to aspects of our relations to others, aspects that are naturally feared or welcomed. These responses all involve risk and uncertainty; and moral training and criticism responds in ways which, if effective, decrease risk of evils of a variety of related sorts, and increase the chances of a family of goods but always at the cost of new risk. Morality is throughout responsive to already given responses, and its norms are reflective versions of natural responses to the risks and opportunities interdependence involves. If we see morality this way, I think we can keep that *critical* element which most normative theorists want to stess without making the critical morality one that cannot make constructive critical responses to the real situation. The role of morality as a criticizer of the real grows out of its more primitive role as a corrector of natural response. But instead of taking one possible higher form of correction, which occurs when we try to codify and justify our sense of right and wrong, and looking at its less intellectual ancestors as mere psychological preconditions of morality, on the approach I favor (which I take to be Aristotle's), we see that intellectualized version as merely *one* of the possible developments of a process of reflective conflict-resolving corrections of responses to ever-widening yet ever more discriminating sources of recognition and acceptance.

Correction always has some costs, but the correction of impulses and motives by the formative influences of parental encouragement and discouragement is, as Plato knew, far less costly than adult correction, and is so even when the psychological costs Freud explored are taken into account. Freud of course saw the costs of childhood acquisition of a set of deontological prohibitions, not of a set of Platonic, Aristotelian, or Humean virtues. As regulators of human tendencies, virtues may have less ugly psychic costs than those of a moral law which has to be burned in, and which tends to provoke return aggression, or more slowly working poisons.

What I have attacked is one way of doing moral philosophy, namely the articulation of a system of moral laws, vaguely anchored to intuitions about particular cases, laws that the theorist presents as valid or acceptable in conditions of strict compliance, hoping eventually to work back, from there, to the actual conditions (which, after all, generated the intuitions). I have charged that the variety of moral theories, and the absence of agreed criteria for choosing between them, make them all look like arbitrary constructions, and that in any case they are utopian constructions, since there is no point in our knowing what would be is fair or what we should do provided everyone did likewise, when, whatever conditions we are in, we can be pretty sure that everyone is not doing likewise. Even as a way of representing a norm and of testing its coherence with others, imagining worlds with full compliance is, I claimed, useful only if the norms have a clear hierarchy that actual moral norms may lack, and only if we assume that the only good moral norms are the precise and definite ones.

Does this mean that we should live by our inherited fuzzy moral intuitions and do no moral philosophy at all? Only if there is no way to think about our morality except by attempting to contemplate a better world with its perfect moral system. There surely are other ways, and many great moral philosophers—Plato in *Meno*, Aristotle, Spinoza, Butler, Hume, Hegel, Nietzsche, Dewey—have shown us these ways. We can try to reflect on the actual phenomenon of morality, to see what it is, how it is transmitted, what difference it makes. We *may*, as a result of the resulting consciousness of what morality is, think we can make some improvements in it; however, these will come not from surveying abstract possibilities, but from seeing how, given the way it is, it can, by some move we can now make, improve itself, work better, correct its faults. Only when we think we know *what* it is, how it is now working, what it is doing, will we be in any position to see how it might really change, let alone know if that change would be for the better. I think we philosophers need to work with anthropologists, sociologists, sociobiolgists, psychologists, to find out what an actual morality is; we need to read history to find out how it has changed itself, to read novels to see how it might change again. To feel any proper confidence that a possible change, a really possible change, a takeable step from here, is an improvement, we need of course not only to understand what it is that is changing, but to have some sense of direction, of where we are heading. We do not need a fully detailed vision of the perfect society to have that sense, and a sketchy vision may misdirect us. We need some sort of moral compass, but a compass that points to true north gives us neither a full nor a sketchy picture of the North Pole. A moral compass to guide us, not only in our individual actions but in our institutional or educational reforms and innovations, is not something we are likely to think up in an armchair, but something that will itself evolve by the testing of generations of people. The most we philosophers will do will be to see ways of tinkering with existing moral compasses, not ways of inventing them *ex nihilo*.

I suggested earlier that ordinary moral attitudes are learned responses to other people who present both a hope and a threat of destroying it, both a threat and a hope for averting it. Moral attitudes are corrections of spontaneous human responses of trust and love, fear and hostility, corrections encouraging some responses, altering others. If morality is, in its least sophisticated form, such an inherently responsive thing, a response to natural responses, then there is inbuilt into it a potential for self-correction, for including moral approval and disapproval, respect and contempt, among its own targets, without any discontinuity. The compass for moral change may be merely a natural development of the compass for morally acceptable action. Hume believed that all of morality was a matter of what he called reflection, turning natural responses, not just on their natural target, but on responses, turning self-interest on the workings of self-interest, turning sentiments on sentiments. Ordinary parental training, the source of all operative moral attitudes, is such a turning of responsive sentiment on the child's responses and expressed feelings. To extend moral reflectiveness we develop responses to such things as parental influence, responses that grow out of their own targets. Hume believed, perhaps overoptimistically, that increasing the inherent reflectiveness of moral responses would *not* lead to a wholesale rejection of moral control; but it is always a possibility not just that bourgeois morality, but morality as such, contains the seeds of its own destruction. The moral sentiment, just as much as that "reasoning" about morals which Hume tried unsuccessfully to dethrone, may subvert itself when it examines itself. I think we do not yet know whether that is so, because we have been so fixated on the *kind* of thinking about morality which Hume condemned as rationalistic and idle, but which Kant successfully revived, building in our heads systems of ideal moral laws or ideal institutions, that we do not yet know much about the direction in which the other sort of moral thoughtfulness would take us. We know that it can take a Marxist form. What Hume describes as the workings of moral sentiment is essentially a dialectical process. It might take other than Marxist forms, if we explored its possibilities. We need not believe that the real is the good or even the best, merely that actual moral processes are the place to start if we wish to determine the better. The utopian blueprint without any method of implementation is morally irrelevant, the utopian blueprint with no regulation of the method of implementation is a renunciation of morality. The unreal, the utopian vision, is at best morally irrelevant, at worst morally destructive.

What does this mean for courses in medical or business ethics? If they are not to be "applications" of Kantian "theories," systems of laws, what can they be? What some of them already are: attempts to understand the roles of doctor, patient, relative, advisory boards, to see what changes have evolved in those roles; what regulations or other controls have come into being and what difference they have made; what grievances are felt by whom, in the process as it is. If you want to call this sort of thing the application of a "theory" *about* morality to our procedures in health care, you are within your verbal rights these days when anything any professional thinker puts on paper tends to get labeled a theory. But it is not a normative theory in the Kantian sense, it is merely a framework for description and attempted understanding. If it links with any theory proper, it is with evolutionary theory, a theory of the costs and benefits of different forms of life, over many generations.

Since in business ethics and medical ethics we are dealing with institutions, where there are legal rights and powers and responsibilities attached to the various roles of, say, producer, entrepreneur, customer, consumer, courses in these fields will study the actual functioning of the recognition of these rights and powers, so will have a place for *essentially representable* moral and legal concepts. But they could also have a place for a study of the virtues of honesty and integrity, humanity and mercy. Beyond the rights, powers, duties, and responsibilities lie the convictions, sometimes, inarticulate, of those who created those artifices, or who accept a life structured by them, convictions about the sort of *persons* who should fill these and other roles our society offers, the sort of person the roles themselves should help nurture. Some history of health care or business practices in different societies would give us a sense of the functions and possibilities of these professions. This will not give us any algorithm for the difficult cases, the hard decision. We cannot and should not ever promise that, and we should beware of those who try to sell us any ready reckoner or decision-making machine. But we might help the decision-makers anticipate the reactions they should expect from different decisions, see the grievances of different parties, see all the actual and perceived interests involved. We can also make them aware of the categories of assessment we have for decision-makers, ourselves, and others—categories like fairness, integrity, considerateness, humanity, vision—the potential development of those categories, and their link with less specialized moral categories, applicable to those merely following good habits or routines, not facing hard cases or new dilemmas.

I have merely sketched an approach in ethics, which has been taken by some of the greatest moral thinkers, which is realistic in starting with functioning moralities, and which tries to understand those moralities—to discover, not prescribe, what *sort* of coherence they have, what links the bits together. I have used Hume's term *reflection* for the sort of thinking which can pick up a feature I think we do find in our least intellectualized moral responses, and can continue to develop that feature, reflective response itself. Reflectiveness about our practices requires at the very least noting whether they are counterproductive to their expressed aims. Teaching comparative normative theory at the introductory level is thus self-defeating, cannot bear reflective survey. We do not yet know whether trying to continue the sort of moral philosophy Hume and other practiced, reflecting on actual moral practices, will or will not end by destroying the things it reflects on. Darwin, who had read his Hume,[6] uses the term *reflection* for the ability we human animals have which gives us that moral conscience which most importantly distinguishes us from other animals. If, for better or worse, we want a philosophy of morality, reflection, continued and turned on itself, can give us that too.

NOTES

1. Richard B. Brandt, *A Theory of the Good and the Right*, Oxford: Clarendon Press, 1979), p. 304. In the preceding discussion, Brandt had made clear how the constraints on the content of what one believes to be the moral code rule out *self-serving* private codes, and require that the code address real world conditions. One must believe that general obedience to it will be better than any alternative general policy. But these more or less Kantian constraints do not, as far as I can see, ensure any coordination between different private versions of what would be best for all. The road to chaos may be paved with conscientious obedience by different moral agents to their different versions of the best scheme of coordination.

2. See John Rawls, *A Theory of Justice*, (Cambridge, Mass.: Harvard University Press, 1971), secs. 1, 39, 53, for his concept of a well-ordered society and for his distinction between ideal theory, assuming strict compliance, and nonideal and partial compliance theory. In his discussion of civil disobedience, as in many parts of his discussion of political and economic arrangements, Rawls assumes not only "that the context is one of a state of near justice, that is one in which the basic structure of society is nearly just" (p. 351) but also assumes in effect that the contemporary United States provides such a context. In his Dewey lectures Rawls makes it even clearer that his theory is intended as "focused on the apparent conflict between freedom and equality in a democractic society . . . . We look to ourselves and our future and reflect upon our disputes since, let's say, the Declaration of Independence." (*Journal of Philosophy* 77, no. 9 [1980]: 518.) The conception of justice Rawls develops is intended to articulate a standard of criticism of institutions shared within this democratic tradition. The Dewey lectures also make clearer Rawls' conception of a well-ordered society (ibid., pp. 521–22). What does not become clear, to me at least, is what relation Rawls sees between the moral task of criticizing or evaluating institutions and the moral task of changing them. His principles are designed primarily to assist one in the evaluative task, but the discussion of civil disobedience suggests that he sees the same principles as capable of directing response to imperfect institutions.

3. Rawls, in assuming that every family has a head, in effect assumes that either patriarchy or matriarchy is just, or that there is some just procedure by which each monogamous family can appoint a head. See *A Theory of Justice*, p. 7, for inclusion of the monogamous family among the major institutions comprising the basic structure of society, and p. 128f. and p. 289f. for use of the concept of the head of a family. Rawls also speaks of parties in the original position as "representatives of family lines" (p. 128) and so one might generously interpret Rawls' "head of a family" as any representative of its interests, so that one monogamous family at one time might have several heads (namely all its currently adult members). There would still be a problem in making the arbiters of the justice of family relationships be representatives of the interests of families *qua* families.

4. Brandt, *Theory of the Good and the Right*, p. 305.

5. David Hume, *A Treatise of Human Nature*, ed. L. A. Selby-Bigge and P. H. Nidditch (Oxford: Clarendon Press, 1978), p. 497.

6. Charles Darwin, *The Descent of Man*, pt. 1, ch. 4. In n. 25 of this chapter Darwin quotes Hume.

12

Doing without Moral Theory?

When one turns from Aristotle's or Hume's moral philosophy to contemporary moral philosophy, several differences are bound to strike one. First is the fact that neither of these two (nor most who come between them) anticipate much disagreement among their readers about the actual moral judgments they endorse in their philosophy—neither Aristotle nor Hume expect any serious dissent from the list of virtues they endorse. (Hume, it must be admitted, is sometimes disingenuous here—he knows that there will be those who refuse to transfer celibacy, fasting, silence, humility, and the rest of the monkish characteristics to the column of vices, but he at least writes as if there is a consensus among all persons of good sense in seeing them in the way he saw them.) They do expect some disagreement on *philosophical* issues—Hume refers to the contemporary controversy over whether moral judgments are based on reason or sentiment, and Aristotle argues against the hedonists, but such disagreements at the philosophical level are not expected to alter the assumed rough consensus at the moral level. By contrast, we today often see moral disagreement as a datum, almost an indispensable prerequisite for the very possibility of moral philosophy. Stevenson, for example, begins with this datum. I think that this presumption of a plurality of conflicting moral outlooks in the audience for whom a book of moral philosophy is intended dates back to Bentham and J. S. Mill, who certainly expected some of their audience to have to be persuaded of some of their moral conclusions. Mill was not merely a moral theorist but a moral reformer—he wanted to change people's views about the rights of women, about sexual freedom, about sui-

---

"Doing without Moral Theory?" incorporates "Some Thoughts on the Way We Moral Philosophers Live Now," *The Monist* 67, no. 4 (October 1984), and material from a talk given at New York University, December 1981.

cide, and other topics. He created or at least fomented moral controversy. Now earlier philosophers, such as Kant, Hume, Locke, Hobbes, or even Aquinas, had certainly taken stands on some controversial social and political issues, but it is one thing to be a political reformer, making moral criticisms of social and political institutions, another to be a moral reformer, criticizing currently held moral beliefs. Mill was both, and his moral theory was used by him to try to change both moral and political attitudes. From Mill on, I suggest, philosophers writing on ethics no longer supposed that there was a moral consensus, a body of agreed moral judgments one could appeal to in support of a controversial political or social cause, or in support of one's particular philosophical theory about moral judgments. Apart from a few sheltered enclaves such as Oxford, where those like Ross, Pritchard, and Ryle still spoke as if there were a consensus, at least among all right-thinking Oxonians who had learned to tell right from wrong at their nannies' knees, and had learned of a few more elaborate and tempting wrongs at their public schools, serious moral philosophers took serious moral disagreement as part of their data. Among such serious thinkers I include Bradley, Bosanquet, Bergson, Moore, Stevenson, Ayer, Schlick, and Frankena.

What is striking about this shift from presumption of moral consensus to presumption of its absence is that the philosophers at the beginning of the transition saw themselves as working for some disputed moral cause, saw themselves as members of the nonagreeing community of moral judges, while more recent moral theorists mostly see themselves as above the moral fray, outside the everyday disputes about what is to be tolerated. Hare, for example, said in *Freedom and Reason*:

> Thus ethics, the study of the logical properties of moral words, remains morally neutral (its conclusions neither are substantial moral judgments, nor entail them, even in conjunction with factual premisses).[1]

Of course, present-day moral philosophers may take stands on disputed moral issues such as abortion, but there are very few contemporary Anglo-American moral theorists to whom one would naturally apply the term "moral reformer." (One such rare practicer of what he preaches in his philosophy is Peter Singer.) Rawls, the best-known moral theorist in this country, does not aim to enter the moral fray on particular issues—he quite explicitly limits the goal he sets himself to that of constructing a theory to accommodate his own considered judgments. He takes these to be typical of Americans, or of some Americans, but says, in *A Theory of Justice* (p. 50):[2]

I shall not even ask if the prinicples which characterize one person's considered judgments are the same as those that characterize another's ... so, for the purposes of this book, the views of the reader and the author are the only ones that count. The opinions of others are used only to clear our heads.

This is an interesting, and extreme, reaction to cultural pluralism. Rawls, as much as Stevenson or Harman, takes for granted that there *are* a plurality of possibly conflicting moral views, or "opinions," as he calls them. But he does not aim even to defend his own against contrary opinions—merely to construct the best possible theory on his own opinions, tested only by their confrontation with a variety of possible constructions. Rawls defends his contractarianism against intuitionism and utilitarianism (as if they exhaust the field of other alternatives) but this defense at the philosophical level is a defense against those with the *same* base of moral opinions, at least on most matters, and who differ only in their philosophical opinions on what theory that base best supports. This turns academic moral philosophy into the intellectual construction business—one attempts to outbid one's competitor constructors in erecting a theory that rationalizes the moral opinion of some group within which there is approximation to moral consensus. In the limiting case, the extreme limit of individualism and pluralism, the group is oneself. This, I suggest, makes moral philosophy into either ideology or into play-ideology. Like most of us, I welcome good ideology for a cause I espouse—I admire J. S. Mill for his cultural crusades and for his effort to use intellectual instruments along with any others he could get. What I am less happy with is professional play-ideology, and with unacknowledged ideology, ideology parading as detachment.

MacIntyre, In *After Virtue*,[3] says that our contemporary style as moral beings is indignation, protest, and unmasking. All that is left for us to do, after the breakdown of a religious moral consensus and the failure of the enlightenment attempt to provide a secular basis for a shared morality, is to react negatively to the contradictions present everywhere in our present moral situation—conflicts between slogans about rights and practices that ignore such rights, between the moral "fictions" to which we give lip service, and the brute facts of the exercise of superior power. While I admire MacIntyre's illuminating version of how we got where we now are, as far as concerns morality, moral philosophy, and their perceived relation to one another, I do not agree with his very gloomy estimate of the prospects of a secular culture, and I shall claim that at least one version of the enlightenment project has not yet been given a fair enough trial for us to know whether it will or will not fail—I mean Hume's attempt to give morality a secure basis, not in moral theory but in human active capacities for cooperation. But I have, in my negative prolegomenon to that claim, exemplified MacIntyre's version of the typical contemporary moralizer— although I may keep my indignation under control, and although my form of protest is harmlessly academic, I have been indulging in that favorite twentieth century sport of unmasking—I have been presenting our twentieth century moral theorists as ideologists in fairly transparent disguise.

As MacIntyre points out, this game of unmasking can be played interminably. Just as I can ask why today's moral theorists like to present themselves, not as parties to moral disagreements but as either detached adjudicators or as solitary thinkers, in retreat from public dispute, as builders of systems for their own private satisfaction, so you can ask why I like to present myself as a critic of the current moral theory and applied theory industry, as if I can stand apart from it, see its self-delusions and its unacknowledged ideological functions, while myself keeping free from these forms of false consciousness. It is as easy to unmask me as a parasite on the moral philosophy I criticize as it is easy for me to criticize moral theorists. Unmasking is a game that has become boring due to the laxness of its rules. When Marx did it, it had some force. When Nietzsche did it, it had more force than most could tolerate—we wrote him off as mad. When Freud did it, and generalized the scope of the charge, then masks became an interesting cultural product, something to cultivate and on which to spend, in analysis fees, considerable sums so that one might understand and appreciate one's mask. To be civilized and to be masked became more or less identical, and the new art was to wear one's carefully studied and even carefully crafted mask with panache, rather than hiding behind it, or refusing to distinguish oneself from it. Once masks became fashionable, the game of unmasking began to lose its point. The sort of unmasking which still survives as a popular form of moral action is not the charge of hypocrisy—that was the form unmasking took when Strachey wrote about the Victorians, but rather the more general charge that, in MacIntyre's words, "behind the masks of morality [lie] what are in fact the preferences of arbitrary will."[4] The will that the wearing of the moral mask advances need not be one's own—or even one of which one is aware. Powerful wills in our era know how to manipulate others to do their will, and to do it unaware of the manipulation and of whose will they are doing. So today's form of "unmasking" is simply showing what cause is in fact furthered by particular moral posturings—and there need be no charge whatever that those taking up those postures are insincere, are *merely* posturers. The charge today is not of insincerity or hypocrisy, but of false consciousness. This is a charge so hard to rebut that it is easy to turn it on anyone and everyone. I therefore take it for granted that I, like the next person, am *not* fully aware of the forces that make me say what I say, nor aware of whose cause I may be furthering by the saying of it. False consciousness can now be taken as the successor concept to "original sin" — of course one is liable to it. That which distinguishes any sheep from the large herd of the goats will be not their escaping it, but their awareness of it and their attempt to find some method of "redemption" from its evils.

A second difference between Aristotle and Hume and most contemporary philosophers is that the latter have normative theories, and I think we find nothing analogous to these in Aristotle or Hume (although we do in Aquinas and Kant). By a normative theory I mean a system of moral principles in which the less general are derived from the more general. I want to attack the whole idea of a moral "theory" which systematizes and extends a body of moral judgments, and attack in particular the idea that the theorist might accept a theory with controversial implications, without thereby becoming a moral reformer, one dedicated to having those implications accepted and acted upon. It is perhaps appropriate that I should exhibit, in my moral philosophy, MacIntyre's mode of moral action — if I am right that there is no room for moral theory as something which is more philosophical and less committed than moral deliberation, and which is not simply an account of our customs and styles of justification, criticism, protest, revolt, conversion, and resolution, then any moral philosophy which is not such descriptive anthropology will tend to merge with moral action. To quote MacIntyre again "There ought not to be two histories, one of political and moral action and one of political and moral theorizing, because there were not two pasts, one populated only by actions, the other only by theories. Every action is the bearer and expression of more or less theory-laden beliefs and concepts, every piece of theorizing is a political and moral action."[5]

I shall now briefly diagnose[6] what I think is the background error of the moral theorists, then I shall explore a different way of being a moral philosopher. Where do we have genuine and useful theories? Primarily in science — but there we find a plurality of them primarily over time, rather than at a time. We certainly do not find some engineers building bridges or spaceships by application of one theory, while others at the same time are applying another different theory. In practical fields, like engineering or cooking, we do not find *theories* of how to do what such practitioners do, merely schools to train people to do it. There may perhaps be theories of nutrition, or of taste, which a cook might consult, and there certainly are recipe books, but it would be a very odd enterprise to try to find the "principles" applied in such recipes, or to unify the rules of cooking into a grand system, from which we might deduce some new recipes, or menus for new occasions. Theories tell us what the world is like, and we need to know that if we are to act successfully in it, either to maintain something in it, or to change it. Engineers need theories of physics and chemistry; cooks need knowledge about what is edible, what is digestible, what tastes will result from certain combinations of ingredients and processes such as grinding, fermenting, baking, freezing. Moral agents also need theories, or rather the reliable facts good theories produce—facts about the way people react, about the costs and consequences of particular ways of life, on those who adopt them and on their fellow persons. We need psychological theories and social theories, and, if we are intent on political change, theories about political power and its working, and about economics. But do we need *normative* theories, theories to tell us what to do, in addition to theories that present to us the world in which we are to try to do it?

Why might we have thought that we do need, and that we can get, such theories? We certainly need some way of deciding what to do, especially in cases we find difficult; and the oldest way, in our culture, was by accepting the guidance of some religious teaching. Here a theory about the way the world is and a set of practical guides were closely interconnected, and it may be nostalgia for this theory-linked practical guidance that prompts philosophers today to construct moral theories, fairly elaborate systems of norms with the less general linked to more general principles. We have accepted, from Moore, the claim that we cannot base our moral precepts on any metaphysical theory, so instead we have tried to let the precepts themselves constitute a theory. The religious thinkers were the ones who really *did* have a theory, in the strict sense—a representation of God's creation. A theory, strictly, is the outcome of contemplating some unified structured world—in the first place a world manifesting the unity of the divine perfections, and so showing the coherence and structure to be expected in such a divine self-display. It is dubious if even our scientific accounts of the way the world is can count as theories in this sense. But scientists seem eternally optimistic that there is some order there to be discerned and contemplated, that such an order-seeking being as a human being must be part of a universe exhibiting the order for which it yearns. It is like the dog's confidence that there are good smells out there—and probably about as well grounded. (That is to say, it is fairly well grounded. To paraphrase Hume,[7] how else would the order-seeking beings have survived unless they, with their needs, *did* fit at least into *some* niche in the world as it really is?) So those religious thinkers, like Aquinas, who outline a whole world-account, and one which entitled that world to the name *nature*, because of what it revealed about its divine creator, could indeed go on and read off a "natural law" which informed us how to pursue our true end. For a religious outlook, moral guidelines can be extracted from the total theory, that is from the contemplation of world-and-God.

But we secular moralists have no such total picture. We have a world view which is expected to reveal a "naturalized" version of some approximation to that order which originally was seen as a displaying divine unity-in-variety. We may also have an optional private religious view, worshipping the free-enterprise deity, the God of our fabrication, or the consumer deity, the God of our choice. Such religious views may impose religious duties upon us, but for our dealings with our fellow persons who have exercised their religious freedom differently, we need some less elite moral guide. Religion no longer either ties or reties us to many of our fellows. In place of the once-shared common morality of a community with a more-or-less shared religion, we have a great void in which a few moral memories echo forlornly. This void is of course a temptation to the moral philosopher, who constructs utilitarianism or contractarianism to fill the free space, and not merely to supplement a given moral guide, so as to get decisions in difficult cases. But what *really* would fill that space would be a moral force that was felt at the time when moral codes get accepted and paradigm moral ties get forged—namely in childhood. Until there are utilitarian and contractarian Sunday schools and pulpits, and until such moral outlooks are learned at the parent's knee, the void will not be filled by such philosophical enterprises. We philosophers are very squeamish about pulpits and knees—we cultivate a cool distant style, and like to think of our influence on culture as safely indirect and long-term. Yet the influence of our introductory classes in ethics may be fairly direct and immediate—exposure to a variety of moral theories, and the varieties of conflicting advice they generate when "applied" to business or medical decisions, is a very effective way to produce a moral skeptic. Our pluralist culture prepares a young person for moral skepticism, and a course or two in comparative moral theory (and application) is the perfect finishing school for such skepticism.

The belief that there was room for normative theory, for a systematic body of moral precepts, dates from Bentham's substitute for natural law, and from the continuity he saw between morals and legislation. In the old view, human morality was continuous with human law, itself continuous with natural and divine law. Even when human law is severed from this theological root, it clearly still was amenable to systemization. So it is a fairly natural move to suppose that, since there is no problem in stating the content of the human law of a particular community as complexly organized and hierarchically arranged set of principles and precepts, the same might be done for the morality by reference to which these laws get made and changed. A natural move but, I think, a bad move.[8] The laws by which courts and judges arrive at verdicts *must* be expressed, must be general and perhaps hierarchically ordered, and must be sanction backed.

Need moral beliefs be verbally expressed, to be beliefs? *Must* they take the form of universal pronouncements perhaps derivable from supreme principles? *Is* there a moral sanction? Affirmative answers to these three questions are usually assumed—since Kant we seem to have found it hard to see how there could be any such thing as moral philosophy if there were no such thing as "the moral law" or "the moral rules." Alan Donagan's opening chapter in his book *The Theory of Morality* shows this prejudice in its full force. "The Theory of Morality," he says "is a theory of a system of laws or precepts binding upon rational creatures as such, the content of which is ascertainable by human reason."[9] Thinkers as diverse as Alan Gewirth[10] and Richard Brandt[11] also take the concept of "moral law" for granted—Gewirth's search for a rationally justified first principle, Brandt's attempt to formulate a ideal moral code, both assume that morality consists in a set of general principles or rules or laws. Today's moral theorists are all Kantians in their prejudice in favor of formulated general rules. Even if some, like Brandt, see inclination as much as reason as the *source* of those precepts, they all see reason as providing both the form and the tests that make them moral precepts. And those, like David Gauthier,[12] who look to the market rather than to the law for moral inspiration, are still Kantian in making *reason*, in the form of rational self-interest in a social context, authoritative for their morality for bargainers. I find all these three assumptions to be mere Kantian prejudices, whose self-evidence does not survive self-consciousness. They might turn out in the end to be justified claims, but it is time that those who think they are justified produce the justification. Until they do, it remains mere prejudice to demand explicitness, universality, and coercive backing, in any moral guide. For any such guide to be passed on it must be learnable, but one can learn from example. For any such guide to be of general use, its precepts must apply fairly generally, but generality is not universality. For any such guide to be accepted *as* a guide, there must be some motive to accept it. But the motive need not be avoidance of sanctions.

On my diagnosis, where we now stand in moral philosophy is among an array of rationalistic systems, all of them aiming at universality, even if sometimes at degenerate versions of it, at personal "rational" moral utopias that are not expected to be shared, even by other utopia-fanciers, or rationality-admirers. The retreat of the theorists from moral problems in the real world to the construction of private fantasy moral worlds is as it were compensated for by the advance of a new breed of professionals, namely all those who assemble all the available theories, then "apply" them to suit their clients' needs. Can we approve of a division of labor in which the theorists keep their hands clean of real-world applications, and the ones who advise the decision-makers, those who do "applied ethics," are like a consumer reports service, pointing out the variety of available theories and what costs and benefits each has for a serious user of it? Does the profession of moral philosophy now display that degeneration of a Kantian moral outlook that Hegel portrays, where there are beautiful souls doing their theoretical thing and averting their eyes from what is happening in the real world, even from what is happening in the way of "application" of their own theories, and there are those who are paid to be the "conscience" of the medical, business, or legal profession, what Hegel calls the moral *valets*, the professional moral judges?[13]

The villain, as I see it, is the rationalist, law-fixated tradition in moral philosophy, which, given freedom from its religious base, breeds multiple and in the end frivolous systems and their less frivolous, more dangerous applications. MacIntyre sees the roots of the present mess to be the failure of Kantian and post-Kantian moral philosophies to defend a secular *rationalist* moral philosophy from Hume's attack on rationalism, a defense to which there seemed no option, on his account, given the failure of Hume's attempt to provide an alternative basis. I dispute that diagnosis, and that estimate of Hume's contribution.[14] As I see it, it is not so much that Hume failed as that his successors failed to continue his project. In the nature of that project, it could not be completed, once for all, by Hume himself, and I see no fatal weaknesses in the project as he launched it. I think that his preferred version of secular morality and his version of philosophical reflection on morality have not really been tried for long enough, and so it is too soon to say if they are or are not viable and acceptable to sensible people. For present purposes, the important aspects of the latter are its nonrationalism, and its version of the relation between moral philosophy and the actual human practices in which appeals to moral judgments are made and in which morality makes a difference to what is done, thought, and felt.

I contrasted Hume's approach to ethics with the post-Kantian and post-Benthamite moral philosophy that went in for theory construction. Hume's way involves no normative theory—it involves a psychological theory, of course, and it also involves a political-economic theory, about the actual workings of human right-determining institutions. But no *normative* theory. The psychological theory, the account of human passions and their potentialities for self-regulation, is empirically testable, and so is the political theory. Hume indeed tested and refined it by his historical researches. What the Humean moral philosopher does is take well-based accounts of human nature, its malleability, its current condition, and equally well-based accounts of the workings of institutions, and of the interrelations between the two—the way institutions express and encourage some passions, the way some passions, or frustrations of them, lead to changes in institutions. Given this factual base, the moral philosopher's special interest will be in the workings of all the *reflective* sentiments, those reacting to other sentiments, and in particular to those that claim to be moral reflections, that is, to be reflections from a steady and general viewpoint. All of this will be "mental geography," as Hume called it,[15] *descriptive* moral and social philosophy, understanding the modes of individual and social moral reflection as they actually exist now rather than an "airy science"[16] that "opens up a world of its own,"[17] be it that of Kantian noumena or any of those full compliance human utopias favored by normative theorists. For such mental georgraphy to be accurate and to yield reliable maps, the philosopher may have to leave her armchair, or have associates who do so.

In the conclusion to Book One of the *Treatise* Hume said that any philosopher whose "system or set of opinions" will prove "satisfactory to the human mind" will have to have "a share of the gross earthy mixture" of the nonphilosophers who do the world's more worldly work. "Of such as these I pretend not to make philosophers, nor do I expect them to be either associates in these researches or auditors of these discoveries . . . Instead of refining them into philosophers, I wish we could communicate to our founders of systems a share of this gross earthy mixture. . . ."[18] Hume has no wish to make nonphilosophers into philosophers, or even to tell them his philosophical discoveries. On the contrary, those philosophers who will have anything worth the telling must first acquire some of the solid virtues of the honest nonphilosophers. Later, in the first *Enquiry,* Hume describes the way he thinks that sound philosophy will affect these honest nonphilosophers, with or without their becoming the philosophers' auditors. "And though a philosopher may live remote from business, the genius of philosophy, if carefully cultivated by several, must gradually diffuse itself throughout the whole society and bestow a similar correctness on every art and calling. The politician will acquire greater foresight and subtility, in the subdividing and balancing of power; the lawyer more method and finer principles in his reasoning; and the general more regularity in his discipline and more caution in his plans and operations."[19] This sounds as if it might be a manifesto for applied philosophy, a proclamation of the value of philosophical and moral valets to other professionals. But this puff for the public benefits of philosophy is carefully limited to philosophy as carefully cultivated, and Hume does not go back on his earlier claim that the philosopher must acquire something of the nonphilosopher to do the philosophical job properly, must become less of an ivory tower intellectual and spinner of airy systems. The Hume who wrote the *Treatise* knew a little law and had sampled the life of a businessman. By the time he wrote the second *Enquiry* he had a more varied experience of the world's affairs, and he went on to be a secretary to a general, a diplomat, and a historian. By the time he made the final revisions to the second *Enquiry*, he was well acquainted with several branches of the common life whose procedures and practices the Humean philosophy was to methodize and sometimes correct.

The brief for "applied" moral philosophy which we get from Hume, then, is one which directs the philosopher to learn from the nonphilosophers before presuming to advise them. Such willingness to learn, to become less of an intellectual judge and more of an apprentice participant, is to be found among contemporary moral philosophers less in the theorists than in those who *have* become associates of the nonphilosophers, in other professions. They are more or less forced to acquire some of the gross earthy mixture Hume prescribed for the philosopher, forced to see what are the procedures they are hired to methodize and correct. If anyone is likely to be doing their philosophy "carefully" in the sense Hume meant, it will be this new breed of moral valets. They are in a position to enact a Hegelian master-slave reversal.

The "careful" moral philosophy Hume practiced was a mental geography of our powers of reflection, and of our reflective practices. His bold methodological claim was that the correction of motives, sentiments, and habits catering to them, can be done by sentiment and custom, and is not the prerogative of a purely intellectual "reason." His sort of moral reflection is empirically informed, that is to say, informed by psychological, political, and historical knowledge, and it is also practical, a reflective version of real motives in real-world conditions. The unfinished task Hume launched, in his bold antirationalist moral philosophy, was to find a better way of being a moral philosopher, a way which avoided unworldly intellectualism, which was as willing to correct its own methods as to criticize the customs of others. Hume's manifesto is a call for a self-critical, nonintellectualist, and socially responsible moral philosophy. His own practice of it was with the pen. Although the member of the republic of letters need not be an intellectualist, the pen or word processor of the Humean philosopher ought not to be her only tool (or weapon). If we are to carry on what Hume began, we should be looking for new and better ways both of designing our own role, and of conducting our reflection on and examination of the moral practices of our time.

Moral philosophers might be expected to be especially self-conscious about their own social role but, apart from Marxists, who like the true Wittgensteinians have tended to transmute their philosophy into more direct ways of acting on the world, they have not recently been very conspicuous for their sense of social answerability. In the analytic tradition particularly, moral philosophers (once tenured) have tended to take their own social niche for granted, and to turn their socially critical eye, and any modest proposals for reform, only on practices in which they are not themselves professionally involved (I exclude, of course, participation in internal university affairs, those local reorganizations that do not change the relation of academic philosophers to the rest of society). But should we not, at least occasionally, consider why the rest of society should not merely tolerate but subsidize our activity, given what we do and how many there are of us who do it? Is the large proportional increase of professional philosophers and moral philosophers a good thing, morally speaking? Even if it scarcely amounts to a plague of gadflies, it may amount to a nuisance of owls.

The fairly recent expansion of the socially tolerated role of salaried moral philosophers beyond colleges into hospitals and into the workplaces of other professions should encourage in us a sensitivity to our own place in the social division of labor. If we are to "do" applied ethics and professional ethics, we should not exclude our own profession from our attention. Is it in accordance with the moral principles we endorse in our philosophy that we should advise other professions before we have examined our own? Our own professional activities, until recently, have been restricted to teaching and writing. Just as most of us teach without having been trained in the art of teaching, learning, if at all, from sorry experience, so those who consult and advise other professionals are learning by trial and error, not usually by any study or expert training in the new areas. I suppose that it is no worse for philosophers to think that, simply by being philosophers, they can make a contribution in a hospital, than to assume, as most of us do, that merely by philosophizing aloud in front of our students we thereby contribute constructively to their education. We have not been notable for our efforts to check and see if this assumption is correct. Even our recent, usually externally demanded, attention to our performance as teachers has limited itself to trying to measure our success in converting nonphilosophers into beginning philosophers. We stop short of asking whether this conversion serves some good wider educational or cultural purpose. Our sacred ability to be critical and questioning seems to have as its limit a refusal to question the value of becoming, in our sense, philosophical and critical.

That any society ought to have philosophers in its midst seems to us an axiom of any possible social philosophy. Probably any society *will* have some reflective people in it, some Socrates or Mandeville or Wollstonecraft to ask awkward questions, but even if this is to be welcomed, it does not follow that any society should have *professional* philosophers in its midst, nor, if it does have them, that their activities should take the form ours assume. The very professionalization of philosophy makes the likelihood more remote that those awkward questions, necessary for a healthy social consciousness, should come from its philosophers. It may make for better philosophy and a better society if they come from a social misfit like Diogenes, or from an anathematized lense-grinder like Spinoza, or from a man of affairs, an unsuccessful aspirant to two chairs of philosophy, like Hume. (Even more conventionally acceptable moral philosophers like Aquinas and Butler earned their living as clerics, not as philosophers.)

The questions we need occasionally to ask are, first, why anyone should be a philosopher (in our sense); second, why anyone else should pay one to be a philosopher; third, how many should be paid philosophers; and fourth, what exact form the professional activity of paid philosophers should take, and in particular what sort of examination of moral practices the moral philosopher should conduct. These questions are, of course, connected — the answers to the third and fourth are obviously interdependent. The answers need not be true for all conditions. It is not *a priori* impossible that we today can put to good use a vastly higher proportion of philosophy professors in our population than did Hume's Europe. Social conditions have recently changed enough to make philosophers welcome in hospitals, playing there a role once played, approximately, by chaplains. Are we the new priesthood? Could good Humeans possibly become that?

As teachers, our activities have usually been anything but pastoral. Although generalizations are risky, I think most teachers of moral philosophy have prided themselves on their success in disturbing the complacent beliefs of their students. We have set out to produce in our students a willingness to challenge old beliefs, to pursue the implications of principles further than they naturally would, and to look at alternative beliefs. We like playing devil's advocate. Does this systematic assault on inherited and conventional moral beliefs corrupt the young? I do not think we know, and some of us can give no sense to the question. How, we would ask, can initiation into rational criticism *corrupt* — surely that can only cure the corruption of dogmatism, not itself corrupt. But most of us do know, by casual observation or by sessions with distressed students, that it can unsettle and upset, and it can also produce moral skeptics and even cynics. Part of our own faith, it seems, is that anything, even a moral skeptic, is better than an unconscious moral dogmatist. Better for whom? For the new skeptic and his fellows? For his children? An introductory course in moral philosophy ought perhaps to include J. S. Mill's *Autobiography,* so that the critical examination of beliefs will include an examination of the faith in reason alone, and the effects of trying to live by such a faith. If Socrates is our martyr in the cause of critical rationality, the young Mill stands as countervictim, reminding us of the incompleteness of critical rationality as a human goal. The examined life may be a sustainable goal, but only if the mode of examination does not destroy the life.

Not only are we dogmatic about the value of critical examination, of challenge to dogmas, but we are also fairly dogmatic in our beliefs about the best form of examination. We examine by lawyers' methods—by challenge, counterchallenge, argument. We give verdicts and pass judgments. For some moral philosophers this aping of legal procedures is self-conscious and deliberate; for others it is more automatic, the result of their analytic training. Among less analytic moral philosophers other styles exist, equally imitative but imitating other models. There is the meditation, the examination of conscience, the confession. And now there is cost-benefit analysis, moral philosophy imitating the accountant and the merchant, and game-theoretic approaches, in which the moral philosopher imitates the military strategist. We need to survey the array of possible styles, and, if we are to imitate, to be aware of why we choose the model we do. Philosophy, these days, seems in its methods not the queen of the sciences, expecting others to listen to her, but the social mime, drawing her procedures as well as her economic support from other sources. Such heteronomy need be no disgrace—by imitating, extending, transferring, and perhaps distorting the methods of other disciplines we may occasionally do something enlightening, useful, entertaining, or even consoling.

The recent struggles in our profession in this country between the self-named pluralists and what they see as an analytic establishment, or ex-establishment, might be seen as involving a clash of models of philosophical procedure. Those who dislike analytical methods are usually rejecting not merely the assimilation of philosophical thinking to mathematical computation, but also the legalist paradigm, the tyranny of argument. (Of course, to replace what Hume disparagingly called "lawyers' wrangling" with political campaigning is dubious advance.) The alternative ways of doing philosophy here and now seem either to be those of the Marxists, modeled on guerrilla warfare, or those of the phenomenologists, modeled on the gentler moves of religious exercises. Few have taken up Wittgenstein's suggestion that a philosophy book could take the form of a series of jokes—and fewer still have brought it off. To get the earthiness Hume recommended, must we choose between being pretend accountants, pretend lawyers, pretend revolutionaries, failed priests, and unsuccessful comics?

Hume had himself to become a real diplomat and a real historian before many found any of his opinions satisfactory to their minds, before he found many auditors for his social philosophy. History and the human sciences could also provide procedures for us to adapt to our purposes, and, for moral philosophy in particular, history seems an indispensable fellow-discipline. Unless we know the fate of communities that tried to implant and live by the moral principles we consider, how can we have any empirically tested opinion about their soundness? The fate of communities that tried living by those principles, their success or failure in passing them on to successive generations, is not decisive, of course, for the validity of those principles for us now, but it does seem relevant data for the moral philosopher. Unless our moral reflections are historically informed, they will be mere speculation.

The difficulty of providing appropriate support for a moral guide is increased if a new untried one. To have any confidence that a proposed new guide will work better than the guides it would replace, will conduce more to the human good of those using it and affected by its use, one would need not merely economic and sociological generalizations confirmed by past history, but also something of the novelist's imagination of the detailed human consequences of its use, its full effect on people's lives. Anticipating such real-world consequences of adoption of a moral principle is different from seeing its logical consequences, or its theoretically appropriate application to concrete cases. In real life the attempts to apply an abstract theory or principle lead to results richer and messier than those foreseen from an armchair. The emotional effects of abortion, for example, and the effects on nurses assisting in abortions, go stubbornly beyond what the liberal defender of the right to abortion envisaged as the consequences of his or her principles. The difficulty of learning, transmitting, applying some new proposed moral guide, or reform of an older one, the frequency of misapplications, the hidden psychic costs of living by it, these are all empirical matters of vital importance to the proper evaluation of that guide, but they are matters which, even with the historians' knowledge and the novelists' imagination to assist us, we can still only guess at from our chairs of moral philosophy, in advance of the actual trial of that guide over several generations. To make even educated guesses here we need more studies not only of the effect on children of moral education of various styles and contents (including the effect on how they try to bring up their own children), but of the effect on adolescents and adults of conversion to new principles. The relative incidence, among the followers of different moral guides, and among those who have changed their moral beliefs in various ways, of suicide, alcoholism, avoidance of parenthood, and other forms of the failure of the will to perpetuate one's way of life, would be relevant information for a philosophical examination of such moral guides—more relevant than calculations about what expert, emotionless bargainers would accept in unreal conditions, or what an uninvolved observer would enjoy contemplating from a god's eye view.

It is not easy, of course, to find out what role is played by moral beliefs, as distinct from bad health or bad economic, political, or personal luck, in driving a person to some form of life rejection, nor indeed should we want to separate too sharply the influence of moral beliefs from economic and political factors. One's moral beliefs may influence one's willingness to put up with economic and political hardship, as well as with bad health and bad luck, but they also affect one's input into the economic and political processes. Relevant to the moral philosopher's examination of a moral code are such questions as "Will the followers of such a code become exploiters and exploited? Will they be led to war more or less often than others? Will they need to restrict one sex to child-rearing roles to ensure the successful transmission of their morality?" Such questions are not easy to get answers to, but without such answers we cannot know what we are endorsing, in endorsing a particular moral guide, nor could we be endorsing it as satisfactory not only to intellect, but to the whole human mind, in all its emotional and historical complexity. To get, or even to try to get, answers to such questions philosophers will have to get their hands a little dirtier, a little more officially familiar not merely with intellectual arguments but with the other forces that drive human life, for better or worse.

The extension of the work of some moral philosophers into consulting and advising in other professions is bound to confront them with some of the real-world complexities a moral guide encounters. This change in the social role of moral philosophy therefore holds out promise as well as problems. The problems arise because of the lack of relevant special expertise with which most of the philosophical consultants enter their new positions. Advisers and consultants are usually those who have some experience-based expertise in the area where the advice is given—we seek legal advice when our problem is with some law-regulated aspect of life; engineering consultants check what other engineers, or builders, are planning to do, and so on. In such cases the one who is consulted is the one with more experience in the problem area. Any expert theoretical or intellectual knowledge the consultant brings will also be experience-tested theory, knowledge refined by practice. Philosophical consultants in the areas of medicine, law, business, are rarely experts in these areas, and any theories they invoke will have been tested merely by argument. Even granted that for some of the moral issues arising within these professions a wider viewpoint is needed than that internal to the profession, why is the viewpoint from a moral theorist's study better for that purpose than that of any morally sensitive intelligent layman? We philosophers, by having given thought, may have help to give, but only if are willing to investigate (or subcontract the investigation of) the actual results of trying

to live by the principles that commended themselves to us in our arm-
chairs and debating halls.

Most of those philosophers with whom I have spoken who are playing
these new philosophical roles in other professions seem to be acutely
aware of the need to absorb at least some knowledge of the host profession
before they can serve it, and seem properly modest about the scope of
their contribution and its tenuous connection with any specficially philosophical special knowledge or special skills. (Arthur Caplan tells the story
of his contribution to hospital practice—the suggestion that patients' pri-
vacy could easily be better respected if a physician on his rounds were
willing to wait until a patient had finished using a bedpan before exposing
that patient to his own gaze and that of his retinue of attendant underlings.
This is a fine contribution, but as Caplan has noted, a Ph.D. in philosophy
scarcely seems a necessary condition of making it.)[20] I think that this new
class of moral philosophers can be depended upon to carve out some
suitable work niches for themselves in their new environments, given
time, sensitivity to wrong moves, humility, and inventiveness. From these
philosophers, who perforce have more contact with life outside the study
and classroom than the rest of us do, we can hope for new suggestions
about method, about ways in which we can better ground our moral
theories on the facts—the economic, historical, and psychological facts.
From them may also come new theories, but I think that the more important benefit to moral philosophy from its current spread into other professions will be new ideas about ways of examining moral theories, systems,
opinions, and practices—ways of continuing Humean reflection on the
principles by which we proceed.

Such moral philosophy would merge with other disciplines, and with
the reflections of common life, and such a merger might help us to escape
from that arrogance of solitary intellect which has condemned much
moral theory to sustained self-delusions concerning its subject matter, its
methods, and its authority.

NOTES

1. R. M. Hare, *Freedom and Reason* (Oxford, 1963), p. 97. Hare in more recent writings
has moved to the view that the moral theory we get when we analyze this neutral language
is one on which all theorizers agree.

2. John Rawls, *A Theory of Justice* (Cambridge, Mass.: Harvard University Press,
1971), p. 50.

3. Alasdair MacIntyre, *After Virtue* (Notre Dame: University of Notre Dame Press,
1981), ch. 6.

4. Ibid., p. 69.

5. Ibid., p. 58.

6. I discuss this further in "Theory and Reflective Practices."

7. David Hume, *Dialogues Concerning Natural Religion,* ed. Nelson Pike (Indianapolis: Bobbs-Merrill, 1970), pt. 8.

8. See my discussion of this move in "Theory and Reflective Practices."

9. Alan Donagan, *The Theory of Morality* (Chicago: University of Chicago Press, 1977), p. 7.

10. Alan Gewirth, *Reason and Morality* (Chicago: University of Chicago Press, 1978).

11. Richard B. Brandt, *A Theory of the Good and the Right* (Oxford: Clarendon Press, 1979).

12. See David Gauthier, *Morals by Agreement* (Oxford: Oxford University Press, in press).

13. Hegel uses the phrase "Kammerdiener der Moralität" in *Phänomenologie des Geistes,* ch. 6, p. 468, in the Hoffmeister edition Hamburg; Feliz Meiner Verlag, (1952).

14. See "Civilizing Practices" for more on this.

15. David Hume, *Enquiries,* ed. L. A. Selby-Bigge and P. H. Hidditch (Oxford: Clarendon Press, 1978). Further references to Hume's writings will be to the Selby-Bigge and Nidditch editions of *A Treatise of Human Nature* (T) and *Enquiries* (E).

16. Hume, E. 12.

17. Hume, T. 271.

18. Hume, T. 262.

19. Hume, E. 10.

20. See Arthur L. Caplan "Can Applied Ethics be Effective in Health Care, and Should It Strive to Be?" *Ethics* 93 (1983): 311-12.

13

Civilizing Practices

MacIntyre's diagnosis[1] of where we stand, as far as morality goes, emphasizes the "arbitrary self-will" behind the contemporary "masks of morality." His story of how we got to this state is a story of loss of faith in a
shared morality, in guidance by what presumably was either not will at
all, or was some less arbitrary and more rational and invariant "will," by
a tradition that nurtured those practices into which individual persons
were initiated, so that they could combine participation in them into
meaningful life-histories. The larger continuing narrative of a cultural and
religious tradition sustained the individual life-narratives of those who
learned those practices, cultivated the virtues needed for success within
them and for that interweaving of them which went into the composition
of significant lives. The real disaster was the Enlightenment, when the ties
that bind were unraveled by impious and curious thinkers like Diderot
and Hume. Once those ties were untied and unraveled, attempts to recon-
stitute and retie them were unsuccessful, and so we have MacIntyre's
scenario for modernity—a sequence of "unmaskings" of the nature of
those ties, and of breakings loose, by protest, from their steadily weaken-
ing hold.

Presuming that MacIntyre is in agreement with most of these modern
unmaskers, that the moral malaise he finds is the lack of any guide except
arbitrary self-will (rather than the determination to unmask, to *find* nothing but arbitrary self-will), I want to raise the question of whether such
unmasking might have gone on earlier, before those older traditions with
which MacIntyre has more sympathy had to struggle against these forces
of modernity to survive—what I mean is not whether it was historically
feasible that unmaskers should appear, but rather whether there was any-

From *After Virtue*, ed. Anton leist, *Analyse & Kritik*, forthcoming.

thing to unmask, whether the morality of Jane Austen's Southern counties, or of Ango-Saxon Becket and Norman Henry II, or of the Benedictine order, or the Greek polis or the Homeric heroes, was a mask for some arbitrary will. Did wills only become arbitrary once traditions were broken, or did morality in those uncorrupted times not serve any will? Is it that the uncorrupt morality is not expressive of will, or is it that the will it expresses is nonarbitrary, so that no "mask" is needed?

MacIntyre's version of moral virtues and the good life in Homeric times, in Athens, in the England of Jane Austen's heroines, does successfully veil the power relationships constitutive of those social worlds. The concept of power plays no important role in his analysis—even the shrill modern self-assertive arbitrary wills are seen as mostly impotent, or are counted on to cancel out one another's power. When MacIntyre discusses the conflict between Becket and Henry II, that is of course seen as a conflict between secular power and the church's power. Their confrontation is meaningful, Becket's martyrdom and Henry's penance have point, because "each had to recognize in the other not just an individual will, but an individual who was the bearer of an authoritative role" (A.V. 161). They "inhabit a single narrative structure," whereas clashing modern wills inhabit none except self-invented, alienating narrative structures (if this is not a contradiction in terms for MacIntyre). Now granted that Becket and Henry each occupied time-honored roles that carried authority, how does that fact make their wills, as occupants of those roles, nonarbitrary? The evolution of the role of arch-bishop, and of English monarch, if not exactly "arbitrary," was as dependent on historical "accident," and as dependent on perceived group interest, as any modern person's will is dependent on accidents of subjective taste and luck, and on perceived self-interest. Do our wills cease to be arbitrary when they serve some larger purpose than our own good? Is Becket's will to oppose Henry nonarbitrary since done for the church he heads, for an institution that preceded his leadership of it and will survive his martyrdom? But if our wills cease to be arbitrary simply by our joining in collectives that last longer than any of their members do, it is easy enough for us moderns and postmoderns to have nonarbitrary wills. All we need is a "cause"in which to unite our will with that of others. Palestinian guerrilla groups, rebels in Central America, members of the armed forces supporting those in power there, all have such collective causes, all are initiated into practices and share "narrative structures" and may indeed see themselves as living unified lives and dying meaningful deaths.

If the recipe for a life that escapes moral corruption is simply to occupy some time-honored role which requires one to do things one had to be taught to do and to show qualities of character one had to cultivate, and to live out a whole life which exhibits some consistency of purpose, in a narrative structure one shares with others, then even university teachers in contemporary America and Europe qualify as MacIntyrean heroes and heroines. Each of us had to learn our trade, had to learn some often against-the-grain functional virtues like punctuality and enough self-discipline to get our classes prepared and our exams graded on time. Our petty ambitions are mutually comprehensible—reading obituaries in the proceedings of our professional societies we recognize the familiar narrative structure of our deceased colleagues' lives—the tenure hurdle, the first book, the entry in the index of citations, the election or appointment to office in the professional association. We teachers each occupy a time-honored position carrying with it a little classroom authority. Perhaps MacIntyre does see present-day universities as communities that continue older traditions of authority and civility in ages of darkness and barbarism, as vestiges of a more civilized past, but I could give a parallel sort of description of the life of my bank-manager neighbor, or my businessman neighbor, or my politician neighbor. They all occupy roles and are not the first to occupy them; they all exercise some role-associated authority, and must accept the role-associated authority of others in their sphere; they all do things they had to be taught to do, and show qualities of character that took some cultivating. Their lives show more or less familiar and typical developments over time, a rough unity of purpose or unified progression of purposes, about as much integrity as Henry's or Becket's; and they all share narrative structures with at least some fellows and colleagues, some who understand what they are doing and why, who can recognize successes and failures in their lives, know what counts for them as tragedy, what as happiness.

But according to MacIntyre we would be deluding ourselves, my neighbors and I, if we thought that our lives met his demands for moral integrity. For our values are masks for arbitrary wills, even when the values are tied to roles we did not invent. MacIntyre is willing to accuse the bank manager of the sin of usury; the businessman of greed; perhaps also the academic of a version of vain self-seeking; those of us who campaign for the better recognition of the rights of minorities, or of children, or the aged, as shrill shouters of meaningless slogans. The debate over nuclear disarmament must be just another clash of arbitrary wills. Why? What is there about the American president's assertion of executive privilege, the American Congress' efforts to protect the powers of Congress, the disputes concerning the implication of the First Amendment, which doom them to be different from and less meaningful than Henry's and Becket's struggles?

Now of course we experience more of the effects of consciousness of cultural diversity than did, say, Jane Austen's heroines. We do not all share the same narrative structure, since some of us are Catholics, others Protestants of various sorts, other Muslims, others Buddhists, others atheists; and this variety of religious and cultural life, which has always existed to some degree, is something we are conscious of in a way past people could sometimes avoid. The cultural mix in many modern nations, the ease of travel, and the access we have to televised versions of the way others live, make each of us necessarily aware that our practices are not the only ones, our lists of virtues (if we have them) not the only ones, our institutional roles only one of many possible sets of institutional roles, our sort of narrative structure one among many alternatives. This doubtless does produce in some of us the emotivist reaction—we see each of the alternatives as equally arbitrary, and so all of them lose their authority, their meaning-conferring power. But I venture to say that, among reflective people, at any rate among philosophers, there are more traditionalists today than there are emotivists, more conservatives than radical skeptics. The reaction to awareness of cultural diversity need not be the urge to demote all the diverse variants to the status of so many expressions of arbitrary wills. On the contrary, one can not only enjoy the variety of forms of life to which one can be no more than an appreciative onlooker (as I am to Maori hakas, American Thanksgivings, and to Corpus Christi processions in Austrian villages), but one's participation as insider rather than onlooker to those forms into which one *has* been duly initiated can be enhanced rather than devalued by awareness that they are only one set of many such sets of life-structuring forms.

I do not think MacIntyre wants to deny this. His reason for claiming that all we have today are moral masks, no longer even succeeding in hiding the arbitrary will behind them, is not the known plurality of alternative such "masks" or postures, but the claimed fact that it is self-will, and emotion not reason, behind the masks. MacIntyre's whole diagnosis seems informed at the deepest level by a distrust of human will, by a demand that human feelings be disciplined, overruled by some "reason" or some "nonself." Other selves like our own are not enough—that merely makes the arbitrary will an equally arbitrary collective will. Some discipliner or denier of human feeling-guided will is what seems required to save us from what MacIntyre calls arbitrary self-will.

But what can and usually does discipline and curb human wills is, of course, a more powerful human will, not anything nonhuman. Typically such power-wielders do claim to articulate the voice of "reason," sometimes of a divine reason. When the power to bend other wills derives from some office the power-wielder occupies, some throne or archbishop's seat, it is that much the more secure, and the authority of tradition backs up the power that is wielded. Why should the decrees of such institutional powers express nonarbitrary decisions and policies? May not the disciplining of human passions and wills serve wills as "arbitrary" as those they suppress?

Where there is an institution, there usually is some inbuilt constraint on how the occupier of a powerful office wields that power. Popes are tied by the infallibility of their predecessors, judges constrained by precedent, constitutional monarchs and presidents by the constitution that both gives them their authority and defines its limits. So there may be a sense in which any wielder of the power that goes with a traditional office expresses a will which is dependable in some respects, is to some degree nonarbitrary in that there are limits to the free discretion such a powerful office-holder exercises. One thing a tradition does is define the limits of the power of the offices integral to that particular cultural tradition. Omnipotent wills are not bound by the rules of any practice, nor by the constraints of any tradition. But those traditions that have created and sustained positions of authority for those licensed to speak for or on behalf of omnipotent wills, be they the positions of king, pope, or simply father, have enabled some humans, with the ordinary array of passions and ambitions, to have very great power over others. Unless there is something nonarbitrary in these traditions themselves, and in the institutions they sustain, then the wills these powerful office-holders execute are essentially just as arbitrary as those of contemporary individualists. That the arbitrariness is institutionalized and continuing makes it no more ultimately acceptable and no less in need of moral masks, and no less ready to employ them to retain power and privilege.

If there is to be a distinction drawn between arbitrary wills and nonarbitrary wills, if we may so speak, it had better be more than simply the distinction between those who do not and those who do occupy positions of some authority in some tradition-hallowed power structure. As Rawls has emphasized, it is the basic structures of a society, and the roles they define, which are the most important sources of injustice, and of arbitrary tyranny.

Does the arbitrary contrast with the just, for MacIntyre? His concept of justice as a virtue is meritarian. To be dealt with justly is to get what one deserves, in light of one's "contribution to the common tasks of that community in pursuing shared goods" (A.V. 233). If my community's practices are of a military type, the shared goods are those of military glory, and my contribution to these is small, I will deserve little from my fellows. Beggars contributed to the medieval Christian version of a shared good, their begging was part of the total common task, the glorification of God, but they apparently deserved little, in material terms, for their contribution. To ask the Rawls' question "Is it fair to allocate some people to the role of beggar, of untouchable, of non-property owner, of slave, and to judge their desert in terms of the sort of contribution such roles allow?" is to ask the sort of question about fundamental social structure, about the basic terms of cooperation, that MacIntyre's version of morality seems almost designed to block. Unless there is consensus in accepting some such structure which defines the roles of those who engage in the different practices, which gives some the right to determine the places of others, some the right to initiate others into their station and its meaningful duties, there cannot be that sense of shared values that is the prerequisite for the sort of narrative structure needed for unified lives and the cultivation of the virtues. A discreet veil is drawn, in MacIntyre's account of our moral decline, over the power-relations that obtained in those noncorrupt communities he cites. He is more willing to raise the question "To whom does power accrue?" of modern societies—the manager and the therapist profit from our moral malaise, get power over us. But what of the old-style managers and therapists, what of kings, popes, and priests? What gave them their power may have been what MacIntyre sees as the moral health rather than the moral malaise of those over whom they exercised power, but the fact of privilege and superior power remains. MacIntyre is better at pointing out whose will lay behind the masks of Hume's version of morality (a Hanoverian elite) and behind post-Humean versions, than at showing whose privilege was sustained by those versions of morality Hume challenged.

Why does MacIntyre give the unsympathetic portrayal he does to Hume's moral philosophy, which in an earlier article[2] he had seen as falling within that approved Aristotelian tradition that sees the moral life as the cultivation of virtues, rather than as obedience to a moral law? Hume also emphasizes the need for shared mutually agreed customs, and his concept of a social artifice can be seen as an ancestor of MacIntyre's (or Wittgenstein's) concept of a practice, a form of life with its own standards and internal goods,[3] an activity that one can learn only by being taught by those already initiated into it. Indeed Hume's essay "Of the Standard of Taste" seems to articulate the need for just this sort of expert authority, by one practiced in the art, and "delicate" in the discriminations relevant there. Hume's essays "Of the Delicacy of Taste and Passion," "Of Eloquence," "The Rise and Progress of the Arts and Sciences," and "Of Refinement in the Arts" all explore the practices whose internal goods Hume himself valued most, the practices of literature, fine speech, "the republic of letters." Such learned and taught activities, which generate their own standards of excellence and their own goods, seem to count as practices in MacIntyre's sense, and Hume does not underestimate their complexity, nor reduce them to efficient ways of getting some practice-neutral pleasure. But Hume of course analyzed (and accepted) not merely the cultural practices of the republic of letters, but also practices concerned with other kinds of publicly recognized goods, namely wealth and political power, and it is here, I think, that he offends MacIntyre, since it is here, supposedly,[4] that he justifies the preferences of a Hanoverian elite.

Hume finds virtue in obedience to the constitutive rules of some moral artifices, like contract, which are essential to capitalism, and to that "bureaucratic individualism" in politics which MacIntyre finds so pernicious. It is Hume's essays on commerce, money, interest, trade, taxes, public credit, his account of justice as obedience to property rules and fidelity to promises, that seem to condemn Hume to MacIntyre's disapproval. All the practices which, on Hume's account, take the natural passion of avidity and transform it by giving it an "oblique direction,"[5] first by inventing property rights that fix possession, then by inventing progressive new forms that property and its transfer may take, are practices essential to that modern world from which MacIntyre advises us to retire. They do provide a narrative structure within which a businessman or a politican may find an entire life's activity, with a typical unity, but they are also practices that enable the rest of us, whatever other practices we engage in, communal or more solitary, to adjust our individual and group activities to one anothers'—to buy and sell, to elect governments. These cultural artifices are those of Hegel's "civil society," they make possible minimal cooperation between strangers, and MacIntyre seems to prefer the closeness of ethical life to the cold, distanced dealings of civil society. But must we choose? *Some* of our dealings must be with strangers, with members of other groups, practitioners of practices alien to us. Nor need we expect to find the whole meaning of our lives in these commercial and political practices, in order to appreciate the role they play, and the extent to which our own particular preferred richer practices are parasitic on those economic and political ones, dependent on them for any chance of peaceful survival. Hume does try to see the relation between economic and commercial activities and other human activites—in "The Rise and Progress of the Arts and Sciences," and in the various appendices in his *History of England*, he explores the historical interconnections between different forms of legal, religious, political, economic, technological, craftsmen's and artists' and game-playing practices, and the virtues displayed in them. In all of this, he seems to me to be doing just what MacIntyre thinks one should do, in order to reflect on the moral possibilities for human beings. But he is also doing something that the earlier, more Marxist MacIntyre would have approved of—giving attention to the economic bases of various more refined cultural forms of life, and attending to the power relationships perpetuated by particular ways of life.

I have suggested that one reason why MacIntyre gives Hume the role of villain in his narrative, despite the large extent to which Hume's position in moral philosophy resembles MacIntyre's, is Hume's "liberalism," his acceptance of commercial and financial practices of which MacIntyre is suspicious. Another reason may be Hume's rejection of many of the practices that MacIntyre admires, those religious practices whose internal goods have essential other-worldly connections. MacIntyre's version of the history of ethics, in this book, is striking for its muting of the question of whether the moral life must also be a religious life. Hume's place in the history of ethics is, most obviously, that of firm rejecter of Christian ethics. He rescues the Aristotelian virtue of pride from its Christian status as first deadly sin, and puts it back among the virtues. He tries to provide an entirely secular account of the virtues, and the practices they enable us to engage in. Although MacIntyre does not condemn secularism, as such, in this book, he is insistent on the need to graft the Christian concepts of sin and of redemption onto the Aristotelian account of the moral life. Hume's role in the book becomes more comprehensible if we see his rejection of these concepts as what really damns him in MacIntyre's eyes.

Hume is no doubt wrong when he says that "celibacy, fasting, penance, mortification, self-denial, humility, silence, solitude, and the whole train of monkish virtues—for what reason are they everywhere rejected by men of sense, but because they serve no manner of purpose."[6] As MacIntyre points out, the purposes of certain sorts of Christian are served by such virtues—they are needed for the kind of practices and other-worldly narrative structure to which, say, Becket devoted himself once he became archbishop. On being made archbishop, Hume writes that Becket

> totally altered his demeanor and conduct, and endeavoured to retrieve the character of sanctity of which his former busy and ostentatious course of life might, in the eyes of the people, have bereaved him. Without consulting the king, he immediately returned into his hands the commission of chancellor; pretending that he must henceforth detach himself from secular affairs, and be solely employed in the exercise of his sacred function, but in reality, that he might break off all connexions with Henry and apprise him that Becket, as primate of England, was now become an entirely new personage. He maintained, in his retinue and attendants alone, his ancient pomp and lustre, which was useful to strike the vulgar. In his own person he affected great austerity and most rigid mortification, which, he was sensible, would have an equal or greater tendency to the same end. He wore sackcloth next to his skin, which, by his affected care to conceal it, was necessarily the more remarked by the world. He changed it so seldom that it was filled with vermin. . . .[7]

A Christian like Becket will see his life on the assumption that, in MacIntyre's words, "whatever earthly community I may belong to I am also held to belong to a heavenly eternal community in which I have a role, a community represented on earth by the church." (A.V. 161). Hume's estimate of Becket's character, and of the narrative structure within which his life and death achieved their unity and meaning, is this:

> This was the tragic end of Thomas a Becket, a prelate of the most lofty, intrepid and inflexible spirit, who was able to cover, to the world and probably to himself, the enterprises of pride and amibition under the disguise of sanctity and of zeal for the interests of piety and religion: an extraordinary person, surely, had he been allowed to remain in his first station, and had directed the vehemence of his character to the support of law and justice; instead of being engaged, by the prejudices of the times, to sacrifice all private duties and public connexions to ties which he imagined, or represented as superior to every civil and political consideration. But no man, who enters into the genius of that age, can reasonably doubt of this prelate's sincerity. The spirit of superstition was so prevalent, that it infallibly caught every careless reasoner, much more every one whose interest and honour and ambition were engaged to support it. . . . The spirit of revenge, violence and ambition which accompanied their [prelates'] conduct, instead of forming a presumption of hypocrisy, are the surest pledges of their sincere attachment to a cause which so much flattered these domineering passions."[8]

These passions and this otherworldly Christian quest are of course ones with which Hume was well acquainted, at least in their Calvinist version, and he is not so much ignoring them, in what he says about celibacy, as deliberately setting himself against them. Men of sense, he says, have no truck with such purposes, which lead one to cultivate character traits that "cross all desirable ends, stupify the understanding and harden the heart, obscure the fancy and sour the temper."[9] This is a considered rejection of one set of virtues, the manner of purposes they serve, and the sort of people they produce.

It is not a rejection of an Aristotelian emphasis on character and virtues, rather than rules or laws. Indeed it should count, for MacIntyre, as one of those internal arguments and conflicts that sustain and advance a moral tradition—MacIntyre does not see the importation of other-worldly ends into the Aristotelian tradition as a break with that, and all Hume is doing, when he rejects the monastic virtues, is restoring the Aristotelian tradition to its origianl *this-worldly* values, removing from it the religious element which, by MacIntyre's own account, had occasioned some incoherence within that tradition, especially in its Thomist version. "What Christianity requires is a conception not merely of defects of character, or vices, but of breaches of divine law, or sins" (A. V. 157). The real trouble with the Enlightenment, for MacIntyre, is not that the Aristotelian conception of virtues and the practices they sustain are challenged, but that the concept of sin is challenged. Hume's ethics does indeed have virtually no place for anything like a Christian understanding of evil, or the Christian conception of a human will that may either sinfully consent to evil or, with the help of cultivated virtues, overcome such temptation. Hume even dismisses the distinction between what is and is not voluntary on our part as a distinction of interest only to official punishers, and to moral philosophers who are "divines in disguise." He includes temperance, but not self-denial, in his table of virtues. Aristotle's concept of weakness of the will gets transformed, in Hume, to the dominance of violent over calm passions, and he sees the determinants of that dominance to be largely situation, temperament, and education, not feats of will by the individual. Despite this de-emphasis on the individual will (which at least guards him against any celebration of self-will), his work in moral philosophy can properly be seen as an attempt to restore something like the original secular Aristotelian conception of the virtues, and to rid that tradition from the effects of the doctrine of original sin and of divine law, which had been grafted upon it, in one of those many historical fusions of once incommensurable moral outlooks that occurred when the Greek and Hebrew conceptions of morality were joined by Aquinas. Just as the tradition Becket and Henry shared was one in which once-clashing traditions of Briton and Roman, Saxon and Norman had reached some sort of mutual adjustment, had created a common measure, so the Christian Aristotelianism of someone like Aquinas or Butler had made peace between once-warring traditions.

Hume's question about monks is precisely the question MacIntyre thinks it is important to ask. Not "what rules they break or keep," but "what sort of *people* are they, what does this pursuit of other-worldly ends do to them?" His answer was unflattering and perhaps unfair. Whether or not the monkish virtues do harden the heart and sour the temper, at least this is a good Aristotelian way to approach the question of wisdom of their way of life. Hume's evaluation of the moral effects of religious belief is not restricted to this judgment about the monkish character traits. In part 12 of the *Dialogues* he diagnoses the effects of "false religion" to be a "habit of dissimulation," a tendency to resort to "fraud and falsehood"; to combine "the highest zeal in religion with the deepest hypocrisy"; to result in a "narrow contracted selfishness" in those understandably preoccupied by "so important an interest as eternal salvation," a manic-depressive alter-

nation between excessive enthusiastic joy and "superstitious terror," not
to mention the pernicious social consequences of "factions, civil wars,
presecutions, subversion of governments, oppression, slavery" and of that
"sacred zeal and rancour" that Hume saw to be the "most implacable of
all human passions," the deadliest vice on his list. The effects of such zeal
are familiar enough to us today, from Belfast to Beirut.

Another reason MacIntyre may have for excluding Hume from the
tradition of moral reflection MacIntyre wishes to revitalize is the centrality, in his own account, of the concept of the unity of a life. Can the Hume
whose *Treatise* worries over personal identity are so notorious have any
place for such a notion, and for that of the narrative structure within
which the unity is discerned? Well, even in the *Treatise* account Hume
does offer us the same sort of literary metaphor that MacIntyre wants,
seeing the succession of perceptions as like the action on a theater stage,
where different actors "pass, re-pass, glide away, and mingle in an infinite
variety of postures and situations." Dramatic unity is a sort of unity there
can be in such a Humean person, one who has a "present concern for past
and future pains and pleasures"[10] and whose history is likened to the
history of a republic. Narrative and dramatic structure in lives and in
nations becomes Hume's main concern in the *History of England.*

MacIntyre chooses narration as the art form from which to project the
sort of structure he finds important for the explanation of human action,
denying that this *is* a projection.[11] Probably one's preference for one
metaphor rather than another here is itself determined by the sort of
practices that structure one's life. Musicians may hope to see their lives
as fugues or free-improvised variations on an emerging theme; Nietzschean free spirits may see theirs as a dance on the edge of the abyss; while
more sober historians will see the basic structure as that of narrative.
MacIntyre's favourite genre among narratives is that of the story of a
quest, and his version of the unity a life may have is that it is the unity
of a quest. The attraction of this metaphor is undeniable, but one ought
to remember all those other metaphors that have been used by Christians—life as a pilgrimage, as a straight race, as a good fight. One's choice
among these varieties of metonymy will be an exercise not in arbitrary
self-will, but in self-expression—which one seems best will indicate something about the content of one's life, about which practices seem most
meaningful to one. Can we allow a thousand flowers of interpretation to
bloom even within one tradition, or must we try to discriminate *the
correct metaphor,* from among the metaphors used to describe the structure and the possible unity of a life? I would hope that we can afford to
be tolerant here, that pluralism is compatible with mutual intelligibility.
We can let MacIntyre describe life in terms taken from the literature of

the Arthurian legends, and also let Hume describe his literary activities in metaphors taken from biological life. Life can have narrative structure, and books can be stillborn.

MacIntyre writes off Hume's evaluations as simply his Hanoverian prejudices or his arbitrary self-will expressing itself, since, on Hume's own account, moral judgments, such as his own judgments on the pernicious effects of "religion as it has been commonly found in the world," are expressions of feeling, that complex feeling he called the moral sentiment. I cannot here go into the justice of MacIntyre's assessment of Hume's philosophical project of showing how human sentiment could, with reasoning from experience as its indispensable slave, correct itself, overcome natural partiality, and achieve a "more stable point of view." MacIntyre judges that this project failed, so that the historical path was cleared for Kant and his formalist version of the moral law. I do not agree with MacIntyre's estimate of Hume's philosophical success, but what I want here to emphasize is something about the project itself, whatever its success or failure. Hume raised the epistemological question of how we recognize moral virtues (and that *is* the main question, as he addresses it—not how we judge actions, or know moral laws, but how we recognize virtues). The answer he gave is complex. Virtues are those traits of character, involving both motivation and ability, to which we give approval when we reflect upon them from a point of view that has overcome the "continual contradictions" to which more partial points of view are prone. The basis for this approval for character traits is their perceived contribution to character itself, and Hume's ultimate moral question is one about character: the good person is the one of whom the moral judge can say "his company is a satisfaction to me," the one who is "a safe companion, an easy friend, a gentle master, an agreeable husband, or an indulgent father."[12]

Now the epistemological question about the basis for our endorsement of some list of virtues or other moral desiderata *is* a typically modern question. One searches in vain in Aristotle for any clear answer to it. All we get there, in the end, is a reliance on one virtue on the list, *phronesis,* for generating the correct version of the other virtues that are to accompany it. (MacIntyre's answer to this question will presumably be given in his promised book on practical reason.) Hume's investigation was prompted by his reaction to the received epistemology, which gave one the choice between conscience, reason, and relevation as the source of moral demands. Convinced that none of these were their real source, Hume set about analyzing conscience and "unmasking" both reason and revelation, to show what passions were served by their spokesmen. He was an unmasker, and not the first. (Think of Socrates, of Jesus against pharisees—

unmasking is no specifically modern calling.) It was precisely because of his confidence that he could discern what passions the received versions of moral reason were slaves to, that he saw his own positive task to be that of showing how violent passions could be calmed, how contradictory passions could correct themselves, with the help of some cooperative practices, to arrive at a stable shared point of view from which moral agreement might be reached among men and women of sense.

Hume does unmask our moral capacities as well as endorse many traditional ways. A traditionalist need not be an obscurantist. Hume tries to bring into the light of reflective good sense both the virtues, the tradition and traditional practices in which they were nurtured, and the human capacities that make possible such virtue-recognition and such participation in shared practices. He resisted attempts to codify and generalize— his "science" of human nature was the historian's science, not the Weberian sociologists's. Unless the big mistake was to examine the virtues, and the epistemology of their recognition, Hume's project seems to be one with which MacIntyre should have every sympathy. Is MacIntyre telling us that only the unexamined tradition is respectworthy, only those practices we have not analyzed or cannot analyze worth engaging in, only mystery-mongering conceptions of the human good, and of human virtues, able to generate the possibility of lives that seem to have point to those living them? I do not think so. His own moral philosophy tries to show us what a practice is, to make us self-conscious about practices, traditions, narrative structures, and virtues. In this sort of history-informed moral philosophy, which makes central the conception of a good person and his or her contribution to a correlative version of a good community with civilizing shared practices, Hume was MacIntyre's predecessor.

Their dispute, if there is one, is one internal to that non-Kantian, more Aristotelian tradition of reflection on morality. I think it concerns precisely the point where Christians disagree with Aristotle, namely whether a secular version of the human good, and of the practices and virtues enabling that good to be enjoyed, is better able to withstand the reflective survey it itself makes possible than are religious other-worldly variants in that tradition.

Hume was a thorn in the flesh for the defenders of religion in his own day not just because of the case against religion he made patiently and thoroughly in all his writings, but because he so obviously in his own life achieved the sort of calm, and grace of spirit, that his opponents thought only supernatural powers, self-denial, and floggings of the flesh could achieve. He managed to live, and live well, and live without any apparent sense of purposelessness, within the very secular practices and tradition he examined, cultivating the virtues he had analyzed. The Enlightenment project, as carried out by Hume, did not fail within Hume's own life. He had no cause, either on his deathbed or earlier, to revise the main lines of his views about the human good. Maybe he was too optimistic about the ability of people in general to live without stupifying their minds, or indulging their love of the mysterious, or their fear of the unknown, their arrogance of power or resentment of powerlessness. But if these are the forces that defeat an enlightened Aristotelian secular tradition of civilizing shared practices and agreeable virtues, the real enemies of Aristotelianism are neither Hume nor Marx nor Nietzsche, but St. Paul and St. Augustine. The City of God is what subverted the Aristotelian earthly city, dissolved its ties, and drained its practices of meaning. Hume tried to make something of the fragments of true Aristotelianism still alive in his culture and did that realistically, helped by his acute perception of the realities of economic, social, religious, and political power, as they had developed since Aristotle's day. In his life and his writings, he tried to show that a good life was still possible, and possible without splitting the human person into masochistic sinful desires demanding to be scourged, and sadistic reason, or conscience, glad to oblige. Hume refuses to admire Becket's sackcloth, refuses to admire either Henry's kneeling to be whipped or those who whipped him.

He accuses the practitioners of religious practices both of hypocrisy and of a stupefaction of the understanding. These harsh words which MacIntyre finds so unsuitable coming from the pen of one who believed that moral judgments have no authority except that of shared human sentiment—as if the religious have a monopoly on righteous indignation, as if one needs a pulpit to thunder from—might be translated into a calmer diction this way: that a certain resistance to full self-consciousness is built into the religious believer's attitude, that the practices of the religious, in as far as they are dependent on religious belief, do not bear what Hume called "reflexion," a turning of sentiment on sentiment, of reasoning on reasoning, of cultural practices upon cultural practices. Hume did want to unravel the ties that bind; to understand how they bound; to see what version of the human good they served, what kind of persons they turned out, and, to his credit, to see quite calmly, and even coldly, what relative allocation of power they entailed. He sees the power relations without, like Marx, becoming so preoccupied by them that nothing else can be seen. His analysis of female chastity, for example, does not blur the power relationships it perpetuates, nor the natural facts that make that asymmetry of power possible. In this particular case, his analysis of a practice, that of monogamous marriage with asymmetry of rights, had a certain recipe for change implicitly contained in it,[13] whereas his analysis of, say, inheritance of property by eldest child, does not. In general Hume seemed to have faith that we would still feel tied, once we understood the ties, that our form of life and catalogue of virtues would bear self-survey, would not be degraded by being understood for what it was. And to understand what it is includes understanding who, on the form of life under examination, gives orders to whom, who profits most, who inherits Ninewells and who does not.

Part of Hume's confidence that, even when one has understood a particular moral order and "balanced the account" as far as the gains and losses go, one will willingly conform to practices by which some profit more than others, in terms of power, riches, and honor (and rarely through any moral "desert" on their part), rests on his trust that the human good sense a decent culture will nurture will see that "inward peace of mind, consciousness of integrity, a satisfactory review of one's own conduct" are more important than "profit or pecuniary advantage"; that compared to "the invaluable enjoyment of a character," superior power and wealth are "worthless toys and gewgaws." The goods internal to the practice of the moral life become more important than any external goods. This should be unworldly and uncommercial enough, even for MacIntyre. But the more worldly side of Hume's acceptance of an inegalitarian set of social practices was his resignation to the need for a certain degree of what might be called "arbitrariness" in human affairs, a limit to the scope of the virtue of equity. He emphasizes the fact that, in any stable scheme of property rights, or of rights to govern others, there will be "frivolous" factors deciding who gets how much of the social powers in question. Any attempt to allocate property or other powers by merit, or on an egalitarian basis, would fail to achieve the end of making possession or government stable, and would lead to the sort of discord and contention England experienced in the seventeenth century, when meritarians and levellers tried to reallocate rights according to their version of desert. If for some norm to be "arbitrary" is for it to be such that it easily could have been different in detail, without being better or worse, both the artifices Hume analyzes and the practices MacIntyre analyzes are arbitrary, and inevitably arbitrary.

Was Hume overoptimistic in thinking we might find forms of cooperation from which all benefit, despite their arbitrariness, and despite the manifest inequality of their distribution of material benefits and worldly power? Hume saw pretty clearly how human beings can react, emotionally, to their own perceived power or lack of power, and he helped us to get clear perceptions of the power relations in which we stand. For all MacIntyre's knowledge of Marx and Trotsky, and for all his reading of Nietzsche on the moral pathology of power-perception, he seems to lack, in his own positive account of morality, any appreciation of the various social, moral, and emotional poisons that can flow from relationships between persons of unequal power, be they divine or human. Hume saw the dangers very clearly, and saw religion as increasing those dangers. If MacIntyre thinks Hume was wrong there, he owes it to us latter-day Humeans to make it clear exactly where Hume went wrong. It is the details of Hume's case against religion that MacIntyre should attend to and rebut, if he wishes to continue to cast Hume in the role of serpent in the Aristotelian garden. For Hume attacked not Aristotelianism, but what he saw as the puritan religious perversion of Greek and Roman morality. Were a Humean historian to retell the narrative MacIntyre has given us, then the fall from Aristotelian grace, the original sin, would occur precisely with the doctrine of original sin.

NOTES

1. Alasdair MacIntyre, *After Virtue* (Notre Dame: University of Notre Dame Press, 1981). References throughout are given as A.V. followed by the page number.

2. In "Hume on Is and Ought," *Against the Self-Images of the Age* (New York: Schocken Books, 1971), p.124, MacIntyre says: "And the virtue of Hume's ethics, like that of Aristotle and unlike that of Kant, is that it seeks to preserve morality as something psychologically intelligible." In a later piece, "How Moral Agents Became Ghosts," *Synthese* 53 (1982): 295–312, he contrasts Hume's Aristotelian gearing of moral philosophy to moral psychology with the later Kantian spiritualization of the moral agent into a mere noumenal chooser. He disagrees with the version of reasons for action he finds in Hume, but it is a version which largely ignores that "correction of sentiment" Hume describes, the move from partial to moral point of view that occurs when "continual contradictions to our sentiments in society and conversation" cause us to be "loosened from our first station" and to "seek some other standard of merit which may not admit of so great variation" (*A Treatise of Human Nature,* ed. L. A. Selby-Bigge and P. H. Nidditch [Oxford: Clarendon Press, 1978], p. 583. I have begun to explore these Humean moves in "Master Passions," *Explaining Emotion,* ed. Amelie Rorty (Berkeley and Los Angeles: University of California Press, 1980), and in "Hume's Account of Our Absurd Passions," *Journal of Philosophy* 79, no. 11 (1982): 643–51.

3. In "Hume on Heaps and Bundles," *American Philosophical Quarterly* 16 (1979): 285–95, I tried to show how the greater power, ability, and security which were the aims of the hypothetical natural persons who adopt the first Humean artifice, that of property, get transformed as new sorts of power, ability, and security become possible. New goods and evils, new forms of trust and mistrust, good and bad reputation for new forms of trustworthiness, while at first valued only for their instrumentality in providing practice-independent goods, come, like the practices whose internal goods they are, to be valued for their own sake.

4. The Hanoverian elite did not receive Hume's *History* with the welcome one would expect, were MacIntyre right about Hume's ideological commitments. As Hume said, in *My Own Life,* "I was assailed by one cry of reproach, disapprobation, and even detestation; English, Scotch and Irish, Whig and Tory, churchman and sectary, free thinker and religionist, patriot and courtier, united in their rage against the man who had presumed to shed a generous tear for the fate of Charles I and the Earl of Stafford."

5. David Hume, *Treatise,* pp. 492, 497. Hume's account of justice, in the *Treatise,* is

an account of how one particular passion, avidity or "the interested affection," restrains itself when mutually advantageous conventions are adopted. These artifices invent the so-called "laws of nature," and so give rise to "natural obligations." Sympathy with the public interest they create, and with rightholders whose rights they create, promotes these into "moral" obligations, on Hume's *Treatise* account. MacIntyre, both in *After Virtue* (p. 47) and in his introduction to *Hume's Ethical Writings* (London: Collier Macmillans, 1965), charged that this account in the *Treatise* based justice on self-interest, whereas in the *Enquiry* altruism and sympathy are also invoked. But Hume's *Treatise* account of justice as a *moral virtue* did invoke sympathy (*Treatise*, pp. 499–500), and all that has changed in the *Enquiry* is the dropping of the hypothetical *sequential* account of how a natural obligation becomes a moral one.

6. David Hume, *Enquiries*, ed. L. A. Selby-Bigge and P. H. Nidditch (Oxford: Clarendon Press, 1978), p. 283.

7. David Hume, *History of England*, vol. l, ch. 3.

8. Ibid.

9. Ibid.

10. David Hume, *Treatise*, p. 261.

11. MacIntyre, *After Virtue*, p. 197.

12. David Hume, *Treatise*, p. 606.

13. See especially his essay "Of Moral Prejudices," which develops the hints in his *Enquiry* account of what powers women possess to make resentment felt, given that no individual has within himself "every faculty requisite both for his own preservation and for the propagation of his kind." (*Enquiries*, p. 191). I have explored this in "Good Men's Women: Hume on Chastity and Trust," *Hume Studies* 5 (1979): 1–19.

14

Poisoning the Wells

I. Methodological Preliminaries

Morality is the culturally acquired art of selecting which harms to notice and worry about, where the worry takes the form of bad conscience or resentment. Were we to keep on our conscience all the harm we are doing, all the risks we are imposing, and to resent all the harms and risks we are subjected to, our moral energies would be, as Hume put it, "dissipated and lost for want of a proper limited object."[1] When is a public policy which entails death for some, risk of death for more, a policy which offends against moral standards? Which deaths, and impositions of risk of death, are wrongful, and wrong to those concerned? It is not merely a question of whose lives we should save by what measures with whose money, but whom, among those whose cooperation and whose taxes we are using, we will with good conscience kill, cause to die, or let die, by what measures or neglect.

Traditional moralities have evolved very complex ways of selecting which harms to focus on, which to turn into wrongs, and different moralities turn attention on different humanly controllable dangers. But since, until recently, our society has not embarked on many large-scale enterprises, other than war, that are known to affect security of life for large numbers of persons in significant ways, our own inherited moral code (or collection of codes, since ours is not a homogenous culture) gives us little direct guidance on the issues now facing us. Is accepting the higher rate

Written as a member of a working group led by Douglas MacLean at the Maryland Center for Philosophy and Public Policy. Papers from that group will appear in *Values at Risk,* ed. Douglas MacLean, Maryland Studies in Public Philosophy, forthcoming, Rowman and Allanheld, Totowa, N.J. A slightly different version of "Poisoning the Wells" will appear in that volume.

of disease and early death among nuclear plant workers and among the population living near such plants like accepting the deaths of soldiers, and some civilian war victims, in wartime? Or is it more like neglecting to do anything about the rising rate of death at the hands of armed burglars and robbers? Or is it like not doing anything about a plague, known to be spread by some human habits? We think we have a sort of rationale for exposing soldiers to death and danger in wartime—our story is that young males are the ones who do best the vital job that carries the danger. But this can scarcely be said of the temporary workers who do the most dangerous cleanup work in nuclear plants.[2] Their position is more like that of those who volunteer to fight in wars because no other job is open to them—it is not that they do a needed job better than others, so must be exposed to the dangers which go with a job that must be done, it is that this is the only job society offers them. The justification of the imposition of risk on them is not that that is an unavoidable occupational risk falling on those who do that vital but dangerous job better than others could. Is the fact that they "volunteer" for it sufficient justification—is the risk they face, like the risk professional prizefighters face, justified since in some sense chosen by the victims? And can we say the same of those, not workers, who are endangered simply by living near such plants—do they too *choose* to face the dangers they do?

The very fact that anyone wants philosophers to address these questions is a sign that our inherited stock of moral guides does not give us ready-made answers to them. Many of the problems are new problems; and moralities, although serving as all-purpose fairly versatile guides, evolved for less rapid change in the human condition that we have had in the last century. What can a philosopher do to help answer the new, difficult questions? Some feel that the very recognition that different moralities focus on different harms is a reason for philosophers to attempt to step back and ask which harms any group should be focusing on, so that even if our own inherited moral guides did give us ready-made answers to the questions facing us, we should not trust those answers, but should appeal to some first principles by appeal to which that morality's dictates are justified, to the extent that any of them can be justified. But the problem that arises then is disagreement about those ultimate principles. Anyone who thinks she knows what the point of morality is, so proposes to judge whether a particular inherited morality is a *good* selector of harms to focus on, must expect some others, in the group whose policy is in question, to reject that version of the point of morality. Some utilitarian readers will have already rejected my fairly neutral Humean characterization of it as a way of ignoring some dangers and of highlighting and coping with others; but even if one does accept that, it will still be a matter of controversy what the point is of such moral focusing devices, or blinkers, what counts as the well- or ill-functioning of such blinkers. Rule utilitarians will see the point as the minimization of total or of the average harm suffered, harm being equated with misery. Contractarians will have a different answer, and Kant[3] believed that the point of morality was the progressive development of rational capacities in our species, even at the cost of war, conflict, misery, and even incapacitation, suffered by the morally good as much as by the less good. Nonphilosophers, if they have any views at all about the point of morality, are as likely to disagree as are the philosophers—many religious people take its point to be obeying or pleasing God, rather than promoting human well-being. So any assessment of a conventional morality's adequacy, and any attempt to appeal beyond it to its point, to get answers to hard questions, is bound to encounter opposition. At this point, the realization that disagreement about metamorals is at least as likely as disagreement about morals, some[4] conclude that the proper reaction is to demote all these ultimate values, opinions about what ultimately matters, to personal preferences, then, at the level of social policy, to maximize expected preference-satisfaction. We are simply to throw the sacred values into the hopper along with every other preference, ignore differences of level among the "preferences" or "tastes" we are taking into account, and measure all of them by the amount of money the preferrer will pay to get her way, ignoring the different sort of *expression* values of different sorts typically get[5] and simply trying to thwart as few people as possible as little as possible. But such a reaction to disagreement about ultimate or sacred values is the reaction only of those whose own sacred value is utility-maximization—it would not be the reaction of the Kantian, who is quite willing to thwart mere empirical wills in the name of the progress of reason. So to resort to utility-maximization is not to get *beyond* clashing sacred values, but merely to reveal one's own sacred value.

I do not think that we can step back from our inherited cultural blinkers, including our moral ones, to examine those blinkers with an unblinkered gaze. At most we can turn our blinkered gaze on one anothers' blinkers, and listen to others' version of our own blinkers, and their judgment of the effect of those blinkers. Even our way of doing this, of studying other cultures or criticizing our own, will itself owe a lot to inherited traditions and practices, and will not itself be free of cultural bias. So I do not see my role, as philosopher, to be to make any pretense of stepping outside the conventional morality in which I was reared to examine its "rational" credentials, to judge it by external standards, nor to replace it by something better. I see my role rather to be to exploit that morality's own potential for self-consciousness and development, aware that it may have multiple potential, so that others in the same tradition may go in different ways, and aware also that there are other traditions, like mine with some techniques for recognizing studying, learning from, communicating with, nondestructively disagreeing with, and sometimes coming into agreement with, those inside and outside that tradition.

I began by agreeing with Hume that concern for human well-being needs a proper, limited object, and suggested that moralities typically provide their followers with just that. Hume also has a version of what goods are furthered by that part of our morality which impose obligations and recognizes rights. He says that such a scheme of rights and obligations is a cooperative social venture in which "By the conjunction of forces, our power is augmented: By the partition of employments our ability increases; By mutual succor we are less expos'd to fortune and accidents. . . . Tis by this additional *force, ability* and *security* that society becomes advantageous."[6] Now this verdict on what goods socially enforced obligations and rights provide is, if what I have just said is accepted, one which might be disputed, and one which is a result of turning on a social scheme or morality a kind of reflection made possible by the social scheme itself— it is not the judgment of an impartial spectator, but of a reflective participant. Other reflective participants might not agree that power, ability, and security are what our morality (and I am assuming that Hume's and ours are close enough to be regarded as the same) promotes. I shall not defend this finding of the formal goods morality promotes, but rather try to use it to do that stretching of the blinkers which seems needed to get an answer to the question of which policy-related deaths and impositions of risk we should have on our consciences. Hume's version of what goods morality promotes is promising for this purpose, since it is not a tendentious claim about the ultimate goal, but a possibly less tendentious analysis of the formal goods that are promoted—it leaves open what sort of power, to do what, we want; what kind of abilities we wish to increase; what we want made secure. It is not an attempt to discern ultimate values, but does look a bit beyond immediate judgment of right and wrong. That much stretching of our moral blinkers, widening of focus, may be enough for us to see when and why we may, in pursuit of our public policies, impose risk of death on our fellows and successors.

Hume applied his thesis that our moral constraints involve a cooperative conjunction of forces, partition of employment, mutual succor, for the sake of increased power ability and security, largely to us as proprietors, concerned to have powers to appropriate, ability to get and own varied sorts of things, and to be secure in our ownership. I shall try to use these categories, as he scarcely did, to the morality of life and death dealing, to the protection morality gives to our concern to have power and ability to live a life of normal length and to do so with security of life.

II. Individual Rights and What Supplements Them

The social schemes Hume looks at, what he calls the "artifices" of property, gift, barter, promise and of government, all create (or enable the transfer of) rights, and impose obligations. One of the commonest ways in which moralities select which humanly controllable harms to treat as wrongs is by the recognition of individual rights, in some area, such as security of life, where danger lurks. Such rights are protection against danger from other persons, through their assault or their neglect. The prohibition of murder is the most obvious way in which we cooperate to reduce insecurity of life. But lists of rights are fairly crude moral guides, since rights sometimes clash, and then we need some way of selecting which rights are the more important, or which of the interests those rights protect are the more vital. Nor is it only when one recognized right clashes with another that it may be overridden.[7] Sometimes it seems to be overridden by a vital interest that is protected not only by a recognition of individual rights, but also in other ways. J. S. Mill discusses this possibility. After arguing that certain vital interests of persons (security of life, property, contractual agreement) ought to be given a special moral status, namely that of recognized and protected individual *rights*, he goes on to say that although, as a class, these interests or "social utilities" are vastly more important and so more absolute and imperative than other parts of morality or of social efficiency, nevertheless in particular emergencies one justifiably puts aside these more "absolute" demands: "Thus, to save a life, it may not only be allowable, but a duty to steal or take by force the necessary food or medicine, or to kidnap and compel to officiate the only qualified medical practitioner."[8] The case Mill takes here is a controversial one and his own position is interestingly complex. It is not, on the face of it, a case in which one recognized right clashes with others, since presumably the injured man whose life we try to save (by stealing and kidnapping what is needed to save it) does not have a recognized *right* to be rescued. He has a right not to be attacked, but in most communities no recognized right to rescue if attacked, nor to rescue if injured in an accident. We do not encourage persons to feel that their rights have been violated if they are not offered aid in such circumstances. (If they are paid up members of the AAA, or some other such organization, they may of course have rights to aid from specific persons.) Presumably Mill's version of "social utility" is to decide whether or not the interest each person has in assurance of receiving life-saving assistance is sufficienctly "vital" for this class of case to give rise to a recognized right to aid. Although formally this case does seem to satisfy Mill's criterion for a right and a correlative duty of justice—there is an "assignable individual" who is harmed if some moral duty is neglected—nothing that he says suggests that he believed that we should recognize an individual right to rescue. Any assistance a person gets in such emergencies will be, for Mill, given to satisfy those requirements of morality which are not duties of justice, that is, duties to respect recognized rights. Nevertheless the moral requirement to rescue is to override the normal requirements of respect for rights of property and rights to liberty, presumably because it is part of that most vital interest, the interest in security of life, which the foremost of recognized rights partially protects.

Both the recognition of the right not to be assaulted, and the expectation of rescue efforts, contribute to what we can call a certain climate of life as far as concerns security of life. The victims of the nonrecognition of such a right or the disappointment of this expectation would not be merely those killed or injured by assault from others, or left to die unrescued, but all persons whose lives are at risk in these circumstances, whose security of life is thereby lessened. "For as the nature of foule weather lyeth not in a showre or two of rain, but in an inclination thereto of many days together; so the nature of war consisteth not in the actuall fighting; but in the known disposition thereto during all the time there is not assurance to the contrary."[9] We want, as Hobbes emphasized, not merely goods but the assurance of getting and keeping them. Even in a Hobbesian state of nature, a lucky person who was not deprived of life by the absence of established rules but who survived to old age, would have been deprived of security of life, and so of most enjoyments. He will have lacked what Hobbes calls "power," and have had no opportunity for "glorying," unless it be a limited case of glorying, say in his proven ability to live a precarious, powerless, and dangerous life. Mill, who was no adventurer, judged that "security no human being can possibly do without; on it we depend for all our immunity from evil and for the whole value of all and every good, beyond the passing moment, since nothing but the gratification of the instant could be of any worth to us if we could be deprived of everything the next instant by whoever was momentarily stronger than ourselves."[10] Even if no individual *right* to rescue, or to safety in the workplace, in public transport, in consumer goods, is recognized, the reasonable expectation that such rescue measures are taken, and such safety standards observed, contributes to the security climate of life in which we live. Nonviolence, general public safety, and the will to rescue, are public goods. Individuals may die unrescued, and die of accidents in the workplace, although these goods *are* provided, but if they are not provided the victims are not merely those who die through the absence of such services but all those who live in fear of this happening to them.

Leaving aside for the moment the question of whose responsibility it is to see that they are provided, I want at this point to consider whether we should speak of *rights* to such public services. Are my rights violated if I live in a community without proper police protection, without ambulance or rescue services, and am thereby deprived of a decent climate of life as regards security of life? Should we allow the concept of a right to cover rights to social climates of various sorts? If we were to, then we could construe Mill's case as a clash between rights—between the individual's property rights (and right to the maintenance of a social climate of respect for property) and the right of the injured man, and others, to a climate of life in which we have assurance that an attempt will be made to rescue us when we need rescuing. If we say we have a *right* to these public services, then Mill's case becomes a clash of rights, although the injured man still has no right to be rescued, only a right to normal rescue attempts. Would it be wise to stretch the concept of a right to include the provision of such social climate controllers as rescue services (and the special rights of rescuers), if we agree with Mill about the moral priority of providing them?

The pressure to say yes comes from a worry about the complexity, perhaps the incoherence, of Mill's unrevised position. Can we both recognize rights as "more absolute" protectors of vital interests we all have and also allow the overriding of those rights? And if we can override some of them for the sake of what another of them protects, namely security of life, why not incorporate in the "right (or rights?) to life" everything that a person is encouraged to expect to be done to protect his or her security of life, both the enforced prohibition of murder, and the observation of safety standards and the provision of rescue services? I shall consider a good and a bad reason for rejecting this attempt to tidy up Mill's position by letting all the highest priority moral requirements generate rights, some of them rights to a "share" in a public good, to the enjoyment of a certain climate of life.

The good reason to reject it is the impossibility of fixing the "assignable individuals" who are the main victims of any violation of a hypothetical right to a certain degree of security of life, and also of deciding who the violators are. The usefulness of the concept of a right, as Mill saw, lay in its being a quick way to determine both the wronged and the wrongdoers. But when we as a community have failed to provide ourselves with any ambulance system, it is not clear, unless some official or authority is charged with this duty, *who* has failed, nor is it clear which accident victims would have lived had there been an adequate service. All who live in fear of dying unaided are the victims of the bad social climate, but there is no way of saying who are those on whom it actually rains, who would have been kept dry had we the proper climate control. Rights without clear victims or clear violators are as much pseudorights as are rights without remedies. So I think it better to leave Mill's views unrevised. Untidiness is better than misleading surface tidiness. What we must say is that we ought to have a certain climate of life, that this "ought" has a high moral priority, but not that we have a right to this good. Only when there *are* assigned responsibilities for tasks concerned with ensuring this required climate of life will it make sense to speak of the public's right to the proper meeting of these responsibilities, and only when those responsibilities are fairly specific will there be any possibility of making good the claim that a given individual is a particular victim of the violation of the public's right, so that some compensation is due.

The bad reason that one might give, that some do give, for rejecting the idea of a right to a climate of life is connected with this assignment of responsibilities. Some believe that no genuine rights are rights which impose on others unconsented-to positive duties as distinct from mere refrainings.[11] If we are to have rescue services and safety standards, someone has to provide and administer them, and so a claimed right to such things may appear, like the United Nations' "human right" to paid vacations, a pseudoright, quite different from real rights like the right not to be robbed or assaulted. We can respect the latter rights simply by inhibiting our aggressive impulses, but to respect the hypothetical right to paid vacations or good samaritan services, inhibition is not enough—someone has to do something, to spend time and effort. Positive pseudorights are costly; negative real rights cost only the inhibition of evil, aggressive impulses.

That is perhaps a parody of the bad reason. There are places in Mill's writings where he might seem to give it some weight. After making room for recognition of rights as recognition of vital interests of persons, he says: "Now it is these moralities which primarily compose the obligations of justice. The most marked cases of injustice, and those which give tone to the feeling of repugnance which characterizes the sentiment, are acts of wrongful aggression or wrongful exercise of power over someone; next are those which consist in wrongfully withholding from him something which is his due—in both cases inflicting on him a positive hurt either in the form of direct suffering or of the privation of some good which he had some ground, either of a physical or social kind, for counting on."[12] Mill's attempt in this passage to distinguish active "aggressive" infliction of a hurt from more passive infliction of a hurt by withholding something is problematic. "Withholding" is intentional nonsupplying, so Mill's distinction is not that between acting in some matter and failing to attend at all to that matter. I do not "withhold" care from those needy persons whom I have never bothered to notice or find out about, but I do withhold from the beggar I refuse. Mill is not, I think, succumbing to the liberal temptation to construe all genuine rights as "negative" rights, all of the core moral rules as prohibitions; but he does seem to want to make the most *important* rights "negative" ones, perhaps rights not to be harmed, and the most serious wrongs wrongings by "doing," whereas the less serious but still serious wrongs are wrongings by withholding—violations of lesser, more "positive" rights, perhaps rights to be benefited. I shall give reasons for doubting that this distinction can be defended when it is thought to rest on the active/less active, positive/negative, or harm/no benefit distinctions. As Mill himself says of his top-priority moral demand, and correlative individual right, namely that others not assault us, it is "the claim we have on our fellow creatures to join in making safe for us the very groundwork of our existence." It is a claim to mutual succor, that they *join in making safe*, not merely a claim that they desist from assault. To prevent all "inflictings of hurt," whether by doing or refraining taking or withholding, persons must join in a cooperative scheme. To thus join is not merely to obey the main normative demand, whether it be phrased as a prohibition or a positive requirement, but also to to obey related demands and to contribute to the enforcement costs any such demands involves.

III. Obligations and What Supports Them

To think that some part of morality, respect for rights, is both more stringent and more easily justified than the rest because it demands of each person no more than the "refraining" from certain "harmful" acts such as murder, while other less easily justified moral demands impose on us "positive" duties or obligations such as aid to the injured, is to make at least one of three mistakes. The first is the mistake of ignoring the positive cooperative contribution each person makes to the enforcement of *any* social or moral demand, be it the prohibition of assault or the requirement of parental care. The "cost" of a prohibition of murder is not merely the frustration of murderous impulses in those subject to them, but also the "training" costs on those educated so as to inhibit, repress, or sublimate aggression, the efforts of the educators, the social costs of getting them to provide such education, and all the enforcement costs (in taxation, effort, and inflicted pain) involved in having police, courts, and prisons, so that violators of the requirement be detected, tried, and punished. This is parallel to the sorts of costs involved in a "positive" requirement such as parental care—the cost here is not merely in the efforts of parents, but in all the educational, propaganda, and enforcement machinery needed to get them to do their perceived duty. The first mistake, then, is to ignore the educational and enforcement costs which *any* moral requirement involves, costs that always do demand active cooperation by large numbers of persons, and "positive" contributions by all members of society. As both Hume and Mill emphasize, morality is a cooperative scheme, for Hume a "conjunction of forces," for Mill a "joining to make safe the very groundwork of our existence." The joining and conjoining includes bearing our share of enforcement and training costs.

The second mistake typically made by those who see our clearest and most stringent duties to be to *refrain* from certain active "harmings," is to let too much weight rest on the fact that some moral requirements typically get expressed in a negative way, "don't kill, don't steal"; others in a positive way, "obey legitimate authorities, keep contracts, care for your children." What is the significance of this surface difference between moral requirements? Is it merely surface?[13] We can, it seems, force all moral requirements into a negative form (to get all in a positive form is harder)—"don't break promises, don't disobey governments, don't neglect your children." But perhaps these are all double negatives, so the contrast has not been lost. Is not breaking failing to keep, disobeying failing to obey, neglecting failing to take care of? Yes, and so is stealing failing to respect property rights. It seems that our effort at transformation succeeds in transforming some surface negatives into positives, but not yet in destroying the contrast unless we can construe "don't kill" as equivalent to something like "show respect for the right to life," as "don't steal" might become "show respect for property rights."

Can we do this? I think not. "The right to life" is a lot vaguer than the wrong of manslaughter. We have no clear conception of what "the right to life" is supposed to guarantee one, as we do have a clear idea of what are our property rights, contractual rights, duties as parent, duties as citizens. We have relatively clear ideas about all of these because all these rights and obligations are specified in determinate law-backed social artifices, as Hume called them. We need conventions to know what counts as stealing, as contract breaking, as treason, as failure to do one's parental duty, but we seem to have and need no social artifice[14] to tell us what counts as killing. This would give "don't kill" a special place among moral requirements, special in its independence of social artifice rather than in any pure negativity. But of course it is not "don't kill" that is our rule. "Don't dispossess" would be an equally artifice-independent rule, were we to accept it, and so would be "don't change your expressed mind," "obey the powerful." But our moral prohibitions are of murder, stealing, promise-breaking, disobedience to legitimate authorities, not of killing, dispossessing, disappointing aroused expectations, disobedience. It is murder and manslaughter, not killing, which we prohibit, and to distinguish murder from execution or warfare we need to appeal to powers and duties which are as "artificial" and as culture relative as are property rights. As behind "don't steal" lie the complex property rules of a society, so behind "don't murder" lie complex rules telling one what counts as murder. The instructions we need to give, and the laws and moral rules we need to recognize, will be framed in the terms our way of life has forged.

Most human ways of life have given a fairly regular and prominent place to killing, whether in societies of hunters and fishers, or of farmers and soldiers, or in industrial societies like ours in which the meat industry, the military, and the weapons industry are central parts of our economy. Restrictions on killing, segregation of the contexts where killing is encouraged and where it is forbidden, have been essential in all human societies which depend, as most have done, on some sort of death dealing for the very possibility of their way of life. The crucial piece of moral knowledge in any human society, and one that war veterans may find very difficult to acquire, is knowing which times and places are the times and places to kill. Equally central in most societies is knowing when, where, and with whom to have sexual relations, and in both cases we have special words for the forbidden varieties—murder, assassination, and manslaughter; rape, sodomy, fornication, adultery, and incest. We also have some words for the allowed or encouraged kinds—self-defense, execution, combat, "wasting"; courtship, marital love. Precise norms expressing our complex attitudes in these matters usually need to employ such special words—our rule is not "do not kill," but rather "do not commit murder or manslaughter"—wherein it takes an institutional and cultural context for us to know when killing, even of human beings, is and is not murder or manslaughter; just as it takes such culture-specific knowledge to tell adultery, incest, fornication, or even rape apart from allowed sexual relations. If our moral requirements about killing are indeed intended to "make safe the very groundwork of our existence," then we must suppose that "we" are a somewhat exclusive set, and that "our" existence does not include the existence of members of enemy nations, nor of human fetuses, nor of animals, nor of those found guilty of capital crimes. Our social and moral attitudes to the deliberate termination of a human life are as complex and baroque as are our attitudes to sex. Behind the short prohibition "thou shalt not kill" lie as many tacitly understood qualifications and cultural and legal discriminations as lie behind "thou shalt not love thy neighbor's wife." Just as the latter presupposes determinate institutions of marriage, determining individual marital rights, so "thou shalt not murder" presupposes a complex set of culturally specified rights, powers, and prerogatives.

Far from giving us some sort of minimal thin version of the right, as liberals would have us believe, any popular version of a short set[15] of moral don'ts, such as "don't kill, don't steal, don't break promises, unless you are an official don't coerce," brings with it a very rich cultural baggage,[16] if it is to have any content at all. Either it is a purely formal moral code, not yet prohibiting or enjoining anything, or else the form gets a determinate filling, in which case we are committed not merely to these "negative" rules but to the rules of the background institutions and ways of life that supply the determinate content to these prohibitions. Their negative form, then, is simply an indication that the behavior they are regulating is complexly organized, so that lines have to be drawn, limitations made clear, the onus of proof laid. All of these apparently simple negatives can be rephrased in a less simple and less purely negative form this way: "You may kill these but not those. You may take and keep these but not those. You may change your mind in these circumstances but not those. You may limit the options of others in these ways but not in those." The simple negative formulation is merely the tip of the full normative iceberg.

The third error which pushes some to see negative rights to various sorts of "noninterference" as more basic than any rights whose respect requires some activity and effort, is that of thinking that if we "leave people alone" we cannot harm them, so the basic rights are rights not to be harmed by others, while the more dubious rights are rights to be benefited by them; the basic obligations, obligations not to harm, the more dubious obligations, ones we need special devices like contract to take on, obligations to confer benefits upon them. On such a view "don't murder" tells us not to harm another, whereas "rescue the perishing" seems to require that we do them a good turn, that we go out of our way to assist them. Such duties seem too strenuous, whereas refraining from murder takes no calories at all.

Now, as I have already emphasized, it is quite a strenuous business to train persons so that they can and do inhibit violent impulses, no less strenuous than to bring them up to spontaneously offer aid to the injured. It just isn't true that helping another always costs more than not harming, especially if we include the costs of training. (And it *may* cost the Mafia real dollars to refrain from wiping out those who threaten their profits.) But what this third mistake primarily concerns is not cost to the agent so much as cost to the patient, what counts as harming and helping another. It is not easy ever to say where not harming ends and helping begins. Some, such as Robert Nozick and David Gauthier,[17] want to make the benchmark relative to which one decides this well-being of the "patient" without any interaction with the agent. If his situation is improved by the interaction, we have benefited him by it, if it is worsened we have harmed him. But this choice of benchmark prejudges a lot of moral issues. If it is used to support the claim that our basic moral obligation is not to harm, it presupposes that there is no obligation to join with others, that reclusiveness is morally unobjectionable, even if our nonjoining ruins the enterprise for those who join. For some pipings and some dances "I have piped unto you and you have not danced" may be moral condemnation, but the Nozick-Gauthier position makes that impossible, unless one had contracted to dance if piped to.

It is easiest to see the unacceptability of a noninteraction benchmark for interpersonal harms and benefits used as a basis for limiting wrongings to harmings, if we consider its implications for duties of child care. Since without interaction a newborn child would die, any interacting adult who does not simply maim or torture the child confers a benefit, by the noninteraction benchmark. The child is not harmed by anyone (parents, let us say) who leave it alone. Unless one has contracted with the child or someone else to care for it, there is no duty to do so if duties are duties not to harm. One might try to see carrying to term and giving birth as a prior interaction, so that for the mother the question would become not "interaction or no interaction?" but "continuation or cessation of interaction?"; however, this would, at best, generate maternal not paternal obligations (which may be what the "no interaction without contract" theorists hope to show). It would generate these obligations only if prior unconsented-to interaction could be construed as implicit promise of continued interaction, which seems absurd. Whatever pregnancy is, it is not a promise. So the outcome is that no one is obligated to care for the child; it must hope that someone will do it a good turn. This methodological solipsism in ethics, espoused by Gauthier and by Nozick, seems to me both question begging and ultimately self-destructive. If there is no harm done to a newborn child by simply leaving it alone, and there is no duty to benefit it, then, by adopting the benchmark of no interaction to determine wrongful harming, we are opting for a morality[18] that cannot ensure its own continuation, since it condones the letting-die of new members of the moral community.

It is hard to avoid the suspicion that this liberal[19] version of morality is a morality for males, parasitic upon an unacknowledged, quite different morality for females. Both the hidden costs of *training* persons to be good capitalists who sublimate violence, respect property, and keep contracts, and the implicit exceptions from the "no duty to benefit" principle fall upon the women. As Nancy Chodorow[20] has acutely pointed out, women's duty includes the training of daughters willing to continue with this version of mothering, so that the double standard, if that is indeed what it is, becomes self-perpetuating—women make one another into accomplices in the system.

I have in this section argued against bad reasons for rejecting a right to public goods such as a climate of life that gives security of life against the dangers of child neglect, assault, dying in accidents without any rescue attempts, dying from unsafe conditions on roads and in the workplace. These bad reasons would, if accepted, be reasons not merely for rejecting the right, but for demoting the obligation to help supply such goods. I have in the previous section allowed that there may be good enough reasons not to speak of a right to many of the services that protect security of life, but, with Mill, I argued that we can still give high moral priority to the duties to support and help supply such services. Rights need not merely the complementary obligations not to violate rights, but the supplementary obligations to support the institutions that train persons to be responsible moral agents, who respect rights and seriously recognize duties; and all prohibitions need the support of the possibly strenuous doing of related duties. Such security of life as our society has provided has been provided not merely by those who obey the criminal law prohibiting murder, but by all those who do their duty as law enforcers, as moral educators, by those who protect the young, the injured, and the aged from neglect and prepare others to do the same, those who observe or enforce safety standards and train others to do the same, those who observe or enforce safety standards and train others to do the same. A complex network of some rights and many more obligations has given us such security of life as we have enjoyed until now. How can this scheme be adapted to cope with new sources of danger? Is there, in the existing scheme, some implicit principle of selection of which harms to give attention to, which can help us get such conservative guidance? I turn now to that question.

IV. Fortune, Accidents, and Ill Will

Hume's cited version of the point of our rights and obligations emphasizes its role in giving us, through mutual succor, security against *fortune and accidents*, but the details of his account make quite clear that some of the relevant misfortunes and accidents are at the hands of our fellows. It is indeed because the goods we would like to keep can be "ravish'd from us" by others that Hume's first artifice, that of property, is seen to be necessary. Although later artifices, such as contract and government, make it possible for people to undertake such cooperative protections against nature, fate, and accident as draining meadows and improving harbors, the first artifice protects people against dangers from one another. This seems to apply to our social and legal reaction to danger to life as well as danger to possessions. We first prohibit assault and pay for the supportive institutions that requires, then think about public hygiene, health service, ambulance service. Is this our choice because this is the most efficient use of our social resources, because we save more lives more cheaply by a prohibition on assault than by other possible measures? Or is it salience that selects this measure—is assault simply a more obvious danger to life than are other dangers? Although it *will* be a salient danger in groups who live by assaulting other living things, I do not think either salience or perceived efficiency is enough to explain the priority given to prohibitions of assault, the near universality and complete uncontroversiality of socially enforced prohibitions of civilian assault.

If, starting from a blank tablet, legislators asked themselves "What can we do, and how best can we allocate resources to reduce risk to life, across the board?" would the prohibition of, or even required compensation for,[21] assault be the obvious first move? That would depend, perhaps, on the psychology of the population, and their situation with respect to access to means to satisfy their perceived needs. If they were not quarrelsome by nature, and if they did not need to physically worst a human competitor to get what they needed or wanted, a law forbidding what is known to be the poisoning of the wells (by careless personal habits, perhaps) might have a much higher life-preserving effect than a law against murder even in a society of hunters, accustomed to deliberately killing animals, and of warriors, accustomed to killing human enemies. Yet it seems to have been clear, not merely to Hobbes and Mill, but to most human societies, that the most vital of our interests in the area of security of life is security against malicious attack. Why? If I am to die because of what others do, should I prefer to die of infection because my fellows defecated thoughtlessly in the wells, than because one of them knifed me with malicious intent? Why, as legislators, have we first prohibited murder, and only later worried about the knowing or unknowing poisoning of our wells? Is it merely because we were first hunters, and only later deliberate poisoners of animals, so that restrictions on assault preceded restrictions on poisoning?

Rousseau pointed out that "the nature of things does not madden us, only ill will does," and our laws reflect what maddens us rather than what merely distresses us. Perhaps Rousseau should have allowed that negligence as well as obvious ill will can madden us, and that all the range of degrees of ill will, from thoughtlessness to malice, need not madden the victims, but can produce that suppressed rage which is resentment. The criminal law prohibits the sort of harming of others which, whether or not it is prohibited, the victims resent, and resent because it displays ill will. Once prohibited, we call such harming with intent "injuring," or "violating a right," thereby implicitly assimilating *all* the prohibited harmings to violent assault, to intent to inflict bodily injury. Security of life is partially protected by the prohibition of assault, itself part of what is correlative to "the right to life," and other duties protect other equally complex rights, such as property rights, or security of possession, and to security of contract, security of liberty (noncoercion) in some areas of life. In all these cases, as with security of life, the recognition of the right amounts only to partial protection, protection only from threats from certain sources. A person can have security of property lessened by inflation and depression as well as by likelihood of theft, can have security of contract threatened by acts of God as well as breach of contract, can have freedom or security of liberty threatened by need and by obligations as well as by any coercion by private or public agents. The threats we are protected against by these rights and recognized obligations are threats stemming from what can be seen as the absence of goodwill in others. I shall use the term *ill will* for this absence of goodwill. Thus ill will includes not merely aiming at harming another (the evil eye), but also ignoring the interests of others, or knowingly sacrificing vital interests of theirs to lesser interests of one's own (turning a blind eye.)

Intentionally killing another who has not asked to be so killed, with any motive other than self-defense clearly exhibits such ill will. Defecating in the wells need not. It could be an ignorant endangering of lives, and the ignorance need not be culpable if attention had not been drawn to the effects of such action. Only children need to have attention drawn to the effects of stabbing and battering—even before such actions are explicitly prohibited, an adult knows what their effects normally are. It does not take social emphasis for these ill effects to be known, whereas, for poisoning, some "labeling" by society is needed. Before that labeling occurs, there can be ignorant poisoning, and the ignorance need not be culpable. Even when the poison label has been attached, that is, when there is common knowledge of the lethal effects, and when a person shares in that knowledge, he may ignore or forget or not attend to that knowledge. There is culpable ignoring as well as culpable ignorance. There can be nonculpable ignoring, but it is harder to excuse one's action by the claim "I forgot that the effects could be so bad," than by the claim "I didn't know they were so bad," even when the claim is true. Whether ignoring what one knows is or is not culpable will depend on whether what one ignored was highlighted common knowledge, and whether, when it is special, esoteric knowledge, one is an expert in that field of knowledge.

What a society invests in making criminal, then, depends not merely on what knowledge of dangerous effects of actions exists somewhere in that society, but on how widely that knowledge is disseminated, on how much that danger has been highlighted, and so on what can reasonably be construed as harming with ill will, with knowledge that one is neglecting the interests of others affected by one's action.[22] Not merely the criminal law's selection of harmings to focus on, but the selection made by other agencies, regulatory, educational, and service, depends on available knowledge, on its commonness, and on what consequently appears as ill will, if done or left undone. It is now common knowledge that people are poisoned by what steel mills and automobile exhaust put into the atmosphere, what many industries and agriculturalists put into rivers, seas, and soil. Despite vigorous disagreements there is a large body of common knowledge about radiation dangers, both from medical diagnostic procedures and from nuclear plants, military and nonmilitary. We cannot, then, as officials and as private agents, ignore such dangers without being guilty of ill will. If our morality is to adapt itself to our new common knowledge we must update our registry of poisons and records of poisoners. We must recognize the new instrumentalities of poisoning, as such.

I see no reason why those who use these lethal methods of going about their business, who knowingly impose on others significant risk of death by radiation-related cancers, by poisoning from slow-seeping chemical wastes, from poisons emitted into air and water, should not be dealt with in the same way and in the same place as we deal with those who, for gain, send poisoned chocolates to their elderly relatives. Once there, their defenders may try to invoke the doctrine of double effect to get them off the hook, but it will take that dubious doctrine to show any relevant difference. And even that doctrine may not succeed in distinguishing the two cases — just as the steel mill owner can claim that he deplores the deaths his mills cause, that he wishes his profit-making did not require such lethal means, and that he is not relying on the deaths, as such, to get his profits, so the chocolate-sender can claim that he regrets the need to adopt this means to come into his inheritance, and relies, for his success, not on the death as such, but simply on the property transfer. Were the laws of inheritance to have been changed so that the mere age of his aunt sufficed for that wanted transfer, he would gladly have spared his aunt. The honors for ill will seem equal.

V. Consent to Risk

Some risks that avoidably or unavoidably are imposed by those with power to do so are not escapable by those on whom they are imposed, although those affected may have some control of their relative magnitude. Declaring war imposes risk of death on members of the armed forces, and risk of death by bombing or invasion on civilians. Democratic processes are supposed to amount to some sort of consent to such risk impositions on the part of legitimate authorities acting constitutionally, and also to empower them to decide which escapable risks they will impose on people, and which imposition of such risks by private agents they will tolerate. I shall limit my discussion to these escapable risks, where, by not "escaping," a person may be thought to have consented to bear the risk.

Some people choose to play Russian roulette, others enjoy watching, and yet others make a living by catering to such tastes. Some choose dangerous sports, choose to ski, box, play football, others enjoy watching, and yet others profit from catering to these tastes for first- or second-hand thrills. Some choose work in coal mines, accepting the risk in return for a coalminer's wage, although few want to watch. Most of us incur significant risk of death on the roads in return for convenient travel. Since some choose high risk, for the thrill, and most choose some risk-involving package deals, what is ever wrong with providing people with the opportunity to "buy risk," or to accept it as a free gift? Is that what the owner of a nuclear power plant or a dangerous coal mine does, namely give residents and workers the option of accepting a risk, or risk package, or else rejecting that offer?

The morality we have inherited puts considerable weight on the difference between self-imposed harm or danger, and danger we have not chosen to face. We are on the watch for paternalism, for those who would deprive us of the right to injure or risk injuring ourselves. Does this respect for individual choice, and the right to self-injury, require us to tolerate or even encourage the provision of opportunities for new forms of risk-taking, even perhaps to welcome a widening of the range of available risks to life which individuals may decide to bear?

I shall discuss some distinctions that we seem to need for thinking about this hard topic. The first is the distinction between *creating* an opportunity for risking life and exploiting an opportunity already there. Nature and normal life provide us with plenty of opportunities to indulge any taste we have for life-risking thrills. The person who runs a ski resort is getting his profits not from enabling persons to take the risks which only such as he make available, but from making the skiing, which could go on without the likes of him, more attractive by amenities of various sorts, including perhaps safety measures and rescue services. It would be a bad joke to see nuclear plants as making it more convenient for people to take radiation risks for whatever reasons they may have to take them. The coal mine owner and the nuclear plant owner create the dangers they "offer" others; they do not merely facilitate or enhance dangerous activities already available. Other things being equal, creating new dangers is worse than enticing persons to take naturally available risks.

The second distinction is between dangers incurred in work, and travel to work, and dangers incurred in leisure activities. What known dangers people incur in their leisure activities are chosen in a stronger sense than are those they incur in the workplace. As Aristotle would put it, the coal miner may take that job "out of compulsion," even when he is not, like a member of a chain gang, literally coerced into working there. Few go down into coal mines for fun. What we do for fun is more freely chosen than what we decide to do to make a living, even when, as always, we have *some* choice in that matter (we can turn to theft if all else fails). Other things being equal, acknowledged risks in the workplace are harder to justify than acknowledged risks in the adult playgrounds.

Thirdly, I think we need to draw a distinction not merely between man-created and naturally available risks, but between degrees of human contrivance in gearing that risk (natural or humanly created) to a particular activity that there is frequent reason (other than desire for risk) for people to perform. The risk of death incurred by skiing in avalanche conditions, or on very steep slopes, is intrinsic to the activity, not engineered by anyone. Anyone who decides that she must bear that risk, to get quickly in some emergency from or to some inaccessible place, faces a risk that skiing carries. Anyone who decides to undergo frequent diagnostic x-rays faces a risk which that carries. But those who decide to face risk in coal mines decide to take a risk which someone has first contrived, then decided not to remove; those who decide to remain residents of an area where a nuclear plant has been built decide to take a risk someone else has decided to attach to residence there. Other things being equal, enabling persons to weigh the risks against the benefits of some activity, and choose for themselves, is suspect when one has contrived the risks, *made* the beneficial activity a risky one.

Fourthly, and relatively uncontroversially, we should distinguish those new risks attached to some activity that are accompanied by some newly attached benefit, from those newly attached risks that are not accompanied by any attached compensation. Problems arise, however, both about how much and what sort of benefit is a fair return for added risk to life, and also in distinguishing added benefit from what it is added to. The worker offered a certain package of wages plus fringe benefits by an employer for dangerous work may be told that some of the money, or some of the rest of the package, is compensation for the risk to life the job carries, and that this would not be offered did the job not carry this risk to life. How can the potential employee test this claim? If there are other employees in the same plant, doing the "same" work, but without the danger, who are being paid less, he can verify the claim that *some* return is made for willingness to bear risk. But if *all* the work in that plant, say a nuclear plant, is unsafe, what does the claim come to? And even if, in other fields such as coal mining, we can compare wages in relatively safe and relatively unsafe mines, and can confirm the claim of those running the unsafe mines that they are offering more, so are offering compensation for added risk, we cannot tell if they are offering *enough*. They may be offering enough to attract workers, but that may be because of monopoly, or because unemployment is high and times are hard, and a worker must take what she can get. If times are hard enough, workers will accept the deal at the unsafe mine even if no more is paid there than at the safe mine. It might be stipulated that fair compensation is whatever difference there would be, in perfect market conditions, between what is offered at the less safe and the safer mine, if both are to get workers, but how, in imperfect market conditions, can one tell what that is? This distinction between added risk with and without adequate compensation may be as unusable as it is uncontroversial.

Fifthly, we need to distinguish those risk-plus-benefit "offers" which can improve the choice-situation of some without that very offer worsening the situation of others, from those in which a welcome offer to one person is to others a threat. When a community has a nuclear plant built close to it, and at the same time gets some community benefits, perhaps parks and concert halls as well as new job openings, some may welcome it, and be pleased to have the choice of leaving the area or staying to enjoy the benefits and bear the risks. Others may interpret that offer as a threat— "leave, or else put up with this." One cannot determine, from the actual choice made by persons in this situation, whether or not having that choice improved their lot. Some who are threatened may stay, some who welcomed the choice may in the end decide not to accept the "offer." Since the importance people put on risk to life varies, there will probably be both sorts of persons in any place where such plants are built. By contrast, some risk-benefit offers can be selectively directed only at those who will not find them to be threats. Even a Russian roulette parlor, unless it is the only employer in town, can restrict the main effects of its offer to interested parties. But in a case where what is "offered" is a risk to life through dangerous air, water, soil, or street violence, combined with some benefits, (perhaps lowered taxes and rates) we cannot prevent the welcome opportunities for some being also the unwelcome change of opportunity for others. Should we count heads, or should we adopt a Pareto principle here, not improving anyone's choice-situation unless we do not thereby worsen another's? Such veto power by affected individuals over any enterprise that reduces overall security of life or increases its cost, would surely be unworkable, unless we could agree on some level of overall risk to life above which this power of veto is to come into force. But there is, in our moral tradition, a strong onus of justification lying on those who increase public insecurity of life. We do not vote on whether or not to repeal the law prohibiting assault and violence, or that making old-style poisoning illegal—we invest in such criminal laws, however many people might welcome the option of being free of both the prohibitions and the protection they provide, and only anarchists are worried by the paternalism we thereby show to such people. So counting heads isn't appropriate—some form of enforced safety standards seems more in the spirit of the tradition I am trying to update.

Let me repeat that none of these[23] morally relevant differences between sorts of risk-increasings decide the hard questions for us. But the deliberation that leads up to the decisions on those hard cases should not ignore those distinctions. Not merely are there different kinds of costs and different kinds of benefits, there are different ways in which the costs and the benefits get combined with one another, and different ways to decide who should do such combining as gets done by human decision.

VI. Partitioning, Coordinating, and Conjoining

In the previous two sections I have looked at categories already implicit in our present moral beliefs that might help us develop beliefs about what to do about the new dangers to life that face us. Now I want to turn to the question of where responsibility lies for such responses.

Traditionally, both at community and at the national level, we have divided the responsibility—the criminal courts and police look after certain threats to security of life, the coast guard and firefighters and ambulance services look after other threats to it, regulatory agencies look after yet others. The agencies are not normally individuated by what is threatened, but are individuated instead by the nature of a *source* of threat to many interests, many rights. For instance, the criminal courts protect not merely security of life, but security of property and security of personal liberty, whereas other courts protect security of contract, against individual offenders. The defense department looks after threats from a different sort of source, both to the security climate of life and to less easily specifiable public interests, often including the climate of trade. Even agencies with specific names like "environmental protection" are not looking at *all* threats to the human environment, but at those that come from thoughtless or ruthless human policies. Acid rain is in their bailiwick, but not the threat of an ice age, nor of a meteor strike, nor of a volcano eruption. Such a division of labor—whereby different public authorities look after different sources of threat, take on different public "enemies," each of which may threaten several vital interests—may mean that no one is thinking about *all* the threats to security of life, nor coordinating all measures to protect it. Someone, of course, is determining the budget of each arm of the public, but there will be no security-of-life budget, nor any security-of-liberty budget, nor any security-of-possession budget.

Is this a bad thing? Speaking of public policies to save lives, Leonard and Zeckhauser say, "full efficiency would require that we are able to allocate funds across areas."[24] Would such greater lifesaving efficiency be a good thing? Only if we are quite sure that it is not even more "efficient" to be able to allocate funds across all the vital interests but only in *one* "area," where an area is individuated by the source of a many-faceted threat. To be trying to deal in one budget, the total lifesaving budget, with the threat to human life posed by a rise in terrorism, and to deal in a different budget, the total liberty-saving budgets, with the threat terrorism poses to liberty, would lead to less, not greater, coordination. Doubtless there are better ways to partition our public labor than we have yet devised, but it may be no bad thing to have difficult "areas" recognized, as well as different public interests that need protection in each area. "Rationalizing," if that amounts to identifying some abstract common goal in several areas, then adopting an efficient total plan to reach it and aiming at consistency in all the areas affected, may be one of those rational strategies which it is even more rational to restrict.[25] The best coordination does not always come from abstraction of a goal and generalization of a method. When I began considering these issues I consulted a systems-analyst friend. His advice was that the important thing is not to go in for "special coddling," reducing risks in one area, such as in nuclear plants, more than we are willing to reduce them in others, such as coal mines. I asked him just how far such area-uniformity of policy was to go—was it to be restricted to energy-production industries, or extended to cotton mills and steel mills? He was uncertain, but was inclined to be in favor of a consistent, across-the-board job safety policy, with some exceptions such as employment in the military. When I raised the question of risk not merely to employees but to the general public, he began to get impatient, and when I asked if the policy of uniform treatment of persons as regards security of life was to apply also to programs concerned with reducing infant mortality, or to caring for the elderly, or to supporting the police courts and prison system, he wrote me off as a typical overgeneralizing philosopher. But of course the move to generalization was not mine but his, and is a proper move within certain limits. It is probably best if the only ones who *do* consider what we are doing for security of life, across areas, are the philosophers and intellectuals, not those in a position to redesign the budget partitions. The dangers that would be involved if we gave the rationalizers a free hand are all too easy to see.[26]

The complex and perhaps inefficient group of methods we have for protecting all our vital interests divides the labor according to the location of multifaceted threats, which give us the "areas," but within some areas, such as the law (and also in morality, which is not an "area" but affects and sometimes criticizes what goes on in all areas), we divide the danger in that area according to *what* it threatens, and so have lists of vital interests and of rights. Different divisions again give us, within "the" right to life, *different* prohibitions and requirements which must be obeyed if that right is to be respected—duties of child care as much as murder-avoidance. The divisions of public responsibility, rights, vital interests, moral duties, cut along different lines. This may give inefficiency, but it may also give insurance against perverse versions of efficiency, and of rationality. The very multiform nature of our public protection of our vital interests is itself a protection.

VII. The Complexity of the Good

This negative defense of traditional partitions and restrictions of power, namely that it gives protection against total lifesaving takeovers, could be strengthened if a more positive foundation could be given for dividing public power and responsibility more by source of threat than by what is threatened. If the various goods that are protected by different agencies against different sources of threat are interconnected it will be no accident that what threatens one of them often threatens others also. Here I must tread carefully to avoid that abstract variety-denying generalization of which I have accused others. I do not mean that we can abstract some one thing which is what we *really* care about, behind life, liberty, property— and that it is *its* enemies we should guard against. On the contrary, I want to emphasize the specialness and individual importance of each of these goods recognized by our traditional lists of rights and their background practices. But these different goods are not a mere collection of things all of which human beings happen to want to safeguard. They are also mutu- ally supportive goods. I shall call on both Hume and Mill to help me express this claim, which, if fully worked out, might give a theoretical basis for the largely conservative intuitions I have expressed in this paper. Talk of mutually supportive goods, or parts of the good, has an idealist ring, and sounds more like Bradley and Bosanquet than Hume or Mill; but it is to the latter two that I turn, or return, for that hint of a moral theory with which I shall end this largely antitheoretical paper (no antitheorist is a consistent antitheorist, for only theorists give first priority to consist- ency). Hume and Mill helped me at the beginning, and I shall also let them have the near to last word.

Mill, although he is in theory reducing the goods of security of life, liberty, and any other goods, to the pursuit of happiness, is no suitable father-figure for those who would equate practical reason with the use of any sort of calculus whereby we strive to maximize some abstract quantity, utility. He says, of his comprehensive and dominant good, happiness, that it "is not an abstract idea but a concrete whole." Its ingredients, he says, "are very various, and each of them is desirable in itself, not merely when swelling an aggregate."[27] Music, he says, is one of those ingredients desirable in themselves, and not replaceable by other pleaure-bringers. Mill does not develop these suggestions about concrete wholes with independently desirable irreplaceable and mutually supportive parts, nor shall I here attempt to do that. Whatever the truth of this claim about the good, it cannot and need not be used to deny that sometimes we have to choose which "part" of the good to lose or fail to get, however indispensable that part for happiness.

This doctrine of the complex unity of the human good may seem unfounded optimism,[28] or displaced theology, and if it is to have a bearing on the fit or misfit between the various ways in which, in the real world, we pursue the good, or at least the better, and flee from the worse, it needs translation into less utopian terms. It is because Hume, who shares with Mill a complex account of human well-being,[29] also has a complex account of the different ways in which we try to improve our situation, that his social philosophy seems to me to be especially valuable. He has an account both of mutually cohering social artifices, and of the mutually cohering formal goods they provide, the goods of increased force, increased ability, increased security. These provide examples, at least, of goods not as "concrete" as music, nor as abstract as utility, and the way they cohere may be suggestive. They are each "irreplaceable" in the contribution they make to improvement in the situation of a person. One can have great power, much ability, yet one's life be ruined by insecurity. One can have security and power, but no ability to use them to any purpose, or have ability and security but crippling lack of power. Separately important though they are, they mutually enhance each other's value when all are present to significant degrees. Each of the artifices Hume describes can be seen to advance all of them, and to do so by all the general means he had specified—conjunction of forces, partition of employments, mutual succor. Mutually supportive means advance mutually enhancing goods, as new levels of power, ability, and security are made possible by the artifices that Hume thought merited moral approval. This is not the place to spell out the details of that Humean scheme of mutually complementary artifices which by complex means advance a complex good. It would, I believe, provide us with an instructive example of the sort of nonabstract coherence possible in social policy, when the complexity of the good aimed at requires a coordinated family of measures. It would also show how the very measures that cope with some dangers create new dangers.[30] Hume claimed that the scheme of artifices he described gave us "infinite advantages," but some of that endless supply of advantages are the advantages of control over the infinitely proliferating dangers which our own previously advantageous inventions, technological and social, keep supplying. As with individual health and quality of life, so with security of life and the measures needed to protect that, we may have to keep running to stay where we were.[31]

NOTES

1. David Hume, *An Enquiry Concerning Human Nature*, in *Enquiries* ed. L. A. Selby-Bigge and P. H. Nidditch (Oxford:Clarendon Press, 1978), p. 229n.

2. Mary Melville, in *The Temporary Worker in the Nuclear Power Industry: An Equity Analysis*, Monograph I, Center for Technology Environment and Development (Worcester, Mass.: Clark University, 1983), quotes one worker who said "You're there because you need the money. Sometimes you have to force yourself to go in there" (p. 40). However she cites surveys showing that most such temporary workers do not resent the risk to health when it is coupled with higher pay than they would get from alternative jobs.

3. Kant believed that each person should aim at his or her own perfection as a rational being, but, as far as real possibility goes, he says: "Those natural capacities which are directed to the use of reason are to be fully developed only in the race, not in the individual" (*Idea for a Universal History,* second thesis). He notes how "the earlier generations appear to carry through their toilsome labor only for the sake of the later, to prepare for them the higher edifice which was Nature's goal . . . " (third thesis). This redeeming achievement of what is otherwise "this idiotic course of things human" involves war and discord as means. "Thanks be to Nature, then, for the incompatibility, for heartless competitive vanity, for the insatiable desire to possess and to rule! Without them, all the excellent capacities of humanity would forever sleep undeveloped" (fourth thesis).

4. Alan Gibbard discusses this move, and the motivation for it, in his paper "Risk and Values," in *Values at Risk*, ed. Douglas MacLean, Maryland Studies in Public Philosophy, forthcoming.

5. Douglas MacLean discusses the appropriate form of expression for different sorts of values in "Social Values and the Distribution of Risk," in MacLean, *Values at Risk.*

6. Hume, *Enquiries*, p. 485.

7. Amartya Sen defends a complex moral theory in which rights are important but can be overridden by what are not rights in his paper in "The Right to Take Personal Risks," in MacLean, *Values at Risk.*

8. John Stuart Mill, *Utilitarianism*, ch. 5.

9. Thomas Hobbes, *Leviathan*, ch. 13.

10. Mill, *Utilitarianism*, ch. 5.

11. See Henry Shue, *Basic Rights: Subsistence, Affluence, and U. S. Foreign Policy* (Princeton: Princeton University Press, 1980), for a vigorous attack on the view that all the basic rights are "negative," and for a discussion of ways of selecting which rights *are* basic. Shue draws attention to the "positive" enforcement costs of so-called negative rights, but does not attend to the training costs all these rights and duties involve.

12. Mill, *Utilitarianism*, ch. 5.

13. Jonathan Bennett, in "Morality and Consequences" (*Tanner Lectures*, vol. 11, [Salt Lake City and Cambridge, Eng.: 1981], pp. 45–116), replaces the surface distinction with what he argues at careful length is a real, and also a morally neutral, distinction between positive and negative instrumentality. He then considers whether causing death by positive instrumentality is worse than doing so by negative instrumentality and concludes that it is not. To tell whether a person brought about some effect by "what he did" rather than by "what he didn't do," we are to consider, for the agent at the time, all the ways of moving or holding still. When the way the agent actually moves (or is still) is one of small minority of those ways that would have produced the given effect, the instrumentality is positive; when it is one of a large majority of ways, all of which would have led to the same effect, the instrumentality is negative. I confess to finding it difficult to count ways of moving, and comparing the number of such ways which would with those which would not be followed by a given effect. To the extent that I can ever draw Bennett's distinction, I find it to be a culturally relative one. For an Eskimo the number of ways of moving that will lead to the hunted seal's death will be much greater than the number of deadly movements I can envisage as possible, so whether a given action turns out to display positive or negative instrumentality will depend on one's culturally acquired abililty to see ways of moving and their consequences in a given situation. This may not introduce any *moral* prejudgment of issues into the drawing of the distinction, but it does seem to introduce cultural bias. (See also n. 14.)

14. Although the possibility of killing depends upon no social artifice, the fact that we have action verbs such as *kill, hit, poison,* shows something about our culture, about which intentions are readily recognizable, and about which intentional actions are recognizable as such. The list of action verbs of a language gives information about familiar activities. The list of prohibitions of a group, and the verbs occurring in it, may give indirect information about special duties as well as prohibitions. It is when killing people is the duty of some that others need to have it made clear that it is the monopoly of those whose duty it is. It is when drinking human blood, with or without transubstantiation, is the duty of a priest caste that the general prohibition of cannibalism gets its point. Mary Douglas in *Purity and Danger* (London: Routledge, Kegan Paul, 1978) has shown very clearly how one's man's (or occasion's) moral poison is usually another man's or occasion's moral meat. So my earlier general formula for moral rules should be revised to "You, but not you others, may, perhaps must, kill (take, etc.) these but not those, now but not on other occasions."

15. Christopher McMahon, In "Morality and the Invisible Hand," *Philosophy and Public Affairs* 10, no. 3 (1981): 247–77, shows how the liberal's short list fits a market economy.

16. Any short list of *don'ts*, such as the liberal's, is historically a remnant from a much longer list of rules regulating all aspects of life, from birth, to burial and grave "security." That middle-sized list, the Ten Commandments, is a selection from the full version of the Mosaic law in which it is embedded—from the rules telling one what one can eat when, where, with whom, and from whose hands; how, with what, where, and when one washes one's body; what one must do to the newborn, the dead, the stranger, the captured enemy; from what group one obtains one's sexual partner, what ceremonies must precede cohabitation, and so on. The liberal lops most of this off, seeing such restrictions as unnecessary, as not serving vital interests. But he usually tacitly retains some vestiges of these more comprehensive regulations. If pressed, he will admit that we should not be left free to eat human flesh; to take our parents, siblings, or children as our sexual partners; to use our dead relatives as compost for our gardens. Such taboos, he is likely to say, are matters of a shared sense of what is civilized or decent, their infringement arouses disgust rather than moral outrage. But whatever the moral emotion that informally enforces these taboos, it is, I think, as much a *moral* emotion as indignation, outrage, or a sense of injustice.

17. Robert Nozick, in *Anarchy, State and Utopia* (New York: Basic Books, 1974), p. 57, says: "A line, or hyper-plane, circumscribes an area in moral space around an individual," and any unconsented crossings of that boundary will count as "losses" to the violated individual, *prima facie* grounds for compensation. This inviolable moral space, the invasion of which harms a person, is supposed to arise out of " the fact of our separate existences," p. 33. This fairly clearly takes interaction to be *either* by consent, for presumed benefit, or to be a harmful "boundary crossing," with no interaction at all between the separate existents being the benchmark. In David Gauthier's unpublished manuscript *Morals by Agreement*, the espousal of a no-interaction benchmark is very definite. See also his "Rational Cooperation," *Nous* 8, no. 1 (1975): 53–65.

18. Defenders of this version of morality typically want to ward off the sort of objection I have raised by claiming that they have described a "core" morality which deals with relationships between human adults, and that this would need supplementation to cover relationships with children, the infirm aged, animals, and any others who might get into the moral picture. Although I do think that there is a "core" morality that concerns relations between those who have, will have, or had, obligations, as well as being ones to whom obligations are owed, I see no good reason, within that core, to single out adult-adult relations as especially central. Our relations to those who are becoming moral agents and to those who have been such agents are as important as any others. In any case no sharp line divides the adolescent from the adult, the competent adult from the infirm aged person, so we need a morality that does not force us first to classify persons as competent adult or not, before we know how to deal with them.

19. I have used the term *liberal* for those who espose a minimal morality that protects the powers exercised in a commercial capitalist society of individualists; but *liberal* is a slippery term, and connotes also the espousing of the cause of individual adult liberty, the placing of onus of justification on those who would limit it. Against liberalism in that sense I have little quarrel, but I think its defenders, Mill included, underestimate the extent to which the liberty of some adults, usually males, has a cost in coercion of other adults, usually females, to prepare new adults for such liberty.

20. Nancy Chodorow, *The Reproduction of Mothering* (Berkeley, Los Angeles: University of California Press, 1978).

21. Robert Nozick, in *Anarchy, State and Utopia*, ch. 4, raises the question of when we should prohibit an action as distinct from requiring the agent to fully compensate the victim of that action. Since his discussion takes individual rights as somehow there prior to any social recognition of them, providing proper side constraints on any state requirement, of compensation or of anything else, and since I reject that dogmatic conception of rights, I cannot use his ingenious reasoning here to any good purpose. I am assuming that the question of what rights to recognize is as social a decision, indeed the same decision as that of whether to prohibit an action (and so regard it as a violation of a right) or merely to compensate any victims of that action for the harm done to them, for what Nozick calls a "boundary crossing," perhaps making the inflicter of the harm pay those compensation costs. To be able to do this, each person will need plenty of fault insurance, and so perhaps the optimal version of the categorical imperative according to Nozick is "Take out fault insurance so that the victims of any unconsented-to boundary crossings you make will receive full compensation, or saleable rights to compensation." Due to the peculiar and, by Nozick's account of it, irrational phenomenon of human *fear* of some sorts of "boundary crossing," even when there is assurance of compensation for them, psychological conditions are not optimal for Nozick's morality, so certain actions, those feared even if compensated for, must be prohibited—penalties as well as compensation and costs must be imposed on those who perform them. Nozick seems to have no account of why we fear and resent some

"boundary crossings" even when compensation is assured. But to have no account of that is to have no account of what makes some constraints moral constraints. If enforced morality is reduced to the protection and the insurance markets, that may be an explanation of the kind which Nozick finds to have "a certain lovely quality" (p. 18) which is intellectually satisfying, but it is only the enforcement, not the morality itself, which is thereby explained.

22. The action verbs in the language will, as discussed in n. 14, exhibit what knowledge of consequences is the commonest knowledge in a group.

23. There are, of course, other important distinctions, including that between fair and unfair distribution of imposed risk, between risk of catastrophe (many lives lost from one event, along with loss of cultural and social "capital") and risk of equally many deaths not amounting to one catastrophe, between that danger in which we know the frequency with which the evil falls, and that danger in which we are ignorant of frequencies.

24. Draft for the *Values at Risk* workshop. Zeckhauser and Shepard, in "Where Now for Saving Lives?" *Law and Contemporary Problems* 40, no. 4 (Autumn 1976), speak approvingly of "a rationalized policy choice process" (p. 6) and see the "accurate" version of the question such policy answers as "Where should we spend whose money to undertake what programs to save whose lives with what probability?"

25. For an illuminating discussion of the rationality of restricting our use of rational methods, see Jon Elster, *Ulysses and the Sirens—Studies in Rationality and Irrationality* (Cambridge, Eng., 1979).

26. One is tempted here to present a new "modest proposal," one on how best to use a given amount of the public's resources for livesaving purposes. The first move will be one in which we determine to use those resources to save the greatest number of lives, weighted, perhaps, so that the lives of the young and healthy count for more than those of older people whose prospects are worse. We will ignore the difference of "feel" between saving the lives of identified persons, perhaps under our gaze, and saving "statistical" lives. So if ten people are clinging to a semisubmerged oil rig and we have seen their plight on the evening news, we will, before sending the helicopters, ask ourselves "Could we save more lives, possibly less visible lives, some other way?" Almost always the answer will be yes—an inoculation program to save children from some disease will save more lives for the same expenditure. So let those clinging to the oil rig drown. We have more efficient uses for our money.

The next move is to consider whether we should spend on the inoculation program or invest to spend more effectively later. Medical methods and technology can be expected to advance, so we will save more children from an untimely death by investing our funds in research than by inoculating now. So let the present children at risk remain at risk, we have more efficient uses for our lifesaving moneys.

At the next step we query whether investing in medical research is the best investment we can make. Medical research has progressed nicely without great subsidy from public funds, so perhaps our best bet for eventually saving more lives is to invest elsewhere, wherever the economic returns look best. That way we will have more funds to use, eventually, on putting to use the then-latest medical knowledge to save lives. So let us invest, say, in oil rigs, or atomic plants.

Once this decision is taken, we, both as public servants and as shareholders, will have to have a view on what safety measures should be observed in our oil rigs and atomic plants. We will, to protect our investment and so eventually save more lives, perhaps sacrifice a few workers' lives to keep profits up and return on our investment high. We have more efficient ways to save lives than to waste potential lifesaving earnings in measures to save workers' lives.

The next move comes later when we face the decision of whether to reinvest, or spend our earnings on actual lifesaving. As long as there are still more lives at risk than we can save with our increased funds, and as long as oil or other energy profits are still high, and medical know-how still increasing without our subsidy, we will of course reinvest whenever we face this choice. We still have better things to do with our lifesaving resources than to save lives.

With luck, our very investments and the hazard they produce may kill off enough people so that a time will come when it will no longer make good economic sense to go on increasing our lifesaving funds. We will then disburse our funds to save whoever is left at risk, perhaps the entire now-much-reduced population. We will then congratulate ourselves on our rational use of our opportunities. From a position where, had we spent, we would have saved only a fraction of those whose lives were at risk, we have, by our clearheaded efficient investment policy, made it possible for us eventually to save all the lives remaining at risk. What more rational course of action for the public good could possibly be dreamed up?

27. Mill, *Utilitarianism*, ch. 4.

28. Ronald de Sousa, in "The Good and the True" (*Mind* 83, no. 332 [1974]: (531–51), has claimed that there is no reason to expect different real goods to be jointly realizable. Ruth Barcan Marcus, in "Moral Dilemmas and Consistency" (*Journal of Philosophy* 77, 3, [1980]: 121–36), has argued on the contrary that the need to choose between evils, or choose which or whose good to sacrifice, should always be taken as a sign that collectively we have reprehensibly failed to create the conditions in which goods are jointly realizable.

29. Hume believed that there were basic needs, "the desire of punishment of our enemies, and of happiness to our friends, hunger, lust and a few other bodily appetites" (*A Treatise of Human Nature*, ed. L. A. Selby-Bigge and P. H. Nidditch [Oxford: Clarendon Press, 1978], p. 439), as well as more general desires for whatever brings pleasure, esteem, and power. His account of the best social means to satisfy these involves a complex interplay between nature, culture, and artifice. In a future work I hope to complete the unraveling of that complexity, which I began in my "Hume on Heaps and Bundles," *American Philosophical Quarterly* 16, no. 6 (1979): 285–95.

30. Although Hume claims that the social artifices he analyzes bring "infinite advantages," each new artifice he describes remedies an "inconvenience" created by the previous one. The invention of property "fixes" possession, but it is a "grand inconvenience" (*Treatise*, p. 514) that persons and possessions are then often "very ill adjusted," so transfer by consent is invented to remedy that. Again, after promise and contract have made accumulation possible, thieves and frauds can escape their fellows' detection and so magistrates become necessary, and themselves bring dangers of tyranny against which the institution of a free press partially protects us. At the end of his life Hume seemed to see a need for another artifice to correct the excesses of a free press.

31. If any progress has been made in the several versions this paper has gone through, it is due to the help I received from my colleagues Robert Brandom, David Gauthier, Shelly Kagan, Nicholas Rescher, and from Douglas MacLean.

15

Secular Faith

I. The Challenge

Both in ethics and in epistemology one source of skepticism in its contemporary version is the realization, often belated, of the full consequences of atheism. Modern nonmoral philosophy looks back to Descartes as its father figure, but disowns the *Third Meditation*. But if God does not underwrite one's cognitive powers, what does? The largely unknown evolution of them, which is just a version of Descartes' unreliable demon? "Let us ... grant that all that is here said of God is a fable, nevertheless in whatever way they suppose that I have arrived at the state of being that I have reached, whether they attribute it to fate or to accident, or make out that it is by a continual succession of antecedents, or by some other method—since to err and deceive oneself is a defect, it is clear that the greater will be the probability of my being so imperfect as to deceive myself ever, as is the Author to whom they assign my being the less powerful" (*Meditation* I, Haldane and Ross, trans.). Atheism undermines a solitary thinker's single-handed cognitive ambitions, as it can undermine his expectation that unilateral virtue will bring happiness. The phenomenon of atheism in unacknowledged debt to theism can be seen both in ethical theory and in epistemology, and the threat of skepticism arises in a parallel manner.

In a provocative article, David Gauthier[1] has supported the charge made two decades ago by Anscombe,[2] that modern secular moral philosophers retain in their theories concepts which require a theological underpinning. "The taking away of God ... in thought dissolves all," said

From *Canadian Journal of Philosophy* 10, no. 1 (1980): 131–48. Reprinted in *Revisions: Changing Perspectives in Moral Philosophy,* ed. Stanley Hauerwas and Alasdair MacIntyre (Notre Dame: University of Notre Dame Press, 1983).

Locke, and Gauthier agrees that it dissolves all those duties or obligations whose full justification depends upon a general performance of which one has no assurance. He quotes Hobbes: "He that would be modeste and tractable and perform all he promises in such time and place where no man els should do so, should but make himself the prey to others, and procure his own ruin, contrary to the ground of all Lawes of Nature, which tend to Nature's preservation" (*Leviathan*, ch. 15). The problem arises not merely when "no man els" does his[3] duty, but when a significant number do not, so that the rest, even a majority, make themselves prey to the immoral ones, and procure their own exploitation, if not their own ruin. The theist can believe, in his cool hour, that unilateral, or minority, or exploited majority morality will not procure his ultimate ruin, that all things work together for good, but what consolation can a secular philosopher offer for the cool thoughtful hour, in the absence of God? If Gauthier is right, either false or insufficient consolation. He says that in those modern theories which preserve some vestige of a duty to do what others are not known to be doing, or known to be failing to do, "God is lurking unwanted, even unconceived, but not unneeded."[4]

I shall suggest that the secular equivalent of faith in God, which we need in morality as well as in science or knowledge acquisition, is faith in the human community and its evolving procedures—in the prospects for many-handed cognitive ambitions and moral hopes. Descartes had deliberately shut himself away from other thinkers, distrusting the influence of his teachers and the tradition in which he had been trained. All alone, he found he could take no step beyond a sterile self-certainty. Some other mind must come to his aid before he could advance. Descartes sought an absolute assurance to replace the human reassurance he distrusted, and I suggest that we can reverse the procedure. If we distrust the theist's absolute assurance we can return to what Descartes spurned, the support of human tradition, of a cross-generational community. This allows us to avoid the narrow and self-destructive self-seeking which is the moral equivalent of solipsism. But Gauthier's challenge is precisely to the reasonableness of community-suportive action when we have no guarantee of reciprocal public-spirited or communally minded action from others. Not only may we have no such guarantee, we may have evidence which strongly *dis*confirms the hypothesis that others are doing their part. We may have neither knowledge nor inductively well-based belief that others are doing their part. Faith and hope I take to involve acceptance of belief on grounds other than deductive or inductive evidence of its truth. Faith is the evidence of things unseen. It will be faith, not knowledge, which will replace religious faith. I shall try to make clear exactly what that faith is faith in, and what it would be for it to be (a) ill-founded or unreasonable,

(b) reasonable, but in vain. I shall be defending the thesis that the just must live by faith, faith in a community of just persons.

II. Faith: The Substance of Things Hoped For

Faith, not knowledge, was and is needed to support those "plain duties" whose unilateral observation sometimes appears to procure the dutiful person's ruin. But faith, for rational persons, must appear reasonable before it can be attained. If it is to be reasonable, it must not fly in the face of inductive evidence, but it may go beyond it, when there are good reasons of another sort to do so. We may have such good reasons to hope for an empirically very unlikely but not impossible eventuality. Reasonableness is relative to the alternative beliefs or policies one might adopt, or be left with, if one rejected the candidate for the status of reasonable belief. One of the chief arguments for the moral faith I shall present is the great unreasonableness of any alternative to it. The *via negativa* which leads to secular faith has been clearly indicated in Hobbes' description of the state of nature, the state of persons without the constraint of justice. Hobbes' modern commentators, including Gauthier, have underlined the futility of the alternatives to morality. Yet if everyone insisted on knowing in advance that any sacrifice of independent advantage which they personally make, in joining or supporting a moral order, will be made up for by the returns they will get from membership in that moral order, that order could never be created nor, if miraculously brought about, sustained. Only by conquest could a Hobbesian *Leviathan* ever be created, if the rational man must have secure knowledge that others are doing likewise before he voluntarily renounces his right to pursue independent advantage. How, except by total conquest, could one ever know for sure that other would-be war makers will lay down their arms when one does so?

In fact Hobbes' first Law of Nature requires every man to endeavor peace, not when he has certainty of attaining it, but "as fare as he has *hope* of attaining it" (*Leviathan*, ch. 14, emphasis added). Hope had been previously defined as "appetite with opinion of attaining" (op. cit., chap. 6) and opinion is contrasted with science (op. cit., ch. 7), which alone is the outcome of correct reckoning or calculation. It is then, for Hobbes, a Law of Nature, or a counsel of rational prudence, to act on hope when what is at stake is escape from the Hobbesian state of nature.

Faith, Hobbes tells us "is in the man, Beleefe both of the man and of the truth of what he says" (ibid.). It is faith in its Hobbesian sense, in men, not merely belief in the truth of what they say which I shall argue is the only 'substance' of the hoped-for cooperation which avoids the futility and self-destructiveness of its alternatives. Faith, in a nonHobbesian sense, that is a belief which runs beyond the inductive evidence for it, when it is faith in the possibility of a just cooperative scheme being actualized, is the same as that hope whose support is trust "in the man."

Trust in people, and distrust, tends to be self-fulfilling. Faith or lack of faith in any enterprise, but especially one requiring trust in fellow-workers, can also be self-fulfilling. Confidence can produce its own justification, as William James[5] persuasively argued. The question whether to support a moral practice without guarantee of full reciprocity is, in James' terminology, live, momentous, and forced, and the choice made can be self-verifying whichever way we choose. Every new conversion to moral skepticism strengthens the reason for such skepticism, since, if acted on, it weakens the support of moral practices and so diminishes their returns to the morally faithful. Similarly, every person who continues to observe those practices provides some reason for belief that they are supported, and so strenghtens the foundation for his own belief that their support is sufficient, and provides some justification for his own dependence on that support. *Some* justification, but not enough, surely, to be decisive, since he is unlikely to be the critical straw to save or break the camel's back. The case for the self-confirmation of moral faith is less clear than for the self-confirmation, the band wagon effect, of moral skepticism. Immorality breeds immorality, but need moral action, especially if *unilateral*, breed more of the same? The sense in which the exemplary unilateral act *does* provide its own support, even if the example it gives is not followed by one's contemporaries, will be explored later. For the moment the best one can say for the reasonableness of willing to believe in the value of (possibly) unilateral moral action is that the alternative, giving up on that crucial part of the moral enterprise which secures cooperation, must lead eventually to an outcome disastrous to all, although those with a taste for gun-running may make a good profit before doomsday dawns. There are different styles of shoring fragments against one's ruin, and some choose to exploit the presumed failure of morality, while others, or even the same ones, retreat into a narrow circle where virtues can still be cultivated. But when, even granted the badness of its alternatives, would it be unreasonable to keep faith in the moral enterprise, in particular in the attempt to achieve a fair scheme of human cooperation? I turn next to consider the coherence of the ideal of justice.

III. More or Less Just Societies

When would an actual cooperative scheme between persons be a just one, one which gave its participants the *best reasons* to support it? When the goods, for each, gained by cooperation outweigh the individual advantage any sacrificed, and where all partakers in the benefits make their fair contribution, pay their dues, observe the rules which ensure production and fair distribution of benefits. Even in a society where this was true, there would still be a place for a descendant of Hobbes' *Leviathan*, to enforce rules, since there may still be persons who acted irrationally, and who have a perverse taste for bucking the system, whatever the system. A stable, efficient, equitable[6] and democractic scheme of cooperation would give its conforming members security, delectation, nonexploitation and freedom, but some may still try to get a free ride, or to break the rules out of what Hobbes called "the stubborness of their passions." His fifth Law of Nature commands "compleasance," that every man strive to accommodate himself to the rest, and unilateral breach of this rule is contrary to Hobbesian reason whose dictates include the laws of nature, since it calculates that the individual can count on preserving himself only if steps are taken to ensure the conservation of men in multitudes, and so to ensure peace. "He that having sufficient security, that others observe the same laws towards him, observes them not himself, seeketh not peace, but war; and consequently the destruction of his own nature by violence" (*Leviathan*, ch. 15, immediately following the passage quoted by Gauthier, which points out the folly of unilateral conformity to the laws of nature).

Both unilateral conformity and unilateral nonconformity are, according to Hobbes, contrary to reason, but man's natural intractability inclines him to the latter. In any state of affairs short of perfect and perfectly secure justice such intractability provides a healthy challenge to an imperfect *status quo*, but if a satisfactory form of cooperation were attained such a character trait would serve no useful function. And even if Hobbes is wrong in claiming that one who refuses to do his part thereby irrationally seeks his own violent destruction, his claim that only a fool believes he can profit by breaking the rules his fellows keep is plausible to this extent, that if those rules were just in a stronger sense than any Hobbes can provide, then however attractive the promised gains of a free ride, or of exploiting others, only a fool would believe that he has more to gain by risking the enmity of his fellows by such a policy than by cultivating a taste for the pleasures of cooperation and regulated fair competition. It may not be positively irrational to break the fifth Law of Nature, especially in a would-be totalitarian Leviathan state, but it would be against reason to think one would do better by breaking the rules of a decent just scheme of cooperation. There is no reason *not* to be sociable in a decent society, and nothing to be gained there by nonirrational unsociability, by going it alone, by entering into a state of war with one's fellows. But some will act contrary to reason, "by asperity of Nature," and be "Stubborn, Insociable,

Froward, Intractable." Such stubbornness is perversity, not superior rationality, when the rules are just. We could define a perfectly just society as one where it takes such intractability to motivate disobedience.

How do we measure how close an actual society is to the adequately just society? Unless we can do this it would seem impossible ever to judge a society so unjust that its institutions merit disrespect, or to have confidence that any change made in existing institutions is a change for the better. Yet there are grave problems in establishing any coherent measure of comparative justice. These problems arise because of the tension between two ways in which an existing state of things may approximate the just society. In one sense an institution is just to the extent that it *resembles* one we expect to be part of the adequately just society. In another sense an institution is better to the extent that it is instrumental in moving the society closer in time to that adequacy. But the institutions a society needs, to change itself, may be quite other than those it needs, once improvement is no longer needed. Yet if we opt for this dynamic measure of relative justice, and say that institutions are good to the extent that they facilitate movement towards adequate justice, we run up against the possibility, explored by Hegel and developed by Marx, that historical movement towards a social ideal may be dialectical, that the institutions which best facilitate movement towards an ideal may be ones which least embody that ideal.

The ideal of *justice*, however, is one which cannot generate a sense of "more just than" in which intolerable exploitation is counted more just than a lesser degree of exploitation, merely because it is more likely to precipitate rebellion and change. Those who advocate making things worse in order that they may get better cannot claim that what their strategies increase is justice. Is justice then an ideal which is committed to a perhaps groundless liberal faith in progress, faith in its own gradual attainment by moves, each of which represents *both* an increase in qualitative approximation to the ideal, and *also* a step closer, historically and causally, to its attainment? If these two measures of approximation are both proper, yet can come apart, can come into irresolvable conflict with one another, then the ideal of justice may be confused and incoherent,[7] may rest on a faith which is false. I think there is genuine issue here, but it is not one which I shall discuss further. Social science, not philosophy, would shore up the liberal's faith, or show it to be false. If it is false, if there is no coherent measure of relative justice, then the modern moral philosophy Gauthier criticizes in even worse straits than he claims. But I shall proceed within the limits of the comforting liberal faith which I take Gauthier to share, faith that some institutions can be judged less just than others, and that improving them can count as progress towards a just society. It is worth pointing out that this is part of the *faith* the just live by, but it is not the part of it which is controversial to Gauthier and those he criticizes, none of whom embrace the radical moral skepticism to which the Marxist argument leads, nor the new nonmoral revolutionary faith which can fill the vacuum it creates.

Where else does faith enter into the motivation to act, in a less than fully just society, for the sake of justice, to conform to more or less just institutions which not all conform to, or to act, possibly unilaterally, to reform salvageable institutions, and to protest corrupt ones? What must the just person believe, which must turn out to be true if his action is not to be pointless or futile? Before we can discuss the question of whether and when personal advantage is pointlessly sacrificed, we must first discuss the nature and varieties of advantage and personal good. I shall in this discussion adopt a hedonist terminology, to stay as close as possible to the Hobbesian point of departure.

IV. Goods: Secure and Insecure

Hobbes speaks not of advantage but of *power*, namely "present means to obtain some future apparent good." Advantage strictly is advantage over, or against, others, and Hobbes' emphasis on man's "diffidence" or need to assure himself that there is "no other power great enough to endanger him" (op.cit., ch. 13) turns power-seeking into the attempt to attain advantage, competitive edge, a position superior to one's fellows, since even in civil society he believes that men "can relish nothing but what is eminent" (op.cit., ch. 17). I shall keep the term "advantage" for this competitive good, superiority over others, and use Hobbes' word "power" for the more generic concept of possession of present means to obtain some future, apparent, possibly noncompetitive, good. (I think that when Gauthier speaks of "advantage" he is using it in a looser way, more equivalent simply to "good," that is to a combination of possession of present good and power or present means to attain a future good, whether or not these goods are scarce and competed for.)

Hobbes says that prudence, the concern for power rather than for immediate good, is concern for the future, which is "but a fiction of the mind" (op.cit., ch. 3), and moreover is based on an uncertain presumption that we can learn, from the past, what to expect in the future. "And though it be called Prudence, when the Event answereth our Expectation; yet in its own nature is but Presumption" (ibid.). Hobbes is surely correct in pointing out the risks inherent in prudence. One may invest in a form of power which turns out to be a passing not a lasting one. Hobbes (op. cit., ch. 10) catalogues the many forms power takes, and it is fairly obvious that accidents of chance and history may add to, and subtract from, this list, as well as determine the relative importance of different items on it. Even if one's choice of a form of power to obtain is a lucky one, one may not live into that future where the power could be spent in delectation, or even in misery-avoidance. At some point, in any case, the restless pursuit of power after power must end in death, so *some* future good for which the prudent person saved is bound, if he remains prudent to the end, not to be enjoyed by him. In theory one might, when imminent death is anticipated, make a timely conversion to imprudence, cash one's power in for delectation, and die gratified and powerless, but persons with Hobbesian, or with our actual, psychology are not likely to be capable of such a feat. One may have advantage, and have power, which is no good to one, or no longer any good to one, if to be good it must be cashed in delectation.

How are we to judge what is and what is not good to a person? Must good, to be such, be converted, eventually, from apparent good into real indubitable good, and from future into present good? These are hard questions, and it would take a full theory of the good of a person, the place in it of pleasure, interest, power, advantage to answer them. I have no such theory,[8] and will offer only a few remarks about the complexity of all goods other than present simple pleasures. In all human motivation, other than the gratification of current appetite, there is a potential multitier structure. In the case of action designed to make possible the gratification of future desires, that is in prudent action, the good for the sake of which one acts is the expected future gratification, but usually also, derivatively, the present satisfaction of feeling secure, of believing that one has taken thought for the future, secured its needs. So even if the prudent investor does not live into that future for which he provided, he may still enjoy a sense of security while he lives. Prudence, like virtue, may be, and sometimes has to be, its own reward. It is possible, but unlikely, that prudent persons take no present satisfaction in their prudent action, that they develop no taste for a sense of security. The normal accompaniment of prudence is the pleasure of a sense of security. I shall call such pleasures, which make reference to other, possibly nonpresent pleasures, "higher" pleasures (Hobbes' "pleasures of the mind"). By calling these pleasures "higher" I do not mean to imply that they should necessarily be preferred to lower ones. The special class of them which makes reference to future pleasures are power-derivative higher pleasures (Hobbes' "glory"). Such pleasures can coexist with regret that the cost of prudence was renunciation of a present available lower pleasure, and even with doubt whether such costs were unavoidable, and whether one will live to enjoy the future for which one has saved. It would be incorrect to say that the prudent person trades in present lower pleasure for higher pleasure— the higher pleasure is merely a bonus which can come with the power for which the lower pleasure was traded. But hedonic bonuses count for *something*, when the rationality of the action is to be judged.

When one acts for the sake of some good for others, be that good pleasure or power, present or future, there is a similar immediate bonus or "glory" possible, the pleasure of believing that someone else's present or future is improved by one's action. Persons who perform such altruistic acts usually do develop a taste for altruism, a fellow-feeling whereby they share in the good they do others. Just as the sense of personal security usually pleases the prudent person, the awareness of others' pleasure and the sense of their security usually pleases the altruist. It may be possible to do good to others because the moral law is thought to require it, without thereby getting any satisfaction for oneself, but such bonus-refusing psychology seems neither likely nor desirable. It is best if virtue is at least *part* of its own reward, and a waste if it is not.

V. Artifices to Secure the Insecure

To be a normal person is to be capable of higher pleasures, both self-derived and other-derived, to be able to make the remote in time and the remote from oneself close enough in thought and concern not merely to affect present action but to give present pleasure. Hume explored the mechanisms whereby concern for the remote, both from the present, and from oneself and one's family, can be strengthened by its coincidence with concern for the contiguous, so that the "violent propension to prefer the contiguous to the remote," (*Treatise*, p. 537), may be combated, its unfortunate and sometimes violent effects avoided. These mechanisms include not merely psychological ones, imagination and sympathy, which turn the useful into the also agreeable, and the agreeable for others into the agreeable for oneself also, but also social practices of training and education, and social artifices. Such artifices—promise, property, allegiance—turn the useful for people in general into what is useful for oneself, and this requires both convention, or agreement between people as to *what* the artifice is, and general conformity to its constitutive rules. Convention requires both communication and coordination. Hume believed, perhaps wrongly, that all of justice was in this sense artificial and that only with respect to the artificial virtues did a person risk being "the cully of his integrity" (*Treatise*, p. 535) if he acted unilaterally, without assurance that others were similarly virtuous. Since the actions of a kind or a generous person do the good they do, to individual others, case by case, whereas just or honest actions *need* do no good to any specified individual, and do what good they do, for people in general, for the public interest, only when they are supported by other just acts, it is an easy but false move from this valid contrast between the ways the natural and the artificial virtues do good, to a contrast at the level of motivation for the agent, and to the claim that an individual always has good reason to display a natural virtue whether or not others do, while one has no reason to display an artificial virtue, unless others are displaying the same version of it. Nonviolence, or gentleness, is a natural virtue, but nonviolence toward the violent can be as self-destructive as unilateral promise-keeping. Moreover, the higher pleasure of knowing that one's attacker has not suffered at one's hands is not merely insufficient to outweigh the loss of life or limb, it will also be lessened by the awareness that, when violence is the rule, the good to the violent man done by one's own nonviolence is short-lived and insignificant, unless it inspires others to nonviolence.

The natural virtues can, in individual cases, lose most of their point if the degree of nonvirtuousness of others is great enough. They still contrast with the artificial virtues, however, in that their good-promoting power will vary from case to case, given the same degree of general conformity. When there is general conformity to nonviolence, one may still have reason not to trust individual persons, if there is reason to believe that those ones reciprocate nonviolence with violence. When there is general violence, one may still have reason to expect a nonviolent response to nonviolence in selected cases, so that isolated pockets of gentleness and mutual trust can grow up within a climate of general violence. The same is true, up to a point, of the artificial virtues, in that respect for property rules, or promise-keeping, or allegiance, may be dependable within a restricted circle—say among members of the Mafia—although they do not observe rules outside that group., The artificial virtues differ from the natural ones, however, in that there is never excuse for *selective nonobservance*, within a generally conforming circle, as there can be reason for selective nonobservance of nonviolence, generosity, helpfulness. A debt owed to a vicious man, a miser, a profligate debauchee, or a dishonest man, is still owed. "Justice, in her decisions, never regards the fitness or unfitness of objects to particular persons, but conducts herself by more extensive views. Whether a man be generous, or a miser, he is equally well receiv'd by her, and obtains with the same facility or decision in her favor, even for what is entirely useless to him" (Hume, *Treatise*, p. 502). To grant that the conformity of others does affect the value of the natural as well as the artificial virtues is not to deny Hume's point here, that selective nonobservance, based on "fitness or unfitness of objects to particular persons," is reasonable with natural but not with artificial virtues. "Taking any single act, my justice may be pernicious in every respect; and 'tis only on the supposition, that others are to imitate my example, that I can be persuaded to embrace that virtue; since nothing but this combination can render justice advantageous or afford me any motives to conform myself to its rules" (op.cit., p. 498).

VI. The Pleasures of Conformity

One must suppose, then, that enough others will imitate one's just action if a just act is to be "advantageous," is to advance any interest, or give anyone, however altruistic or public-spirited, rational motive to perform it. When that supposition or faith is reasonable, then there will be a new higher pleasure obtainable by virtuous persons, the satisfaction of knowing that they have contributed to the preservation of the condition of general conformity needed for justice to deliver its utility. The higher pleasure of conformity will be obtained not only from acts conforming to established more or less just artifices, but also from acts displaying those natural virtues whose full point requires the reasonable expectation that others will not return vice for virtue. The higher pleasure of confirmity can, in those latter cases, be added to those of altruism and prudence, and it exceeds them in "height." As prudence and altruism facilitate delectation, so conformity facilitates prudence and altruism, as well as extending their range through artifices.

There are, then, a series of hedonic bonus pleasures which we can enjoy, if we cultivate our spiritual palates and develop a relish for them, as Locke puts it (*Essay*, bk. II, 21, 69). They can accompany the nonhedonic goods which are powers, the non-self-directed goods, and conformity to those artifices which create public "powers" to increase the powers and pleasures of individuals. Such present occurrent pleasures, once obtained, cannot be taken away from the prudent man, the altruist, or the conformist, even if the nonpresent or other-dependent good *in* which the pleasure is taken does not eventuate. Bonus pleasures are non-negligible contributors to the goodness of a life. As pains are indicators of other ills, these pleasures are indicators, not guarantees, of other presumed goods, and they add to them as well as indicate them. But the indication may be false, and the glory may be vainglory. Only in so far as one can reasonably hope for the success of one's prudent policy, altruistic project, or for the successful achievement of *general* conformity to an institution, can one derive a higher pleasure from prudent, altruistic, or conforming action. Should the hopes on which they were, reasonably, based become later known to be false, the already obtained bonus pleasures may be devalued. They cannot be canceled, but they may count for less, perhaps count negatively, in the person's proper assessment of the goodness of the life. If hopes turn out to have been what Hobbes calls vain "presumptions," the pleasures dependent on them may come to have been vainglory. If, on one's deathbed, one were persuaded that the person whose apparent love and devotion had given one much pleasure had really been uncaring, perhaps even had despised one, it would not, I think, be reasonable to react with the thought "thank God I didn't know till now." False pleasures, pleasures based on what comes to be seen as a lie, can, if the lie is serious and has reverberating implications for many of one's concerns, be worse than the absence of pleasure. Better no glory than vainglory.

Would the prudent man's bonus pleasure of feeling secure come to have been, like the friend's trusting pleasure, fool's gold, if he comes to realize that he will not live into the future for which he saved? If the bonus pleasure had been pleasure in the anticipated spendings of his savings, it would certainly be degraded by realization that he will not spend it, but to the extent that his bonus pleasure in his sense of security was in that which freed him from anxiety about his future, that bonus pleasure is not devalued by any knowledge he may acquire about his imminent early death. The power he had was a good, even if not exercised, because its absence would have been an ever-present felt evil. One might say, of the trusting friend, that his trust that his love was reciprocated was a good similar to the prudent man's security, in that its absence would have been an evil for him. But could the evil of suspicion or distrust, or of the absence of affection, be as great as the evil the friend suffers if he bases his life on a false trust? The difference, I think, lies in the fact that the unnecessarily prudent man is not *betrayed* by events, as the friend is by the false friend. The prudent man saves, because of the *possibility* that he may live long, but the friend loved in the confidence that love was returned. Prudence is, and knows itself to be, a reaction to risk and uncertainty, so its goods are not devalued if the possibility the prudent man provided for does not come about. But friendship does not, typically, see itself as content with the mere *possibility* of returned trust and love.

Can the man who acts for the sake of justice, when he knows or suspects that others are *not* conforming, get any bonus pleasures which are not fool's gold? We need to distinguish the cases where most but not all others are conforming from the cases where the conformists are in a minority, and, within the latter class, between the few who are trying to *inaugurate* a needed practice, and the few who are clinging to a once accepted but now imperiled institution. The last case, of fidelity to a once supported practice, faces less severe problems than those of the moral innovator, who must both get agreement on what should be conformed to, and also try to get sufficient conformity to it to secure the rewards of conformity. At least the moral conservative, the would-be supporter of a once established practice, does not face what have been called[9] the isolation and coordination problems, he faces only the problem of assurance of compliance. I shall not discuss the problems, faced by Hobbesian natural men, of simultaneously achieving communication, agreeing on what institutions are desirable (what coordination scheme to adopt) and also getting assured compliance to them. Let us, optimistically, assume that we have got, by the fact of past established conventions, their later reform, and their agreed need for specific further reforms, a solution to the isolation and coordination problems, that is, we have agreement on how we *should* all be acting. The compliance problem then arises—namely whether to act as we all should if we all are to get the best state of things for us, when there is no assurance that the rest of us are going to comply. If I comply and the rest of you don't, then the main good, for the sake of which that cooperative scheme was seen to be acceptable, will not be fully obtained, by any of us. To the extent it is partially attained it will be attained by noncompliers as well as compliers. I will have been the cully of my integrity. So, it seems, the pleasure of conformity is fool's gold unless others do in fact conform in sufficient numbers.

One thing which might save those pleasures from becoming false is the psychological taste of the individual for conformity. Not everyone can enjoy gun-running. Just as the prudent man who doesn't live to enjoy his savings may nevertheless have been saved by his prudence from unpleasant anxiety, so conformity to the old ways may soothe the timid who would be alarmed, not gratified, by the immoralists' life style.

But suppose I *could* develop a relish for gun-running, would it be irrational for me to decide to stick by, not to abandon, the threatened moral practices? Can unilateral (or minority-wide) conformity to just, or potentially just, institutions have any genuine lure for me?

VII. The Higher Pleasure of Qualifying for Membership in the Kingdom of Ends

Hume's point, a valid one, is that only a fool supports widely unsupported institutions whose only good depends on their getting wide support. But support from whom? My contemporaries and only them? It is fairly evident, I think, that the support of the majority of his contemporaries is not *sufficient* to guard the conformist from being taken in by fool's gold, especially when the institution is one which *conserves* goods for future generations. Whole generations can be retroactively made into cullies of their joint integrity by later generations' waste and destruction. What I want to stress is that conformity by the majority of one's contemporaries is not *necessary* to save the moral man from having been a fool.

Here, at least, I turn to the obvious source of a reply to Gauthier: Kant. He spelled out more clearly than any other modern philosopher the wholly secular basis for a strong set of plain duties. It is wholly secular, and it is also faith-requiring.

Kant says that although a rational being, when he acts on the maxim he can will as a universal law, "cannot for that reason expect every other rational being to be true to it; nor can he expect the realm of nature and its orderly design to harmonize with him as a fitting member of a realm of ends which is possible through himself. That is, he cannot count on its favoring his expectation of happiness. Still the law: Act according to the maxims of a universally legislative member of a merely potential realm of ends, remains in full force, because it commands categorically. And just in this lies the paradox, that merely the dignity of humanity as rational nature without any end or advantage to be gained by it, and thus respect for a mere idea, should serve as the inflexible precept of the will. There is the further paradox that the sublimity and worthiness of every rational subject to be a legislative member in the realm of ends consists precisely in independence of maxims from all such incentives" (Kant, *Foundation of the Metaphysics of Morals*, trans. Lewis White Beck). In this remarkable passage Kant appears to be claiming that the willingness to act as *if* one were a member of an actual kingdom of ends, when one knows that one is in fact a member of a society which falls short of this ideal, alone makes one worthy to be a legislating member of an actual kingdom of ends, or just society. But unless there can be such sublime and worthy persons, no just society is possible. The kingdom of ends is "possible through oneself." The existence of persons with the ability to act from respect for that "mere idea," is, then, the condition of the idea's actualization. Apparently just institutions would not guarantee a just society, if those persons living under them fail Kant's motivational test. A just society must be comprised of just men whose lives are ordered by just institutions.

On this account, apparently futile unilateral and possibly self-sacrificing action is neither futile nor unilateral. Not futile, because it keeps alive the assurance of the possibility of qualified members for a just society. Not unilateral, because the one just man has a "cloud of witnesses," all those others whose similar acts in other times kept alive the same hope. The actions of individuals who, unsupported by their contemporaries, act for the sake of justice do not necessarily hasten the coming of a just society, but they do rule out one ground on which it might be feared impossible. In this very modest way the just man's actions confirm his faith, demonstrate that *one* condition of the existence of a just society can be met, that human psychology can be a psychology for sovereigns. And the one just man is not alone, his isolation problem is solved if he recalls that enough others have already acted as he is acting. Thus every action in conformity to a just but threatened institution, or in protest against an unjust but supported one, furthers the cause, keeps the faith. The highest pleasure or "relish" of all is that of qualifying for membership in the kingdom of ends.[10] It is not just a priggish pleasure if the demonstration that there are and can be qualified members has the role which Kant as I interpret him claimed for it. (The blood of the martyrs is the seed of the church.)

VIII. The Faith the Just Live By

The secular faith which the just live by is, then, a faith in the possibility of a society for membership in which their just action theoretically qualifies them. They believe, in part, because of the previous demonstration that there can be such qualified members, so they join a movement already started. Each new member gives other potential members new assurance that the faith is not in vain, and it also confirms the faith of that new member himself, in that, after his act, the club of which he is an "honorary" member is the larger by one, and its point depends on the size and persistence of its membership.

The qualified, so honorary, member of the kingdom of ends, usually hopes that some actual society, perhaps long after his death, will embody the kingdom of ends on earth, that the possible will become actual. Such a society would, in general intention, honor all those who acted for the sake of justice, who qualified for membership but did not survive to be members. They would be participants in the secular variant of the communion of the saints. This higher pleasure is a variant of that pleasure of imagination, delight in the prospect of a posthumous recognition, which even Hobbes allows as a real pleasure. "Though after death there be no sense of the praise given us on earth, as being joys that are either swallowed up in the unspeakable joys of heaven or extinguished in the extreme torments of hell, yet is not such fame vain; because men have a present delight therein from the foresight of it and of the benefit that may redound thereby to their prosperity, which though they see not, yet they imagine; and anything that is pleasure to the sense, the same is also pleasure in the imagination" (*Leviathan*, ch. 11). Hobbes would not be content with anonymous recognition—presumably only the foresight that one's name will live on, preserved on some honor roll, could give Hobbesian man this pleasure of imagination. Fame is one thing, membership in the faceless communion of the saints quite another for one who values nothing but what is eminent. Still, the qualification for praise and recognition by a posterity to whom benefits redound is at least part of what the Hobbesian can glory in, and for a Kantian it suffices for glory.

Does this pleasure of imagination require expectation that posterity *will* benefit? Does the faith the just live by include confidence that some society on earth will some day actually be just? As already acknowledged, the ideal of justice includes a demand, which may be utopian, that its historical approximation coincide with its qualitative approximation. In addition to this demand, which the just person must, for the moment at least, merely *hope* can be met, there is another more serious difficulty in the idea of an actual just society which would meet the Kantian requirements. This is that, to the extent that there *is* conformity among one's contemporaries to apparently just practices, to precisely that extent none of the conformers can be assured that they, each of them, qualify for membership in the kingdom of ends. If they are acting, not for a mere idea, but in support of an actual practice, they cannot be sure they meet Kant's paradoxical test for qualification for membership in a just society, that is they cannot be sure how they *would* act if there were not general conformity. But the apparently just conforming society will not *be* just, in Kant's sense, if its sovereign-subjects are not qualified to be members. Kant's paradox is real, and so, once again, the ideal of a just society threatens to become incoherent. The threat, this time, is not one which can be allayed by sociological and historical findings, but is more fundamental—a *necessary* conflict between the criteria for qualification as the just society comprised of qualified members, and the criteria for its actualization.

Must the just man then conclude "credo quia absurdum est?" He might—as he might develop a relish for acting for necessarily lost causes—but he can keep his faith from being the absurd hope for the impossible, by acceptance of the fact that one can live without certainty. As the just man *now*, in an unjust world, has no certainty, only faith and hope, that there really can and will be a just society of the living, so, in any apparently attained just society, that is in one with just institutions, its members will rely on the faith and hope that they could if neccesary act for a mere idea, and so that they really qualify for membership. A new variant of Hobbesian faith in man will be needed. Both in the absence and in the presence of an actual just society, then, the just will live by faith.[11]

NOTES

1. "Why Ought One Obey God, Reflections on Hobbes and Locke," *Canadian Journal of Philosophy* 7 (1977): 425–46.

2. G. E. M. Anscombe, in "Modern Moral Philosophy," (*Philosophy*, [1958]: 1–18; reprinted in *The Definition of Morality*, ed. G. Wallace and A. D. M. Walker [London: Methune 1970] claimed that all deontological moral concepts are empty words unless there is a divine lawgiver and duty-determiner. Gauthier's thesis concerns not *all* moral laws and duties, but only those involving "moral convention," where mutual benefits depend upon

general observance. I accept his assumption that all moral duties require some rational basis, that we do not simply intuit moral absolutes.

3. Throughout this paper I use "his" to mean "his or her" and sometimes use "man" to mean "person." This is especially regrettable in a paper about justice, but needed allusions to the words of Hobbes and other sexists dictated my usage. I am not, it seems, willing to make the sacrifices in communication needed to help gain as much currency for 'the one just woman' as already gained for the one just man.

4. Gauthier, "Why Ought One Obey God," p. 428.

5. William James, "The Will to Believe," in *The Will to Believe and Other Essays in Popular Philosophy* (New York and London, 1897). In this paper I am really saying no more than James said about moral faith. I suppose the justification for saying it again, and adapting it to a Hobbesian context, is the perennial character of the issue. I have benefited from discussion with Richard Gale on James' position, and from his comments on an earlier version of this paper.

6. It is not an easy matter to formulate an acceptable criterion of the equitable, but I have assumed that we can get a stronger test for justice than that provided by Hobbes— "What all men have accepted, no man can call unjust." If we cannot, then maybe only the fools says in his heart that there is more to justice than fidelity to possibly forced agreement. If the ideal of the equitable or fair is empty or incoherent, then the more inclusive ideal of justice in a strong sense, which I am invoking, will also be empty or incoherent.

7. As has been pointed out by a reader for this journal, coherence could be preserved by letting one test apply on some occasions, the other on others, whenever the two tests would give conflicting decisions if both were applied. This would preserve only a weak formal coherence, unless some clear principle could be formulated which selects which test is applicable, and unless this principle itself expressed some component element in our hazy intuitive idea of justice.

8. Although in what follows I try to depart as little as possible from the hedonism of Hobbes and Locke (not because I agree with it, but because of the context of the present discussion), I do however depart very significantly from Hobbes in accepting, as rational motivation, not only self-preservation of the natural man, or "nature's preservation" but also preservation, not of Leviathan, but of a moral community, and of the very idea of such a community. A special "pleasure of the mind" would have to be added to Hobbes' list to accommodate such Kantian motivation.

9. Kurt Baier, "Rationality and Morality," *Erkenntnis* 11 (1977): 197, where the "isolation," "coordination," and "assurance" problems are distinguished.

10. I have not discussed the question, raised by Gauthier's example of unilateral abstention from preemptive nuclear strike, of what should be done when the decision taken may commit others besides the decision-maker to the higher pleasures of martyrdom for a good cause. This is the *really* difficult question.

11. I have tried, throughout this paper, to evoke some Biblical echoes, to show how the secular faith I describe parallels its theological forerunners. The effort to speak both the language of Hobbes and that of the King James Bible has resulted in a style which some readers have found obscure. This I regret, but I do want to keep, for those in a position to recognize them, allusions to, e.g., St. Paul's Epistle to the Hebrews, chs. 10 and 11.

Index

Index

Actions, basic, 4, 5, 47-49
Acts, higher-order, 45
Animals. *See* Beings, sentient
Anscombe, G. E. M.: and Hume, 177, 178, 182, 183-85; on intentional action, 34, 37, 44, 115-16; on moral concepts, 307 n2; on promises, 174, 182-85; on reason, 176, 177
Approval, 134, 149, 151, 154, 158-60, 221
Aquinas, Saint Thomas, 43, 130, 138, 229, 232, 233
Aristotle: cited by Danto, 49; on common sense and imagination, 43; on friendship, 95; and human passions, 123; and Hume, 261; and the moral life, 251, 253, 257, 258, 259; as moral theorist, 138, 228, 232; on unnatural love, 97
Artifice. *See* Hume
Atiyah, P. S., 175, 200, 202-5
Augustine, Saint, 95-96, 259
Austin, J. L., 40, 42, 177, 197
Authority, 69, 83

Baier, Kurt, 308
Barwise, Jon, 5
Beings, sentient, 171-73
Belief: and change of mind, 120; and changeability, 8; and its reasons, 110, 117, 119; and knowing, 22, 23; as mental state, 52-56; and narcissism, 9
Bell, M., 24
Belnap, Nuel, 24-31
Bennett, Jonathan, 54, 66, 67, 288

Bentham, Jeremy, 228, 234
Bergson, Henri, 229
Body-mind relation, 35-36, 76, 79-90, 91 n5
Bosanquet, Bernard, 229, 285
Bradley, A. C., 229, 285
Brandom, Robert, 167
Brandt, Richard, 103, 138, 211-12
Broughton, Janet, 91
Butler, Joseph, 161, 255

Caplan, Arthur, 244
Castaneda, Hector-Neri, 15
Causes, 3, 38-39, 127-28
Cavell, Stanley, 174-81, 197, 200-201, 106
Change of mind: belief and, 120; examples of, 56; and the "half-wanton," 53-54, 62-63, 65; and judgment, 63-64, 65-66
Children: compared with animals, 151; Descartes' views on, 83-86, 89; and moral training, 214, 219, 220-22, 242, 243
Chodorow, Nancy, 275
Christianity, 97, 99, 130, 209, 210, 254-61, 308
Clark, Stephen, 141, 144
Commitment, 174, 178-81
Considerations, 60, 63, 114-15
Contractarianism, 137, 139, 146, 151-52, 204
Conventions, 60-63, 67, 68, 69. *See also* Hume
Cooperation, 260, 266, 295-98, 300-304
Correction: and Descartes, 77-78; and

311

Born in Queenstown, New Zealand, in 1929, **Annette Baier** earned her bachelors and masters degrees in philosophy at the University of Otago, and her B. Phil. at Oxford University. She has taught at the universities of Aberdeen, Auckland, and Sydney and at Carnegie-Mellon University. Baier is now professor of philosophy at the University of Pittsburgh.